A SPIRAL LIFE

"Jean MacPhail's personal journey through child abuse, art school, medical practice, and religious institutions leaves you with a burning curiosity to read the next book in this series.

In many ways her story resonates with my own, for I was also a nun (though several decades prior) in the same Vedanta order that she enters toward the end of this first book. And as an artist, I particularly identified with the author's early struggle to make a decision between her career as an artist or the medical profession. I, too, faced a similar choice early on when I became deeply involved with a form of acupressure and the service of my clients. Instead, I chose the arts and allowed my engagement with it to expand until it became global work for peace. Seeing the author's artistic talent in this book, it is obvious that she could have chosen that same direction.

But she is serving in a different way, and it is a privilege to travel with her through the inner workings of her journey. I am sure many others will find this same resonance, experiencing the truth in her voice, a truth the world needs to hear, not only about spirituality but also about religious organizations, with their pitfalls and need for revision.

I am left with a rich fabric of cultures, personalities, and spiraling transitions of a fascinating and deeply spiritual woman."

- **Vijali Hamilton**, environmental sculptor, fellow of the World Academy of Art and Science, and founder of *World Wheel, Global Peace through the Arts.* She is author of *World Wheel, One Woman's Quest for Peace,* and *Of Earth and Fire,* available on: www.worldwheel.org.

"Many writers send me books to review and manuscripts they hope I will write a blurb for. While almost all of them are things I would like to read and share with others, I can seldom find time in my busy life of research, teaching and writing to even glance at them.

But *A Spiral Life* caught me up after the first pages; four days later I had read all five hundred pages and was very disappointed when it ended. I certainly hope there will be a volume two some day!

This is the real life story of a modern Western woman discovering and deepening her spiritual life in spite of numerous personal tragedies that would defeat most of us, and, especially interesting, in spite of powerful biases against women in the Vedantic path she choose to follow. Fascinating reading and valuable lessons!"

- **Charles T. Tart,** Professor (Emeritus) at the University of California Davis and Professor at the Institute of Transpersonal Psychology; author of *Altered States of Consciousness*; and *The End of Materialism: How Evidence of the Paranormal is Bringing Science and Spirit Together.*

A Spiral Life is an excellent book; a multi-layered story of Jean MacPhail's search for spiritual congruity in a world where even those who are teaching spiritual opening and deepening may have difficulties in being congruent with their teachings.

You will find much wisdom and inspiration in the responses to the life-challenges the author shares. There are also thoughtful suggestions for exploring patterns within life experiences that may contribute to your comprehension of meaningful patterns in your own life.

It is rare to find a literary gem like this that is a good read, a historical set-piece, and a provocative sorting of the 'what' of the 'how' and the 'how' of the 'what' in our lives.

- **Daniel J. Benor,** MD, American Board of Integrative Holistic Medicine; author of *Seven Minutes to Natural Pain Release* and *Healing Research, Vol. 3, Personal Spirituality.*

What a gift Jean MacPhail has given us with this first volume of her autobiography! Not merely evocative of three generations and three cultures over three continents, *A Spiral Life* is at once more intimate and more universal.

As we travel with "wee Jean" through her bitter and ecstatic journey, we are struck over and over by the two qualities that make autobiography so compelling, vivid detail and unflinching honesty. Her remarkable memory brings the book to life, while her brave candor speaks directly to her deepest questions and desires—and to ours.

We read this book both to learn what will happen to its author and what will happen *to us*, whether we are Hindu, Christian, Buddhist, or atheist. That living universality is the greatest gift autobiography can offer the reader and *A Spiral Life* offers it to us with open hands and an open heart.

- **Franz Metcalf**, Ph.D., author of *What Would Buddha Do?*

A number of worthy spiritual memoirs have been published in recent years, but few treat the reader to the rare combination of virtues of Jean MacPhail's *A Spiral Life*.

For lovers of strong, compelling narrative, the book offers a rip-roaring tale with Dickensian characters and scenes of comedy, tragedy, and high drama. For students of religion, mysticism, and the historic intersection of East and West, the author's journey provides a vivid glimpse into the experience of a woman of science who plunges deeply into an ascetic Vedantic lineage. She reveals the treasures of that ancient tradition, enhanced by a systematic exploration of advanced states of consciousness; and she exposes its dark side as well, with a disturbing account of her life inside the convent walls.

As Western culture continues to adapt and integrate India's spiritual teachings, it is imperative that we understand both the immense gifts that the enterprise promises and the perils that it can entail. Jean MacPhail's thorough, unflinching memoir lets us see both in one woman's gripping story.

- **Philip Goldberg**, Ph.D., author of *American Veda* and *Roadsigns on the Spiritual Path*.

A SPIRAL LIFE

Jean C. MacPhail

To order additional copies of this book, contact:
Xlibris Corporation
1-888-795-4274
www.Xlibris.com
Orders@Xlibris.com
58270

DEDICATION

This book is dedicated to all who seek to know who they truly are and to find and hold on to the conviction which keeps them in the saddle till the end.

CONTENTS

FIRST TURN OF THE SPIRAL
DARK MOTHER: 1941-1960

First Quarter: Laying the Groundwork

Second Quarter: Wild Reactions

Third Quarter: Facing the Music

Fourth Quarter: Back to Ground

SECOND TURN OF THE SPIRAL
MOTHER OF THE DAWN: 1961-1980

First Quarter: Groundwork, Again

Second Quarter: Clear Response

Third Quarter: Another Big Decision

Fourth Quarter: Ground It Is, Again

ILLUSTRATIONS

INTRODUCTION

In this book I seek to show how my life was molded and shaped by many difficult outer experiences and at the same time was held together by recurring glimpses of the inner world.

Such glimpses took forms from different religious and spiritual worlds, but all of them were soothing, invigorating, and empowering. And they all held together in what seemed to be a spiral pattern, shaping me up from a tot being whirled around by untoward circumstances during the Second World War to a maturing woman, much more consciously working with my fiery emotions and becoming aware for the first time of the pattern as it unfolded itself.

I believe that all of us can discover such resources as were made available to me in the crucible I had to pass through, because ultimately they come from within every one of us and can be used to cope with our own riddles, defeats, and moments of despair. We learn that in a sense we permit difficulties to affect us and can summon the determination and strength to rise above them. And also, of course, in savoring our moments of triumph and joy we get the additional bonus of knowing that all we are enjoying is coming from within us and cannot be taken away.

This book gives an impression of what is possible if we are open to the innate resources we have within us. The patterns we follow may be different, but I believe we can all reach the same state of self-assurance and conviction that is so vital in negotiating the jungle we call human life.

APPRECIATIONS AND A DISCLAIMER

This book was written at the behest of Phil Goldberg, a dear friend and writer on spiritual subjects. I was extremely reluctant to talk about my inner life and how it grew in the face of endless obstacles and resistance from the outside; but he convinced me that it would be interesting and beneficial for others as well as helpful for myself. And so I took the plunge.

In addition to Phil, there have been others who have tremendously encouraged me and helped me with the book as it moved forward. My long-standing friend and spiritual sister, Pat Walker, has read every page as it was written, counseled me on numerous technical issues related to editing and publishing, and generally been extremely supportive. Marjorie Kewley is another dear friend and mentor whose balanced view of what I was doing helped me to shape up the work and see it in a wider perspective than I had had before I got her comments. The same is true of Lily Hayward, another long-standing close friend and well-wisher.

Professor Charles Tart, the well-known doyen of consciousness research, and Laurel McCormick, a Ph.D. student at the Institute of Transpersonal Psychology, both saw merit in my attempt to describe the unfolding of my life in a repeating pattern of noetic experiences forming what I call a spiral. Professor Tart's remarks in a personal letter—

> I must confess to being completely ignorant about there being regular patterns in spiritual unfolding, I've never heard anyone talk about [that]. That does indeed make it especially interesting! As a former engineer, I think that if one knew there was a certain pattern one could adjust one's practices to it, "ride the wave," as it were, and get stronger results

—gave me considerable encouragement to attempt to describe and comment on my experiences in public, not an easy task, to say the least.

I have also received much encouragement from Dr. Daniel J. Benor, the holistic psychiatrist and healer who understands my story in a very deep way, and Dr. Amy Thakurdas, a naturopath, healer, and dear friend, whose knowledge ranges over a very wide spectrum, and who in her extensive shamanic practice has also observed life patterns similar to my own.

My family has also been tremendously supportive and helpful in many different ways, particularly Dr. Jean Thomson and Grace Dempsey.

I am deeply indebted to Phil Goldberg, Professor Tart, Dr. Benor, Franz Metcalf, who writes in a very accessible way on Buddhist subjects, and the remarkable artist and creator of sacred spaces, Vijali Hamilton, for agreeing to write a blurb on this book. Together they bring to bear on the book a wide range of expertise, ranging from creative art through science to experiential religion, all subjects which I personally worked through and explore in the book.

In telling this story I have had to include a number of characters and situations which presented tremendous difficulties for me, challenges which I had to surmount and work on to understand, digest, and weave into a broader, more compassionate understanding of what had happened and why. I have made every effort to be accurate and factual in my account of these people and situations as I perceived them (relying on the diaries I kept at the time); but as this book is an extremely subjective account, it is natural that my descriptions may seem rather stark at times, as that is how they seemed to me as I encountered them. I have no intention of maligning or "exposing" anyone; my purpose in writing this book is to show how even the worst situations can lead to inner light and understanding and help us to grow as individuals and members of society. I was very happy when one of my commentators said of the book, "Your spirit shines through, as well as your ability to consider the different points of view and circumstances of the others involved (i.e. empathy), giving a nice, balanced quality." This is a perfect paraphrase of my intention throughout.

I have, however, changed the names and in some cases the locations of those individuals who posed the most serious challenges to me. I trust that as the readers of this book proceed through it and its sequel, they will find that I seek to empathize with the difficulties with which my adversaries seemed to be struggling and to arrive at a deeper understanding of the dynamics from both sides which created the difficulties between us.

FIRST TURN OF THE SPIRAL

DARK MOTHER

1941-1960

FIRST QUARTER

LAYING THE GROUNDWORK

CHAPTER 1

NAN AND WEE JEAN: 1941-1944

I was born in Glasgow on February fifth, nineteen forty-one, just six weeks before the German Luftwaffe strafed the engineering and ship-building installations in and around the city on the River Clyde in southwestern Scotland. This was a hotspot of intense war effort, crucial to the resistance Great Britain was putting up to German and Italian forces in World War II; and so intense was the German bombing that the area was devastated and a large percentage of the population was killed.

Clydeside and its principal city, Glasgow, was a bastion of gritty, working-class people, many of them from Ireland or the Scottish Highlands. It was a hotbed of Socialism and even Communism, as the area had been hard-hit during the Depression. Hard drinking and heavy smoking was a way of life, worked out against a background of appalling industrial pollution, for Glasgow was prone to the "pea-soupers" more commonly associated in the popular mind with the better-known city of London. Another ever-present threat to life and limb was Protestant-Catholic rivalry, largely fuelled by the immigrant Irish. They would slug out their differences in razor-slashing Friday night brawls; indiscriminate mayhem on Orange Day, July 12th (the commemoration of the victory of the Protestant king William of Orange over the Irish Catholics in 1690); and vendettas that, as late as the interwar years, would lead Protestant gangs to kill any Catholic who dared to come on "their" side of the street.

In our highly uniform ethnic world, a "mixed marriage" meant one between a Catholic and a Protestant, a fate we Protestants would regard as one of the very worst. The priests were everywhere, telling the impoverished immigrants how many children they were to have (as many as possible), how much of their pitiful earnings were to go to the Church (a lot), how their children were to be educated (at Roman

Catholic schools, a Protestant parent notwithstanding), and preventing their parishioners from getting into shows deemed detrimental to the faith—such as a movie on Martin Luther, to which Protestant school-children went in long "crocodiles" for what was considered their religious uplift. In the milling sea of Protestant school children around the box office the black figures of the fathers stood out rather ominously as they peered around looking for any errant Catholics trying to get in under cover of the Prots.

Such was Glasgow and Clydeside at the time of my birth. Dour, dark and dismal, from many standpoints. But along with that went a tremendous personal kindness and generosity, loyalty to the family and to Scotland, as well as a very pragmatic way of thinking. And then there was the humor—dour, dark and pawky, to use an indigenous word. The Glaswegians had learned to react to the unremitting gloom of their lives—from the unspeakable industrial slavery at the beginning of the capitalist revolution in the eighteenth century (for which Scotland itself was largely responsible), through the misery of World War I, the Great Depression and on to the ever-present terror of German bombing and submarines coming up the Clyde to "get" the warships under construction—with an arch, tongue-in-cheek and at the same time quite direct and even forward sense of humor. A few specimens of the art of put-down may suffice to give a flavor of our daily interactions: "Put that in your pipe and smoke it!" "That'll put your gas on a peep!" And then, the item which struck horror into my American friends when I arrived in the States in the nineteen sixties: "Aw, go bile yer heid" (Go boil your head)." In our direct and boisterous world, no one paid any attention to such expressions—they were very familiar, perhaps rooted in some horrible form of punishment from the past, and all part of a day's work. Yet, with all of that, overt violence was never much in evidence. The police were still unarmed and actual killing was a rarity. Brawls there were a-plenty, but shootings, stabbings and drugs (other than the alcohol that seems to practically pickle all of Northern Europe) were all but unknown.

I saw the light of day at 2 am in Govan Hospital in south-central Glasgow. My mother was born Agnes Barnes Laughland, a typically Irish name, pronounced *Lochland*—though my father's father loved to call her Miss Laffland, at which he would laugh (or laff!) uproariously. Her family had come from Ireland some generations back and settled in Ayrshire, south of the Glasgow area, and then moved to

Dumbarton, on the Clyde estuary down-river from Glasgow. My mother's father was in the business of printing supplies and at times did quite well. Somewhere around the time of World War I he was well enough off to have a large car and a driver, a relative rarity in economically depressed Scotland.

In addition, my grandparents did all they could to give their four daughters the best education money could buy. Their oldest daughter, Jane, took her basic arts degree, but could go no further on account of her parents' early death. Married to Bill Thomson, the proprietor of the *Lennox Herald,* one of the oldest newspapers in Scotland, she was fairly comfortably off and helped her other sisters complete their education and get a start in life. Eileen, who had trained as a ballet dancer but had to work in a lawyer's office to make a living, attracted attention from the firm she worked with and was trained at their expense as a lawyer. Later she married my Uncle Robert, a man who became one of Scotland's leading psychiatrists. Leila earned a Ph.D. in philosophy and later ran as a Labor candidate in the north of England, where she had settled with her husband Billy Muir, a much-loved general medical practitioner.

My mother was the youngest of the four, losing both of her parents by the age of twelve. Her sister Jane, even as a young married wife, took her into her home and cared for her like her own daughter, for she had the tenderest affection for Nan, as my mother was called. Nan was very attractive, not only physically but personally. She was gifted intellectually and artistically and had such an enchanting personality as a little girl that

My mother about age eight.

a well-known, elderly writer and artist took a fancy to her and featured a portrait of her in the book he was writing. After a desperate bout with meningitis in early childhood, however, her naturally sunny disposition was marred occasionally by emotional swings that seemed to get worse as she grew older. And, although the family was of liberal persuasion politically, Nan stood out as quite the rebel. She used to take delight in telling visitors to their middle class home that her Irish ancestors had been tinkers, the itinerant menders of pots and pans, who did odd jobs, some crafts—and, people would say, sleights of hand with other people's property. Like the gypsies, of whom they were the Celtic counterparts, the tinkers were said to abduct children—for what purpose I could never fathom. All in all, they were considered low class and highly unrespectable, and my mother would get great satisfaction from shocking everyone with her assertions!

As she grew older and saw the devastation of the Great Depression which hit Clydeside very badly, my mother became deeply concerned with the plight of the working people. Her impulsive nature would lead her to give away anything she could find to the poor souls she would encounter. Sometimes she came home in her underwear, having given her clothes away to the pathetic women and children begging on the streets. And as time went by she, like many intellectuals of the period, became a Communist. These idealistic young people believed that politics could solve issues of human exploitation and that the Soviets were embarking on a new world order that would bring justice, economic fairness and stability to the world. She came to regard the values of her middle-class family as "bourgeois", and refused to go to university, which she regarded as a training ground for the Capitalist values which had caused so much suffering, not only worldwide, but particularly in Scotland. She rejected the liberal religious values of the family in favor of atheism and, a fluent German speaker, opted to study the Froebel system of education in Munich during the nineteen-thirties.

Friedrich Froebel was a German educator who introduced the kindergarten system in eighteen thirty-seven. Influenced by the Swiss educator Pestalozzi, he embraced the emerging idea that children are not mere blank tablets to be written on from the outside, but are motivated from within and, given an appropriate environment, will learn naturally and spontaneously. His methods included emphasis on directed play and providing children with a structured environment which they could explore and learn from, at the same time revealing to the teachers their temperaments and inclinations as well as stage of development. The final ingredient in the work of these men was pantheism, the notion that everything is suffused with divine presence, characteristic of the pagan religions and also of Indian philosophy, which was being avidly studied in Europe in the late eighteenth and early nineteenth centuries.

Furthermore, these educators were religious dissenters and political radicals—no doubt the feature that attracted my mother to their work.

Her parents had been Unitarians, which in the rather fundamentalist religious environment of early twentieth century Scotland must have seemed extremely counter-culture. Just how much my mother had absorbed before her parents' death is not clear, as she was only twelve when she was fully orphaned, but it certainly seems that she was like her parents in her tendency to independent thought and alternative philosophies. Her attraction to German thinking and culture was no doubt due to the fact that Germany was a hotbed of experimentation with indigenous paganism, esotericism, and oriental thinking—a revolt, perhaps, against what remained of Christianity after its devastation by the Inquisition and later the rapid onward march of science, of which the Germans had in many ways become masters. As we know historically, this fermentation, having thrown off the restraining limits of the Christian tradition, was to take an ugly turn in the nineteen twenties and thirties, culminating in the Third Reich of Hitler and all of the unrestrained atrocities that the human mind cannot conceive of.

As of my birth in nineteen forty-one, the developments in Germany over the preceding ten years had of course been deeply disturbing to Nan Laughland; but for the moment she was now a mother with a daughter of her own to care for and educate. And she was alone, in a profoundly troubled way. Married at the beginning of the war, she had seen very little of my father, Dr. Colin MacPhail, for he was in active military service as a captain in the Medical Corps with the Gordon Highlanders. Indeed, because of the war and its aftermath, I was not to see my father for any length of time until I was seven or eight years old; and for my mother, it was to mean tremendous loneliness, anxiety and ultimately despair. But, for the moment, she had her "wee Jean", on account of whose unsuspecting head many a flagon of whisky was doubtless quaffed in some barren military outpost, no doubt briefly brightening up the lives of the officers and men upon whose existence the dice game being played worldwide was depending.

After the devastating bombings of March nineteen forty-one, Clydeside was no longer a safe place to live. Perhaps because of that, or perhaps because of some other scruples in my mother's mind (or perhaps just due to lack of money), she and I embarked on a sort of hegira, moving further and further west and down the river away from Glasgow. One of our earliest homes was in Luss, on Loch Lomond of sentimental ballad fame, where my mother and I lived in a prefabricated hut-like structure behind a large stone house with a monkey-puzzle tree in the front garden.

At that time I was at least able to toddle, for I recall many happy hours splashing in the ever-present puddles of rainy Scotland with my wee friends. This ability, combined with the British idea of how to restrain infants, resulted in a rather dramatic episode which also throws some light on my personality. One sunny day my mother, busy with something else, put me in my pram and left me to my own devices. For those not familiar with the British pram, let me say that this is a baby carriage of princely proportions in which proud parents perambulate their offspring—hence the colloquial *pram*. At least three feet off the ground, something like four to five feet long, with four wheels and a collapsible hood, it affords the prized occupant quite a bit of wiggle room—or, in my case, shoogle room. In Scotland, we shoogle when we are restless. That is, we wriggle, rock, and—may I add—roll. I certainly seem to have been in fine fettle that morning, for when my mother returned, the pram was lying on its side and I was nowhere to be seen. Family folklore has it that wee Jean had rocked the pram so vigorously that it fell over and she was able to make her escape.

From my side, what I recall is heading for the wood behind our house, exulting over my freedom. I was delighted by the sun dancing on the fair-sized burn or creek that bubbled through the woods and by examining all of the shrubs and trees as well as the flowers alongside the path I was following. There was a moment of terror as I passed some sort of electrical installation, humming rather ominously in a dark space under the trees, but the next moment I came round a bend and into a clearing where the sun was unobstructed. I sat down beside the burn and felt wonderfully joyous—alone, free and sitting in the lap of what was nothing but my very own mother. Somehow it seemed the most natural thing in the world to start taking off my clothes and throwing them in the water. The wee wool bonnet—that nice bonnet knitted in those lovely patterns and with the ribbons—off it came and into the water with a satisfying plop. As I watched it bob away, I started in on the equally lovely cardigan. The buttons were a bit difficult, but I managed them after a tussle and off it went, an offering to the water. Next was the dress. Getting it off was going to be more work than the bonnet and the cardigan, but it seemed to be the most important thing I could ever do. It was as if some primal instinct were urging me on, that giving up these hard-to-come-by clothes was what was required of me above all else.

As I was struggling with the dress, I heard my mother's cries in the distance. She had found the empty pram and was distraught. What had happened to her wee Jean? During the war years there were many deranged men roaming about, and it was dangerous for children to be alone. Somehow she had understood where I might be—perhaps she saw little footsteps in the ever-present mud—and had run into the woods to find me. I thought that she would be angry when she saw that my clothes were floating down the burn, but of course she was so relieved to find me alive that it was nothing but hugs and kisses. Still, the urge to throw things—even important things—away was a feature of my life, and this was the opening act, as you might say.

Another feature of "wee Jean's" personality made itself known on a visit to my father's parents' house in Glasgow. My mother occasionally went to Glasgow, I think in connection with her part-time work as a superintendent of kindergartens, and would drop me off at my grandparent's home in Glasgow. We rarely went into the city and, coming in on the bus, it was easy to see why. Block after block of the ubiquitous tenements of Clydeside and Glasgow were lying in heaps of rubble, a truly shocking sight. Worse, in some ways, were the walls that were still standing. In what had been the different apartments you could see the selections of wallpapers still on the walls, most of them a grubby cream, but some murky green or shocking pink, perhaps hangovers from the Victorian period, when such colors were in vogue. Here and there a shattered picture was dangling from the wall, the remains of a chest of drawers perched on a remaining fragment of the floor, or a toilet twisted and mangled almost beyond recognition. As a three-to-four year old, I could not of course have any idea what the official explanation for all of this was, but what I saw filled me with anguish. I could at once visualize the mangled bodies that had been so recently salvaged from the rubble, the children left without parents, the terrible loss of income and the hopes crushed beyond redemption. Why? Why? Why? It was my first inkling of the callousness and cruelty that so mysteriously follows humanity like a dark and ominous shadow.

I was one of the fortunate ones, still alive and on my way to my grandparents' home. Arriving there my dark mood would pass, for this was a haven of the affection and love that just as mysteriously is part and parcel of the human condition. I was simply entranced by my grandfather,

Murdoch MacPhail, a Gaelic-speaking man in his mid-seventies who had worked as a quartermaster in the HLI or Highland Light Infantry Regiment, having been posted all over the world and particularly for at least two years in what was then East Bengal. On retirement, this good-hearted man had become an inspector for the Society for the Prevention of Cruelty to Children, tragically a job that was never slow or dull. His military bearing—and he was what we used to call "a fine figure of a man"—his cane held under his arm, and particularly his long, waxed

My Grandfather, 1901.

moustache would strike such terror into the hearts of miscreant parents that he had no trouble in bringing them round to more decent treatment of their starving, ill-educated, and often tuberculosis-ridden broods of children.

My grandpa had somehow hit on the idea of entertaining me with a routine I called "Granpa splashie windies". Setting me up on a tall chair behind one of the huge long windows that graced the immensely high-ceilinged rooms of his home, he would fill up a bucket of water and toddle outside, shouting to me to tell him when to let the water go. We would shout back and forth and then he would throw the water with all of his strength against the window, to shrieks of delight from me. The best part was seeing his face when the water had cleared from the window—I just loved his pure white hair, his twinkling blue eyes, the dimples deeply creased in his benign, smiling and happy face.

On this particular visit our routine was over and Grandpa and Grannie had gone to the kitchen, perhaps so Grandpa could have a well-earned cup of tea. I slipped out into the cavernous dark hallway, looking for something new to play with and mischief to get up to. I was thrilled to find an umbrella stand, which contained, along with the usual colored brollies for women, a huge, black man's umbrella, which doubtless was my grandfather's and indeed might well have come from India, as it had what looked like an ivory handle. I managed to pull it out. It was taller than I was, perhaps over three feet long. I opened and closed it with difficulty, but with a great sense of achievement. Then came the feature of my personality that has gotten me into trouble several times since. Pushing the envelope of discovery, you might say. I thought: "Why not put the handle in my mouth?"

No sooner thought than done; and remarkably easy, considering the handle was so large. It slipped in, effectively holding my jaws so wide apart it hurt me terribly—and of course, it was too firmly wedged in to be taken out. Dim visions of carrying this thing around for the rest of my life beset me—how was I going to eat, for one thing? Of course I started to yell and my grandparents came rushing out of the kitchen to see wee Jean dragging Granpa's umbrella round the hallway in her mouth and tripping over it as she did so. "Ov! Ov! Machrachs a chanaig! What will we to with wee Cheen!" Grannie cried.[1] Grandpa, though a

---

[1]   Gaelic for Oy vay! What a disaster! Gaelic speakers cannot say soft consonants, so *do* becomes *to* and *Jean* becomes *Cheen*.

military man, was so upset to see me in such distress that he was simply paralyzed. He was an extremely soft-hearted man; everyone in the family knew that when there was a spanking or some other disciplinary action to be done, it was his wife, Mary Anne, who would give it, never he. No doubt Granpa would have gotten his act together, but for the moment he was in tears at the sight of his little pet in such an incredibly strange and painful situation.

Who knows how long this would have gone on, if the doorbell had not rung and there was my mother who, though a loving woman, was more down to earth than my Highland relatives. She got the umbrella handle out quite quickly and gave me a good scolding for causing my grandparents so much trouble and distress. Again, there were lots of hugs, kisses and the inevitable tea, scones and shortbread with which so many things came to a happy end in Scotland.

One last episode from this early part of my life foreshadowed yet another aspect of my life that has recurred again and again. I was perhaps going on four when my mother took me on a visit to the home of her elder sister Eileen and her husband Robert. They were living in Killearn, where one of the largest psychiatric facilities in Scotland was situated. My uncle was involved in some research work there, laying the foundation for what was to be a quite distinguished career in psychiatry. As ever, I was delighted with a new house to explore, which I began as soon as I was alone. It was a single story bungalow, with the usual features of a middle class home. However, at the back of the living room I was mightily surprised to see several cages stacked up against the wall. As I got closer I saw that each cage contained a stoat, a small relative of the weasel. Of course, I had no idea what they were for and I wondered what my uncle could possibly need with so many stoats. They were all running frantically round and round in their cages, the very picture of misery and fear. I wished I could do something to calm them down, but it was obvious that they were afraid of me. What could my uncle be up to? Knowing what experimental animals go through was reserved for twenty years down the line.

This was my first exposure to the world of science. I looked out the window and saw the sun rising over the hills, shimmering on the hoar frost that was everywhere. As I moved my head, the color of the frost would change from red to orange, darts of green and blue, and yellow and turquoise, sending shivers down my spine and thrilling me to the core of my being. Then I remembered the stoats and wondered, "Why, why, why?

Perhaps the same morning, I learned another big lesson—in my three year old way. Somehow I had been shut into the room by myself, along with the stoats rattling away in their cages. I desperately wanted to get out, but was too small to reach the handle of the door. I strained and strained, but it was obvious I was not going to succeed. I sat down on a chair facing the door and stared at the door knob intensely. I concentrated on it all the willpower I could command, expecting it to understand me and obey: "Open! Open! Open!" The human mind has its ways, and so does the material world. The door remained exactly as before, not even a smile or even a rattle to let me know it understood. This made me all the more determined and I began to glower at the doorknob. "Come on! You know what I want—now just please do it!" I may have been sitting like this for a quarter of an hour, getting really angry, when suddenly the door did open and my mother came in. "Jean! Why are you in here all by yourself! Come on, it's breakfast time."

This little episode helped me to see that the material world obeys its own laws, not my needs or desires. It was a stern lesson, no doubt, but then you could say that my mother coming in was maybe the way my command was answered. The human heart speaks through doors, hears unspoken cries, creates networks of communication which exist before, during and after physical events and is ultimately in command of the physical world. Or at least so it seemed at the time. And still seems to be true, despite all that has happened.

CHAPTER 2

"LET HIM GO OR LET HIM TARRY . . ."
1945-1946

In nineteen forty-five Germany was under siege as the Russians moved toward it from the East and the British and Americans from the West. Britain was breathing rather easier than it had for some time, and more energy was beginning to return to our everyday world. My Aunt Eileen and her husband Robert were moving into new housing in a suburb in the northwest of Glasgow, and my father had agreed to pay for the upstairs floor of the two-storied house so that my mother and I could move in and have a more stable home than we had had for quite some time.

Myself, age 3.

It seemed like a wonderful idea. My mother was close to her sister Eileen and my cousin Caite was just about my age and would be a playmate for me. The house was near the top of a hill on Hillview Road which, although it had houses on both sides near the main road, looked out onto a virgin field up at our end. The field was made up of little hillocks, valleys and shaded areas, with a small burn running through it, full of minnows, frogs and other essentials to keep children engrossed by the hour. Further up the hill was a wood with a fair-sized lake or loch, fascinating but, our parents warned us, the haunt of "bad men". We were warned never to go there without someone else.

But as always, there were difficulties—and this time not from the Jerries, as we called the Germans. Having got rid of them, more or less, we had to turn to the troubles within our own house. And in my case it was with my Uncle Robert, he of the stoats. Unlike the rest of my family, who were of medium height, fair-skinned, brown-haired, blue-eyed, and for the most part very jolly, Robert was dark, tall, and thin, with a large Adam's apple, a deep voice and a saturnine temperament. Over the fireplace in the living room on the ground floor he had arranged in concentric arches his collection of daggers, knives, pistols, shotguns and instruments of torture. I found it quite threatening and was always glad that we seldom had occasion to go into the room.

As a progressive psychiatrist, my uncle had decided that spanking children inhibited the growth of ego, and he would never spank his daughter Caite. This, again, was something unusual, as in all of the rest of our family (as indeed in the rest of Scotland) spanking was taken for granted and, as far as I am concerned, did nothing whatsoever to our egos, except perhaps to give them a healthy respect for law and order. There was, however, one feature of my uncle's theory which I was not too keen about. Whenever he was angry with Caite—something which occurred quite frequently, due more perhaps to his angry temperament than to anything else—he would thrash the living daylights out of me. Caite's ego was taken most seriously but mine seemed to be able to stand the risks of spanking! I do not remember my mother spanking me—I think it was likely unnecessary, given her insight into children and her close relationship with me; but I was aware that spanking would follow misbehavior and expected it on a number of occasions. What made me furious with my uncle was that I was punished for the offences of my cousin and also that he thrashed me so viciously. Even at that age I sensed that he was taking out on me all kinds of anger and revenge that should have been going to someone else.

This was my first personal introduction to the injustice of the world. My mother would protest to my uncle, but he would laugh callously and tell her that he would do what he thought was right. I am quite sure that this caused my mother tremendous anguish, coming as she did from a totally different concept of how children are made up. For her, a child was full of creative and joyful potential that was to be drawn out through love and play, and with the greatest respect. And that is how she always behaved with me. In view of the threatening darkness downstairs, which made playing with Caite anything but attractive, it was only natural that my mother and I would enjoy each other's company as much as we did.

My mother did one thing which left a permanent mark on my mind and molded the rest of my life in a very creative way. All round our dining-cum-living room she pinned postcards at about my eye level, so that I could take them in. Some were pictures of Scottish wildflowers—primroses, snowdrops, ladies'-smock—which I would delight in finding in

the field and woods around our home as the seasons came and went—but most were reproductions of art works.

Red Horses by the German Expressionist Franz Marc were an especially big hit with me, later influencing my own art work profoundly. This was a contemporary work of horses depicted in a quasi-abstract way and colored bright red and other unexpected colors, which tickled me immensely.

My mother had definitely created an oasis in our upstairs apartment, where I could feel some security and happiness. Yet even there, there was sadness breaking through from time to time. My father was still not with us, and of course the situation with my uncle was indeed oppressive. And, as a four-year old child, I could not appreciate how devastating it was for my mother to hear about the atrocities in Germany and Russia, both cultures which she had idealized and idolized as counterweights to the patent dysfunction of the Capitalist West. As the war began to run down, eye-witness reports of the concentration camps in Germany and the result of the pogroms in Russia were reaching us and shocking us to the very core.

Who knows what was passing between my parents at this time. Whatever is was, it was causing my mother a great deal of pain. she would sing, with me joining in enthusiastically:

> Let him go or let him tarry, let him sink or let him swim,
> For he doesn't care for me, and I don't care for him.
> He can go and find another, which I hope he will enjoy—
> For I'm going to marry a far nicer boy.

We would sing this together, sometimes casually, sometimes assertively, sometimes angrily, but increasingly in a minor key, leaving me filled with sorrow and a dread that I could not at all comprehend.

Although the sun was shining as it always had, it seemed as if there was a darkness hanging like a veil over everything. How many more times would I pass through this experience in my life! But one of the great blessings of my life has been that when such darkness closes in on me, light suddenly bursts out in unexpected ways, moving me forward or perhaps inward, lifting me above the clouds and the pain. This I was about to experience for the first time.

One night I had a vivid dream. I was walking in a dark wood, full of anxiety and feeling utterly lost. No need of deep analysis on that one! Gradually I saw a little light breaking on the horizon and revealing a huge oak tree in my path. The diameter of its trunk might have been ten feet, it was so large. Trees always make me feel welcome, so it was natural that I would run to it to shelter under its huge, embracing branches. As I got closer, I saw a little door in the trunk, just above eye-level. Standing on tiptoe, I reached up and opened it. As I did so, light began to stream out and I leaned forward to see where it was coming from. Inside I saw Jesus, from whom the light—so clear, bright, and yet serene and reassuring—was radiating. He was looking directly at me, smiling and filling me up with what felt like an infinite ocean of love. I woke up feeling light, happy and free.

Using my ordinary mind, I could easily explain this dream. My mother had been getting tired, no doubt quite exhausted by all the burdens she was carrying; and, despite the fact that she was an atheist (and perhaps to get a little respite), she hit on the idea of sending me off to Sunday school on Sunday afternoon. Someone had a gathering of little imps like me in their home further down the road, loosely referred to as "Sunday school". We were all tots and what we got there was pretty simple: some little pictures of Jesus or scenes from the Bible, a bit bigger than a postage stamp, and a few jingles, which we sang together with great gusto. From one standpoint, it was all quite corny; but to my four-year old mind, the pictures of Jesus, smiling and so happy (and so blonde and blue-eyed!) were really quite entrancing. My mother no doubt felt that not much harm could be done in a four-year-old spending one hour a week with simple-minded Christians, but see what it did for my dream life!

But I believe there was much more to it than that. The pressure that was mounting in my life was truly massive, though of course I had no idea how much or why. Because this has happened to me three or four times now, I know that something from within me was speaking to me, reminding of who I really am—and, naturally, taking the form that most appealed to me and gave me a sense of security. I regard it as nothing but a blessing that I had the chance to be exposed to those simple images, the merry jingles and the patent faith and kindness of the good souls who gave up their Sunday afternoon to host a group of noisy wee children, shouting their heads off and messing up the house.

I could also say that this dream was preparing me to face the next scene of the drama: My father was coming for a visit. They tell me he had come before, but I had no memory of it. As far as I was concerned, this was the first time I was to see him. My mother was in a state of high excitement, maybe with a touch of hysteria. I felt a bit anxious and puzzled at her behavior, which was usually so cheerful and sunny. On the morning of his arrival we had early breakfast and my mother was restlessly running in and out of the house. At one moment, while she was out and everything was quiet, my eye was attracted by a little crystal vase with a white rosebud sitting in the center of the table. The table was covered with a white cloth, so I was looking at white on white, the early summer sun streaming in the window and making it all glow. Suddenly all my anxiety and even fear about meeting my father melted away and I felt I was dissolving in a warm, supporting, gentle ocean of happiness that had no boundaries or limits.

"Jean! Daddy's coming!" I heard my mother's agitated voice coming up the stairs. I got up and ran out to stand with her on the road. Visitors had to get out of the tram at the bottom of the road and trudge up to our house and I could see my father quite a ways down, walking forcefully up. He was wearing a tweed jacket and his Gordon Highlanders' kilt, with an army rucksack over his shoulder. He was quite a good-looking, athletic man, but for me he was a total stranger. He ran the last few yards, picked up my mother and whirled her round, shouting. Then it was my turn. Up I went, him shouting something unintelligible. I knew he was happy to see me, but I felt afraid. I wasn't used to such boisterous behavior, and perhaps thought that he was going to thrash me, like my uncle. Somehow I picked up anxiety, pain and exhaustion in his behavior.

I wasn't really clear what fathers would be good for. My mother and I had had to live in our own world up till then, and all of this was a new experience for me. However, in a day or two I did get a clue, for which I was heartily grateful. My parents and I went for a walk round the loch, where the proverbial "bad men" were. It was early summer and the rhododendrons were in bloom. Their huge clusters of lavender-pink flowers were a symbol of new life, days out of doors, happiness. From my trips up there with my new buddy Sylvia Macdonald and others I knew that there were eggs in a nest in one of the big rhodies, which I wanted to show my Daddy. But despite my repeated pleadings to come with me, he was taking his time. He and my mother wanted to walk slowly, both enjoying their brief time together.

I ran ahead, hoping that the birdies might have hatched by now. I went inside the bush, straining up to see the nest. Suddenly a man's hand grabbed my wrist and I felt myself being dragged away. I could not see his face, but I realized I was in the clutches of a "bad man". Unfortunately this was the first of what was to be quite a series of this kind of thing—for the war had disrupted the behavior of an awful lot of men—but equally fortunately I established the precedent right then and there of screaming at the top of my lungs, a habit which has saved me many, many times. My father, hearing my shrieking, let out what I can only describe as a bellow and charged like an enraged bull. The Scots are known for their ferocious attacks in war; as they fought in their kilts in the Napoleonic wars, the French dubbed them "the ladies from hell". My father was quite a sprinter—as he charged along the path, his kilt swinging, his reddish hair on end and bellowing at the top of his lungs, my would-be molester thought better of his intended project and darted away.

This was the first time my Daddy saved my life. I began to realize that daddies have their place and felt a little less afraid of him. My relationship with my uncle continued to deteriorate, however. One day I was out for a walk with him and Caite. We were in the field over from the house, and Caite was sitting on his shoulders, with her legs dangling down on his chest. My uncle was taunting me cruelly and Caite was smirking at me from her perch way above me. She had her Daddy, and I didn't!

Suddenly I had had enough. I started to run away, planning to go home without them. As I sped along I noticed that there were some particularly fine cowpats lying on the grass. A change of plan occurred, and I stopped to find the ultimate cowpat for my purpose. Soon I found a huge one, firm on the outside, but by palpation, suitably liquid in the middle. I ran back to my uncle and, when I was within range, let it fly. Now, I played rounders, cricket and other ball games most of my youth and was never noted for accuracy of pitching. But this time—maybe five years old, but guided by some destiny or perhaps an avenging goddess—smack dab I hit his face, some four feet above my head. My uncle let out a roar and lunged at me, but of course he was a little handicapped! I took the opportunity to escape and hid out in the fields and woods till dusk, knowing that showing up early was likely to land me the thrashing to end all thrashings.

I have no idea what child psychiatrists would make of this one, but I do know how the family responded to the story when I told it as an adult. To a man or woman, they all smiled, applauded or congratulated me telling me that they would have loved to do what I did. My aunt Jane, my mother's oldest sister, an extremely kind and forbearing woman, said at first, "Oh, dear! Jean!" and looked at me with her blue eyes twinkling. Then she got serious and said in a quiet voice, "Your aunt Eileen was the most beautiful, vital, intelligent and gifted girl! Her husband broke her to pieces, he drained the life out of her and left her a domestic slave." I was simply stunned at this most unusual outburst, even though it was quiet and very low key. It was clear just how much devastation my uncle's behavior had caused his family and how deeply it had hurt my aunt. I began to understand how relevant my "naughtiness" had been. Perhaps I had saved my mother from a similar fate at his hands. Who knows what would have happened if we had stayed there much longer? But of course a lot of damage had been done, and was soon to work itself out in a rather catastrophic way.

I cannot say what the exact sequence of events was, but definitely my mother and I were soon moving on. Uncle Robert had forced us out, despite the fact that my father was still paying for our share of the house. Naturally, my mother was very upset at this turn of events, but off we had to go, this time into the heart of the country at Shandon on the Gare Loch, where we were to stay with the mother of one of my father's boon companions.

My mother and I lived at the top of a turreted gatehouse of a "stately home", concealed behind a dense wood up the hill from us. After my mother had tucked me in bed at night, I would get up and stand on my bed to peer out of the turret window at the night sky. I would love to see the stars reflected on the Gare Loch, the moon rising or setting in its calm, serene way—and, this being Scotland—clouds constantly passing by, creating strange and lovely formations on whatever light was ambient. This was the country, no doubt of it. We were part of a tiny village, frozen in time. I went to an old-fashioned school, where children from five to fourteen shared the same classroom, supervised by one teacher. She was an older woman, a bit portly, and like so many Scots, extremely kind and humorous. Somehow everything went on quite well. The older children coached the younger ones and we managed to learn without much trouble.

Shandon was also a haunt of the tinkers my mother had made so much of when she was younger. The night we arrived there I ran out to the beach, just across the road from where we lived. There they were, sitting in the early autumn dusk, complete with their brightly colored wagon, horse, dogs, pots and pans. Seated around a fire whose smoke curled into the darkening sky in delicious patterns, they were working away on baskets and what looked like artificial flowers made from wood shavings. I was utterly fascinated by them and watched for a long time. They were busy talking among themselves and paid no attention to me, though occasionally the man working on the flowers would look my way and give me a friendly smile.

This scene etched itself in my mind. There was something so free, so natural, so vitally real about these people whom my middle class family looked down on and was rather afraid of. Perhaps my mother had been right, perhaps we really were descended from Irish tinkers—otherwise, why was I so attracted to them? My reveries were brought to an end by the call to come home to bed. The next day and many days after I worked prodigiously to depict the night-time scene in colors which my ever-loving mother had scrimped to provide me with. I was becoming more and more of an artist, and my indefatigable doodling was burning up more and more paper, pencils and colors. But my mother understood the value of such work, and kept me supplied with these things, not so easy to come by in nineteen forty-four or five.

My work around age 5.

That was the happy side of Shandon. The other side was the prisoner-of-war camp up the hill behind us. As far back as I could remember, my mother and I always went for a walk every day. On our way up the Back Road, over the one-track railway line, we saw several rows of Nissan huts, aluminum shells, looking cold and uninviting, with a central observation post and surrounded by a huge fence with barbed wire. One day we saw the men that lived in the huts—young, blonde, German! My mother, always responding to the underdog—as she saw these prisoners—immediately started to talk with them in her fluent German. Their bleak faces lit up and they crowded to the fence to speak with her. Although I was only five years old, I could see that these were not really men; they were boys, teenagers at best. Could I understand that a European government would send out these boys to die as cannon fodder, or to be trapped in this dead end? My mother spoke with the camp commander and got permission to bake cookies for them and provide them with cigarettes, which she herself would deliver, to their obvious delight. It was really wonderful to see these poor children come alive when they saw my mother!

My father visited for a few days while we were living at Shandon. I don't remember much of what happened, though my mother seemed a lot less stressed than she was at the previous visit in Hillview Road. There was one dramatic incident, which made me beholden once again to my father. One evening my parents were sitting together talking on the couch. I was behind them on the floor sooking, as we say in Scotland, on a lollipop. Suddenly the lollipop separated from the stick and got stuck in my windpipe. I could not breathe nor talk and realized I was dying. A black tide was rising above my head and I tried to say goodbye to my mother and father. My parents turned round to see why I was making such a strange noise, and my father, a medical man, realized at once what was happening. In a moment he pulled me to my feet and walloped me on my back. The lollipop shot out of my mouth and halfway across the room, landing stickily on the carpet near my mother. Once again he had saved my life and I realized what it meant to have a father.

But there was another side to this, there was another experience that was to dog and persecute me for a long, long time afterwards. One day in autumn as mother and I were gathering hazelnuts in the woods behind our house, a man quietly stepped out of the woods and approached us. He seemed to know my mother quite well and greeted her affectionately in German. Then he turned to me and said, "You must be Cheen." A quiet man, of medium height, browned by the sun, with calm eyes and a soft voice. I liked him immediately. He seemed to belong in our world, not boisterous and angry, like my father. It was quite natural that he would start to pick nuts with us, affectionate, kindly, humorous, and *connecting* with me, making me feel that I was loved. I wondered, "Why isn't Daddy like this?"

I have no other memory of seeing this man who, in hindsight, could easily have been a university professor, a scholar of some sort. That was the manner he had.

Days I was at school, and I have no idea whether this man ever came into our house. It would be easy to imagine how the local people felt about my mother's fraternizing with the Germans—probably most of them had lost relatives on Clydeside or had boys fighting in Europe. Who this older German was I have no idea, nor how he was free to move about. What I know for certain is that one day in December my mother brought in the mail and sat down at the table to read it. After reading one of the letters she began to sob convulsively and without stopping. She laid her head down on the table and just spilled her soul into a huge ocean of pain and misery. This was utterly devastating to me, for Scots people do not show their emotions overtly. Of course I had known for some time that she was in great pain, but I had never seen her cry like this. There was absolutely nothing I could do: I had no idea what the matter was, I was so unused to scenes like this—and I was only five years old.

After this episode, she was what can only be called fey. It was as if she was under a spell, not living in contact with this world, listening to some call that was leading her to her doom. She took care of me, but she was not with me. I felt a heavy, heavy load on my soul, not knowing what was happening and fearing the worst. A few days later, about four o'clock in the evening, she started to put on her coat. It was nearly dark, for Scottish winter evenings draw in very early, and it was pouring with rain. "Where are you going, Mummy?" I said. "I am going out." "But it is pouring with rain! You can't go out in this rain!" She said nothing, but started to button her coat. "Let me come with you!" She looked at me for a while, her eyes not really seeing me. "I'll be back in a wee while. Wait for me."

That's what I did. She wasn't there for the evening meal, which our landlady fixed for me. Nor was she there at bedtime. The landlady put me in a bedroom next to hers, so she could look out for me during the night. I lay in a large double bed, with a gas mantle burning above my head. I don't believe I cried, but I certainly did not sleep. I could feel my mother's anguish, I could feel her stumbling in the dark, and I knew that I would never see her again.

The next day my father showed up around lunchtime and took me by bus to Glasgow, where Anne Dunlop, my mother's closest friend, was waiting to take me into her family. As she recounted it much, much later, her doorbell had rung at some ungodly hour of the morning and there was my father, looking haggard and distraught. Anne had not met him previously, but of course she had heard a lot about him. He was unable to speak at first, and Anne said, "Colin MacPhail! Come on in." My father was mumbling incoherently, but Anne could understand that he was saying, "Nan has disappeared." Anne was one of those salt-of-the-earth Scottish women who did so much to help me grow up normal. Her immediate response was, "Colin, why are you standing there? Get on the bus immediately and bring your daughter here!" Which he did—but not before a good breakfast and several cups of tea.

This was the first really major turning point of my life, the first turn of the spiral of my childhood. There were to be three more shocks like this spaced out in twenty year intervals, but this one in many ways was the hardest. I was just a little girl, and could not understand what was happening. At least, intellectually. But in other ways I knew exactly what was happening. I had known for a long time that my mother was deeply unhappy, hide it though she might. And I had feared, without putting it into words, what was about to happen. And that night when I lay awake in the big, unfamiliar bed, shut off from the stars that inspired me, I could see in my mind's eye what was unfolding in the dark, boggy hills behind our house.

After she died, I never mentioned my mother's name to anyone. There were no questions, no crying, just silence. The family was amazed; and as the years passed with not a word from me, they thought that I had forgotten her. But children don't forget their mothers, particularly one like mine, to whom I had been so very, very close. The silence continued, but eight years later, when I was fourteen, I wrote this "poem":

> On the mountain, shadows
> Pass and re-pass, over blue rocks
> And black,
> Where lies a broken temple
> Silvered by the weak moon.
> A wreath of curling locks
> And an arm stretched out,
> Cold, cold and heavy,

Soaked with the dews of night.
Peace in the now still body,
Devoid of life and sadness.
No trace of joy, yet it is there—
Silent, still, true bliss and happiness.

Fleeting wings bring the sighs
Of a child;
Teardrops fall as drops of gentle rain
On eyelids white as marble.
A light dim and yellow
Glows in the town.
The eye of love and a heart cries
In the still, warm night.

As it turns out, when I got the facts about twenty years after my mother's death, I had seen exactly what had happened. That, I think, is why I never mentioned it. I already knew and didn't need to ask. When you love someone truly, that is the way it is.

SECOND QUARTER

WILD REACTIONS

CHAPTER 3

GRANT STREET: 1946-1948

Moving in with Anne and her family began the second turn of my childhood's spiral. They lived in Glasgow proper, so I finally experienced the city around which my mother and I had been revolving for the previous five years. Because of the circumstances of the war and likely also on account of my mother's increasing depression I had lived so hermetically that this was the first time I was exposed to community, and a very jolly one it was. Anne's children John and Jem, who were about my age, were extremely energetic and mischievous, always on the go and never giving me time to be sad. Anne herself and her husband John, whom I got to

Anne and Jem Dunlop, around 1944.

know later, were the essence of goodness and kindheartedness and treated me as their own child.

Then there was the larger community of my extended family and friends, whose support I felt shortly after I arrived at the Dunlops'. One morning I woke up on the cot Anne had set up in the living room, and saw several large piles of packages next to it. They had not been there the night before and I wondered what they meant. It was cold and I was inclined to stay in bed, contemplating the packages. Then Anne came in. "Get up, Jean! You have all these Christmas presents to open!"

Christmas! I had no idea that it was Christmas. And who could have sent me so many presents? This was something new for me. I am sure my mother did something for me at Christmastime, but I had never seen anything on this scale. Of course, now that the war was over, it was a little easier to buy such things as gifts, but something like this was utterly new. In a dim way I also understood that people had felt great sorrow at my losing my mother just before Christmas—but that they would express it like this! What was important was that I was made to feel that there were a whole lot of people who loved me and would look out for me now that I was the proverbial "motherless child".

Anne taking me in was all the more remarkable on account of the fact that she was in the middle of preparations to move to Edinburgh. Her husband John was returning from service with the military police and was about to start work in his hometown, where his family ran a chain of upper middle-class tearooms. I was to experience Edinburgh in depth later in my life, but for the moment, the main thing was moving to a nice, quiet, clean neighborhood and having the company of John and Jem. There was really no end to the mischief we got up to, led by the mastermind, John. Anne had to step out one day to pick up some groceries at the corner. When she returned she found us stark naked and painted from top to toe with her best lipstick. We informed her that we were playing at Red Indians. Red, indeed! I often wonder how Anne got us clean again.

At Easter I moved back to Glasgow, where I was to live for the next eight or nine years. A new home had formed itself for me, brought together by other sad events in the family, for by some coincidence, two other family members passed away at almost the same time as my mother. On my mother's side of the family, my Uncle Bill Thomson had succumbed to cancer, despite all the care lavished on him by his wife, my mother's sister Jane. Highly respected for his honesty and decency, Uncle Bill was an unusually dour Scot, keeping to himself the fact that he had a growth on his testis, perhaps because at the time he noticed it, Scotland was again under German attack and he felt he should not take away from his duties with the Home Guard. His death left my Aunt Jane in less favorable financial conditions than previously, and she had to take up work as a schoolteacher to support herself and my cousin Jean, a few years older than I. Jane always poignantly regretted that she was so taken up with her husband's care that she had no idea that my mother was in such deep distress, and that she had been totally unable to help her in any way. She always looked on my mother as her own child, and had longed to adopt me when she died. But she could not now afford it financially. Nevertheless, Aunt Jane was to play a big role in my life, being one of the four or five "mothers" who "adopted" and cared for me during the difficult period of adjustment I was going through.

The other death—on my father's side—was of my beloved Granpa, who died shortly after a massive stroke which hit him around the same time as my mother's death. There was to be no more "splashy windies", though of course by that time I had probably outgrown that particular pastime. My grandmother, now seventy-five or seventy-six years old, was alone in the house in Glasgow, with a weak heart, and it was felt that she should have someone with her. Having me live with her seemed like the best solution to my situation, and also my father, as and when he was fully demobilized from the army—but who would be the person to take care of the household?

The tradition in such situations is to call on the unmarried daughter of the family to do the needful. Our family, being very traditional, did just that, summoning my father's sister Mary back from London to take care of her mother, brother and niece. And she came, the never-to-be-forgotten *Mary*, as I always called her; it was never *Aunt Mary*, because I could never believe she was old enough to be my aunt. She was a dynamo of energy, capability, ingenuity and humor, so lively that even in her old age I could never think of her as anything but a young woman and would humorously suggest that she run for the job of Prime Minister.

The new home was in Grant Street in the heart of Glasgow. It was a rather dingy street of three-story tenements black with the all-pervading soot and superimposed white pigeon-droppings that made most of Glasgow look like an iced cake. Despite its unprepossessing appearance, the street was an island of middle-class, Protestant respectability in the huge ocean of a large Irish Catholic ghetto. Moreover, it belonged to a Mr. Grant who was empowered to prevent children or other rowdy elements from living in his property. My grandparents, both staunch Free Church Protestants and models of propriety, had gone to live there when my grandfather was fully retired. Both were known as pillars of their church, God-fearing and decent citizens much respected by their neighbors and certainly never people who would introduce any undesirable elements into Mr. Grant's oasis. However, a certain amount of jawboning had to go on to get permission for me to live there, no doubt carried on by my aunt, who was one of the fastest and most persuasive talkers in the West. But we did get permission and I arrived there from Edinburgh just in time for the opening of the Easter term at school.

My father, now demobilized from the army and temporarily living at Grant Street, took me to school a few days later. The Glasgow Girl's High School was on a hill not far from us, so getting there provided me with a mile or so walk up and down, a routine that was to become part of my life from then on. Nineteen forty-seven was a severe winter; although it was Easter time, there was about two feet of snow on either side of us as we wended our way along Shamrock Street, one of the key points in the Irish ghetto, me burbling away and stopping only when my eye was caught by a strangely beautiful book that was sitting in solitary splendor in the window of a shabby shop on the corner. Beautiful, rich colors, specially red and green, iconic figures with an irresistibly compelling quality. I could read enough by then to spell out *The . . . Book . . . of . . . Kells*. I had no idea what it was about, and my father did not enlighten me. But a chord had been struck in my soul that I was not to hear fully or really respond to for at least another fifty years. In the meantime, I had to put my energy into a whole new world, a world without my mother, a world that knew nothing of her nor what she had meant to me. But there

Cover of the *Book of Kells.*

was my granny and Mary, the two women who were to care for me, and also the extended family, full of kind aunts and uncles, and a few of my teachers, who would take a special interest in me and help me develop my natural abilities.

My grandmother, Mary Anne MacPhail, was, in one sense, a cultural dinosaur, unlike my sophisticated and avant-garde mother.

My Grandmother, 1901.

Born in eighteen seventy, she had grown up on Lewis, an island off the north-western coast of Scotland where the way of life was crofting or subsistence farming, supplemented by fishing in the hazardous, turbulent North Atlantic. Her family had had a couple of cows, perhaps a horse, a few sheep and hens and maybe a small plot of land where oats and kitchen garden vegetables were grown. From an early age she had done hard farm work, knitted and sewed, making with her own hands the knobbly tweed suits the men wore, and also their leather boots. She had known, like all of the other families on the island, the tragedy of losing most of her brothers to the wild Atlantic as they tried to wrest a living from it in their pitifully inadequate little boats. And, with all that she was related, on the one hand to Duncan MacAskill, the author of the definitive Gaelic-English dictionary, and on the other to the well-known British litterateur and politician, Thomas B. MacAulay.

The islanders were also living in the aftermath of the Highland Clearances, the notorious ethnic cleansing that had taken place since the end of the eighteenth century. The Highland gentry, keeping abreast of modern developments, had calculated that their large, agriculturally unproductive property could turn a profit if made over to large-scale livestock grazing, principally sheep. In order to bring this about, they had decided that they must get rid of the indigenous people, living on the land as their ancestors had done since time immemorial. Although the savagery varied from one property to the other, the basic strategy was to burn down the houses of the crofters and herd them on to ships which took them to the British colonies or ex-colonies—Canada, Australia and the Southern United States—where they were unceremoniously dumped with their pitiful belongings and most of them not speaking a word of English. Gaelic, that ancient tongue, was the language of most of the crofters, as incomprehensible to their English-speaking torturers as English and the mindset that went with it was to these throwbacks to a much older time. For the Gaelic speaking people of the Scottish Highlands belonged to a much, much simpler social order, where family loyalties and living religious faith were the mainstays of social life, and learning was less in reading and writing and more in the stories and legends handed down from generation to generation.

Although these people had not escaped the Reformation—being, for the most part, staunch Protestants—their faith was far from the contemporary mainstream. Living so close to nature and depending on her as much as they did, they kept alive the mystical communion with the forces of nature that we tend to think of as "primitive" and specially associated with the Celts, which is precisely what these people were. Without a written tradition until the Middle Ages, we know them mainly through the materials gathered in the nineteenth century by Alexander Carmichael and known to the world as *Carmine Gaedelica*, or Gaelic Songs. There we find them speaking to the Christ pervading the skies and the oceans, to his mother Mary to make their minds right as they went about their daily tasks, and for help and guidance as they faced the many terrors of their dangerous way of living. Of course, Christian missionaries had arrived from the mainland, bringing some sort of literacy and modernity to their religious belief, but even in my grandmother's youth it was whispered that quite a few folks would slip out at dusk to worship at the many standing stones and other sanctuaries that dotted the island and harked back to millennia before the Christian era.

Their formal religion was the Free Church, so-called because it had freed itself from the compromises made by the Presbyterian Church, the indigenous church of Scotland. The Presbyterian Church itself was fiercely anti-clerical, ruling itself though ordained presbyters or elders. The "meenisters" were deeply revered, but their job was limited to preaching sermons and tending the flock. The actual running of the Church was in the hands of the lay elders, who also did some pastoral work. This was a no-nonsense church, rigidly against any privilege or suggestion that anyone was intrinsically superior to the other. It has been called the most democratic church ever—before its time it seems, for during the seventeenth century it had been mercilessly persecuted by the more aristocratic Episcopalians, adherents of the state church of England.

Despite its heroic history, by the end of the eighteenth century the Presbyterian Church had somehow permitted the landowning gentry to appoint its ministers, thus giving them a large say in how the church was being run. The full impact of this arrangement became apparent as these same gentry started destroying the crofting culture and forcibly expatriating the native people, while the ministry could only stand by and watch helplessly; to speak out was to lose their post and income.

Several ministers found this totally unacceptable and broke with the Presbyterians, setting up the Free Church and dedicating themselves to the fight to end the atrocities. Most of them speaking English as well as Gaelic and being sufficiently literate to write to the press, they began a campaign, not only as go-betweens of the Gaelic crofters and the English-speaking agents of the gentry, but also as writers of quite impassioned articles which first appeared in the newspapers of Inverness, the largest town in the Highlands. From there word spread south to Edinburgh and Glasgow and on to London. The various organizations that had been fighting for independence in Ireland got wind of what was afoot in Scotland and began to arrive there to add to the agitation and help organize it more effectively. Finally action was taken; a Crofters' Commission was set up under Lord Napier in 1883, which, after lengthy investigations, came up with what might be called the crofters' bill of rights, giving the indigenous farmers more security of land and tenure.

The "war" had been fought, from the gentry's side, with policemen and even the military, though there were few if any deaths. The dirt-poor crofters were armed with clods of peat (the fragrant turf they burned in their fireplaces), perhaps some stones, and their native wit and familiarity with the terrain. Though the worst atrocities occurred on the mainland, where there were large tracts of land under dispute, there were also troubles on the Hebridean islands, including Lewis. My grandmother's brother Murdo had been know to throw a clod of peat or two at the police and to lead them a merry dance in pursuit of him and his teenage friends.

By the nineteen forties all this was over. Sheep roamed the Highlands wherever the eye could see and a few crofters still hung on, eking out a bare living, supplemented by the tweed industry which they pursued in their little black houses, where a loom would take up whatever space was not occupied by hens, sheep or farm implements. But the Free Church had proven itself in battle and held its head up proudly. Like their Presbyterian kin, they were dour people, God-fearing, Sabbath-observing and against all forms of frivolity. Clothes were dark and simple, all forms of luxury were non-existent, and "fal-lalls" such as the movies, lipstick, perfume or dyeing your hair were out of the question. We did listen to programs like the news on the radio, but visits to the cinema were not really approved of, Sunday newspapers were verboten and alcohol was in theory not a part of our life (though, of course, a wee glass of sherry at the New Year was all right. Nobody wanted to spoil the party).

This was my grandmother's lifestyle. We had a roast on Saturday and ate cold cuts on Sunday, as cooking on the Sabbath was not acceptable. However, maybe because my granny was a loving soul and maybe because Mary had lived in London so long (and was so darned persuasive!), we did have freshly boiled potatoes and hot tea, rather necessary in the cold, drafty house in which we lived. People reading this may think that I am about to tell them how I suffered in this puritanical atmosphere, how it stunted my life and suffocated me spiritually. Not wanting to disappoint, I have to say that this was the most vibrant and highly spiritual atmosphere I have ever lived in, bar none. Despite, or perhaps because of, the austerity of their outer lives, these were the most fervent and joyful people I have ever known. There is no doubt that for those who were not ready to live like this, the only way to cope was hypocrisy and pretense, and there was plenty of that, too; but for those whose minds were ready to "love the Lord" the austerity and discipline of this way of life really seemed to work.

Grannie's church was next door to our house. On Sundays we would see the congregation arriving in large numbers, mostly clad in black, but relieved by the bright kilts that some of the men were wearing. In they would go and in no time we would hear the penetrating voice of the precentor intoning the psalms of David—for the Free Church did not believe in musical instruments for divine service, nor in the frivolity of singing anything not written in the Bible. The human voice would suffice, and like the Jews and the Muslims, there was one man's voice that cried out the lines in an incredibly powerful way. And this was a Lewis congregation, singing in their highly ornamented style, with arabesques, trills and glissandos, suggesting the Middle East or maybe Japan more than dour and plain-Jane Scotland. No doubt this was a very ancient way of singing, harking back maybe to prehistoric times. Hearing these strange wailing sounds would stop you dead in your tracks if you happened to be passing by. Was this Glasgow or Baghdad? But, just as you were recovering from the strangeness of the precentor's voice, the incredible response from the congregation would begin. Like a tsunami incorporating all forms of sounds and tones, men, women and children's voices in a whole range of keys and little individual trills and arabesques would rise up slowly, build and build in intensity, peak at a heart-stopping climax and then spread far and wide as it melted away in a minor key. Then the precentor would begin again, slowly and majestically pounding out the sacred words of the royal prophet. Again the thunderous response, which made you understand what the phrase "raising the roof" means.

Listening to this, I would long to have the intensity and fervor that these formidable people had. And when they came out afterwards, they were all smiles, no doubt the better of the cathartic and achingly long sermon they had just heard. For the Gaelic preachers would really lean into their sermons, relishing their vanishing language as much as going over the themes that held these people together in a world that was tending to leave them behind. As the group dispersed slowly, I was struck by the fine bearing of the men and women, probably originally country people like my grandparents, and very, very proud of their heritage. A special treat was to see the meenister's son striding homeward in his green Lovat jacket and red kilt, which swung left and right with just the sharp flicking movement that marks out a true Highlander. Thankfully (and no doubt in character) he was totally unselfconscious and blissfully unaware of little Glasgow keelies like me, naughtily trying to see if our carrot-haired hero had gone the whole hog and was not wearing underpants, which was said to be the hallmark of a true Scotsman, no matter where he hailed from.

These ardent people would have communion services only a few times a year. It was a huge event, and religious fervor was at fever pitch. Grannie used to have her close friends come by the house, perhaps to wait for the next service, of which there seemed to be several in one day. These elderly ladies, all clad in widows' black, would read out the Bible in Gaelic by the hour and then they would sing together, rocking back and forth as they intoned the psalms in their inimitable way. They would sing for a long time, creating an atmosphere of tremendous spiritual intensity that made me feel as if I was in the presence of a powerful God of a time beyond the present. There was absolutely nothing "modern" about these women—they were communing with a great God that could not be defined or measured by any of the instruments that we wield nowadays.

When she was alone, Grannie would sometimes sing in English. I distinctly remember her sitting in our small kitchen beside the coal fire, with its fire-irons and singing kettle. In her widow's black from top to toe, a small velvet band around her neck, the brooch Granpa had given her pinned at the front, and her long black hair tied up in a bun, she would croon over and over from a popular hymn, "Peauhtiful, Peauhtiful Cheesus!"[2] She would rock back and forth, passing into an ecstatic mood, with her blue eyes full of tears. This was something utterly novel to me, for my mother and her family were all sophisticated atheists, more or less, and Mary was a hard-headed businesswoman from London who, despite being the best of people, was not in the least interested in religion. Nevertheless, I could relate to what Grannie was doing, because I knew just how beautiful Jesus was. Hadn't I seen him before my mother died? I would watch in mute wonder, silently sharing her feelings, but unable to put anything into words.

And she was not just an eccentric old lady living in a fantasy world. She was deeply rooted in a powerful tradition, though others might think it primitive or retro. She was kind and generous to the marrow of her bones, infinitely loving, though not pushing it on to anyone. And she had the second sight, another feature of the Highland culture. Perhaps because they did live so simply and close to nature, these people had the ability to see things in a heightened way. Mary Anne especially was known to have the ability to read minds, foretell the future, see and hear what was happening somewhere else, though she never spoke about all this or used what she had learned for anything but the welfare of others.

Her balance of mind, heightened powers and basic common sense and wisdom were highly prized in her community and she was considered a holy woman. She had a constant stream of visitors coming to consult with her and get her blessings. When I would get home from school around

---

2   Beautiful, beautiful Jesus.

four thirty, I would find her ensconced in the living room where Mary had started a new coal fire. Grannie would be sitting, as usual, quiet and absorbed in herself as she waited for her visitor. Soon the doorbell would ring and there was another earnest soul coming to have her straighten out the complexities of his or her life. My job, which I relished, was to put on the kettle for tea and get together a tray with the cups, milk, sugar and cookies that I would take in and set on a wee table in front of Grannie, so that she could offer the tea that preceded the infinite sympathy she had to offer to all to turned to her.

Occasionally, if the visitor spoke in English, I was allowed to sit in on these visits. No matter how troubled or even excited her visitor was, she was always calm and quiet, focusing on the core of what was troubling her visitor's soul. Her common sense was really remarkable, even to a seven or eight year old like me. I would empathize with what was troubling the visitor, feeling crushed by his or her difficulties and wondering how the problem would ever be solved. After a short pause, her soft, lilting voice would ask a simple question, so to the point and so direct that it was like a bucket of water thrown on a fire that was going out of control. In no time the visitor and I were relaxing, beginning to see what all of this was about, and yes, I will have another cup of tea, Mary Anne, thank you.

What my Grannie was showing me was that it is possible to cultivate love of God and the wisdom that proverbially goes with it. Her incredibly austere and self-sacrificing life was all about finding the inner light, finding her bliss in her beloved Jesus, and keeping the flame alive through practices supported by the religious community of which she was such a vital part. From the outside it all seemed dark and dour, but inside those black-clad people was a tremendous energy which could not but attract my interest. But of course, most of it was in Gaelic, so how it was expressed in words escaped me. I longed to speak the language, but amazingly no teacher could be found. Certainly it was not taught in our school curriculum, because it was considered a dying language, a remnant of a primitive past. People like my Grannie were considered quaint and old-fashioned, dinosaurs that would soon be extinct.

The great grace was that this wonderful woman did speak English, which she had taught herself, more or less. From the standpoint of my own spiritual life, the blessing was that I saw, from our daily routines which were carried out in English, just how she sustained her spirituality. We never ate without saying, "For what we are about to receive, may the Lord make us truly thankful", a rather barebones grace, perhaps, but one that through constant repetition made me realize that there was more to the world we live in than just the material objects we see before us. Also, of course, that underneath there are indeed the "everlasting arms" which support us and provide us with what we need. Then there was the fact that whenever she added her contribution to any discussion at the table, it was always shot through with references to her spiritual life. One day I mumbled to Mary, who was sitting beside me at the table, "What is wrong with Grannie? She always talks about God!" It really was most unusual, even strange. In this day and age, when we have our wireless, our airplanes, our antibiotics, our automobiles, our movies, our TVs, our Stalins, our Hitlers, our Mao Zedongs, our families destroyed by senseless war, who talks about God? What does it mean? But one look at her calm, smiling face, and her clear blue eyes focused on an infinity that was so palpably here and now, would silence me completely.

One night as Mary was settling me into bed, Grannie came in and said to me, "To you say your prahyersh, Cheen?"[3] "No, Grannie." How would I? I had lived in a purely secular culture thus far. Then she sat down on the covers and said, "I'll kive you a prahyer. Pe sure to say it every night pefore you go to sleep." Then she taught me the most ridiculously simple prayer: "Now I lay me down to sleep, I pray the Lord my soul to keep. If I should die before I wake, I pray the Lord my soul to take." Of course, I was only six or seven and had no pretensions to sophistication, so I took it all in, caught in the glow of her sincerity and perhaps hungry for the key to another world where the pain of my mother's death would not hurt me so much. I would repeat it, night after night, connecting it up in a dim way with the beautiful Jesus I had seen and sometimes feeling that yes, someone very wonderful was listening and was responding.

My Aunt Mary, the other woman who was caring for me in Grant Street, was another pillar of my early life. Though Grannie's second daughter and like her, a model of goodness, loyalty and generosity, she was of a different type. Down to earth, life-and fun-loving, she had found her parents' pious lifestyle not at all her cup of tea and ran away from home when she was fifteen. In search of a more interesting life, she had made her way to London, which the Scottish meenisters of the time, quoting their beloved Old Testament, would not hesitate to call "the whore of Babylon". London was "the big city" in a way Glasgow wasn't. It had theaters, cinemas, nightlife on a scale that Scotland could not

---

3   Do you say your prayers, Jean? . . . I'll give you a prayer.

My Aunt Mary, probably in the nineteen-thirties.

conceive of, fuelled by rich entrepreneurs and businessmen and also the wealthy aristocrats that were a feature of English life almost unknown in Scotland. Whatever aristocrats we had stayed in their fastnesses in the Highlands and hunted game, or even went to the local pub for "a wee dram" with the locals.

Mary would have arrived in London around the end of the First World War. The terrible toll in lives that the war had taken meant that large numbers of women remained unmarried, and also that they became more adventurous in seeking employment and taking charge generally. Mary trained as a nurse, specializing in newborn babies and lunatics and soon became a private nurse, tending the rich and famous. She had had intimate access to the lives of film stars, wealthy business people and the aristocracy, and was a truly bottomless pit of stories about their shenanigans. But she was not lacking in intellect. Once I found her reading a book by Joad, whom I later learned was a quite distinguished philosopher.

And she was an astute businesswoman. Between the world wars she set up her own private nursing agency in London and, as far as I know, was doing quite well when the summons came to return to Glasgow on the death of her father. Although an attractive woman, with the dark wavy hair and greenish blue eyes of the Celt, she had remained unmarried. She had had plenty of offers of marriage; but, she told me, she wanted her freedom to enjoy life as she wished. She loved nice clothes, perfume, going out and having fun, so different from her mother. But underneath it all, she respected tradition, and the call of her family overrode her personal preferences. Looking back at it now, the degree of her self-sacrifice in coming back to dingy old Glasgow to care for her troubled niece and later her even more troubled brother, was simply enormous. But, like the rest of our family, she was a great one for making the best of it, and she took satisfaction in the fact that Glasgow was a much better place to shop than London. This, she felt, was one of Britain's best-kept secrets. And she did like to shop, dragging me along Sauchiehall Street, the grimy and pigeon-dropping-covered main street of Glasgow, always in search of a killing. There again she was close to being a saint, as I would complain and complain and complain, wanting only to go home and having nary a flicker of interest in anything we were doing. Of course, I would be fascinated by the women flipping over potato scones on the huge griddles in the kitchen of Ross's, a dairy and bakery chain that would advertise itself as "If it's Ross's it's right", if it's right it's Ross's"—which, in this day and age of vanishing punctuation, might be a good test to put to schoolchildren. Sometimes Mary would leave me standing outside Ross's while she went off to get a bargain in a nearby store, knowing that she would be sure to find me still there when she got out.

We also differed radically on my appropriate self-image. Mary, like other women of her generation, still clung to the idea of femininity (though she had already breached almost every canon of it). She was always trying to coax a curl out of the slight wave in my hair and liked to dress me up in pretty clothes, which I detested. She was supported in this mission by the fact that many of my clothes were hand-me-downs from my cousin Jean, some three years older than I and living in considerably more comfortable and conventional circumstances. I didn't mind the blue and white striped dress too much, nor the white Mary Janes, but the straw bonnet with the artificial flowers and ribbons hanging down on either side! For one thing, it was much too young for me, and for another I just did not want to look like a little girl, or any kind of a girl, for that matter.

One day Mary and I were going to visit some old relative. She insisted that I put on my best clothes, including the much-dreaded and reviled bonnet. We had a heated argument—I may have shed a few angry tears—but when we left the house I was indeed wearing it. We were taking the tram down Great Western Road, one of the few boulevard-like streets in Glasgow. In a sulky mood, I insisted on standing on the landing at the door, while Mary went in and sat down. The tram picked up terrific speed, whistling rather than rattling along. Trams in those days did not have closed doors, so I was able to lean out and feel the terrific draft being created as we whizzed along. How exhilarating! Pulling back in for a moment to catch my breath, I had a sudden epiphany. The bonnet! The bonnet! This was the moment of truth! Holding firmly to the rail I leaned way out and with my other hand pulled off the bonnet, leaving it to its fate. What happened was extremely interesting in and of itself, for the bonnet caught the wind and started to revolve like a helicopter blade, rapidly disappearing into the back draft we were creating. But what was more glorious was my final liberation from the tyranny of femininity. I felt like Arthur pulling the sword out of the stone, or Icarus flying to the sun on his artificial wings. But I was certainly in the emotional doghouse with Mary for several days, licking my wounds, but secretly rejoicing that I had struck a blow for freedom, no doubt the first of many to come.

Mary and I were definitely on different wavelengths: she liked *things* and working with things, but I was more interested in imagination, ideas and principles, though I could not put them into words at that time. What I did do was put images down on paper—in ballpoint, pencil, crayons, pastels, water-color, whatever I could get my hands on. And, whatever our differences in makeup, Mary loved me intensely and made heroic efforts to help me grow in the direction most suited to me. Not long after I arrived in Grant Street she had me up at the Glasgow Art Galleries having an interview with Miss Jean Irwin, one of the gallery's curators and leader of the free Saturday morning art class for underprivileged children.

As we waited on an upstairs landing, echoing and re-echoing as patrons traipsed over the marble floor behind us, my attention was drawn to an exhibit of what looked like gas mantles similar to the one that had been burning over my head the night my mother died. Why would they have gas mantles in the Art Galleries? This was much more on my mind than the imminent meeting with Miss Irwin. As I read the caption to this strange item, I was amazed and also repelled to find that what I was seeing were actually earrings made, in true Victorian style, out of a woman's hair. So that was why the "mantles" looked blonde rather than white! And why on earth would anyone want to make earrings out of hair, or wear such a thing—or put it in an exhibition?

As this momentous thought process was going on, Miss Irwin appeared and was talking with my aunt. Mary was telling Miss Irwin that I had lost my mother; that we were living in a street with no children;

that I needed to be with other children; and that I seemed to be talented in art. She may have told her quietly that she wanted to cheer me up, but I didn't catch that directly.

Miss Irwin came over to me. She was tall, with prematurely white hair, deep brown eyes, a slight lisp and "arty" clothing, with lovely rich colors unusual in Glasgow. She bent down to talk to me. "So you want to join the Art Class?" "Yes." "What do you like to draw?" Without a moment's hesitation: "Horses!" I had fallen in love with the glorious Clydesdale horses that were still pulling delivery carts in Glasgow, particularly coal and sometimes milk. A coal delivery was for me a sight for the gods. The horses with their huge fetlocks pulling up, the delivery man black from top to toe and with a thick leather cape on his back onto which he would pull a big sack of coal, then clumpety clumpety clump down the hallway and into our house, into the back where the kitchen was and our bunker was standing open. He would bend over the bunker and Clooooosh! Rattle! Thump! The coal would pour in, sending up clouds of black dust. I just loved the animal power and grace of all of this, and was almost obsessive about representing it in my artwork.

Though all I said was "horses", something of my excitement seemed to have conveyed itself to Miss Irwin, for I saw her eyes light up. Very enthusiastic herself, she always warmed to the enthusiasm of others and, rather than trying to squelch it, as so many "grownups" tended to do, encouraged us to develop ourselves with it. She stood up. "So, that is settled. The class starts in two weeks. I will see you there, Jean." I felt tremendous rapport with her, and from the first class never missed a day for the eight years I lived in Glasgow. She was indeed a pioneer in children's art, which nowadays is quite taken for granted, but was not in those postwar days. She would allow us to do more or less what we wanted, though sometimes she would suggest a theme, such as illustrating her visits to Brittany, where the peasants wore such colorful costumes, or occasionally playing some music and asking us to create something that corresponded to it in color. When we were a bit older she would have us work together on pieces that were several feet long and as tall as we were, working it all out among ourselves.

While in the class I was so absorbed with my work that I did not really talk much with the others, nor did Miss Irwin encourage us to do so. Though most of the children came from poor backgrounds, all were talented and it was exhilarating to be in an environment where there was so much enthusiasm, originality and accomplishment. My senior classmates, George Devlin and Alasdair Gray, have gone on to become two of the most distinguished artists in Scotland. But we all benefited from Miss Irwin's methods of teaching. Although she gave us almost *carte blanche* in what subjects we chose, she would always challenge us in some way or another. She would look at the piece and ask, "Do you think you are really expressing the idea you had when you started? How could you do it better?" Sometimes she would say, "You are just copying something else. I expect something of your own here." And if you were in the least self-deprecating (which, on account of my unhappiness, I often was), she would at once say, with great verve, "Is that any way to think? How is that sort of thinking going to help you?" In short, there was no nonsense, which I have always found to be true of really great teachers.

One thing was clear: she genuinely wanted to help me. For one thing, my work was good (she later told me that she regarded me as one of her most promising students); but I also feel that she sensed and empathized with my difficult situation at home. I always felt that she loved me more than anyone else, but so did all of her other students. She took a really genuine interest in all of us, as if we were her own children. And her inspired work was to bear great fruit, not only in Glasgow but all over the world: Our work traveled far and wide in Europe, Australia and America, perhaps reaching its greatest height in an exhibition at the Uffizi Gallery in Italy. She helped to put children's artwork on the cultural map, and of course, inspired generations of Glasgow children.

My relationship with Jean was in a way a reprise of what I had had with my mother. She lived in a world of imagination, ideas and adventurous creativity, which my heart has always craved. Saturday mornings were for me one long bliss. After breakfast I would walk through Kelvingrove Park, situated not too far from our house, thoroughly enjoying my solitude. I followed the seasonal changes in the trees and the flower beds, the activity of the ducks and other aquatic birds in the duck pond, all of which I would capture in my art work and, increasingly, writing. Arriving at the Art Galleries on the other side of the park, it was straight to work, two hours of total immersion in blissful creativity.

When we finished for the day, we put away our paints and laid our work on the gallery floor to dry. We would all walk round, looking at what others had done, enjoying the different ideas, styles, and ways of executing them that our gifted group had come up with. Then, after the last goodbye, I would go around the galleries, either by myself or with a friend from the class, absorbing the work of the great masters, of which the gallery had quite a good collection. There were works by Rembrandt, Caravaggio,

Degas, Renoir—a representation of the best of Western art—but the one painting that really caught my attention and would hold me mesmerized was by two of our Scottish artists, George Henry and Edward A. Hornel. This was a canvas of a procession of druids coming down a hill with the sacrificial bulls and other paraphernalia of ritual, their faces strangely calm, serene and dark, set off with heavy layers of molded gold. I suppose the idea was to look like an Eastern orthodox icon, but this had a quality all of its own. Bright reds, greens and blacks stood out against thick obvious white brushstrokes indicating surrounding snow. The overall effect was, as I say, hypnotizing. I could not for the life of me understand why, but whatever else I looked at, a visit to the Hornel druids was a must.

The Druids—Bringing in the Mistletoe, 1890
by George Henry and Edward Hornel.
By permission of Culture and Sport Glasgow (Museums)

Now I think that this evocation of our Celtic heritage was speaking to me through all of the modern noise that surrounded me. At Grant Street we used to talk about druids, meaning someone who was unusually wise or with the second sight. There was one family joke which ended with the punch line, "Your grandfather was a druid!" I have no idea to whom this referred; the point was that the idea of a druid was still living in our minds. But the strange, iconic image in the art gallery was not making a joke about druids—it was showing them as powerful shamans engaged in rituals of vital importance. At the time the word shaman was totally unknown to me, of course, and our Celtic culture was indeed considered mainly a joke. It took me fifty years to rediscover it for myself.

Jean Irwin was one of the blessings Mary gave me right from the word go. The other was enrolling me in the Sunday school of the Presbyterian Church around the corner from where we lived. Like my mother, Mary was not a churchgoer, but for different reasons. While my intellectual mother was an atheist on principle, Mary had just outgrown religious organizations and wanted to get on with her life. She did, however, think that it was good for me to be part of a religious group, particularly as there were children there of my own age. One of her Holy Grails was to give me as normal a childhood as possible, a goal somewhat frustrated by Mr. Grant's refusal to let children live on his street. And, of course, me playing with the Irish Catholics who surrounded us on all sides was out of the question; any children I was going to be around had to be educated and civilized—and that, in the popular mind, was not what could be said of the Catholics. Only a Protestant environment would do.

Although I would have liked to go to church with Grannie, all of the services in the Free Church were in Gaelic, which I did not understand. So I ended up with the Presbyterians, about which I was to be ribbed quite a bit after I came to America. The public image of Presbyterians is of a terribly humorless, dogmatic, and puritanical people, impervious to ordinary human needs and weaknesses. When I hear people speaking in this vein, I sometimes think that I was not really cut out to be a true "Presbyterian", for I never felt in the least oppressed or cowed by dogma. It might have been that the good souls at our church were not very good "Presbyterians" either, for my memory of them is only of simple-hearted, kindly, good people, with whom I spent many happy years. This was a working-class congregation, not "educated" in the sense that my family was, but full of common sense, simple-hearted, good natured, and with a great sense of humor. In some ways I was the egghead in the group, but they accepted me and worked me into all of their activities, which included, by the time I was finished, not only Sunday school but also the Girl Guides and the Youth Club.

An important part of my relationship with the church was that I met adult men with whom I had cordial relationships. When I arrived at Grant Street I had had no real experience of a father; and as unfolding events will show, was to be in need of one for a long time. But in the meantime there was Mr. Meek, who led the junior Sunday school. Mr. Meek was in early middle age, unmarried, tall, thin, deep-voiced, with a receding hairline beyond which his brown hair stood up electrically. He was extremely serious and utterly devoted to the church, where he played the organ and seemed to be involved in everything that was going on. What was most important for me was his always kind and serious ways with me. Whenever I had any reason to speak with him personally he treated me with the utmost respect and made me feel valid and even precious. To be taken seriously by an adult man was, of course, something quite novel, though, of course, there was still the faint memory of the German.

I was so taken with Mr. Meek that I decided he would be the ideal man for Mary, still unmarried and, I felt, deserving of some kind of love and support. I told her several times how I thought he was just the man for her, to which she always responded gently, but no doubt suppressing her laughter. Looking back on it now, it was indeed rather funny—he so devout, serious and proper and she so life-loving and free-spirited. One small episode about Mr. Meek says it all: one day when he was presenting pictures from the missions in India, he stopped at the picture of a little Indian girl brushing her teeth with a twig flattened at the end. "We should pray for her," he solemnly told us, "Look, she doesn't have a proper toothbrush!" At the time I was maybe eight years old, but I thought, "What has that got to do with anything? What difference does it make what kind of toothbrush she has? Maybe it's better than the ones we have." This was the beginning of my difficulties with orthodox religion and the agenda it tends to carry. I still loved and respected Mr. Meek, but realized that there was a way of thinking that didn't make sense, despite the fact that my hero seemed to take it seriously.

The other "man in my life" at this time of my childhood was Mr. Lachlan MacLachlan, one of our elders, who was indeed elderly, in addition to being a prime office bearer in the kirk. I met him some years after I met Mr. Meek. Around the age of eleven or twelve I suddenly started to attend the Sunday morning church services all by myself. What motivated me I have no idea. Perhaps I was seeking some kind of stability and solace from the demanding situation at home. Certainly, the sermon bored me stiff, but I loved the many psalms and hymns we sang, which really spoke to me and gave me an outlet for all the emotion roiling in my soul. Our singing, accompanied by Mr. Meek on the organ, could not compare with the rousing roar at Grannie's church, but nevertheless it gave me a sense of belonging, of having a place where I felt safe and loved.

And Mr. MacLachlan was a part of it. Whatever the reasons for my coming, I was absolutely regular and steadfast in my attendance. Mr. MacLachlan, whose job was to greet people as they came in to service, was tickled pink at the idea of such a young girl coming on her own and coming every Sunday without fail. He would greet me like royalty, giving me candies, little bookmarks, and other trinkets. "Here's our wee Jean!" he would cry as he saw me coming up the church steps. He would make quite a ceremony of stamping my attendance card, and would rhapsodize over my winning the prize for church attendance, which I did every year. One part of me felt a bit silly with all of this palaver, but the other just basked in the affection of the old gentleman.

These were Lowland people, not intellectuals like my mother's side of the family, nor mystics like my Highland relatives. Everything was foursquare, including what we did. We learned little passages from the Bible, on which our teacher would quiz us on Sunday morning, giving us an opportunity to express our ideas about what it all meant. I took to this like a duck to water, because it was an opportunity to learn what Jesus was like and what he said. Memory work was still part of our educational curriculum at that time, and for that I am greatly thankful. And I found it all very helpful. Even the phrase from the Old Testament—"Tell it not in Gath, publish it not in the streets of Ashkelon, lest the daughters of the Philistines rejoice"—came in handy as a comment under certain circumstances, even up to the present. But the beatitudes, the core of Jesus's teaching, went deep into my soul. We of course learned the Lord's Prayer, which I took to repeating in addition to Grannie's little bedtime jingle. And St. Paul's marvelous passage on love: "Though I speak with the tongues of men and of angels, and have not love, I am become as sounding brass or a tinkling cymbal . . . Love suffers long and is kind, vaunts not itself, envies not, is not puffed up . . . Love never fails." [4]

---

[4]   I Corinthians, 13.

All of this was the essence of Christianity as I understand it; the ethical and spiritual teachings of Jesus, which I took to heart and tried, in my childish way, to live up to. But the passage that really spoke to me and still gives me goose-bumps, was Jesus's saying, "Inasmuch as you do this to even the least of my brothers, you do it to me." Here I was meeting not just Jesus, but the Christ, the indwelling spirit that is the rationale of all well-doing and happiness. In a dim way it thrilled me to feel that the same beautiful Jesus was in the hearts of everyone else just as much as in mine, and that doing something for them was doing it for him. There was also the unarticulated thought that because of this shared blessedness, everyone was a friend, someone to love and be loved by—although my actual experience was not really supporting that very well. But more of that later.

CHAPTER 4

THERE'S ALWAYS A FLY
IN THE OINTMENT: 1949-1951

This, then, was the center of my world from the age of six to fourteen. Despite the tragedy of my mother's death, I had landed in the most caring and supportive of environments, which ended up supplying me with several mothers, four of whom I talked about in the previous chapter. And behind it all there was another figure, a Mother who spoke to me from the pages of George Macdonald's *At the Back of the North Wind*, a Victorian tale in which a mystical boy called Diamond is befriended by

The North Wind: Illustration by Arthur Hughes, 1871.

the North Wind, who carries him far and wide, showing him the dark as well as the light sides of life and filling him with a sense of rapturous meaning and bliss. Finding this book on my father's bookshelves, I was totally mesmerized by the illustrations, one of which has remained with me even six decades later: the vast goddess, sheltering in her streaming hair little Diamond, so often shuddering at the terrific situations his beloved Mother took him into. I have no doubt whatsoever that this was precisely the image of myself as I stepped up to the plate for my own share of difficulty and suffering. For sailing is never smooth; there will always be the terrible storm that drowns, as Diamond discovered. As one wag put it, when they make the ointment, the first thing they put in is the fly. And my case was no different, because, despite all the support I received, my father was also part of the blueprint for Grant Street, though he did not live there permanently until about nineteen forty-eight or nineteen forty-nine, when I was seven going on eight years old.

Looking back on my father Colin MacPhail, his story was in many ways quite tragic. He was the youngest of Grannie's six children, born in nineteen fourteen after my grandparents left India, where they were stationed for about two years. Brilliant intellectually, extremely sensitive emotionally, and perhaps somewhat handicapped as the youngest of a large family, he was drinking heavily even while in high school. In some ways, that was not so remarkable, for heavy drinking is one of the scourges of Northern Europe, including Scotland. But it was out of character with his family, for his two sisters and three brothers were all quite moderate in their habits, including drinking. Perhaps, like Mary, he was in revolt in some way against the strictures of Free Church living—certainly he was a political radical, though not committed to Communism like my mother. In falling in love with my mother, he was not only taking on a woman who had a tendency to emotional instability (due to the meningitis she had suffered as a child), but also her intellectual, more "upper class" family, for whom he later had no time whatsoever, with the exception of Aunt Jane. In Britain class distinctions were and still are important; and though nothing was ever said on the subject, I could well imagine that in some subtle way my father was made to feel a little "plebeian", a fancy word for low class. From the other side, my mother suffered from the classic weakness of thinking that she could reform him after they married. How many tragedies have been built on that one!

But that was all just preliminary. Marrying his school sweetheart just as he graduated from medical school, he was rushed off to the army to serve as a medical officer for just about the whole duration of the war. Wounded twice in the head and winning the Military Cross for bravery, he was devastated by the terrible conditions of the soldiers and by seeing his friends blown to pieces, one by one. But what most permanently affected him were his encounters with the work of the Nazis. He seldom spoke of his war experiences to me, but he did once tell me how he felt when, after sewing up the abdominal wall of a wounded SS officer, the fanatic took a knife and ripped the stitches open, crying that he wanted to die for his Fuehrer. However, what seems to have really thrown him off his mental balance was his assignment to go ahead and, as a medic, assess the situation at a concentration camp that the British were about to liberate. What he saw devastated him completely. He returned from the war a confirmed alcoholic and wracked with what was then known as shell shock and nowadays as post-traumatic stress disorder.

At the age of eight or so, when I first lived with my father, I had of course no way to know all of this nor to understand it if I did. All I knew was that he was extremely moody, sometimes being a fascinating and entertaining conversationalist, and at others a sullen and treacherous opponent. To begin with, it was his charming side that showed. No doubt he was happy to be reunited with his family after about eight years knocking about in the army and medical institutions. At Mary's suggestion he was working toward a postgraduate degree in epidemiology and preventive medicine, "starting over", and possibly feeling a ray of hope after so much suffering and darkness. He was fascinated by me, and maybe hoped to find in me the happiness that had thus far eluded him.

My main time with my father was at the weekends, when we would go out for the day, either on Saturday or Sunday. Right after art class or Sunday school, we would head west in the bus, either for my Aunt Jane's home in Dumbarton or to visit with family friends in Balloch on Loch Lomond. Aunt Jane and my father got along very well, she being so kindhearted and non-judgmental, as well as totally dedicated to anything to do with my mother. When we went to her place, my father and I would get out of the bus before Dumbarton and walk for a few miles along a little path by the edge of the Clyde. We would be talking a mile a minute, hashing over all sorts of topics, to begin with in mostly a friendly way. As the eternal clouds of Scotland flew over the water its color would keep changing from blues and greens to purples, even red and orange, all of which I was noting for future work at the art class, even as I argued tenaciously with my father. For I never was one to accept anything at face value, and my father did tell an awful lot of tall stories. For the most part he would take it good-naturedly, but sometimes there was quite an edge to our conversation by the time we arrived at the foot of the hill that led us up to Aunt Jane's house.

Aunt Jane always received us with the utmost cordiality. "Come away in!" she would always say, as I noticed the delicious smells coming from the kitchen. She was a really good cook, and served us food that we could not afford in Glasgow. The whole house was full of things I had never seen before, and what particularly drew me was the gramophone, a luxury that I could not have dreamt of in my life that far. As my father and aunt talked, talked, talked in the dining room I would go to the living room and play my favorites: "Take a pair of sparkling eyes"—my first introduction to Gilbert and Sullivan—"Red sails in the sunset", and "Plain Mary Jane", all old chestnuts, the words of which are still flitting about like bats in my belfry. Then there was the "dressing up"; Aunt Jane's box-room was stuffed with old clothes from the twenties, hats with feathers, even her wedding dress and huge long train with sparkles through it. Dressing up in various combinations of these was my idea of total bliss, for it brought out in me grandiose fantasies, some of which I played out with my cousin Jean, who sometimes joined me in my forays into the box-room.

But the real business was dinner, an evening meal we could never aspire to in Glasgow. Wonderful home-made soup, followed by exotic entrees, sometimes including rice, another new experience and—ta da! Trifle. Aunt Jane would bring the traditional dessert in a huge cut crystal bowl, which had been part of her dowry, and lay it on the table for inspection. Through the cut flowers in the crystal we could see the layers—sponge cake soaked in sherry, fruit, a thick layer of custard, topped with an equally thick layer of whipped cream and finished off with glacé cherries and angelica. My cousin Jean and I, though already loaded with all we had eaten, would sit up attentively and brace for the drama we always knew was going to take place.

The fact was, our parents were locked into such a fascinating discussion that food had ceased to exist for them. Aunt Jane would finally stand up (for she was tiny) and pick up the heavy silver serving spoon. "Trifle, dear?" she would ask—as if it was necessary! A silent nod loaded with mouth-watering anticipation. The spoon would rise—and then,

"By the way, Colin, the point you just raised is really most interesting.
I have been thinking about it myself recently" . . . Down would come
the spoon and my aunt would sit down, the better to get a grip on the
conversation. At least fifteen minutes of analysis would follow and then,
her motherly instincts coming to the fore, she would notice the faces of
Jean and myself. She would get up again, ask the same question and—if
we were lucky, we would get our trifle. But sometimes this pantomime
would go on two or three times. If she lit up a cigarette at any point, Jean
and I would know the wait was going to be unusually long!

Looking back on the relationship between my father and Aunt Jane,
this brilliant woman was most likely starved for conversation at her own
level. Her own education had been curtailed by the death of her parents
and taking up responsibility for her sisters—particularly my mother—
while the premature death of her husband had made it necessary for her
to take up a teaching position with very young children. She was a great
storyteller and would regale me with yarns about her pupils and their
antics, some of them not so pleasant; but behind it all was an active mind
that no doubt enjoyed the company of my brilliant, original, and free-
thinking father. Another side of the relationship was that Aunt Jane was
an extremely kind woman, who no doubt felt for my father's mental agony
and loss of direction. I have no doubt she extended to him an acceptance
and forbearance that helped him immensely. Certainly, my father never
misbehaved at Aunt Jane's, and my memories of our frequent visits are
nothing but very, very happy. Her house was one place he was welcome
long after the rest of the family had shut him out.

On alternate weekends my father and I would walk through Balloch
Park, where there were some magnificent old trees and beautifully
tended gardens. The huge canopy gave me a sense of security and peace,
which contrasted with the increasingly difficult conversations I was
having with my father. He was becoming more and more querulous,
nit-picking and nasty as time went by. I simply could not fathom what
his problem was, and would let my mind rather go to the red squirrels
with the tufted ears, which I loved to feed, and also the azaleas, which
flourished in the damp climate and acid soil of the park. Sometimes
we went rowing on Loch Lomond, which helped to defuse some of the
tension and gave me the satisfaction of learning how to row, thus getting
great exercise and making my father pleased. Whatever difficulties we had
had during the day, going home on the last bus to Glasgow was usually a
moment of reconciliation, as we dug into huge fish and chip suppers—a

venerable Scottish tradition—swaddled in newspaper and reeking of fat and vinegar.

Our occasional trips to Hillview Road were another story. There we visited the Macdonalds, parents of my friend Sylvia. Mrs. Macdonald had been a friend of my mother, a cultured woman who had been a piano soloist with the Halle Orchestra and had given me two years of piano lessons. She was another of my inspired teachers, who insisted on my relying on myself and also memorizing my pieces so that I could concentrate on executing them better. In retrospect, she was deeply frustrated at her suburban life and increasingly unable to get along with her husband Dougal. Dougal was severely disabled by the worst stammer I ever heard, almost incapable of getting out any meaningful statements. It was really agony to listen to him speak. I think it likely that this was something the war had either brought on or made much worse. Whatever its origin, he, like my father, was meeting his challenges by increasingly heavy drinking.

As soon as I arrived, Sylvia and I were out the door and into the field or up the hill and round the loch, where "bad men" were either no longer present or did not want to take on the strapping young girls we were becoming. As we went up to the top of Hillview Road, I had epiphanies, which may relate to the increasing anguish I was feeling about my father. One of them related to the exquisitely bluish-purple primroses so many people had in their rock gardens. I have never seen anything so deep and vibrant anywhere else—though it is true that all colors seem so much more vivid in Scotland, perhaps because of the damp air or the way the sun's rays diffract through the ever-present clouds. At any rate, as we were gunning up the hill talking a mile a minute and me feeling some sort of oppressive emotion, my eyes suddenly fell on a clump of those primroses and instantly a mass of energy began to swirl out of it toward me. It caught me up in itself and for a moment lifted me into a completely different space where there was quiet, calmness and a deep sort of joy.

Maybe just as well—for when I would get back from my forays with Sylvia, we would invariably find our fathers blind drunk and her mother beside herself with anger. The two men seemed to have reinforced each other's weakest points and had simply allowed themselves to go to pot. Seeing my father alternately laughing mindlessly or cursing in the most vulgar language was a terrible shock. Where was his brilliance, his learning, now? I have no idea how he and I got home on the tram at night; but fortunately I did not have to go through this for too long, because my father's visits soon stopped. Mrs. Macdonald and her son Bob had put their foot down about my father's visits and that was that. However, I continued to visit Sylvia as long as I lived in Glasgow, and would enjoy getting out to the relative countryside, where I could breathe much better air than in Glasgow. I remember one unusual sight that caught my eye as I was going there by tram. It was just before Christmas and Glasgow had an uncharacteristic fall of snow—for Glasgow was close to the Gulf Stream which brought warm water across the Atlantic from the Caribbean. As the tram lurched and clattered around a corner, I saw roses still blooming in a garden. On one bush there was a large, fat pink bud, bending over under the weight of about three inches of snow. The sight affected me deeply—was I the bud, trying so hard to express itself, and yet held shut by abnormally difficult circumstances?

My father was, in many ways, going down in a spiral into whatever personal hell was consuming him. Where it really came out in its true colors was on our visits to the Hoggs. My mother's radical friends were all of them the nicest, kindest and most honest people you could ever want to meet, and Pearl was one of them. Her husband, whose name was Hogg, was quite a bit older than she, and was trying to run a small farm in the countryside near Loch Lomond. My father and I would go there from time to time to help with various farming chores, particularly the harvest. I just loved humphing the stooks of grain and stacking them up in the haystacks. I was the only child working with the adults, but felt that I was pulling my weight, and certainly got a lot of encouragement from the mostly city people who were helping out. I was not, therefore, very pleased when, at suppertime, Pearl's husband said to her, "Don't give her so much to eat; she hasn't done much work." Like my uncle Robert, he was of a saturnine temperament, with quite bit of volatile anger into the bargain. I kept my distance from him.

Although the work was wonderful, I simply hated the aftermath of supper. The adults would convene in the living room and start the heavy drinking. Pearl's husband would start agitating about politics, getting vehement and at times abusive. As a farmer, he had shotguns standing against the wall, and occasionally he would grab one of them and start brandishing it as he spewed out his anti-government tirades. I got in the habit of sitting on the floor behind the sofa where no one could see or hear me, sometimes wondering if I would make it out of there alive. Never slow to take a dram, my father would get into this hateful act, starting off with the government, but more and more drifting on to tirades against Mary, whom he depicted as the dragon woman to end all dragon women, using vulgar language and horrible epithets that simply made my blood boil. Mary was my *de facto* mother, and how could I take this detestable stuff? I was sorely tempted to jump up and have my say, but then I remembered Hogg's shotguns and how he didn't want to feed me properly, and decided that it was safer to keep quiet behind the sofa.

This sort of thing began to affect my behavior. They tell me that when I was a tot I was a sweet, sunny child with a great sense of humor, but around this time I began to get angry and prone to denunciatory outbursts. Mostly I let off steam to Mary, but unfortunately she wasn't always able to help me. Once I was telling her with great verve what I thought about my father and his drinking. She looked at me for a while and then she said, "Jean, try not to lose respect for your father. He is, after all, your father." This was, of course, noble counsel, particularly as she herself had plenty of difficulties with him. I never remember her criticizing him or discussing him with me in a negative way. I think she probably understood the overwhelming difficulties he was struggling with and was trying to make space for him. On this particular occasion, I took in what she had just said and then remarked, "You should hear what he says about you!" She must have been tempted to ask, but she didn't. She simply left me with the ideal of rising above the situation.

That was not easy to do at all, particularly as his difficult behavior began to manifest itself at home. I would come home from school to find Mary and my father locked in conflict. He slept on a fold-out bed in the living room and, on account of his late night reveling, was often still in it in the late afternoon. Our tradition was that in the afternoon Grannie would come into the living room to receive guests; but my father's snoring presence made it impossible. Mary could not set and start the fire, nor get my father to move. Mary, however, was an executive woman, fiercely devoted to her mother and niece, and she did not back down. "Colin!" she would say in her best staff-nurse voice, "Your mother and daughter need to use this room. Just have some consideration for them and get up!" She would not let him alone and persisted until he grumpily moved himself. While he was in the bathroom Mary got the bed up, the room cleaned, a fire started in the grate and Grannie installed, so that there was no question of him getting back into bed.

This ritual became more and more frequent, almost a routine; and at the same time my father became more and more ugly and abusive.

He would shout obscenities at Mary, using the most hateful language, and occasionally threaten her. I was simply appalled and feared that he would hit her. I had not forgotten my Uncle Robert and his modus operandi! However, he never did use physical violence, either against her or me, for which I am eternally grateful. In retrospect, I feel tremendous empathy for the poor man, basically decent, but in such emotional turmoil that he was losing control of his life. But, as a little girl, already so traumatized, this horrible threat to Mary—the symbol of my security—was increasingly unbearable.

Tension was mounting and mounting in my mind, but I would say to myself, "At least he is decent to Grannie", and take some sort of satisfaction in that. But of course, it was only a matter of time. One day at lunch he was in a particularly bad mood, abusing Mary and myself, and obviously totally out of control. Grannie, the most forbearing of souls, usually remained quiet during his tirades, which were mostly directed at no one in particular. But when he started to spew out his invectives against Mary and myself, she could remain quiet no longer. She quietly asked him to stop it. To my horror, he turned on her and started abusing her in strong, strong language! She remained silent, but her eyes filled with tears. This was too much! Mary was beloved, but Grannie was divine. There is nothing worse than to hear one's ideal reviled. I seethed in fury—but as at the Hoggs', I felt it safer to keep quiet, with my father in that terrible mood.

My father's behavior became more and more erratic, his outbursts alternating with periods of tremendous self-pity and maudlin sentimentality, both of which offended me greatly. This was my Daddy! Why couldn't he be strong and manly, someone I could look up to! Things came to a head one day when, after one of his self-pitying monologues, I gave him a bit of my mind, characteristically hitting hard. He looked very upset and said to me, "You shouldn't speak to me like that. I am your father." I looked at him for a moment, not sure whether to burst into tears or laughter. At that moment one of my besetting faults was preparing to strike, unbeknownst to me, but nevertheless a terrible failing: *Speaking Harsh Words*, which all of my various religious mentors have cautioned me about. What is so devastating is that Harsh Words seem to come of themselves, without any premeditation. Indeed, often one oneself learns for the first time what is brewing in the mind. When, much later, I read in a book of Celtic wisdom that anger is one method of knowledge, I smiled ruefully; for by then I had learned quite a lot that way, and had lived to deeply regret it. We simply do not realize how much damage we do with words, which can cut so deeply into souls that are tender and insecure. But at that moment I only knew one thing: "You are nothing but a drunken old sod!"

Out it came, and then it was nothing but war! I don't think he ever forgave me for saying it. His attacks were now turned primarily on me, reviling, denigrating and abusing me whenever we were together. Meal times, when I saw him most, were just torture. Encouraged by the example of Grannie and Mary, I managed, for the most part, to keep my mouth shut and to try to feel for him and his suffering. But it was difficult. I was an eight or nine year old child, already badly traumatized by the loss of my mother, and desperately needing the protection, love and guidance of a mature adult man. And when he began to shout obscenities about my mother, the screw was turning almost to a point I could not bear. He would call her a whore, a bitch, and all manner of intolerable names. I could never fathom where all this was coming from, even in the moments when I could calm down enough to think. But the vehemence, the hatred, with which he was shouting it were hitting me very, very hard, and it was impossible not to respond in kind.

One day he said something that shook me like an earthquake. Along with the usual profanities about my mother, he added that she had had an affair with "some German bastard". At first I had no idea what he was raving about and looked at him closely. Was he going completely over the top? Only when I was alone did I remember the face of the lovely German man I had met on the railway track the fall before she died. This is what my father was on about! What had made him think they were having an affair? Who had told him? And, indeed, were they having an affair?

I really could not handle this and tried to drop it from my mind. But once my father started, he would not stop. Again and again and again he would compulsively rant on about her and the German. I felt he was simply crazy, that he had imagined the whole thing. But I never once responded directly to what he was saying. I kept my own counsel, both with him and with Mary. Never once did I say anything about my mother and those German prisoners, nor the man—whom in my heart of hearts I would much have preferred as my father, given any choice in the matter. And another unspoken thought began to form: I am being punished in her place. I looked like her, of course, and I had the same, outspoken and self-assertive personality as she. But the idea never really came to the surface, nor did I ever so much as suggest it to anyone else.

The pressure was getting intolerable. There was no way at that time I could know how demented he was—how, when he went to the morgue to identify her, he had pulled off her wedding ring and thrown it in the gutter where the blood from the autopsies collects. But I did see from time to time the full horror of his shell shock. Occasionally he would start speaking about the terrible things he had seen in the war, in a strange, high-pitched voice, his eyes looking as fey as my mother's the night she went out in the rain. The slightest remark from me would send him into a towering rage, his eyes protruding, his hair on end, the veins on his neck standing out, and him bawling loud enough to burst my ear drums! Once he came right up to me and pushed his face into mine, roaring like an enraged gorilla. He was a strong man physically, much, much bigger than I. I felt at that moment that it was my last, absolutely paralyzed by terror. But he was my grandparents' son. No matter how angry or upset he was he was never physically violent. Having heard the stories of a number of women friends whose fathers were alcoholic, I never cease to be thankful that my father had that degree of control—indeed, if he hadn't, I would not be here telling this tale.

Like some inexorable Greek drama, day passed after day, the screw winding tighter and tighter. I was moving toward my ninth year, and my ability to express myself was becoming better and better. One day at lunch I was laying off my chest, as we used to say, about something, my poor family patiently waiting for me to finish. When I did, my father suddenly turned to me and said, in a cutting voice, "We don't care what you think! We don't care whether you live or die! We don't care about you at all!"

Now it was my turn to be mortally wounded. His words had hit the sorest spot in my whole being, one that I did not even know I had. I felt as if I were bleeding to death and remained absolutely silent. I do not doubt that Mary and Grannie went out of their way to console me, but the damage was done. I felt so utterly rejected, not only by my mother, but also by him. Why children make such a fuss over their biological parents, even when they behave so badly as many of them do, is totally beyond my comprehension. I had a whole family of loving people to support me and make me feel valuable, and yet I let my poor, afflicted and devastated father injure me so mortally.

Scottish people tend to be taciturn about their feelings. I was a Scot, and I was myself—bottomlessly silent about what was in my soul. But this incident was not allowed to pass without effect. I became a little hellion. Up till then I had been a model student, getting top grades and also recommendation for my good and cooperative behavior. But now I was disobedient, argumentative, and confrontational to my friends, teacher and family. I would lash out at everyone and refuse to cooperate with any. My poor teacher, a nice but inexperienced woman, was at her wits' end with me. I was put out of class a number of times, sent up to the principal (who was unusually kind, wondering why her star pupil, with the unprecedentedly high IQ and proverbial good behavior, was doing so poorly); and finally my father was summoned to a number of interviews with the principal.

These were the solutions of the grownups. But destiny and I had other plans: I got involved with the Roman Catholics. Or at least, a group of Irish rowdies. Only a middle-class Prot from Glasgow of those days can understand what a desperate thing that was. Irish of any stripe was hardly socially acceptable, and *Catholics* were considered the lowest of the low. But that was it: I was in with the wee hooligans from Shamrock Street and nothing was going to stop me. In no time I was hanging out on Shamrock Street or ranging all over our section of Glasgow through people's back yards. We would scramble over walls, jump over fences, no matter how tall, and yell our heads off almost without stopping. One night we decided to give the folks in the tenements a wee concert and launched out into our repertoire at the top of our lungs. Not surprisingly, in no time a policeman showed up and told us to move on. But, despite the noise and rowdyism, it was all pretty harmless. Although I was maturing early, the others were really children. Just to show off, some of the boys would occasionally light up a cigarette, but there was (surprisingly) no alcohol, drugs were unknown and certainly there was no violence. Mostly we listened endlessly to John Biggins weaving his Irish yarns, at which we laughed noisily.

Every once in a while I went into their homes and was shocked to see the conditions these people were living in. Families of up to twelve living in one room, with all but no heating and sharing with everyone else in the tenement a faucet and toilet situated on the landing of one of the floors. I could readily understand and empathize with their restlessness and irreverence. My father, who at that time was doing research into the causes of the epidemic tuberculosis that was carrying off so many, would occasionally turn his anger toward the Catholic Church, which he perceived as locking the misery of these people in place. Encouraging them to have huge families (some said by paying them money), insisting that they have only Catholic education (which could not compete with the standards of the rest of the country), and filling their heads with all sorts of myths that bore little relationship to the stark realities of their lives, the Church was condemning these people to live on the lowest rung of society, with no hope of rising. I began to understand why these kids were wasting so much time in so much daftness. They didn't know any better. And the tragedy was, kids like John Biggins were really intelligent and could have done so much with themselves if they had had better health, education and opportunities.

I do not remember either Grannie or Mary asking me to stop seeing my friends; Grannie was too forbearing and Mary, with her psychiatric background, almost definitely understood that any veto would simply make things worse. But they and the rest of the family were deeply concerned that I was neglecting my schoolwork and acquiring an Irish brogue to end all Irish brogues. It may seem trivial or even charming to acquire an Irish brogue—especially as my Gaelic-speaking relatives spoke with one that was somewhat similar; but in those days (and maybe even now) the way you spoke could make or break you. Getting ahead was often determined by your accent—in London, where the best jobs were, a Cambridge accent was the standard, but other "provincial" accents might get you by. A Scottish accent could be considered a bit of a handicap, at least in some quarters, but an Irish brogue was, across the board, a sentence of doom. In our upwardly mobile family, it was nothing short of disaster that I was wantonly gadding around with these Irish kids and thereby cooking my professional goose.

Mary was one of the most resourceful women I have ever met. She did not harangue me; she simply signed me up with Ena Paterson. Miss Paterson was the leading voice and drama teacher in Scotland, conveniently giving classes at the Highlanders' Institute quite near our home and the school I was going to. Her students had included the film star Robert Donat, and also Stanley Baxter, who was currently rising in radio, TV and film. And, like all good teachers, Miss Paterson stood for no nonsense, which was probably the most important aspect of my relationship with her. Her imperious manner and stringent and demanding methods were just what I needed, and responded to enthusiastically. I had joined a class of three other girls who were also in my class at school—Shiona, Joyce and Sheila, who had been studying with Miss Paterson for some years and were therefore used to her and her unusual demands. I felt the difference one day when Miss Paterson, taking her seat at the piano, announced that she was going to play chords suggestive of different emotions, and we were to make appropriate movements. I was simply flabbergasted to see my friends—as far as I knew, perfectly normally repressed like all of the rest of us—throwing themselves about, on the floor, over chairs, clutching at their throats, knees and God knows what else. Was I supposed to do that? Well, yes. "Jean!! Get up and participate! Express what the music is conveying!!" I got up rather shakily, not trusting myself at all. I was a dour Scot, not at all used to expressing myself and this—! To make a long story short, in no time I was throwing myself about as much as if not more than the others and Miss Paterson was crowing enthusiastically, "I see you have a gift for this!"

Miss Paterson was as whimsical as she was magisterial. One day someone knocked on our door during our class at the Highlanders' Institute. Rising seductively from her seat, she wove her way to answer the door, waving her hands about in Egyptian fashion, and whispering over her shoulder, "Here comes Cleopatra to answer the door!" When she got there, she slid one arm up the door jamb, leaned on it sexily and with the other slowly opened the door. "Ye-e-e-e-e-es?" she intoned in a sultry voice. The poor man who had knocked was one of the husky Highlanders from the Institute, in full regalia with kilt, sporran, plaid, tam, and toorie (the red pompom on the top, which it was said, during the Second World War, scared away the Jerries far more than the tommy guns)[5]. The contrast between him—so foursquare, uncomplicated and honest—and Ena, all dressed up to kill in her usual flamboyant harem pants and flowing cape, or some such thing, was really terribly funny. We all started to snicker. "Oh, Missus! I'm soooooorry", the poor man stammered, stepping backwards to avoid this snare of a woman. "I think I've cot the wrong room!" And off he beetled, as fast as his brogans could take him.

Such energetic fun and serious work was good for me. It helped blow off the tension that was building and also got me started on my own line of impersonations and character sketches, with which I entertained my family and friends. There is nothing a good laugh can't help! But Mary had more remedies up her sleeve. In addition to my art and voice classes,

---

5   "It wasn't his tommy gun that made the Jerries run, But his red toorie oorie, his red toorie oorie, his red toorie oorie oorie ay!" A popular song in the Second World War.

she signed me up for swimming at the pool three times a week, for the Girl Guides at my church, and also the Church Youth Club, for which I was now nearly old enough. She was determined to keep me out of the house in the early evening before my father left for his work and/or pub-crawling. In addition, now that her brother Willie had just moved his family up to the Black Isle, across the Moray Firth from what is now world-famous as Findhorn, Mary jumped at the chance to get me out of Glasgow and away from my father for as long as possible. She and I set off for Fortrose the Easter of I think my tenth or eleventh year. It was bitterly cold and snowy, unlike the southwest where we lived, but I thoroughly enjoyed the rambunctious company of my three cousins, Murdo, Seumas and Angus. Murdo was a year and a half older, Seumas and Angus about seven years younger than I. After being in such a feminine environment—for I attended a girls' school and had little to do with men in Grant Street—it was exciting and enjoyable to be interacting primarily with boys and of course my father's brother, Uncle Willie. The visit was short, but the seeds were sown of friendships with my uncle, aunt, and cousins that were to blossom in the many visits I was to make up north with my "Hielan' cousins".

That summer I returned to Fortrose to spend some three weeks. The main event was connecting up with my Aunt Bet, the mother of my three cousins, who were themselves still very young and not up to the great outdoor activity we would get into in summers yet to come. She was a girlish, good-natured, fun-loving woman, who had married a man quite a bit older than herself, the serious-minded "Mr. MacPhail", my Uncle Willie and her classics teacher at school. It rained a lot that summer and she and I sat by the fire, knitting, drinking tea and consuming large numbers of homemade cookies, while she told me the whole story of her life. She had so longed for a little girl, but instead she had three sons, a house full of men, for the most part uncommunicative or terribly rambunctious. She thought I was the child she had longed for, and she always treated me as her daughter, in whom she felt she could confide the whole romantic story of how she snagged my uncle as her husband.

All of this was something utterly new for me. I was what is now called a tween, but my family still treated me as a child. Not surprising, as they were all so much older than I, for our family married late and the difference between the generations was about thirty years. I had with Aunt Bet something like the relationship I had had with my own mother—a friend, a confidante—though now in a more adult key, and without the intellectual counterweight that my mother had. She quickly became yet another "mother" to add the richness of my experience.

Perhaps because I was in the pristine countryside, so quiet and free of smog; perhaps because I was away from the conflict with my father; perhaps because I was being treated in such a friendly, open way, I seem to have relaxed considerably up in Fortrose, and enjoyed myself immensely. This visit was the first of many, many more, and was to end on an important note, nothing less than the turning-point of the spiral of my childhood. And it happened in a quite unpremeditated way. My cousin Murdo seems to have felt too "grown-up" to identify with the shenanigans of his younger brothers, or the hen-parties that Bet and I were having, and so I rarely saw him. But occasionally he would ask me to go for a walk, and on this occasion I set off with him toward some hills north of the town.

Murdo was, is, and no doubt always will be, the world's worst tease; he ribbed me so constantly I sometimes wondered if he was capable of being serious at all. My attention therefore wandered to the countryside we were passing through. We were going up a hill, walking on the heather that stretches in an unbroken pink or purple carpet as far as the eye can see, with here and there a clump of white heather, just for luck. On all sides were silver birches, with their slender, shiny white trunks and myriads of tiny leaves, green on one side and silver on the other, rippling like cascading water whenever there was the slightest breeze. In between were rowans or mountain ash, loaded in early autumn with glorious orange-red berries, contrasting sharply with the color of the heather. It was, in short, a wonderland of natural beauty, painted with the most vivid palette of colors, and thrown into relief by the gathering, dark thunderclouds coming over the horizon. We were in a clearing in the woods surrounded by the trees, and I stopped for a moment to take it all in.

Murdo apparently decided that this was the time to play his trump-card of tricks; he totally disappeared. I thought he had gone to take a leak, but no sign of him after several minutes. I realized he was trying to get a rise out of me, knowing I had no idea how to get back home, but decided I was better off enjoying the view, while I had it in this amazingly celestial mode. Everything had become utterly quiet. There was no breeze, the trees were still, there were no birds singing, the black clouds had taken over the sky. I felt myself relaxing completely in this wonderful stillness, which somehow offered so much solace and support.

Suddenly, a ray of sunlight appeared through the clouds and spotlighted me as I stood there in that enchanted mood. And with it came a ripple of breeze, which set the leaves of the birches fluttering like cascading water. Somehow I was caught up in the flowing movement of the trees; the whole scene disappeared completely and I felt myself disappearing into a huge, enveloping, golden light, endless, joyful and real, real, Real. I have no idea how long I was there, but bit by bit I began to feel that I was "coming down", though I had not been "anywhere", actually. Slowly I felt that I was above the trees, looking down on their canopy. Then I saw my body standing in the middle of the clearing. "Oh, I don't want to go back into that!" I said. "It is so miserable. Why can't I just stay here?" But whether I wanted it or not—bang! There I was. And Murdo was coming across the heather, grinning in his inimitable way. Whether he had seen me in that state, or was just pleased with his pranks, I have no idea. We managed to get home before the rain really got going.

THIRD QUARTER

FACING THE MUSIC

CHAPTER 5

PROBLEMS AND SOME SOLUTIONS
1952-1954

When school resumed for the autumn term, I was in the seniormost class of the junior division. Suddenly I was no longer interested in the rowdy Irish kids, and I settled down to work, cooperating readily with the rather experienced and sensible teacher we had that year. There were no more outbursts and confrontations, I had no difficulty remaining at the top of the class, and my report cards again included excellent points for behavior and deportment.

What had happened? The family was amazed, and of course, mightily relieved. But nobody could explain what had happened—including myself, of course. I was too young to understand what was going on inside me, though there were to be several pointers in the next, turbulent five years of my ongoing drama. In essence, I had found something that was grounding me in a way that nothing had up till then. I no longer felt as abandoned and angry as I had after my mother's death, aggravated so terribly by my father's behavior toward me and his attacks on my mother. And then again, I was old enough to travel by myself; I would go to visit relatives and friends without my father, who in many ways began to drop out of my life. School work was taking up more of my time, and I was getting more and more involved in my various special classes and activities, just as Mary had planned. Particularly, from going to the church youth club I was developing friendships of a much more stable and acceptable nature than the wild gallivantings with the Shamrock Street kids. I was also developing friendships with my schoolmates, young people from the art class, and with my cousins, especially Jean, whose mother I still continued to visit regularly, with or without my father. Jean and I loved to play with words and would spend hours making up limericks, spoonerisms and speaking in rhyme, which would convulse us with laughter of a much healthier type than the bawling on Shamrock Street.

Things were definitely stabilizing. My father had graduated with his master's degree in epidemiology and public health and was now working at the university as a lecturer, while continuing on with his book about the causes of the near-epidemic tuberculosis devastating Glasgow. He was also continuing to drink, but somehow it was not so apparent as before. No doubt he continued to bait me, but my recollection was that I was able to rise above it and think of him with some degree of pity and to make attempts to understand, with which Mary would help me from time to time, drawing on her knowledge as a psychiatric nurse, and relying on her own remarkable detachment and goodness of heart.

It was as if I had folded up all the anger and turmoil of the previous five years and put it into storage. But that, of course, did not mean that things were easy or peaceful. Evolution is seldom peaceful, though of course there are occasional plateaus on which you can rest for a moment. What was coming out of the woods now was the Qualies. That was what we called the qualifying exams, part of a rather draconian system which divided us, at the age of twelve, into three streams: those who left school at fourteen and went on to unskilled work; those who left at sixteen and went to technical schools to learn domestic science, typing, or in the case of boys, low-end engineering and carpentry; and those who left school at seventeen or eighteen, having passed the university entrance exams, the doorway to careers in teaching, law, medicine, and other "professional" subjects. What was so intimidating was that the results of the Qualies were the final word on the rest of your life, and there was no recourse. For students whose work was near the middle or toward the lower level, the Qualies were utterly terrifying, and there was a great hullabaloo going on to do away with what was seen as an unnecessary challenge to such young children, putting too much weight on only one set of exam results. My generation, subsequently dubbed the "lost" generation, was the one before the baby boomers; what characterized us was that the old, British stiff upper lip model still applied, though in many ways we were moving on to something more contemporary and flexible. With regard to our education, we had to face the Qualies and make the best of it, as had so many of our forebears.

For me there was no doubt that I would pass in the academic stream, my grades had been so outstanding for so long. But the whole uproar around the exams did start me thinking about my future. Granted I would pass the Qualies—where would I be aiming after that? I had already decided that I would never marry, for one so young a rather sad fact, fuelled by my father's repeated, "Never get married—it's a mug's game." I was not sophisticated enough to understand where that remark was coming from, but I did know how much I had suffered and felt very strongly that I never wanted to bring any child into the world to suffer as I had. That matter being settled, it therefore was of first importance to decide just how I would be spending the rest of my life. Obviously, I would want to do something that was natural to me and could support me financially.

Would that it were that simple! I was to discover many layers to the question as time went by, and am still wrestling with it fifty years later. It was natural, however, that the first layer was laid by Grannie, who had become not only my inspiration, but also my mentor. Although I adored her as a small child, I was rather in awe of her and that, combined with her hardness of hearing, had prevented me from talking with her a great deal. But as I grew older I discovered what a wonderful friend she was—so wise, so kind and so to the point. She would look at me with her clear, blue eyes and speak to a deep part of my soul, just as I had seen her do with her never-ending stream of visitors. Although I do not remember the words of any of our conversations, I know that she instilled into me the ideal of living for the well-being of others. Whatever you do, she had made me understand, do it so that others are benefited, are happier, are the better that you lived. In many ways such thinking was part and parcel of the community I lived in, but coming from her in so many words it acquired the authority of a moral imperative, which I believe has never left me, even up to the present.

The other advice, coming from Mary and the other members of the family who had all suffered through the Depression, was that, whatever I did, it should be something that would provide a reliable living, no matter what was happening to the economy. This was harder for me to relate to in principle, but what it meant in practice was that I should consider a career in either teaching, law or medicine, the primary "professional" careers at the time. Faced with that menu, it was easy. Teaching, I had already seen, was fraught to a large extent with the issues of maintaining classroom discipline. Law was, by its nature, dishonest and corrupt. Medicine, however, was more interesting and familiar. My father was a doctor, as was my Uncle Robert and my Uncle Billy Muir, while my cousin Jean was making up her mind to take it up when she graduated from High School; and of course Mary was a superb nurse, medicine in action and at its best. In addition, I used to read my father's textbooks and, perhaps even more telling, would spontaneously use my dolls to perform surgery—bellybutton amputation, brain surgery, and the like. Any sentimental lady who would be inclined to froth over "dear little Jean" would be quickly silenced when she saw my dolls, heads shaven for their surgery, scars all over their bodies, all sewn up like latter day mini-Frankensteins. Finally, and maybe foreshadowing more than anything else what I was to end up doing, I was simply riveted whenever I saw fishmongers filleting fish, a sight which, in our pre-supermarket economy, was rather frequent. I was so impressed by how they would separate the flesh from the bone with the minimum of waste and would do it all with so much skill and artistry.

So far so good with regard to my inclinations toward medicine, the art and science of handling the human body. But the fact was that, for the moment, my talents were overwhelmingly in the creative and performing arts. Along with others, I entered the annual art competition for Glasgow schoolchildren, and was winning medal after medal. Jean Irwin and I were becoming closer and closer and would talk together sometimes after all the other students had left. She told me that I was one of her best students ever and that she foresaw for me a great career as an artist. Naturally I was happy and loved the idea; but then, there was the problem of what my family was saying. How was I going to resolve this? Miss Paterson, too, was very enthusiastic about my work with her and insisted that I take the final exam. I pointed out that I had only studied for a few years, that I was just a teenager, but she insisted that I had reached professional status, should take the exam, and go on to the stage forthwith. I was absolutely stunned, and could not get up enough courage to take the final exam. She compromised by preparing me for the intermediate exam, which I passed, nervous and flustered as this was the first oral exam I had ever had to take. She kept pressing me to consider a career as a professional actress, but I would counter with the thought that I did not want to have to sell my body to get ahead, something which I took as an inevitable fact in the life of an actress. She looked at me for a moment and then declared in her most dramatic voice, "My dear, you will never have to do that. You are so good you will go right to the top and stay there!" Heartwarming, no doubt, but terribly at odds with the mores and advice of my family.

A big conflict was definitely building up. How could I decide between a life in the world of art, which came to me so effortlessly and spontaneously, and the world of medicine, which was much less natural to me? Family and friends would tell me that I could do my artwork in my leisure time, which I only half-believed, knowing intuitively that to do really good art requires full-time commitment and constant practice, as well as absorption in what was going on around me in the art world. I felt terribly oppressed that I had to deny what was most myself in order to make a living, and struggled to find a way to solve this increasingly pressing problem. I would think of what Grannie was conveying to me: Live in such a way that others are blessed and happy. There I found relief—but, again, in what way could I make others happy? Here again the Calvinist and the this-worldly thinking of the culture I was living in stepped in and made what seemed a good case: As a medical doctor everything you do is geared toward the relief of suffering, but what does art contribute to human well-being?

This maxim came from elders whom I deeply revered and loved, and seemed, to my immature and inexperienced mind, to hold water. I was thoroughly acquainted with suffering, pain, disease and death, even in my early teens, and relieving or lightening them was quite obviously something desirable. My heart warmed to the idea and vision of contributing in this meaningful way to the welfare of my fellow human beings. But art—what does it contribute to well-being? Well, of course, I knew how much it meant to me—the hours of happy absorption in creating a work of art, of imagining new works and of making mental notes and sketches as I went along of things that were beautiful, meaningful, and likely to be good for another composition. But did it really make any lasting impression in the lives of others? What, if anything, did it contribute to the overall progress of humanity? I could not come up with an answer at the time, pulled as I was in two apparently opposite directions. Nor was I able to understand that the emphasis on medical work over art came from the fact that my elders were thinking largely in terms of bodily comfort and security rather than on the value of living and creating in the inner world.

This was an acute dilemma, but one that I had to put on the back burner as other, more immediate and rapidly-moving events blew up like a large thunderstorm. But before returning to the dark side of my life, I want to mention the trips with Mary to the Isle of Skye and to our ancestral home, Lewis, which left a permanent mark on my soul. For the first three or four summers in Glasgow, Mary would take me for a few weeks to the Isle of Skye, made famous as the place where Flora MacDonald, the romantic friend and protector of Bonnie Prince Charlie in the mid-eighteenth century, organized his escape from the pursuing English military. Skye, like most of the Hebridean islands, is a wonderland of ocean, mountains and changing sky, at that time almost without people. Mary and I would walk or sit on the beach all day and see not another person.

On one of our long hikes I had an epiphany that has remained evergreen. As we were moving towards the divine fragrance of a peat fire in a house somewhere near but unseen, we suddenly came round a corner and saw below us a sheer drop into the ocean. The water was feeding a little inlet, a sheltered cove, where the sun was reflecting into the water as pure aquamarine. In the water were three or four seals, joyfully playing in the sheltered area. Moving like winged creatures through the water, everything about them spoke of sheer freedom, awareness and bliss. For a moment I felt myself transported to another realm of being; and for a long time afterwards, during the terrible loneliness and at times despair I had to face, I would visualize myself as playing in the ocean just like them, enraptured in a Reality I could not name, but knew for sure was there. Sometimes it was dark, sometimes it was in the sun, but always very joyful.

I loved Skye with a passion, but when I was twelve years old the idea of going to Lewis to meet with our relatives was certainly intriguing. Unlike Skye, Lewis is mostly flat and has practically no trees. It is a mass of ancient rock, pitted with small lochs, bodies of shining water connected to each other by endless meandering burns creating primeval bog, with a carpet of heather stretching as far as the eye could see. As we had no car and buses were less than infrequent, Mary and I hoofed it from relative to far-flung relative, for these people lived on tiny farms dug out of whatever workable soil there was.

Their homes were a revelation to me. Known as black houses, they were one-story piles of stones with thatched roofs held down with ropes weighted with heavy rocks. How they withstood the winter gales coming in from the Atlantic was a mystery to me. Inside the entrance way there were chickens and sheep as well as dogs and cats, while the main living area had an open peat fire where all the cooking was done. These houses were a bit more advanced than those my grandparents grew up in, in that they had chimneys—formerly the smoke found its way out through the thatch, and hence the name black houses—and also had rudimentary electric lighting. Our own house in Glasgow could never have been considered sophisticated, but when I saw the black houses I realized just how tough and resilient my grandparents had been, and what an effort it must have been for them to come as far as they had.

But one thing was the same—these were the most welcoming and generous people ever. "Primitive" communities seem to have a code of hospitality that we more modern people cannot really begin to comprehend. From one standpoint it is no doubt related to survival of the group, but in human terms it is really most endearing. We spoke in English, as Mary's Gaelic was pidgin at best, and so I was able to enjoy the yarns our hosts regaled us with, interspersed with lots of jokes, songs, and innuendos.

These were devout people, for the most part. But there was another side to it, for there was a tendency to sanctimoniousness, particularly about Sabbath observance. On Sundays going to church was the only permitted activity. As Mary and I did not speak Gaelic, we skipped church and went for a walk and, as we went along, Mary pointed out to me how the lace curtains on every window were being raised a mite. She said, "They're making sure it's Mary Anne's daughter and the wee girl, Colin Og's[6] daughter from Glasgow, and they're saying, 'Would you look at it! It's Mary Anne's daughter, after walking on the Sabbath! What would Mary Anne be saying about it! Ov, ov! What is it coming to, the world!'" But to our faces they were nothing but gracious and welcoming, and I loved every minute of it.

As with most events of my life, there was a shimmering, endlessly changing surface and a silent, motionless depth, and the same was definitely true of Lewis. Lewis is one of the most northerly parts of Scotland, and in August, when we were there, there were perhaps four hours of darkness at night. As I was lying in bed in broad daylight trying to get to sleep, I would hear a drumming sound coming from a distance, passing by and then disappearing in the opposite direction. For the first few nights I thought it was a kind of dream, but on the third night I got up to see what was going on. To my amazement, it was a herd of wild horses pounding over the heather, their manes and tails streaming behind them and catching the rays of the declining sun. I was utterly thrilled to see these wild creatures, so free and untrammeled, and made a point of looking for them every night. They evoked in my soul the same feeling as the seals in Skye—a sense of boundlessness, of joy and very, very real being. Through them was flowing an energy connecting me with life in all of its forms and also with the specific, ancient, and enduring fact that we call Scotland.

---

6   "Young Colin, an epithet for my father.

A few days before we left Lewis, we went on a trip to Callanish, on the west coast of the island not too far from Carloway, my grandfather's ancestral home. There we saw the circle of standing stones considered by some second only in importance to Stonehenge, which had been built by the unknown people who inhabited northwestern Europe some millennia before even the pagan Celtic era. For whatever reason, we arrived there at around ten at night, still daylight, though with a suggestion of the lengthening of the sun's rays which begins the long, slow twilight of the northern evening. I had seen pictures of megaliths many times, but actually standing next to these huge, ancient memorials of a culture long gone and laden with tantalizing possibilities of meaning, I was awestruck. What were these stones lying on the ground? An altar? Perhaps a place of human sacrifice?

Standing in the middle of an endless southern expansion of moor with nary a tree nor any other landmark to distinguish it, the starkness of the circle was mesmerizing. To the north was the ocean, the restless, cold Atlantic, which had become for me a dark and energizing mother from whom I sometimes felt I had arisen, like the selkies or sea-maidens, who sometimes take a human form and live among the sons of women. There was perhaps a cave underneath or close to the megaliths, because we could hear the ocean echoing and re-echoing below us, singing mournfully, rising and falling in cadence, and sometimes letting out a particularly agonizing cry. I felt my skin goose-bumping: were we standing at the junction of earth and the next world? As if to answer my question, there was a sudden increase in the light, like a spotlight suddenly going on, and the aurora borealis, the northern lights, began to ripple across the sky. The effect is nothing short of supernatural, the whole sky flickering, as what looks like colored curtains move across it. Their occurrence at this particular moment and in this particular place was, of course, catalytic. So many strands of my life—Scotland, its history, its myths, my own meaning and destiny, all merged into a moment of blinding clarity, which has never dimmed or left me in the intervening fifty or more years. No wonder it was whispered that the locals would steal out at dusk or twilight to pay their respects to the old gods, perhaps "the Shining One" who, legend says, would walk among the stones on the old druidical festival of Beltane or May Day, brought there by the call of the cuckoo.[7] These activities were,

---

[7]   Claterbos, Nel van Weijdom. Standing Stones. *http://www.theosophy-nw. org/theosnw/world/anceur/my-clat.htm.*

of course, not approved of by the Christian meenisters; but the powerful, stark land has a charisma all its own, tied in the human mind to certain archetypal gods who, no matter what "educated" people say, cannot be forgotten or totally neglected.

Yet, no matter what epiphanies you have, there is always the return to the everyday. We had to return to Glasgow and to the realities at Grant Street, where the moving hand was writing clearly on the wall. Grannie's health was deteriorating. She had had several heart attacks, from which she had made a good recovery; but she was now in her mid-eighties and in basically delicate health. Most unfortunately, as Grannie's health declined Mary had to take a part time job, leaving Grannie to the ministrations of myself and my father. How could I know that my father's drinking and deliberate withholding of money had forced my aunt, now in her early fifties, to take up work again in order to keep the household going? But Mary was ever resourceful and capable. She took a night job so that she could be present for our meals and available for any emergencies during the day.

Mary had signed up for the night shift on the obstetrics ward, but as a consummately executive person she was often drafted for the emergency room, from which she would come home with all kinds of hair-raising tales about the battles of the night before. Friday night was payday night, the high holy night when the denizens of Glasgow headed to the pub and as instant a nirvana as they could find. Once they had primed themselves at the pub, the Watsons and the Foleys—no doubt the Protestant and Catholic gangs respectively—would step outside and get down to the business of cutting each other to ribbons with cut-throat razors. One after the other they would appear in the emergency room, where Mary, among others, would sew them up and get them out as fast as possible, before they picked quarrels with any other patients. These people were running high on rage and violence (though it cannot compare to the mayhem we live with now, when firearms are available to anyone who wants them), and the free-floating hatred between Catholic and Protestant that they used as their verbal weapons was a highly flammable commodity. With their abusive shouting and carrying on, it was not at all impossible that a riot could break out, right there in the emergency room.

All this made me realize just how tough my aunt was, and in retrospect, how callous my father was to condemn her to having to work in such terrible conditions. One day she came home in high dudgeon at the events of the night. She had sewn up one wound that was particularly bad, running from the base of the man's neck to the crown of his head. One of the Foleys had gotten him and was shouting through the door, "Missus, that's the best I ever done! Don't you f—it up, now!" She got the job over as quickly as possible and had the man rest a while, for he had lost a lot of blood. Then she sent him off, telling him to go straight home to bed. She turned to something else, for there was no letup on a Friday night. It was only a few minutes later when she saw the same man come in again, streaming with blood. The Foley was at the door. "Ha, ha, ha! I told you to leave him alone! I got every one of your f—ing stitches with only one slash!" And indeed he had. Mary was really angry at this senseless violence, the loss of time, resources and, above all, human dignity. For myself, I thought of the SS man who had ripped open the stitches with which my father had saved his life during the war, in order to die for his Fuehrer. In some ways, he was better, because he had a sense of purpose, no matter how warped from our point of view. What was so tragic with these Glasgow gangsters was their sense of purposelessness, of being forgotten, left behind and hopeless. No matter what was done for them, their anger never stopped, they kept on stoking their hatred and took out on others just as helpless as themselves the revenge that most probably should have gone somewhere else.

Meanwhile, back at the ranch, as they say, Grannie and I were managing as best we could. I hated coming home from school and not having Mary there. Grannie, as often as not was praying or reading in her room and oblivious to anything outside, while my father, as was his custom, was out on the town, not to be seen or heard of till the following day. If Grannie was up and about, she was most welcoming and would make me a cup of tea, but of course I would worry about her exerting herself too much, in view of her health. From her side, she was vexed at not being able to pull as much weight with the kitchen work as she had been doing. She was a wonderful traditional cook, serving up Scotch broth made from scratch and loaded with vegetables; potted head (head cheese); herrings, salted or fresh; potatoes; and of course, in the morning steel-cut oatmeal porridge lovingly stirred over the flame for over an hour and belonging to an entirely different taste-world than the wallpaper-hangers' paste that is called oatmeal in America.

She was, however, not doing well. One evening while Mary was out working, I had been doing something in the kitchen by myself, maybe my homework, for my father and Grannie were talking in the living room. As

I came into the hallway on the way to my bedroom, I heard their voices and stopped where I was. Grannie was speaking in a high and clear tone, quite unlike her usual soft, low voice. Her voice was almost like a trumpet, gathering intensity and volume as it went along, for my father had stopped speaking completely. "The anchels are with me, they are crowding my room and I am not sleeping any more. The Lord has sent them for me. They are getting me reahty . . . I am getting reahty to co." The whole house was reverberating with the intensity of her mood, as she spoke of her impending death. I felt the same, fey feeling that my mother had had

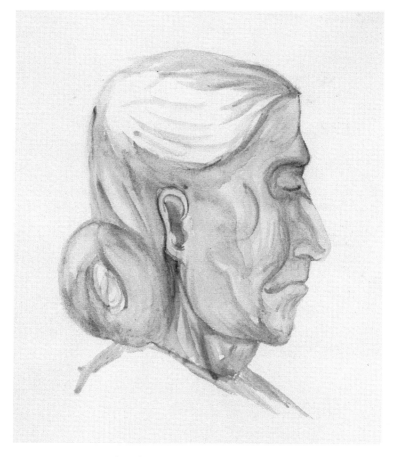

A portrait I made of my grandmother sleeping by the fireside toward the end of her life. Her hair was jet black, but in deference to her sensibilities as to what was proper for an old lady, I painted it white. Watercolor on paper.

just before she died, but not the sadness. For my Grannie was with the angels, those companions of her whole life, who were now with her constantly, lighting up her room as we snored in ours. She had lived a life of intense communion with the divine, looking directly into the light that made it possible for her to read human hearts, hear cries at a distance and know, from the depths of her wisdom what was about to happen.

Not much later she had her last heart attack and died in a few days. Mary kept me out of her room, apart from one visit when Grannie looked at me with the utmost kindness and blessing, but was unable to say anything. Immediately after she died, Mary wanted me to look at her in her coffin, but I was very unwilling to do so. I did stand on the threshold of the room and could see her face, so pale and still and monumentally beautiful, even at eighty-five crowned with jet-black hair. Then I was whisked off to Aunt Jane's, no doubt because Mary knew just how crowded and emotional—and almost certainly inebriated—our house would be as the Highlanders moved in for a wake and funeral. So I was deprived of being with her right to the last; but Mary did tell me about the funeral and what happened. It seems that the church was packed to the doors and as many had to stand outside. It was not surprising that there was a tremendous turnout, for Mary Anne had high status as a holy woman in the Highland community; but what was unusual was that at least half of the people at the funeral were Lowlanders or Irish, folk whom the family had never seen before. Mary spoke with some of these people and asked them why they had come to her mother's funeral. "Oh, Mrs. MacPhail was such a wonderful lady! Whenever we saw her at Mr. Ramage's bakery, she would speak with us, take such an interest in us and our families, and sometimes help us with a little money." The same story was repeated again and again: wherever she went, whether to the local shops or to some other part of the city, on the trams, the buses, she would make everyone around her her very own, as if she was their nearest and dearest.

Her epitaph, written by one of our Highland cousins in June of 1954 for the *Stornoway Gazette* in Lewis, said it all: "She was the finest type of woman one could have the privilege of knowing, and the writer deeply regrets that it is not within his powers to do adequate justice to one he so highly esteemed . . . It would be too much to expect to meet her like, so good, so kind, wise, patient and altogether saintly in this world."

I was blest in living with such a woman. Humble, not highly educated, and with a simple but living faith whose roots went deep into the whole Celtic heritage I grew up in, she was nothing short of a refuge for me from the terrible storms of my early childhood. She more than compensated for the loss of my mother, not only giving me love but also an example of how faith in the divine can give tremendous strength and resilience that holds up under any pressure whatsoever and can give constantly to others. She gave me a sense that I was not only loved but loveable, even though my parents' behavior sent me exactly the opposite message. She was, for me, nothing short of a spiritual teacher, a person on whom my whole childhood turned and on which the remainder of my life has rested as on an unshakeable foundation. Every time I think of her, I see her as a huge presence—though dark physically, on account of her dark hair and widow's black, she is a center that bends the gravity of our world acutely around a central core of light. And, as an interesting item in the penumbra of what she meant, we found among her spiritual books an unusual booklet about an Indian swami. It had a beige cover with a drawing of a young Indian man in a turban looking out to the rising sun. The title was: *Swami—, Awakener of Modern India.* What it had meant to her, we had no idea (though of course she had been in India for two years, and with her ability to communicate spiritually with people, anything could have happened)—and what it meant to me at that time, even less. Why would I, so utterly uninformed about India, notice this booklet or remember its title so vividly? She had never said a word about anything like this, so I had no reason to consider the book of importance in the context I was living in then. In retrospect it seems that some buried memory was awakened when I saw this book, that somehow it was an unspoken message from her to me, the meaning of which is still unfolding as I write.

In addition to what she was personally, Grannie was the focus of a whole network of people, family, friends and workmates, who were living in a certain mindset—of the twentieth century and yet not of it. We had electricity, wireless, and whatever other modern comforts we could afford in the lean years after the war, but our way of thinking was not what I have come to think of as "modern". We were affectionate, concerned about each other, kind and more or less honest, with a sense of responsibility to others which ensured that marriages lasted (divorce was unheard of), children were taken care of and educated properly, and violence and uncontrolled sexuality was not on the cards, even with someone as emotionally damaged as my father. Religion was accepted, even by my mother, and no one was ashamed to speak openly about their faith or to live it out in their day-to-day dealings with other people.

But that was soon to change. With Grannie's death, that enchanted world disappeared and I was force to adjust to a more "with it" mode of living. First, there was the great sorrow that Mary was out working more and more. My father was simply not supporting her, and so I had to live with the desperately empty house that met me in the evening now that Grannie was gone. Worse, my father took to bringing his boon companions home with him in the late evenings, and they would hooch it up, as we say in Scotland, until the wee hours. One night this whole desperate situation came to a head. There were several of them, yelling their heads off and banging the furniture about. Lying in my bed in the next room, I was terrified to hear their angry shouting and repeated smashing of glass. There were sickening thuds, rattlings and bangings, some of them apparently moving toward the hallway door. I thought they might come in and beat me up or—heaven forbid—rape me. It was a desperate night, which finally came to an end in the wee hours, when they decided to move on to wreck someone else's home. After they left, I could not sleep at all, but shivered and shivered with terror until the morning. I felt so terribly alone, with Grannie gone, Mary with the razor slashers and my father out on a dead-drunk binge. In the morning the living room was covered in shattered glasses and liquor bottles, with empty sardine cans dripping on to the carpet. A nice sight for Mary as she came back from the night's work at the hospital.

By this time I was in my early teens and feeling very, very lonely. My days were so full of tremendous tension and grief and my dreams of terror of being murdered or mutilated, that I took to living in a twilight zone of imagination, which would keep me awake for hours as I tried to shake off the pain of the day and the terror of the night. Almost always I daydreamed about meeting a man who shared my ideals, usually a doctor with whom I would be working in some dirt-poor place, such as Africa, India or even the slums of Glasgow. Together we would put our whole hearts into serving, healing and uplifting the people we were caring for and would find a shared belief in the deepest, most valuable core of what it is to be human. On that would be based our mutual love and commitment to our arduous work.

Although I had met several women who loved and inspired me, I had not yet met any men who could touch my heart. On the contrary, the behavior of the men who had been nearest to me had been bitterly disappointing, even abusive, and I had not really experienced what it is to have a father I could love. There had been a few lovely men—the

German, a family friend called Bob Reid, and a few others, who were gentle and kind and made me feel comfortable and accepted; but they were the minority and not major players in my life. I was definitely in quest of a father, and perhaps it is not a coincidence that the spouse of my dreams was usually considerably older than myself. In one daydream he was actually Russian, an art dealer, and at the same time a free soul living on principles similar to my own. This was to prove prophetic, but of course played out in a rather different way that I could conceive of in Glasgow of nineteen fifty-four.

Within a short time of Grannie's death, my father announced his plans to get a job overseas as a professor in preventative medicine—Baghdad and Khartoum were on his short list. By this time his book on the epidemiology of tuberculosis had been published, to critical acclaim and considerable flapping in the establishment, for it laid bare the terrible conditions of those who lived in the slums of Glasgow and demonstrated conclusively that they had a direct bearing on the soaring death rate from tuberculosis.

Along with this decision went another: I was going to be sent to boarding school. "Oh, no, Daddy!" I cried. "I like the Girls' High, my art and drama classes. I have so many friends here!" "No," he said, "I am not leaving you here with Mary, that bitch of a woman. She has had too much influence on you already, and is poisoning your mind. You will turn out just like her if I don't separate you." My grief at having to leave Glasgow struggled for dominance with the anger at his speaking that way about Mary, who had stood by me through thick and thin and gone out of her way to protect me from his worst excesses, without uttering a word of criticism of him. And behind both was the dark feeling that the words *boarding school* brought into my mind, for I was a voracious reader of Rudyard Kipling and my knowledge of what boarding school meant was colored by his *Stalky and Co.*, which revealed the dark and hateful side of the training schools of the British élite.

But my sentence was not immediate. It was too late to enroll me for that year, and so I had one more year of "borrowed time" in Glasgow. What I did not know was that my father was leaving Mary without a penny, as they say, giving her absolutely nothing for the immense sacrifice she had made to support both him and his daughter. She was going to have to work full time, though I did not immediately know it. The atmosphere in Grant Street was not very happy, to say the least. After a few stormy weeks, my father finally left—for the Sudan, via many a pub and lounge, no doubt, and to my vast relief. No more wild nights of shouting or mornings of bitter accusation and reviling. One side of me cried for his suffering, but the other wanted to move on, to grow and express myself without the blight of endless criticism and attempts to make me feel guilty for a crime I had not committed. Or so it seemed to me.

After he was gone, Mary worked hard to create some cheer for both of us. She had Grannie's room painted and refurnished so that I could at last have my own room with space for my ever-increasing art and reading projects. As Grannie had died at the beginning of the summer, I was soon on vacation and Mary did all she could to distract me and lighten my mood. One day she took me to Dumbarton, where we went to the fair and rode on what we called the dodge 'ems, electric cars which banged into each other. We were rammed from the rear and Mary was thrown forward and then backward, hitting her back in a nasty way. She did not say too much about it at the time, but the next day she was in obvious pain.

She had planned a short holiday for both of us at Dunbar on the East Coast, but it seemed to me that she was in no condition to go. I pleaded with her to cancel our reservations, but she insisted that we go, to cheer us both up. So off we went for a week or so to stay at a nice family hotel and go for walks and sit on the beach. There is no doubt in my mind now that Mary desperately needed to get away from Grant Street with all of its memories, but truly she was in no condition for the trip. She was rather silent and broody, but every once in a while, when she had to make a sudden movement, she would let out a terrible cry. The situation reached crisis proportions in the hotel, where Mary's cries would resound through the dining room, riveting the attention of all of the guests. With typical teenage insensitivity, I would mutter, "Mary! Be quiet! Everybody is staring at you!" How could I have any idea what she was suffering? Her self-sacrifice was beyond my capacity to understand. But I did get an inkling after we got back to Glasgow. One morning as I went in to her bedroom with her breakfast, she was trying to get out of bed. As she did so, she suddenly fell forward with a sickening groan and I finally saw her back. It was a huge mass of terrible, black bruising with a central area of actual blood under the skin. I realized that she had a really serious injury and insisted on calling the doctor. I felt utterly ashamed of my previous behavior—but who could have understood the situation? She was so determined to cheer me up that she had been walking around with what may well have been a fractured vertebra.

Furthermore, she had more plans to get me moving on. Despite all of my protestations, she insisted on my carrying on with the program she had crafted to divert me that summer. I was to spend much of the next couple of months with relatives, especially up in Fortrose, where the boys were now old enough for long walks and playing tennis, golf, and football with me all day long. Much as I agonized over how she was doing in Glasgow without my help, the fresh air and animal spirits at Fortrose certainly lifted my mood and the huge burden of doom I had been feeling began to seem lighter.

While there, Uncle Willie, my father's brother, and I became closer. The oldest of my paternal uncles and the third child of my grandparents, he was in many ways closest to my grandparents' culture, being a staunch Free Church member and elder, as well as speaking Gaelic fluently and going for his vacations to Lewis, our ancestral home. As the headmaster of a large school in a very conservative part of Scotland, he had to behave as our "meenisters" all comported themselves: as rather aloof, righteous pillars of society. With his sons he was a rather distant and unavailable father, again like our meenisters, whose sons were proverbially over-disciplined and rebellious. In this mode, he was quite taciturn, though occasionally he would come away with a remark so percipient and so wry that we would all burst out laughing. When I visited, I was quite definitely the "city cousin", full of the blethers of Glasgow and the results of Miss Paterson's drama class (where I was acquiring a rather posh accent), while my country cousins would gaze at me wide-eyed, or make some brief remark in their thick, north-eastern brogue: "Aye, Jean, ye're a verra, verra sad case!"

THE SHORE BRAE FORTROSE.

Uncle Willie would sometimes warm up to me and tease me, laughing uproariously and then looking at me expectantly for the inevitable retort his citified niece would be bound to give him. This was quite a bit different from my father, whose tolerance for my pert turn of phrase was rather low. I enjoyed this little game, which took place at most of our meals, though sometimes he was brooding on something and we all ate in silence. For the first time in my life, I felt secure with talking with an older man.

My uncle had a good library, much of which was the classics in the original Greek. I used to admire the characters, but of course could not read them. However, I did find an introduction to Greek philosophy in English, which I started to read and found interesting. As I was reading, curled up in a large chair, he came in for something and saw me there. He said nothing, but I felt him looking over my shoulder to see what I was reading. I looked up and saw him staring incredulously at me. "Do you understand what you are reading?" he asked me. "Yes, it is very interesting. I am so glad I found this, as Greek philosophy is so important for the West." His eyes grew even wider, but he said nothing. I think he was just not used to early teenagers having an interest in anything but football or popular music.

After that, he would occasionally come into the living room and talk with me about philosophy or some related subject. The following Sunday he asked me if I would like to go with him to the Free Church, where he was an elder. There I saw for the first time just what had gone on in the church that Grannie had been so devoted to. The proceedings were in English, as Gaelic has not survived so well in Eastern Scotland as in the West, but it was definitely dour, very, very dour, focusing almost entirely on the Old Testament. Puritanical, without musical instruments and everyone dressed in black or dark colors and the decor plain white walls and dark, stained pews, with nary a touch of color to lighten it up. But when the singing began, all the emotions of the group came pouring out in the huge waves of sound that had so arrested my attention in the Duke Street Church in Grant Street. My uncle, standing next to me, was quite exalted, bellowing out in his tenor voice the psalms of David, the meat and drink of these traditional, conservative people. I sang along, marveling at the power of sound to elevate the human spirit, and after a few times came to quite enjoy the hour or so we spent in the kirk on Sunday.

Uncle Willie also asked if I would like to go for walks with him. This was something new, as usually I was left to the mercy of the boys—although occasionally I would go out with Aunt Bet, with whom I would always have a marvelous time. I agreed, curious as to what he would say to me. He was in the habit of going to what we called the Point, a peninsula jutting out into the Moray Firth, from which you could see Findhorn on the south side and the water full of seals and dolphins playing their ecstatic play. At any time of day or night it was a paradise, where we all loved to go. On most of these walks, he said little or nothing at all, which I didn't mind in the least. It was a congenial silence, very soothing for one so traumatized as I was by my father's endless tongue-lashings. Once again I felt assured that it was possible to be with an older man and not be assaulted in some way.

One evening he was in a particularly quiet mood. We walked for a long time in absolute silence, me just flowing into the natural beauty all around us. Then he started to talk, telling me about his troubles, the insoluble problems he was having to face. I was at first rather surprised, as this was the first time an adult had confided in me, but soon I was caught up in what he was saying and tried my best to give him some consolation and advice. He became more relaxed and the subject shifted to a discussion of our inner life. He was, like Grannie, a devotee of Christ, and I was happy to find that I was in tune with him there. He asked me if I liked to sing hymns, which surprised me a little, for the Wee Frees generally sing only the psalms of David. We discovered that the favorite hymn of both of us was the old Celtic chestnut, *Be Thou My Vision*, which we launched into without any more talk. By this time the sun was beginning to disappear, creating the copper and golden glory that is sunset in Scotland. As we walked into it, we sang:

> Be thou my vision, O God of my heart!
> Naught be all else to me, save that thou art.
> Thou my best thought, by day or by night,
> Waking or sleeping, thy presence my light.

Darkness was beginning to descend, and we had to watch where we were stepping on the rough path we were following. His voice became very strong and emotional:

> Be thou my battle shield, sword for the fight,
> Be thou my dignity, thou my delight.
> Thou my soul's shelter, thou my high tower;
> Raise thou me heavenward, O power of my power.

It was clear where he was getting his unusual strength from. We managed to get to the paved road as the last glow of light disappeared. We reached the last verse, which seemed so appropriate as we were enveloped in darkness:

> High King of heaven, after victory won,
> May I reach heaven's joys, O bright heaven's sun!
> Heart of my own heart, whatever befall,
> Still be my vision, O ruler of all.

I had always loved this hymn, which brought me so close to God without any theology implied—except perhaps, heaven, which even then I felt was within me. Using the old imagery of the Irish high kings, it spoke of God as being the nearest of the near, the dearest of the dear, removing the separation I kept feeling in my relationships with other people, no matter how much I loved them. The melody is one of the most haunting and memorable anywhere, easy to sing and difficult to forget. The hymn had always been and would always remain one of the great consolations of my life, but sharing it with my uncle and seeing how it supported him in carrying the large burdens of his professional and family life gave it whole new meaning and importance.

To be able to share like this with anyone, far less an older man, was a moment of great joy. The moment welded me to him, not just as an uncle, a father-figure, but as a spiritual soul friend, the rarest and most precious of all relationships. My nature is not to enthuse over things when they happen; the experience sinks down inside and works internally. As time goes by, the meaning begins to appear and the results become apparent. This was the case here. In the course of time the fruits of my relationship with this noble man became evident. But for the moment, I was silently joyful that at last I had a father.

FOURTH QUARTER

BACK TO GROUND

CHAPTER 6

IN THE LAND OF THE PICT AND SASSENACH: 1955

The autumn school term of nineteen fifty-five was the beginning of the next turn of my life's spiral, and of the new life I had been dreading even since Grannie's death and my father's pronouncement of my doom. It was off to the East, away from my beloved Atlantic Ocean, the Hebridean islands, the "Celtic twilight" of my Gaelic family, and into the hills in south-central Scotland, where live the modern descendants of the warlike Picts—*the painted ones* who terrorized the Roman occupiers in the first century CE—and the down-to-earth, businesslike Anglo-Saxons, whom we refer to disparagingly in Gaelic as Sassenachs. Just as a diversion, as we start out on the next via dolorosa, my father often used to sing in the bathroom—along with operatic arias—a Glasgow student song set to the tune of the Welsh *Men of Harlech*, about the woad or indigo blue with which the Picts used to paint themselves in order to terrorize the invading Romans. The chorus goes something like:

> Woad will scare the Roman!
> Woad will scare the foe-man!
> Mix it to a brilliant blue,
> Rub it on your bum and your abdomen.

You might well ask why we keep all of this old stuff alive so long after the fact. It seems likely that our ancient culture is like the rock it stands on: it changes very slowly. And then again, as soon as I arrived at my new school, I was immediately treated as somewhat of a pariah, as the Sassenachs in the east just quite simply regard the folk from Glasgow as nothing short of barbarians. Partly it was a class thing—the Glaswegians are predominantly working class, while the east is more white collar and middle class. But at the age of fourteen I was still not ready for all of these distinctions; and certainly it was not pleasant when other children did not want to sit next to me in case I slashed them with a razor!

There I was at Dollar Academy, a school founded in eighteen eighteen by a Captain John McNabb, who is said to have made his fortune "on the seas"—which we always used to joke meant he was a pirate (a not implausible theory, given that untrammeled adventurism was the order of that particular day). Captain McNabb was a multimillionaire at the time of his death, but nevertheless remembered his Scottish origins, for he stipulated that the interest on his fortune was to provide "a charity or school for the poor of the parish of Dollar, wheir I was born."[8] The school had started out modestly to serve the needs of boys in Dollar, a tiny little town in the peninsula situated north of Edinburgh, but later expanded its catchment area to include the sons of British people living and working overseas, as so many did in the days of our empire. As time went by, the families of the overseas pupils sought to have their daughters admitted also, and thus the school became the oldest co-educational boarding school in the United Kingdom. Later, the school admitted children of the non-British, such as the emperor of Ethiopia, Haile Selassie, while scholarships for deserving students brought in young people from the surrounding areas, including Tillicoultrie, Kinross and the bigger towns of Alloa and Dunfermline.

The school was, therefore, quite heterogeneous in its makeup, though in my day we did not have the really exotic foreigners. But we did have enough students from overseas to divide our sports events into foreigners versus British, a distinction which was avidly kept up and passionately rooted for. There were, then, basically three populations at the school: boarders, day students, and travelers or scholarship students, which meant, in shorthand and respectively, prestige, the in-betweens, and brains. The boarders were mostly from overseas, the sons and daughters of British officials, engineers and other professionals working in what remained of the British Empire. Many of them were scions of the British aristocracy, used to a degree of prestige and noblesse oblige, though others came from professional families in England or Scotland, whose parents were well enough off (such as my father) to give their children a boarding school education, which in those days meant kudos. The impact on my life was

---

8   *http://dollaracademy.org/history.shtml*

mainly that the girls with whom I boarded came from well-to-do families with social pretensions, and their main goals in life were to go to finishing school, "come out" socially, and get a secretarial job while waiting for an appropriately wealthy husband. In my group I was the only one destined for university, a fact that marked me out as a real curiosity—or more accurately, a real non-entity or bore.

The day-students, the beneficiaries for whom the school was originally intended, came from the tiny little towns in close proximity to the school and were for the most part nice country youngsters, who seemed immune to the factional struggles that went on between the boarders and travelers. What distinguished the travelers, of course, was the fact that, as scholarship students, they had brains and almost always dominated the school academically. But again, they were more or less from the lower middle class or even blue-collar backgrounds, and were considered by the more upper class boarders to be rather undesirable. I learned about this directly because, as an egghead myself, I naturally inclined to spend my time with the brighter travelers. I was taken aside by the authorities and told that it was not appropriate for a boarder to associate with such low-class people—a warning I chose to studiously ignore, as my boarding friends, though nice girls, were altogether not able to keep up with my intellectual gymnastics.

This was really my first exposure to the British class system. In Glasgow I had been blissfully unaware of it, perhaps because I was too young. The only inkling I had had was listening to a radio program, *The MacFlannels*, in which the class of anyone involved was denoted by the fabric name they carried. The MacFlannels—Willie and Sarah—were themselves honest working class people, the mainstay of Glasgow and Clydeside; but their friend, Mrs. MacCotton, considered herself a notch above and affected the pseudo-English accent of such people. Mrs. MacVelvet was of a sufficiently higher status that she could afford to be more natural, while Mrs. MacTaffeta and Mrs. MacSilk, acknowledged as way beyond the MacFlannels socially, were occasional players in the humorous unfolding of the MacFlannels' life. If my memory serves, Mrs. MacFustian was the only player who was actually socially inferior, a woman of great common sense and no nonsense, of whom Sarah MacFlannel was very fond. But this was all entertainment, which thus far had no bearing on my day-to-day life.

Dollar was a different world. In addition to our loyalties as foreigners, British, boarders, and whatnot, we also were divided into four "houses" named after the Scottish aristocracy and each denoted by a color, which we wore when playing games. My house was Atholl, for which I wore a red waistband and with which I was supposed to root at any group occasion. Then there were the monitors and prefects, seniors who were entrusted with maintaining discipline, and empowered to "give lines", or make miscreants write out the school rule they had breached up to three or four hundred times—and that in the days when we wrote with pens dipped in ink! In short, ours was a highly structured world, no doubt originally meant to train us for dealing with the intricacies of administration of the British Empire, a goal to which the British boarding school system was still devoted. More generally, though, this type of education oriented us less toward the needs of the individual and more toward the demands of the group and solving the kinds of issues that arise in inter-group activity, something which I have come to appreciate as I wend my way through the relatively amorphous American social landscape, where the emphasis is so overwhelmingly on the individual and his or her pursuits, even to the detriment of the social group.

Another characteristic of this type of education was a high degree of physical austerity, which the authorities had tried to offset by the arrangement that boarders lived in relatively small "more homey" houses than the huge dorms of the past. Playfair House, where I lived, had fourteen girls ranging in age from five to eighteen. While we did not have the floggings and other horrors of the more traditional boarding school, we had rigid routine, more or less military in character. If we did not get out of bed within one or two minutes of being called in the morning, our bedclothes were ceremoniously pulled right off the bed and dumped on the floor. Not a very inviting prospect, given that the temperatures were in the thirties and forties and there was no heating! But again the two inch horsehair mattresses were not exactly inviting either, giving us some degree of incentive to get moving and zoom into the bathroom, where we were assigned a toilet and sink for precisely fifteen minutes. The bathroom was also unheated, so there again we had reason to keep moving. The fact that there were three other naked girls going through the hoops with you was a bit unnerving at first—but part, no doubt, of the kind of military training we were getting.

Before breakfast we had to run round the local war memorial several times, or go down the main street to pick up the rolls for breakfast, still hot from the oven, tantalizingly fragrant, and steaming in the freezing morning air. As soon as the daily newspaper arrived, we had to memorize a news item to be presented at breakfast. It would be rather funny in our large common room as we struggled to get access to the paper and find something no one else had. "I've got the murder in London!" "I've got the economic crisis in the Middle East!" "I've got Elvis Presley's newest song!" "Do you think the housemistress wants to hear that one?" "She'll just have to like it or lump it! What else is there?"

Glasgow Teddy Boy, gouache on paper.

Our housemistress was also the headmistress of the school. One of the many women whose fiancés had been killed in World War I, she had spent her whole life in and around the school and was simply riddled with the class distinctions and other minutiae that so many women who have never expanded their minds are prone to. The most damning word in her vocabulary was *vulgar*, which she used liberally, and in my case, applied to my luxuriant ponytail, which I had been cultivating for a few years. Those were the days of the Teddy boys and girls, the boys in brightly colored zoot suits and the girls in very full skirts, bobby socks and ponytails, all of which I assiduously documented in my art work, along with the Irish navvies or laborers, whose animal energy never ceased to

Irish laborers or navvies, gouache on paper.

fascinate me. The teddy boys, dressed so conspicuously, were like tropical birds in grimy Glasgow, but when they spoke, their heavy Scottish drawl gave the lie to their American attire and amused me intensely.

I never quite understood what made something "vulgar", but now realize that, on the whole, the word applied to anything that had come from America. And certainly the rage over Elvis, to whom we listened at every opportunity, and the craze for American dressing, was radically foreign to our indigenous values. This perception of things vulgar impinged on me oppressively, for I was constantly under surveillance as to how high I wore my ponytail. The guiding principle was: Do you want your head to look like a horse's rear end? Frankly, I saw nothing wrong with a horse's rear end, as I spent my days documenting them in my artwork, nor did I think that anyone would indeed mistake me for a horse, but I had to go along with my superiors and make an attempt to lower the offending "tail". If for any reason—and usually it was that I had thousands of other things to think about—my ponytail rose even half an inch above the approved height, I was liable to be sent out of the room or grounded. Grounding was indeed hard. As our life was so regimented, getting out into the surrounding countryside was the only way we could have a breather. I found it difficult to see how the height of my ponytail could be considered a reason for such severe punishment. But then, what to me was, if anything, a misdemeanor, was in the eyes of my headmistress nothing but defiance. This was the beginning of a lifetime of being accused of crimes I have never consciously given any thought to, far less wished to carry out. Perhaps because certain issues simply did not exist for me I seemed to be trying to defy my superiors; maybe they were indicators of something more important, but I have never succeeded in discovering what.

The flip side of all of this was our penchant for practical jokes and adventures of various kinds. One of the girls in my boarding house was from Ireland, an archetypal trickster if there ever was one. She was always stirring us up to various pranks, of which our favorite was the chips at night number. One of the absolute mainstays of Scottish cuisine is chips, or what are known as French (or, recently, freedom!) fries in America. We all loved them, but of course, for some reason—for they most assuredly were not American—they had been pronounced "vulgar". We were, therefore, deprived of our favorite treat by decree. However, we were not about to take this lying down and our Irish Rosie was more than equal to the occasion. From time to time, as all fourteen of us were sitting together in our common room after we had finished our homework, we would decide that the time had come for a round of chips. Money was always forthcoming without delay, and Rosie was off through the large french windows, through the bushes in front of the house and into the dark street.

We would wait in great anticipation, wondering if she would get busted this time—for she had to pass right by the windows of the matron, whose room was on the ground floor also—but she had the luck of the Irish and never failed to come through. There would be a tap on the window, a rush to get it open, and in she would step, beaming from ear to ear and carrying a huge bundle of bags of chips. We would get started at once, for who knew when the matron would get a whiff of the pungent treat and come barreling down the hallway to cashier all of us. Occasionally she did indeed come in to see what was going on, but fortunately the hallway was long and she was heavy on her feet, so that by the time she threw open the door the chips were safely stored in our lockers, the window was wide open to clear the fug, and we would all be sitting demurely, reading, knitting or otherwise engaged in activities

beyond reproach. Sometimes she would say, "What is that smell in here?"
"Smell, Miss Flemington? Smell? We don't smell anything." Then we
would look at each other: "Do you smell anything?" Rosie, blessed with
the gift of the blarney, would say, "Perhaps it's the fog", or some other
equally irrelevant suggestion, but always with such conviction that Miss
Flemington would take it as a reality and leave us alone to finish off the
chips before they became stone cold.

There was some degree of protection in being part of a group. But
there was also the stark fact of group dynamics. I got rather fed up of
listening to Elvis over and over and occasionally would pull out one the
of the old seventy-eight records of which there was a stash. One of my
favorites was by George Formby, an English comedian, whose number *I
Knew What to Do with Me Gas Mask* tickled my funny bone immensely.
This song was obviously a wartime effort to help people get along,
particularly with those gasmasks that had so terrified me when I was a
tot. George sang to a ukulele, telling us that "I'm getting very fond of me
gas mask, I declare—it hardly ever leaves my side." He put it to all sorts
of ingenious uses, including:

> I bought a farm because I like fresh air,
> At milking time I thought I'd do my share—
> But when I found the bucket wasn't there,
> I did what I could with me gas mask.

From there he went on to even more demanding tasks. Referring to
the fact that some short haul railway carriages had no outside corridor
and therefore no access to bathrooms, he told us:

> I once went for a very tiring ride.
> There wasn't any corridor outside.
> And when I felt the turning of the tide—
> I knew what to do with me gas mask!

Although the ditty became more and more off-color as it went along,
it was innocent and inoffensive, and I just loved the down-to-earth humor.
I played the record over and over. But the others were not amused. Not
much was said verbally, but their verdict was clear when I found a pile of
smashed seventy-eights one Saturday morning. The group had spoken.
Valuable early lessons in the way a group operates.

Like everything else in the school, our life in the boarding house was highly structured. In particular, seniority was a big thing. From one standpoint, I was used to observing seniority, having been trained to stand up whenever an older person entered the room and (more or less!) keep my mouth shut whenever my elders were speaking. American youngsters would probably die at the very idea, but I feel that I gained a lot, learning how to listen to others, to follow a mature line of thought, and generally to acquire self-control and a sense of my relationship to a wider world than my own little subjective one. What I was not used to was having youngsters not much older than I telling me what to do. It was particularly galling because these young women were, for the most part, rather muddled in their thinking and unclear on many of the concepts under discussion. Fortunately, the "head girls" in our house were good-natured, so although I was a thorn in their side, always questioning what they said, they somehow put up with me and were quite fond of me.

Then there was the "foreigner" aspect of things. More than half the girls in our house had grown up overseas and, while British nationals, had developed an intense love for what they looked on as their home. I came to understand what a white African was, when I heard Jinty, she of the Celtic black hair and blue eyes, agonizing over her separation from what was then Nyasaland, the wide steppes which she loved and where she longed to be; Junior Anne rhapsodizing over the Indian ghats and holy rivers, and others from the West Indies eagerly gathering and dancing round a record player playing calypso, that wonderfully mellow Caribbean sound which I think is now called reggae. All of this was very interesting and exciting, exposing me to a universe way beyond anything I had experienced thus far. This was one of the reasons my father had opted to send me to Dollar, and I was thankful for it.

The girls were, on the whole, nice youngsters from good families, though there was one girl whom I later realized must have been a psychopath. She tantalized and tortured the younger women almost to insanity, disrupting their lives considerably. This was my first experience of how one bad individual can cause so much trouble in a group situation. One or two of her victims would ask me to help them. As I had never met anybody like her and as she seemed generally "normal" (as psychopaths generally do), I really did not know what to answer, other than to encourage the girls to stand their ground and make themselves familiar with how she got under their skin, so that they were ready for her whenever she started her operation. Knowledge is power! Whenever I looked at her, she would drop her eyes and turn away her head. It was as if she felt I was looking through her. Certainly, she never touched my life—but then, I was senior to her. The seniority system has some advantages! And it gave me a grounding useful later on in my life.

Anne, my closest friend at Dollar, had one of the sunniest dispositions of anyone I have ever met. So benign and contented was she that she had been nicknamed Daisy, a common name for cows in Britain—and cows, as we all know, are nothing but contented! She was endlessly humorous and loved to play, characteristics that fitted perfectly with my temperament and somewhat neutralized the intensity of my personality. We played endless word games. One day we took a vow to speak in nothing but poetry for the whole day, which got us into considerable trouble. As we conducted our science experiment of the day we were babbling in poetry and getting more and more hysterical. Our teacher, an unusually dour, solemn and decorous Scot, regarded us with a cod's eye for some time and then informed us in a level tone that we would have to leave the room if we couldn't behave better.

We brought our method to bear on our home reading, which as often as not was something by Sir Walter Scott. He told rousing tales, no doubt, but in convoluted, long-winded and faux-archaic English, with which we had a hard time. Daisy and I sweetened the task by reading his novels out loud with the maximum of dramatization. When the weather permitted we would sit outside for our performance, which we hugely enjoyed. Daisy was gifted dramatically and I, of course, had my drama diploma, so we made a good team. I distinctly remember sitting rather precariously on rocks in the local creek on a sunny spring day, declaiming and laughing so much that we nearly fell into the water. "What, Sir So-and-So! Do you challenge me to a duel?" "Fair sirs", cried the lovely Lady What's-Her-Name, "I beseech you, do not sully your honor in such nefarious doings! Look to the higher cause!" and so on and on and on. Great movies have been made out of modernized versions of these tales, but Daisy and I gussied them up long before the movie studios got hold of them.

In the evenings, cooped up in that common room with the other girls we had to work on smaller "productions", which we found in the newspaper advertisements of the day. There was a fashion in the fifties for little picture strips telling some tale to illustrate the value of the product being promoted. Daisy and I would dramatize these tales with the maximum of exaggeration and laughter; and our top favorite was for a toilet cleanser which miraculously removed the odors from a house that guests had been shunning, much to the dismay of the good housewife (the heroines were always housewives in those days of the fifties). The punch line was, "Look, dear, what about the lavatory?" with which a close friend would introduce the disconsolate would-be hostess to the miracle-working cleanser. The final strip would be a happy hostess graciously entertaining her guests in her now fragrant house. Daisy and I worked assiduously on this one, trying it out in various accents, from English to French to German, Russian, Indian and as far East as we knew. It always reduced us to helpless hysterical laughter, much annoying the aficionadas of Elvis who were reverently drinking in the latest offering, be it "Love Me Tender" or "Don't You Step on My Blue Suede Shoes!" at the other end of the room. "Look, dear, what about the lavatory?" became a code for Daisy and me, which we would simply intone whenever we needed to be cheered up, diverted, or were being summoned to the front of the class for some misdemeanor, as often as not for giggling and laughing helplessly in the back row.

On the whole a wholesome, invigorating and happy environment, not only supporting our ongoing studies (of which art was still my

Portrait of a Friend, pencil on paper, 1955.

first love), but also introducing us to the way of life of the administrators of the British empire and the team spirit that supported it and made Britain a great power in the first place. I never regretted the experience, so different from everything that had gone before, encouraging not only the development of the individual, but also a sense of how to fit into the bigger picture without losing self-esteem or reliance on one's own judgment — a skill that I was later to find so hard to come by elsewhere and so much needed in the world I had to live in.

CHAPTER 7

THE SCREW KEEPS TURNING
AND TURNING: 1956-1957

There was much to like about Dollar, there is no doubt about it. But there were other things that troubled me and challenged me in ways I had not yet experienced. And there was, behind that, the slow turning of the evolutionary screw that was propelling me forward, whether I liked it or not.

People were always wondering if I was homesick, a common problem for children at boarding school. I could never say yes with any reference to the question as asked, for the truth was that I did not at all miss Glasgow or my "home". What had been my home, after all? Mary had tried so often to have me bring my little school friends over for tea, but I would refuse, knowing that my father was likely to be around, smelling of alcohol and shouting angrily. And, despite so much love and support from my grandmother and aunt, Grant Street had not created in me the sort of attachment my Dollar mates had for their parents in Africa, India or the Caribbean, their days playing under the palm trees or trekking over the plains with their friends.

What did call to my soul was the Atlantic Ocean, which was now totally beyond my ken. We lived near the Ochil Hills, wooded, inviting and a lot of fun to scramble over and explore. There were burns, lochs, all basic Scottish landscape, with the changing colors of the seasons; but what my heart craved was the huge expanse of the dark, restless water, my dark mother, where my soul would swim like a blissful selkie, one of the seal-women who could also become human and live as wise and fey in an uncomprehending fisher community. Who knew when such a being would once again hear the call of the ocean and, finding her seal-skin, jump into it and disappear into the unknowable vastness of the ocean?

But I was living with the Sassenachs, people largely of Anglo-Saxon heritage, and culturally of the Western Enlightenment, which in many ways took its most modern and effectual form in such figures as Adam Smith and David Hume, as well as the great Scottish inventors and instigators of technology, banking and finance, for which the Scots were famous, and which they exported all over the world. These were people interested in results, performance and no nonsense. The mythology, literature, music and art in which I had been steeped in Glasgow had to give way to hard-headed practicality and income-producing subjects. There was no place for the mysticism, the second sight, the Celtic twilight I had lived in up till then. Religion was a dirty word and God something to snicker at.

As a Communist, my mother had talked such talk, but her innate human feeling had counteracted them in practice. My Dollar classmates—mostly travelers—were lacking in the affection, kindness and love I had become so used to in my world in Glasgow. Was it because they were hostile to the "upper class" boarders, with whom I was identified? Was it teenage affectation? Was it the beginning of the dehumanizing wave that seems to have hit the West since the end of World War II? Or was I just missing Grannie and Mary, who by any standards were unusually loving people? The boarders I lived with were a little less blatant, but in general they, too, were agnostic—though we were all bundled into church to sing in the choir every Sunday morning. All of them hated any sort of discussion of emotional, intellectual or religious issues and would summarily shut me up if I tried to talk about anything other than Elvis, clothes, or boys.

Going back to Grant Street for the Christmas holidays was also rather depressing. Mary was working full time and I was, therefore, alone most of the time in the rather dark and dingy house, the first floor in a tenement of three stories. The emptiness and silence, particularly the absence of Grannie, saddened me immensely. Where was the pot of intensely sweet honey that had basically turned Grant Street into a hive of happiness?

Mary had arranged for me to spend most of the three-week holidays with Aunt Jane who, as a schoolteacher, was on vacation. This gave me an opportunity to get to know her better and start to hear in some detail about the connecting historical links of my mother's side of the family. I naturally felt reluctant to go back to Grant Street for the last few days, but it was an opportunity to be with Mary, who had a few days off work—and, though I did not know it then, a chance to see my home for the last time.

I had been back at Dollar for just a few weeks when I was called to the matron's office to be told that my Aunt Mary would be getting married in about six weeks and that my home henceforth would be in England, with her husband's family. I was absolutely stunned. Mary had said nothing whatsoever to me about having a fiancé—and here I was, being uprooted to England, the land of the out-and-out Sassenachs, and not a chance of going to the wedding! The matron explained that the distance I would have to travel alone, as well as the severe snow and ice we were having that winter, had made it impossible for me to attend the wedding, which was taking place in England. It was too great a responsibility for the school to let me travel so far by myself in such bad conditions.

On the surface, what bothered me most was not getting to the wedding. But the truth was that I was terribly hurt at not being involved at all in the whole process. I always felt that Mary would marry some day, but assumed I would be part of the drama. But this—having no preparation, knowing nothing whatsoever about who the man was, and having to move to England—was very difficult to take. I felt terribly alone and abandoned, the second major support of my life gone. Grannie was dead less than a year, and me in this cold place, physically, emotionally, intellectually and spiritually! But of course, I had to assume the traditional, British stiff upper lip, as any emotional discussion or display was out of the question in the environment I was living in.

Mary did write to me, explaining that her husband-to-be was a wealthy farmer living in what was then the county of Rutland, the smallest county in England. I wondered: How did Mary meet him? How on earth did they get together, considering she had been living in Glasgow for the last nine years and not going to England at all? At the time I could have no idea what the romantic story was: Something like twenty years before, she had been a private nurse for his wife, afflicted by bipolar disorder in the days when there was little effective treatment. He had fallen in love with Mary and asked her to marry him; but Mary was a true child of her mother. She told him, "Your wife's disorder is intermittent. When she is OK you get along well. There isn't a cure now, but there may be, very soon. In a few years, she may be perfectly all right. I would feel bad if you divorced her and then she recovered. I think you would, too." So she went back to her nursing agency in London and carried on her life until she was summoned to Glasgow to care for our little family. As it happened, his wife died shortly after Mary came to Glasgow, and George immediately phoned her and asked her to marry him. "George!" she had said. "I have a mother, brother and niece to care for now. There is no one else who can step in, and I can't leave them to fend for themselves." So he waited nearly another decade. When he learned that my father was not supporting us financially, he began to send money regularly to keep us going. And now, after at least two decades, he was going to marry her. He was in his early seventies and she in her early fifties.

This story would be unbelievable, were it not true. As I learned the ins and outs from Mary over the ensuing years, I marveled at her unselfishness, both in her attitude to his relationship with his wife and toward us, particularly my father. At any point during those abusive years she could have walked out and gone to live in comfort in England, but she chose to remain, putting up with my father's condition, my teenage turmoil and Grannie's declining health, as well as the Glasgow razor slashers. Only living with someone like Mary could possibly make the impression of the intense moral honesty and self-denial she possessed, despite her cigarette smoking, liking for a snifter and her sharp tongue.

But all of this unfolded over time. In the winter of nineteen fifty-six, unusually dark and cold, I felt that another part of me had died. I was, no doubt, happy that Mary had found a way out of the terrible darkness and oppression that Grant Street had become after Grannie's death, but at the same time she had been "my mother", and it was hard for me to share her with someone else. I was not bitter, just deeply sad and lonely, for there was no one at Dollar with whom I could share my feelings. I took some consolation in the school trip to Italy that Mary had signed me up for, maybe to cheer me up. Apart from a trip to London when I was about eight, this was the first time I had been abroad and it was, of course, an exciting prospect, even if the expedition was being led by the headmistress who, I felt sure, would not let go of my ponytail and other sartorial deviations, even when we were on holiday.

There were about fifteen of us teenage girls, traipsing around Rome, Florence and Venice at Easter time under the surveillance of the headmistress. We were allowed to wear "civilian" clothes, but were always under the threat of being pronounced vulgar and being sent upstairs to put on something more seemly. The result was that we were a supremely dowdy group, but that did not prevent the ever-present young men of Italy from trailing us constantly on their scooters, wolf-whistling and shouting suggestive comments in Italian. Many of the girls enjoyed it immensely, but I found it utterly ridiculous and boring. I could never see the interest in relationships with men that were not based on mutual understanding and appreciation. No wonder my housemates would tell me I belonged to the twelfth century, that I was hopelessly grownup already!

We went to all the obligatory sights in the three major cities, including art galleries, basilicas, fountains, and so on. But, although I was deeply involved in art and was seeing many works that I love actually "in the flesh", somehow it made little impression on me. Maybe I was really rather depressed, though not able to understand it fully. What did make a huge impression on my mind, however, were the mummified remains of seemingly innumerable saints that were preserved under glass in the churches. I found them utterly repellant. I couldn't help thinking, as I stood in some huge, ornate basilica: Such a huge pile of ornate masonry, paintings, gold, crystals, jewels, and whatnot to the nth degree, just to hold a decaying corpse! I suddenly saw why the Protestant Reformation had occurred—to get beyond such superstitious clinging to the physical world. Prior to these experiences, I had never understood the Protestant animus toward the Catholics, but seeing these grotesque remains, I understood fully why Luther hammered his theses to the door of Wittenburg Cathedral in fifteen seventeen.

I also dimly connected this sort of worship to the dreadful conditions the Irish Catholics were living in in Glasgow—uneducated, impoverished, and riddled with tuberculosis and other diseases due to malnutrition and poor hygiene. This was the first time I consciously identified myself with a specific religious viewpoint. Christianity had meant for me an inspiring relationship with Christ, but what I was now feeling stemmed from the Protestantism I had grown up with. Although I was not fully conscious of it in my teens, Protestantism is tied in with humanism, robust character development and self-reliance, the questioning attitude behind the scientific mindset, and with the idea of progress in the material world which characterizes the modern worldview. This moment of encountering the superstitious side of Catholicism began my awakening to my religious identity, as contrasted with my inner life thus far. This was to be a long, long story, far from finished as I write—and maybe a dialectic we are all engaged in, between two different ways of thinking about the world.

Our trip was brought to a conclusion by an Italian tradition—a rail strike the day we were meant to leave. We spent twenty-four hours in

Rome's railway station, waiting for a train to get back to Britain. Once there, I was to make my way to my aunt's new home in the center of England—a trip complicated by the fact that I got on the wrong train and found, when I finally got out at a town a long, long way from home, that the local telephone exchange could not forward my call to Mary. There are always kind people to help in such emergencies, and this was no exception. A local English couple sitting on a bench on the platform took me for a nice cup of tea and a sandwich and saw me off on the next train to the destination I was intended for in the first place. The mistake was not my fault; I had been given the wrong instructions by a porter I had made inquiries of—but in a way, it was rather symbolic that I should have gotten lost on my first visit to Clipsham, Mary's new English home. However, in the process I had learned that the English—the dreaded Sassenachs—are human beings like everyone else, and very kind at that.

The same was true of Mary's new family. Uncle George, her husband, was a patriarch who had been born in and lived his entire life of seventy years in the same farmhouse in a remote and traditional part of England. He was a man of few words, but deeply in love with Mary and, although he could not fathom where I was coming from, kind and supportive of me. His three children—about the same age as Mary—were also good-natured and kind; and their children, about my age, were jolly companions. This was a family of long-established farmers who also owned a quarry, of which the stone had been used in building some of the historic buildings of England and was at a premium for repairs or any new construction. They were, therefore, comfortably off financially, and I now experienced a standard of living that I could never have dreamt of in Scotland. I not only encountered beef for the first time in my life, but huge slabs of it and for practically every meal. I began to understand the phrase "the roast beef of old England", which I had encountered in children's stories. I also began to understand the English feudal system, for this was a bastion of English aristocracy, the most important of whom were the descendants of Lord Burleigh, the chief advisor to Elizabeth I of England. They lived in a huge Tudor mansion with interior decorations that were almost beyond my capacity to digest. The luxury and opulence reminded me a little of Rome—but of course with more restraint. This was draughty England, not the exuberant Mediterranean. On balance, I cared more for the five hundred year old chestnut tree growing outside the baronial pile, spreading its branches far and wide.

Our family would refer to Lord Burleigh as "Lordy", but with the utmost deference and circumspection. It did not pay to cross His Lordship, as they well knew; and, as I was amazed to see on the first occasion of our participating at an event at Burleigh House, they actually touched their forelocks when greeting him. I had read about this in children's books and seen illustrations of it for nursery rhymes—the local yokel in a farmers' smock and boots, holding his cap in his left hand and touching his forelock with the right as Their Lordships went by. I had thought this was a thing of the past, but here I was witnessing the feudal system still in action, despite the fact that the farmers in question were extremely astute and successful business people, more than likely capable of outwitting His Lordship, should the chips go down! But not, of course, without a lot of planning and discussion, which I was in on at several family gatherings. This was so utterly different from our Scottish ways, where, as our national poet, Robert Burns, said, "a man's a man for a' that"—a statement of the equality of all human beings, made possible by the fact that the European feudal system never got much of a hold on our society. We have the warlike Pictish blood in our makeup to thank for that! It kept out the Romans; it contained the Anglo-Saxons and the Norman French; and their successors, the English—though Scotland paid the price of economic backwardness. But then, we have our fiery humanism, our sense of equality, and that is good enough for many of us. Some say that it was the Scots who brought these ideals to America.

Another aspect of Merrie England that I had occasion to see was foxhunting. I went along to cubs' day—the day the foxhound cubs went out hunting for the first time. That day the quarry was fox cubs, and the hunters youngsters out for their first hunt. Although I could ride horseback, I did not feel myself up to the jumping involved in hunting, and so followed along as far as we could in the car. There was a lot of shouting and jumping about, hounds running around and baying, freezing cold, hot tea from a thermos, and finally, several dead fox cubs. I took it all in my stride—after all, this was a primal urge in human beings—but I did blanch when it came to the blooding, smearing the faces of the new hunters with the blood of the fox cubs. When I saw the cherubic face of Uncle George's grandson—maybe ten years old, pure blond, pure white skin, angelic blue eyes, smiling rather inanely—being blooded, something in me gave way. I strenuously refused to be blooded, no matter that I was breaching protocol very badly.

I was fond of Mary's English family, but of course they were down-to-earth, practical people without an inkling of the mystic twilight I tended to live in. In the long walks I took in the surrounding woods I would let my mind roam over the various questions that were preoccupying me, one of the most recurrent of which was whether I would ever find someone I could love and who would love me. So many things had happened to undermine my self-esteem; those I really loved had stayed with me for such a short time; and I was turning into a lumpy, overweight teen, overeating to somehow compensate for the emptiness I felt within. Daydreams about Rudolph Nureyev or Marlon Brando, who had really taken my fancy, did nothing but enhance my sense of loneliness and of being an outsider. I read voraciously, of course, at that time mostly fiction, the classics such as Dumas, Kipling, and increasingly the Russian novelists, who introduced a more metaphysical note into my ruminations; but overall, I was finding really nothing that could satisfy the deep-seated cravings I was experiencing.

As far as my recollection goes, I believe that that summer (nineteen fifty-six) I went to Bulgaria. The trip was organized by my father, who was, perhaps, trying to upstage Mary's promotion of the Italian trip, or perhaps to keep me away from her, at least for that summer. Bulgaria was, of course, a Communist country behind the Iron Curtain, and a trip there was more than a rarity. It was made possible only by the fact that my father's brother Donald was a military attaché to the British legation in Sofia, and was good-natured enough to take on his self-conscious, rather emotionally challenged niece for three weeks.

When Mary heard the arrangements for my trip, she was outraged. What was Colin thinking, sending a fifteen-year-old girl into the bowels of Communist Europe by herself? This was the first time I had traveled abroad alone, and no doubt the trip was daunting. I had to spend a night in Zurich, and had two stopovers, in Prague and Budapest. This was the heart of the Communist world, and the idea of a rookie like me navigating through it all was, to Mary's mind, unconscionable. However, one of my father's favorite phrases was "character-molding". He would bring it out whenever things were particularly dire—as often as not on account of his own behavior—and tell me how lucky I was to have these opportunities to develop my character. In retrospect, he may well have felt that his erratic lifestyle had been justified on the basis of how his daughter had had chances to work on herself!

As for myself, I could have no idea what would be involved, though my name as rendered on the Bulgarian visa—Gina Makofalia—was perhaps a hint that I was destined for a world quite other than what I was used to. I was thrilled at the idea of staying with my favorite uncle for three weeks, and that was it. So off I went, a pudgy teenager in a Donegal tweed suit getting on an airplane for the first time. I got to Zurich without untoward event, and from there set off on schedule for Prague, the capital of Czechoslovakia. The flight was uneventful, but the stopover was more than memorable. In flight and into the airport, the air-hostesses were delightful. They spoke English, looked out like mothers for the Scottish haggis in the tweed suit, and gave me clear instructions as to what to expect. But at the airport my passport was taken away,

Passport for Bulgaria.

which terrified me. The hostess assured me it was all routine, but I felt as though I had been stripped naked. Nor did it help to see, as I came down the steps from the aircraft, the cleanup crew standing stiffly in line holding their brooms and buckets with one hand and a military salute with the other. Getting into the airport, the hostess took me to a lounge adjacent to a large dining room, where there must have been about two hundred people, or at least so it seemed. As I entered, they all stood up and stared at me fixedly. I froze in my tracks, but the hostess kindly urged me forward. "They are not used to seeing people from the West", she told me. As we passed a few people, they reached out and fingered my tweed skirt. "They want to know where this fabric comes from", said the hostess. "We do not have fabric like this here." This was a reversal! I was so used to being the frump, and here my clothes were being regarded as something special, or even luxurious! I realized how austere their living conditions must be, and wished I could have spoken to them, those thin, pale faces with big blue eyes and hunger in all of its forms writ large. But I was in a place where English was non-existent, and had to be content with just smiling. Inwardly, however, I was terrified.

The hostess asked me if I would like to eat something, which I declined. I was not keen on sitting in the restaurant, where everyone would be fingering my clothes or eyeballing me fixedly. She sat me down in the lounge, and asked me if I would like to go to a movie that was being shown. She pointed to a door close by, from which was emerging the sound of noisy, military music, with guns going off and lots of shouting. That in itself was scary enough; but more than that, we were all stuffed with ideas of how the white slave trade was rampant in Eastern Europe, and I was afraid that entering that dark room might end up in my being whipped off to some brothel in the Balkans from where I would never return!

The hostess had to go, so I had to content myself with sitting next to the noise of the military movie, being stared at by the people in the restaurant. I had a book with me, but did not dare lower my eyes for fear of being taken off to some terrible destination, such as a work camp or brainwashing facility. I was in a total paralysis of anxiety. After a while an official came with my passport, which helped a bit, but by that time I was in end-stage terror and was vastly relieved when it was time to get on my flight to Budapest.

Thus far I had traveled on Western European airlines. Now I was getting on to a relatively small, Eastern European line, and I could tell the difference at once. Much dowdier, more down home—the hostess was a come-hitherish chub, good-natured and having the time of her life with the East German football team which made up most of the passenger list. Besides myself, there was one other Westerner. This was a large, fat and very loud American woman, dressed from top to toe in pastel blue and carrying what looked like a large hat box. As I recall, she also had a small poodle, but how that was in the main cabin, I cannot tell, unless the Eastern European airlines worked on totally different premises from those of the West. Of course, that was quite likely, as I quickly discovered. To begin with, the vomit bags were at least twice the size of those on the Swiss Air planes I had been on thus far. And then, when the hostess brought round the candy that used to be given out to suck on (in order to relieve ear pressure during takeoff), instead of the hard candy of the Swiss, we were offered chocolate liqueurs, for which I had a purple passion. Rather hungry after my difficulties with the Czechs, I unwisely loaded up on the rich candies. That alone might have upset my stomach, but in addition we got into severe turbulence as we passed over the mountains and to my chagrin I filled up not just one but two of those huge vomit bags! The members of the football team found all of this highly entertaining and laughed uproariously every time the heaves would begin again. All in all, a journey of sorrows, and not knowing what would await in Budapest—a foreign language, of course; everyone staring; and who knows what terrors from the Communist way of life.

As I came rather shakily down the steps from the plane in Budapest, I could see a small group of people standing at the bottom and apparently looking up at me. I had a moment of terror—the secret police! They were going to get me for the white slave trade! A rather mixed bag of terrors, but nevertheless quite petrifying. One side of me wanted to bolt back into the plane—but of course, I had already explored that and found it wanting. There was nothing to do but to keep going. When I reached the bottom, sure enough a man stepped forward, about to speak to me. Eek! What was a nice, normal girl from Glasgow like me doing in this den of iniquity!

"Miss MacPhail?" A cultured English voice, speaking English, English, English! "Yes?" "How do you do? I am from the British Legation here in Budapest. Your uncle instructed me to meet you." I practically fell into his arms, I was so relieved to hear my own language and know I was with someone who (presumably) would not whip me off for the white slave trade. (Obviously this was a big item in the recent news about the Communists, for I was really quite obsessed with it!) I must have been incoherent by this time, I was so tired and famished, but like a true gentleman he saw to it that I got something to eat, a little moral support and a great sendoff for Sofia, the capital city of Bulgaria which was my final destination. When I arrived there I was ecstatic to see my uncle and aunt, who gave me a heroine's welcome.

Bulgaria itself was one of the most beautiful and interesting places I have ever seen. The people, I felt, were also quite beautiful. Although their skins were dark from the sun, and their hair dark brown or black, they had the greenish-blue eyes that I associated with the people back home. The combination of dark hair and light eyes is rather unusual, and I wondered if there was a racial link between them and the Celtic people. Because of the utter blackout at that time on education about our Celtic heritage, I did not know till nearly fifty years later that the Celts had originated around the Danube river which forms the northern boundary of Bulgaria, nor that Bulgaria had historically been the source of so many of the "heresies" of the Middle Ages, which were, as I see it, in many ways, survivals of the old Celtic worldview. Perhaps I intuitively responded to this link—certainly I liked the Bulgarian people I met, and particularly Ivan, who was my main escort around the city. Ivan's family lived in the ground floor of the mansion we were living in. They had been aristocrats and owned the house before the Communist revolution, when they were demoted to being the concierges. His mother was a vibrant, lovely, cultured woman and he himself was an ebullient, self-assertive youngster. He was terribly proud of escorting a Westerner, and did all he could to draw attention to himself as we wended our way through the highways and byways of Sofia. Because of him I am sure I saw a whole lot that most visitors could never have hoped to see.

Christmas card from Ivan.

The city is perched in the mountains, and one day I went on an expedition to Mount Vitosha, one of the nearby peaks, with my uncle, aunt and other friends. We walked the first part, buying bread from a stall on the way. We stopped at one point to drink from a gusher and take a bite of bread. An insignificant moment, perhaps; but the purity of the water, the tastiness of the bread and the vast, encircling mountains radiating the light in what felt like reverberating circles spreading out into infinity etched themselves on my mind indelibly. The trip up to the peak on the funicular was wonderful, but not as meaningful as that moment by the roadside.

In and through these adventures I was encountering at first hand the life of the diplomatic civil servant. My uncle (my father's brother), was a "military attaché", and was, I have no doubt, spying for the British government. Certainly, he had one of the prime qualifications of a spy: he could down a whole bottle of whisky without losing any of his mental acuity, which was itself of the highest order. The idea is that during a political drinkfest the spy remains sober while the victim succumbs and spills the beans. My uncle had a droll way of telling "secrets": he would twist his mouth completely over to one side of his face and say, "Speak sidey-ways!" Being with him was always a delight, but of course he was busy much of the time and I had the experience of sitting around with the rank and file, endlessly gossiping, finding fault and complaining. I felt as if their minds were trapped in some small, dark space, held down by an unknown fear that they could not shake off. Despite so many negative experiences thus far, this was the first time I had experienced this particular kind of petty smallness, and I was always so glad when Ivan would show up and bounce me off on some adventure in his boisterous way.

We spent something like a week up in the legation's dacha in the mountains. We drove up, encountering an almost fairyland scene as we went. There were peasant women in the fields harvesting sunflowers with sickles, or tending the huge, fragrant fields of roses for which Bulgaria is famous. The women were dressed in traditional costume—lacy hats, bodices, heavily embroidered skirts, and frilly petticoats hanging down below. In the streets of the towns we saw the men dressed in fur hats, flowing jackets and baggy pants, with the upturned toes on their shoes that we usually associate with the East. In one place, a group of horsemen galloped by, their cloaks streaming behind them. With their fur hats they looked for all the world like a group of Cossacks riding out on some military adventure. I was, of course, absolutely transfixed by all of this, furiously sketching in my pad and planning several watercolors for when I got back home. Everything was so different that it felt more like a dream than reality—but these were indeed flesh and blood human beings, with no doubt the same passions and aspirations as I had.

Of the dacha and its enchanted location in the high Balkans I have only one memory, very comical and perhaps an illustration in an odd way of the idea of maya or cosmic illusion I was to encounter later in my life. Our cook there was a Bulgarian woman, whose name was Rosa. She had a terrible crush on my uncle and would ogle him any time they were in the same space. She was middle-aged, with what can only be described as a horse-like face. One day my Aunt Connie said, "Jean, would you like to see Rosa making strudel pastry?" I had no idea what was involved in making strudel pastry; but off we went, to discover Rosa manually pulling the dough so transparently thin that we could actually see her on the other side. "The dance of the seven veils!" I thought. My uncle had come along behind us; when Rosa saw him she began to grin and ogle him through the dough, actually swaying and gyrating about, just like a belly dancer or something of the sort. Inwardly I was convulsed with laughter, though I restrained myself outwardly. Here was this woman, in some ways so skilled and gifted (for she was, indeed, an excellent cook) making such a spectacle of herself—and for what? Somehow the scene seemed like a droll commentary on our lives, which are driven along by all sorts of desires and urges that lead us either nowhere or into endless complications.

My forays into Europe had indeed been diverting and character-molding, opening my eyes to the fact that there are many different ways of life (though human nature remains the same) and, of course, inuring me to the sorts of challenges one meets in the course of travel, either through the physical world or indeed through any other world. And at that time I had certainly been called upon to travel on some very difficult paths. There had been several wonderful highlights, but the loss of my mother and my grandmother had hit me hard. After Grannie's death my father's cruel parting shots had hurt me deeply and, despite the laughter on the surface, I could not but feel that Dollar was a sort of prison or penitentiary to which I had been sent, like some princess in a children's tale, to atone for crimes I had certainly not intended and indeed may not even have committed. He had gone off into his own world, leaving me entrapped in a gilded prison; while Mary, seeking a better life for herself and me, had all unintentionally opened up the wounds of abandonment I had felt so keenly when my mother left me completely alone in the world.

Always one who enjoyed her own company, after returning to Dollar I took to going for long solitary walks in the countryside. These were not totally approved of by the authorities, but perhaps they had a dim understanding that I was troubled and needed privacy. Or perhaps, because I said nothing, my activities passed under the radar. Behind the village at the foot of the hills was the Back Road, covered over for the most part by dense tree canopy. I would walk there for miles, turning everything over in my mind, crying some and from time to time singing *Be Thou My Vision* with great intensity, remembering that precious moment with my uncle, also walking in the twilight. As often as not it was raining or drizzling, enfolding me in the same sort of cocoon that my mother had disappeared into on that December night. Evening after evening I would go through this ritual, this threshold zone, trying to find something solid to support me and give me back my sense of purpose and meaningfulness as a person, which had been so undermined by the collapse of the world as I had known it.

Little by little I began to feel a small stirring inside. A moment of calm, a moment of happiness, would suddenly intrude into the general misery I was struggling with. Bit by bit I tapped into an inner source of meaning, which began to assume its own identity, independent of my surface mind. Particularly when I was singing *Be Thou My Vision* I would feel enveloped in an immensely supportive energy, something calm, loving but also dark, perhaps a vast Mother like the North Wind who understood me and loved me in ways beyond my knowing. Who knows where such energy came from? Perhaps from the dark, restless ocean which so attracted and encompassed my mind and filled it with strength; perhaps from the love I had actually experienced with so many people in the external world. These experiences on the Back Road definitely seemed to be a continuation of the same epiphanies of joy and blessedness I had been privileged to experience at other moments of crisis in my life. What was more, this was not just one, isolated peak experience, but a state of being I was tapping into on and off. Could it have been that it was all coming from inside myself? But I did not ask this overtly. There was just a faint knocking at some door of awareness. What was crucial was to keep going, to keep up my studies, my efforts to work out my destiny and to serve humanity in the way that I craved and Grannie had encouraged me to dream of.

Facing that challenge could no longer be postponed. Now fifteen, I had to decide which academic stream I would enter—the arts and humanities, or the sciences. Would I follow my natural bent and go on with art, English, French, Latin, history, in all of which I excelled—or commit to physics, chemistry, biology and math? When I arrived at Dollar the previous year, the biggest challenge I had to face intellectually was the fact that the Girls' High in Glasgow had not prepared me for a really rigorous course in science. I was way behind the students at Dollar, where boys outnumbered girls by two to one, and math and science were more or less the default. In Glasgow I received a wonderful grounding in language, the arts, history, mythology, music and even math, where my teacher was really outstanding. But in science there were several subjects, such as heat, mechanics and light, to which I had not even been exposed. At Dollar I all but failed my first term exam in science, much to my chagrin. My science teacher may have thought that I was just another female dim bulb, but I determined to catch up with the class, no matter what. If I was going to be a doctor I had to be able to handle science. I borrowed Daisy's notebooks and applied myself to the science textbook with a will. In the next term exam I was second, surpassed only by Jan, the school's best girl student in science. My science teacher was an exceptionally dour and understated man, but even he showed a flicker of amazement. He commented, "We will be expecting these kinds of results from you from now on." He also sent me up on the "white list", students who had done particularly well and were to be congratulated by the principal.

In math, too, I could hold my own near the top, so I knew that I had the capacity to perform in the sciences, though maybe not with as much distinction as in the arts. In a way, this was a blessing, because it gave me the potential to see things from two sides. But at that moment in time, it caused me tremendous grief and struggle. Which way would I direct my life? Would I follow my natural bent and gift and become an artist or a writer? My English teacher at Dollar was forecasting a brilliant career for me as a journalist, adding weight to the already huge resume I had in the arts. Or would I go with science and indeed become a doctor?

Self-portrait, gouache on paper, 1957.

This was not simply a question of personal preference; in my mind, it was a choice between self-indulgence or service of humanity, framed by the priorities of the puritanical and also highly pragmatic society I was growing up in. One side of me longed to express itself through art, writing and my dramatic abilities, but the other asked me, "Will your life have contributed substantially to the well-being of others, if you simply follow your own talents and inclinations? This drama was fought out in a massive way up in the bedroom, where I was now allowed to pursue my studies, for my homework was now so overwhelming that the two hours assigned to quiet time in the common room was simply not enough.

Again and again, as I sat at my table piled with books, my mind would wander from the subject at hand and start pick, pick, picking at my central issue. A huge wave of longing for the sheer thrill of creative work, of expressing my inner understanding in concrete forms, would rise up and carry me off, only to be met with a counter-wave of stern duty and commitment to service. The meeting of these two behemoths would create a huge whirlpool that sucked me down, down, down, almost suffocating and even actually gasping. This was indeed a major turning point in my life, a coming into conflict of the two sides of my personality. I simply had no idea which would win out, because both were very firmly part of who I was. As time wore on, a certain amount of light began to enter into these struggles. I would feel that it was indeed possible to reach a solution—but the question was: how could I decide? What slowly gained ground was the belief that becoming a doctor would be a greater service and behind that, my grandmother's behest to me to live for others.

The crisis came one day around Easter time, which is always an intense period for me. Apart from the Easter story, which of course is one of final self-surrender and sacrifice, setting a norm for the life of a Christian, I intuitively understood that simply the time of year had a strange effect on me, making me more psychic, mystical and fey than at any other time. That particular year was no exception: the heightening of my perceptions and feelings was almost overwhelming. I felt that I was reverberating with some cosmic pulse, being drawn into a power that was infinitely greater than myself. On that particular morning—a Saturday—I was toiling away at my studies in the peculiarly penetrating light spattered with rain that is so much a part of the Easter season. I kept stopping, dragged away by the intensity of the inner struggle, to agonize briefly over my decision. Then, remembering my deadlines, I would force myself back to my books. Suddenly I felt myself filling up with a huge energy, very radiant, loving and gentle, but nevertheless irresistible. It spoke silently in Grannie's voice, "Serve others." These unspoken yet clear words lifted up the gathering energy, which rose like a tornado and carried me off, sobbing and still struggling, into a final decision.

Math and science it was to be. I signed up for the whole program: physics, chemistry, biology and math. I was glad to have reached a decision, but nevertheless in anguish at closing the doors to my creative side. However, shortly after writing to my father about my decision, I received a letter from Africa telling me in no uncertain terms that he would not permit me to become so one-sided. I was to continue with English, French, Latin and history along with physics, chemistry and math. I therefore ended up with an academic load nearly twice that of everyone else, as well as a combination of subjects that would make it much less likely that I could win a scholarship to university.

From where I am now I can see quite clearly that my dilemma was created by the divide that our society holds in place between science and the humanities. My priorities were based on the false idea that art and the humanities were not of importance to human growth and development, far less happiness, a goal which of course I rejected long ago. I owe it to my father that he intervened at a point when I was for all practical purposes sealing my doom in the closed sarcophagus of science, where I would have suffocated completely without the balance of the arts. No matter that my chances for distinction were compromised—I was launched into a two-pronged path which, of course, was difficult to negotiate, but nevertheless was truer to my nature. In the long run, this apparently schizophrenic approach was to be immensely fruitful, though over the shorter haul it was to create huge problems for me in a culture where black and white identity was the order of the day.

I think it likely that my father had himself gone through a similar struggle. He was well versed in a number of subjects, writing professionally for various journals. One of these subjects was, interestingly, his collection of children's songs from Scotland, one of which he would sing with great gusto:

> Ho, Mrs. Bumblebee!
> Come awa' and play wi' me.
> And I'll gie you a wee drap tea, [9]
> To keep your belly war-um!

It seems likely that he, too, had had to work hard to keep his balance under the huge load of medical studies, which focus one's attention so relentlessly on the human body at its most basic level and shut out the more creative aspects of life.

And again, as I found out much later, he was almost embarrassingly proud of my accomplishments in the world of creative art. It seems likely that he wanted me to keep open the doors to the world of imagination and creativity. Certainly, when I had cleared the hurdles of my huge load of subjects in the finals exam, he insisted that the following year I take art as a seventh final subject, something unheard-of up till then in the school. That again fragmented my resume and put me at a disadvantage in the scholarship competition, but it did "round me out" in ways for which I have subsequently been very thankful.

---

[9]   I'll give you a little drop of tea.

CHAPTER 8

ARISE, DAUGHTER, AND GO FORTH
A WOMAN: 1958-1960

Although I was what would now be called "financially challenged" for most of my childhood, my family background had given me native intelligence, ability to stick to my guns and quite a bit of cheer, which kept me going through all of the difficulties I had to face. But the most important gift was the mysterious power that seemed to rise up whenever I was facing particularly difficult turning points.

Whatever it was that made me tick was expressing itself in and through all of my experiences and propelling me forward, taking its own, unorthodox forms. If there was any comparison to the Great Mother as the North Wind as in George MacDonald's book—other than the immense support and meaning—it was in the relentless challenges she kept throwing at me. In the book, Diamond is immensely attracted to the North Wind, but again and again dismayed at the adventures and perils she carries him into. She was, after all, the North Wind, and her job was to blow so hard that ships sank and other disasters befell. And again, though she was very loving, she had a way of abandoning Diamond and leaving him to trek through endless snow and ice on his own. Certainly, I was in the clutches of a Power that had no intention of giving me any rest, though I had not worked that out in so many words when I was fifteen. All I knew was that I had to keep moving forward, being true to who I was and trying to live in a way that not only did not harm others, but actually contributed to their happiness.

My first inkling of how strenuous this was going to be was the sheer load of work I had to do to prepare for my final exams in a couple of years—what we called the Highers, the dreaded sequel to the terrible Qualies. *Highers* stood for the Higher Leaving Certificate, a document necessary to proceed on to higher education. Students could present themselves for examination on either a higher or lower level, the minimum requirement for admission to college or university being three Highers and two lowers. Because of my consistently good grades, I had been given the opportunity to sit a total of six subjects at the higher level. Stolidly I kept up cramming my mind full of the facts and figures that were so prominent in our education; but I would wonder from time to time, "Why don't they teach us some philosophy to hold all of this stuff together? It is just a big jumble of facts that lead me—where?" I did read a few books of elementary philosophy which I found in the school library, but did not find them particularly helpful in integrating my studies, I must say.

But I was in the top stream, with the best teachers and the cream of the students, so classes were indeed interesting and challenging. Derek Burrell, our English teacher, took us beyond the more prosy materials on the curriculum to Gerard Manley Hopkins, Dylan Thomas, *Mad Magazine*, J.D. Salinger, Aldous Huxley, and other controversial figures. Jock Milne, our French teacher, was an endless source of entertainment to me, with his strange sense of humor. Occasionally he would stop talking about French to go on a disquisition on how Scotland's greatest contribution to world culture was the invention of the "flush lavvy" (flush toilet), which the English called a water closet or WC, and which also happened to be the initials of Prime Minister Winston C. Churchill. Who knows what political thinking lay behind all that! But we also read French classics by Moliere, Racine and Anouilh, and were introduced to Camus, Sartre, and Simone de Beauvoir, who, as a liberated woman, was quite a heroine of mine for some time. In Latin we read Caesar's *Conquest of Gaul* and the poetry of Ovid and Virgil, the latter two of which I translated into English verse. History continued on its way, continuously revolving round Britain and its exploits over the centuries in Europe and its own colonies. America existed for us up to the Boston Tea Party, after which a curtain fell on "our American cousins". Anyone who chose to drop out of the British "system" was simply sent to the lumber-room to collect dust. Even the United States of America!

The rewards in math and science were of a different order. We did experiments, solved problems and got a completely different perspective on life than the speculative and imaginative world we inhabited as we discoursed on Shakespeare's sonnets, Anouilh's *Antigone*, the unification of Germany or Italy, and couplets from Ovid. I personally loved both worlds, enjoying the splash of cold water science and math brought to the sometimes rather arcane realms we were exploring in the arts classes.

Science demanded an awareness of the physical world, an accuracy and precision that is not part of literary thinking, and I enjoyed it hugely. I loved working on math problems, particularly differential calculus, which opened out to me a whole concept of reality that I could have gotten in no other way. I understood how any given entity could be related to others in a consistent pattern, thus introducing a systematism into what otherwise appears to be an irrational and confusingly diverse universe. Even at the time, I felt that math and Latin were the most important subjects I was studying, because both gave me a key with which I could open up so much; math to the structure of logic and Latin to the structure of language, at least as we understand it in Western Europe.

Along with that went a total craze for the *Goon Show*, which we all used to gather round to hear on the radio. Spike Milligan, another Irish lunatic, was the moving spirit behind its zany humor, its endless wordplay, ad-libbing and improvisation. You could never be sure, as you heard the first part of any program, just how it would end up; and I think the three goons—Spike Milligan, Peter Sellars and Harry Secombe, the Welsh nut job who kept bursting out into frenzied arias in his high tenor voice—weren't, either. Sometimes they, particularly Harry Secombe, would dissolve into helpless laughter as the "plot" took some insane, unpremeditated turn. As I understand it, the whole of Britain was in the grip of the Goons, maybe as a reaction to the austerities we had gone through during and after the war. Or maybe such humor is just part of our makeup.

At this time, a full-blown teenager, I was intensely interested in the cinema, though my lifestyle did not make it easy to go to the movies. Apart from selected screenings at the school on Friday nights (which included *The Little Rascals* series, a classic if there ever was one), movie-going was not permitted at Dollar, and the theaters in Rutland, catering to the local farmers and small businessmen, carried mostly potboilers and light entertainment. In Scotland at that time there was a tendency to regard the movies as the work of the devil, catering to the lowest human instincts; but though there was a British film industry, movies were dominated by the Americans, whose lifestyle we basically disapproved of intensely. At Grant Street I had been permitted to go to occasional movies, carefully selected by my family. I remember seeing *Little Women* with Katherine Hepburn, endless Walt Disney movies, to which I became addicted early on, and *The Kon-Tiki Expedition*, to which my uncle Donald had taken me. This movie, along with my voracious reading about the Amazon, had given me the notion of adventure, of one day traveling down the Amazon from its source to its estuary on a raft! The movies certainly were a great source of stimulation, and attracted me intensely. But, on the whole, I was shielded from the "work of the devil" that lurked in American movies.

That changed, however, in my Shamrock Street days. On Saturday afternoon my Irish chums made a weekly pilgrimage to the movies, where the fare was quite indiscriminate, mostly Westerns and romances. In defiance of my family, I went along, not caring a jot about what American culture would do to me. This was certainly a totally new world I was entering, a revealing section through the human soul that only the unfettered, brash world of Hollywood could dare to present. However, as you went in you would have had no idea what was in store, for the foyer presented the most unsophisticated, primal scene. For these dirt-poor children in the days right after the War money was a scarce commodity, and "jeely jaurs" (empty jelly jars) was the currency for entry into what they must have seen as some sort of nirvana. The cinema foyer, therefore, was stacked high with jeely jaurs, through which you had to negotiate before entering the abode of bliss/devil's workshop. My own family could afford the few pennies needed for the cinema, but no doubt were loath to give them to me. But Mary, who had professional psychological insight (and had probably seen quite a few American films in London, if the truth be known!), did not make it difficult for me to "go with the flow".

Once inside, all hell broke out. There was continuous yelling, spitting, shooting of peanuts and launching of missiles of various sorts. In many ways, the movie itself was merely a backdrop for this cathartic drama. But occasionally something on the screen would attract attention—some showdown between cowboys, or a smoochy romantic scene—and there would be a momentary lull in hostilities. The showdown would attract more yelling, but rather more focused and purposeful than the background noise. The smooch would elicit sucking sounds and ululation, and doubtless imitation in the dark bowels of the cinema. I have absolutely no memory of these movies, except for a huge exposure to John Wayne and Robert Mitchum. I found them boring and silly, for the most part; and I think I remained pretty much immune to the virus of American culture. As did my Irish friends. For them, this was simply an opportunity to blow off all of their repressions beyond the ken of the priests—though, who knows, maybe there were priests sitting in the dark, purportedly supervising the flock, but no doubt getting their own, surreptitious kicks.

How I acquired such a deep interest in the cinema I have no idea. There certainly were plenty of obstacles in the way. However, before I left for Dollar Mary would take me once a month to the Locarno Theater on Sauchiehall Street for what she called a flick and a tea. The tea was an interesting part of the treat, for the theater had its own bakery and tearoom, where I would order either a Victoria biscuit or a flies' cemetery. Flies' cemeteries are a specialty of Scotland, for I have seen them nowhere else. Basically, they are two slabs of pastry enclosing tiny raisins in a sort of jelly, looking exactly like—a mass of dead flies between two tombstones! Such were the sophisticated delights of my youth. I surmise that we saw a better class of movie at the Locarno, for by the time I got to Dollar I was a huge fan of Marlon Brando, dedicated to seeing every movie he made.

At Dollar, my occasional visits to Aunt Jane on the West Coast must have been my opportunity to pursue my interests, for there was no other way I could have seen the movies I was interested in. At our boarding house lunch I remember one day the headmistress asking me what I planned to do on a weekend visit to the West. "Oh, I am going to see *A Street Car Named Desire*, was my ingenuous reply. For me, anything Marlon made was A-OK. But the headmistress froze in horror. Such a vulgar, American film! Up to that point, all I knew was that it was a movie with Marlon in it, and that was enough. The headmistress's reaction, however, made me realize there was more to it than I had understood, and of course piqued my curiosity. What could be so dreadfully vulgar?

When I finally saw the movie, it was definitely a turning point in my education. The raw, brutal emotion of the working-class Stanley Kowalski (played by Marlon Brando), as he tangles with his sister-in-law Blanche DuBois (played by the hyper-sensitive English actress, Vivien Leigh), was the first time I had seen such explicit emotional expression, despite my many verbal brawls with my father. The movie enacted the conflict that arises when people of entirely different backgrounds are brought close together—in the case of the movie, Stanley, a working class man of Polish immigrant origin and Blanche, a southern belle fallen on hard times, but unable to give up her social pretensions. When Blanche descends on Stanley's home to be with her sister Stella, the two grate on each other from the word go and, as the drama proceeds, Stanley finds out that "Miss Blanche" is far from the image of the proper, upper class lady she tries to project and control people with. She is living a complete lie and Stanley, intensely resenting the wedge she is trying to drive between him and his wife Stella, moves in for the coup de grâce, forcing a brutal climax and totally unhinging the mind of Blanche, who ends up being led off to a mental institution.

On account of the social and other important issues that the movie explores, it was considered a cultural watershed when it first appeared. At that time I had lived too confined a life to know much about what was going on in the world—my father had forbidden me to read the newspapers because the reports of the Korean War were giving me terrible nightmares—and was largely in the dark about just why Stanley was behaving so cruelly to his sister-in-law. But I was deeply impressed by the psychological interchange between them. As the more or less uneducated, but nevertheless intelligent Stanley was systematically dismantling his sister-in-law's ego and pretense at gentility, I kept thinking, "Why does she let him do this to her? She keeps setting herself up for his attacks, and plays into his hands with every word she says." Blanche was radically flawed and insincere, and therefore Stanley's success with her was so complete; and for me the big lesson was that loss of objectivity is the key to doom. Blanche could not see herself as she was, and was therefore totally vulnerable to whatever others superimposed on her. If she had been more honest and less prone to fantasizing about everything, she could have seen where Stanley was coming from and met his attacks with more dignity and control.

For me the importance of this rather brutal lesson was as a tool for dealing with my father's often cruel attacks. He had hurt me so much, had dragged me so often into bruising encounters which, when looked at objectively, were thoroughly unnecessary. Watching the movie made me realize just how thoroughly I had to objectify my father's behavior as well as my own in order to retain my self-respect and composure. I was not going to be another Blanche, beaten into insanity by the violent, angry attacks of a dominant male. Just because I was young and dependent on him in many ways did not justify his behavior. I remembered another tale I had read when younger in one of the lovely books friends had given me. This was about a little goat, Blanchette (French for "the little white one"), who was attacked by a huge, black wolf and put up such a tremendous fight all during the night that the wolf began to doubt that he could kill her. However, she became so exhausted that, as the sun rose, she lay down and gave herself over to death. I was sorry for her death, and constantly bore in mind that that might be the end of my struggles, too; but I was certainly determined to fight right up to the very end, not to succumb meekly and give over my self-respect on a silver platter to whomever was bullying me the most.

Another insight I had around this time, perhaps before I left Glasgow, was that living in a fantasy world was, in the long run, not going to help me. For several years I had dreamt of meeting someone (always a man) who would understand me, share my dreams and love me enough to commit to the ideal for which I was working. But of course the reality was quite other, now that Grannie, the only one who had understood me spiritually, was gone. While my fantasies had given me some solace from the difficulties of my daily struggle, I began to realize that they were creating in me expectations which were preventing me from dealing effectively with the harsh realities of day-to-day living, and I made a decision to put an end to them. In some ways, these were "Blanchefying" me, introducing unrealistic notions which no doubt made me more vulnerable to the attacks of my father and other, lesser opponents, such as my headmistress, who (we all felt) was like an old bat out of hell flitting around and creating so many obstacles to everyone's healthy growth.

The routines at Dollar were strenuous, involving a lot more physical activity than I had had in Glasgow, more outdoor exposure and demands from the hierarchical system we lived in. Quite likely that is one reason why my bedtime fantasies subsided at Dollar—if I had any fantasies at all, it was to create something comfortable and warm from the two-inch horsehair mattress and the just enough blankets we were supplied with! Bed was instant sleep, a chance to be alone for once, and escape from the all-seeking eyes watching our every move. Nothing like boarding school for a reality check! No doubt this was all a normal part of growing up, and certainly I did not question the system or its relevance to my life. What did hurt was the dull remembrance that I was there as a "punishment", a banishment from my family and the love I had experienced there. In its place we had loyalty to the school, to our boarding house, to the emblematic houses we had been assigned to, and to our school teams.

I continued to commune with myself on the Back Road, re-finding the identity so many events seemed determined to rob me of. One drizzly winter evening as I was coming home from my walk, for some reason I took the way that led to the main street of Dollar. Usually I came home the quick way, bypassing the village, but something moved me to walk by the café that catered to the students. This was where the boarders and their hench-people liked to hang out, endlessly chattering and shouting. I had been in a couple of times, and felt nothing so much as the need to get out. On this particular evening, perhaps approaching Christmas, everyone who was "anyone" in the school hierarchy was present. Hot chocolate was the "tipple", for of course alcoholic drinks were not served; but the kids were making themselves high with their off-color jokes, flirting with each other, battles for status on the hierarchy of the élite, and general sense of entitlement and superiority, for here the boarders reigned.

I stood outside in the drizzle, looking in through the steamy window. At first I felt a pang that I was not a part of what was going on. I was a boarder, but more or less on sufferance, for was I not one of those dreadful folk—maybe even a razor-slasher—from Glasgow? Then again, I could not identify with the British superiority trip that still held sway, despite the fact that we had lost almost all of our colonies. (I never let on, but in Glasgow I had been known to remain seated when the national anthem was played, so deep was my resistance to what I perceived as nonsense). And, though I longed to eventually find love with a man, I was totally uninterested in the boisterous horsing around that went on. Through the smoke (for many of them were smoking) and steam I could see that some of our senior girls were actually sitting on the laps of the dominant (read rugby-playing) boys, quite at ease with it all. Who knows what they got up to together in the recesses of the Back Road! This was the very picture of student life among entitled British youngsters. I stood there for quite a while, peering in. They were all too engrossed in the rituals they were going through to see me, and I could take my time. I asked myself, "Do you want to go in? You will be much more accepted if you play the game and be 'normal'. You will have influential friends, clout and status. And you will be warm and jolly. Do you have to go on and on in that cold, draughty bedroom, slogging away over your books? Why not go in and have a little fun!" Such thoughts were circling round and through me, like the proverbial bats in a belfry.

This was definitely a defining moment in my life. Though my background did not qualify me for British kudos and entitlement—for the Celtic world to which I belonged was still regarded as backward and inferior—here I was, standing on its threshold. All it would have taken to become accepted by the dominant hierarchy would have been to push open that door and join the festivities within.

The answer came slowly and gently. I quite simply did not belong there. Trying to identify with it would mean turning my back on everything that had meant anything to me thus far. In the long run, I would feel emptied and exhausted. I had to follow my own path, however "low" and "worthless" it might seem to the British élite. How long would they be élite, anyway? The British Empire that gave them credibility was almost a thing of the past, and was running out the bottom even as we enacted the whole scene. Really, it was easy for me to get going, leaving it behind and returning to dry, warm clothes, my books and my mystical egghead identity.

I heard from my father from time to time. He was now Professor of Epidemiology and Preventive Medicine at the University of Khartoum in the Sudan. This was, in a way, quite a distinguished position, but of course in one of the two cities—Calcutta and Khartoum—notorious to the British for their unhealthy climate and hideous culture. But for my father, in the clutches of shell shock and alcoholism, it was definitely a step up. He was now in a position to initiate action for the well-being of others, a goal he had pursued with enthusiasm in the tenements of Glasgow, where the suffering of the Irish was so palpable and at times even grotesque.

More than three years had now passed since Grannie's death and my father's angry exit from Grant Street. They say absence makes the heart grow fonder, and in addition my father was now on his own, making his way without the trammel of womenfolk he had had to hassle with in Glasgow. No doubt he was feeling more benign toward me than previously, and also more sure of his own position in the world. Presumably some such dynamic lay behind the invitation he extended to me to visit him in Khartoum that winter, where, no doubt, my character could undergo a little more molding and he could demonstrate to me his own achievements. Why he should have been so agonized over my criticisms of him has always remained a mystery to me, as has the whole fact of how profoundly parents and children affect each other, not only for good but also bad. I had been a preteen child when I really let him have it—why in the name of God should he have taken it so seriously? Couldn't he understand how much I had suffered by losing my mother, and how his uncontrolled behavior was hurting me? Of course, I have to concede that he really did love me and love, in some of its forms, can be very, very irrational.

It was with such mixed feelings that I set off for the Sudan in December of nineteen fifty-seven, just before my seventeenth birthday. Africa at that time was still referred to as "darkest", a land of exquisite beauty and unknown terror, its people still largely tribal and beating their drums to a totally different tune than the military bands of the British Raj. And, of course, the Sudan, at least the North, was a Muslim country. However, for Europeans at that time Islam did not hold the threat that it does now for Americans. Islamic culture had played a large part in the shaping of Europe, first by its invasions of Europe as far west as France in its early days, and later by the diffusion of culture that brought about the Renaissance and the development of natural science, for the Muslims had kept Western culture alive as Europe auto-destructed in the five hundred years of the Roman Catholic Inquisition. The Muslim culture that took root in the south of Spain had given the world the exquisite blossom of Western Sufism, which in turn had influenced the Medieval troubadours, the legend of the Holy Grail, and the development of the whole humanistic Western tradition.

This, of course, was a longer trip than that to Bulgaria, to a much less familiar culture and to an unknown situation with my father. But, after my jaunt behind the Iron Curtain, I was what you might call a seasoned traveler, while my training in self-sufficiency and team playing at Dollar had made me more ready to face the storms that might come up as I reconnected with my errant parent. Another strike in my favor was the fact that I now had a stable, financially secure and loving home with my new family in England, so that I was not so insecure and dependent on my father. In retrospect, I think he was really keen to rebuild our relationship without the direct influence of Mary, whom he saw as intensely hostile to him and a blight on my mind.

I was weary of confrontation and struggle, and, as I say, more sure of myself than I had been at Grant Street, where my mother's sudden death was eating away at me, though I never spoke of it or even fully understood what was going on. I was, therefore, ready to meet my father halfway, and was happy to note that, though he was still drinking, it was much less than in his desperate days in Glasgow. I don't recall seeing him dead drunk during this visit, and was therefore more able to relax and enjoy the visit than I had expected. No doubt his new social status, both as a white sahib in black Africa and as a professor at the university had done much to rebuild his self-confidence and sense of responsibility.

Khartoum, being near the equator, presented conditions so utterly different from what I had grown up with that just the details of day-to-day living were quite absorbing. Daily life was organized around avoiding the intense heat of the sun. The day began around six, as I recall. After a light breakfast, my father left for work and returned before noon, when the heat of the sun was so overwhelming. We had lunch and then retired to bed for several hours. Perhaps around four pm we had tea and my father left again for work. He returned in the late evening, when we had dinner and would then sit on the verandah chatting with his friends. Our "boy" was Abdul, an amazingly self-sufficient middle aged man who seemed capable of doing anything, and was an excellent cook. I enjoyed the exotic foods we were eating—for a girl from Scotland, peanuts (which Abdul made into a delicious soup), guavas, and goats' milk rather than cows'. Abdul washed our clothes every day and brought them in in the evening, immaculately clean and ironed to perfection. I felt rather strange being the center of such focused attention and service; but this was, of course, the norm for sahibs in their imperial domains, though the Sudan was then independent. Occasionally I would peek through the screen at the back of the house which separated us from Abdul's domain, and would marvel at how he managed in such a cramped space and with such primitive equipment. He was always smiling, calm, and ready with information and needed help, and I took to feeling that if my father got out of control, I could rely on Abdul to help me. His English was rather limited, of course, but I could feel great strength of character and goodwill, which supported and comforted me, particularly on the few occasions that some of the old edge came back into my relationship with my father. After such episodes, Abdul would always smile at me with particular kindness and offer me some delicacy he knew I especially liked.

My father was very friendly with his students, who would come to see him at home quite regularly. As Muslims, they were all men, of course. They may, perhaps, have been coming around more than usual out of curiosity to see his daughter. Be that as it may, I became quite friendly with two of them, Ahmed and Abdullah. Ahmed was a sunny personality, happy and carefree. My father had taught him to play the bagpipes, to which he was utterly devoted, and he would readily entertain us with a medley of Arabic music, his eyes beaming and his whole body expressing joy. Hearing such music for the first time and on our national instrument, the bagpipes, was of course quite an experience. My father had occasionally played the pipes at Grant Street, deafening us in the confines of our living room—for the pipes are meant to be played outdoors—and loading the air with the smell of whisky and honey, the traditional means of keeping the bag (the stomach of a sheep) flexible. I had had a more esthetic experience up at Fortrose, where my cousin Murdo played pibroch, the old, traditional improvisational music, on the beach. I have distinct memories of him walking slowly back and forth in his kilt, the endlessly inventive music skirling over the water and creating what I can only call a cosmic experience. In so many ways, the pipes are the embodiment of the Scottish soul. The world is more familiar with the martial music of the Scottish regiments, but the pibroch is intensely moving, soulful and varied in its expression. I rather think that Ahmed's music was improvisational, too; certainly it moved me almost as much as Murdo's pibroch. And, of course, I enjoyed the enthusiasm of the young man, no doubt coming from an educated and entitled background and with all hopes and aspirations for his own and his country's advancement.

Abdullah was a different type. Smaller in build that Ahmed, he was quiet, intense, and deeply ambitious. He dreamt of a strong and modernized Sudan, of a great national medical service and of his own future career as a radiologist. He engaged me in intellectual discussions and was keen to show me various aspects of Sudanese life. My father readily agreed to Abdullah's taking me to various places in Khartoum, one of the most memorable of which was a visit to the home of one of his friends or relatives.

We went in the evening—a time which is always dark close to the equator—and were ushered up to the roof, where so many activities take place in very hot countries. As it happened, a relative had just died and the family was in mourning. A large number of men and women were sitting cross-legged on the roof, the women on one side and the men on the other. In the center, a thin, ascetic man in pure white robes and Muslim skull cap was intoning a prayer in Arabic.

The equatorial night is truly spectacular. Somehow the darkness is so absolute (maybe a dearth of street lights?), and the stars so near and brilliant. It seemed that you could reach up and pull down a star with no effort at all. There was, in addition, almost total silence, apart from the chanting. The family was still and quiet, apparently totally focused on the words pouring out from the officiating religious. The intensity with which he was intoning the Arabic text was really quite startling; he was, as it were, knocking hard on some inner door, speaking directly and intimately with the departed soul, and carrying the whole family with him to a last, intense conversation with their beloved. The effect was stunning. I felt that I was squarely in a totally different realm than anything I had experienced thus far. I was way above the earth, surrounded by what the Bible calls "a host of unseen witnesses", the souls of the dead, perhaps even of the living. It was an immensely assuring and loving place to be, in which I felt quite at home. I wanted the moment to continue for ever, so peaceful and uplifting it was.

This experience, so utterly new to me, made a huge impression on my mind. The intensity and apparent integrity of the chanting man and the silent dignity of the family impressed me as being very, very valuable and important, and created in my mind a positive attitude to Islam, though in many ways this was a primal situation, which I imagine was independent of any organized religion. Its impact may well have been more connected to African culture than to Islam, but at the time I saw it as part and parcel of the Islamic world I was living in. My experience had been of a straightforward, kindly and good-natured people, generous in their hospitality and respectful of me, though I was a mere teenage girl. And this sudden, direct connection with a more intense inner world was something no experience I had had in Christian lands had given me. I felt that this was a culture more tapped into the inner world (which I already knew was so real and meaningful) than the secular West, and was left, on the whole, with a positive image of Islam.

But of course there was a negative side, as there is to everything. One of the most immediate illustrations was our experience of polygamy, as lived by our neighbor. We were living in what must have been a pretty upscale part of Khartoum, with huge houses surrounded by gardens filled with the gorgeous, brilliant bloom of bougainvillea. Despite the distance between us and our next door neighbor, we could not help hearing what was going on of an evening, when we were sitting on our verandah. We would hear his two wives talking with each other, fairly amicably at first, but rapidly escalating into a shouting match, then on to screaming, with dishes and glasses being smashed. Then we would hear his voice, angrily demanding silence. There would be a momentary lull, followed by a reprise of the shouting, his voice rising above it with exasperation. The threesome would spiral and spiral into utter chaos and then—the sickening sound of the lash, with the women screeching and screeching until they suddenly became silent. After this there was total silence, hideously loaded with the vibrations from the sound of the lash hitting human flesh and crushing the human soul. I had never thought that polygamy was a good idea, but this experience made me realize just how bad it could be, as well as how far male domination and oppression of women could go. I was grateful that I had grown up in Scotland where such behavior was not tolerated by law, and on the whole women were treated with considerable respect and permitted to have their own personalities and aspirations.

Another negative of which I was aware in the Sudan was the oppression of the people from the South. The northern Sudanese were a mix of black African and Arab and were, of course, Muslims. They were inordinately proud of their Arab ancestry and regarded the black Africans of the South as vastly inferior. The Southerners followed either the animist faith of their ancestors or were Christian, and were physically quite different from the people from the North. These were the natural lines of demarcation in this large country along which the British had worked, assigning the two sections of the Sudan to separate administrations and thus making political the racial and cultural separation that already existed. Almost as soon as the Sudan had acquired independence, civil war had broken out and, as we now know to our sorrow, was to continue on and off up till the present, becoming more and more brutal and unrelenting.

Despite our relatively grand social status, we, like most everyone else, did not have the advantage of the flush lavvy, that gift to the world from Scotland, according to Jock Milne, my French teacher. We did have a rather grandiose toilet, a large room where we ascended a flight of stairs to crouch over a hole and make our contribution to a large bucket below. I found it rather amusing, this grandiose structure, totally without any modern amenities. What I was not so happy to hear was that in the evening, the Dinka, the people from the South, would come and empty the buckets, and that their social status was nothing better than slavery. At dusk I would see them walking along the streets, carrying their huge buckets on their heads. These were tall, slender people like the Masai, whose dancing I had seen on film and was totally entranced by. They moved slowly and with the utmost grace, their bodies beautifully balanced and harmonious. I felt a pang that such beautiful people should be forced to do work that was worse than menial, in any way I could understand the word—for this work was dangerous to health in a country where hideous diseases were transmitted by human waste.

And it seems that their presence of mind was rather unusual. There was a story about an English lady visiting the Sudan. Somehow she had not been warned not to use the toilet at dusk and was "doing her thing" one evening. She heard rattling below her and peeked through her legs to see what was going on. To her horror she saw a man standing below her, about to move the bucket. He, however, was totally equal to the situation. He realized she was there and looked up with a charming smile. "Good evening, madam", he said as he graciously withdrew until she had finished her "meditation". This story impressed me immensely. No doubt these oppressed people had to develop a professional attitude to their work, but somehow the grace and composure of the unknown Dinka was above and beyond anything one would expect in such a situation. (And one shudders to think of how other "donors", less refined than the English lady, might have behaved with the unfortunate man).

Our family was not racist in the least, though some of our members disliked the way the Catholic Church was lowering the dignity of the Irish people. That was the way we saw things—in terms of human dignity and decency, which for us were the acid test of the value of anything. One telling illustration of this aspect of my upbringing is the fact that I gladly owe my debt to Abdullah for his introduction to the ideas of feedback systems, my first exposure to the rudiments of holistic thinking, which has now become so central in my life. He gave me a copy of Norbert Weiner's seminal book, which I devoured with intense interest. Many people would have looked down on Abdullah as a "black", or detested him because he was a Muslim; but to me he was an important guide in my intellectual life and a very worthwhile friend. Looking back on him now in the light of how people generally behave with foreign cultures and ideas, I am simply amazed at his breadth and depth of understanding and his dedication to humanistic values. Who would have thought that I would have found such friendship in "darkest Africa", as we always referred to that continent? I believe I owe such serendipities to the upbringing our Mary Anne gave us, generous, loving and accepting, qualities which had rubbed off on my father, at least as far as people other than myself went. Through some grace, he and I had managed to get along quite well and I had understood better than previously that he loved me almost insanely. But why could he not express it in a more supportive and helpful way? I was grateful that things had improved, however, and began to hope that over time we could build up a more normal relationship.

However, I was in for a rude shock and in short order. One day, not long after returning to Dollar from Africa, I received from my father a rather formal-looking letter. I was puzzled—as he was not one to go in for formalities—and perhaps had a moment of foreboding; but opened it anyway. An invitation to his marriage! He was going to marry Pat, a public health nurse who came from a part of Scotland fairly near Dollar. I was truly stupefied. How could he foist on me an invitation to his marriage without telling me beforehand, without introducing me to his fiancée, who lived so close to me? He had had all the opportunity in the world to tell me about it while I was with him in Africa! Coming on top of

Grannie's death and Mary's marriage (also without my active participation) and in the space of less than four years, the whole thing was just too much for me. I had somehow adjusted to Mary's marriage, for her family had accepted me and made me feel at home; and, of course, I had no doubts of how much Mary loved me. But coming from my father, with whom I had had so much difficulty, and whose love for me was, in my mind and at that time, highly in question (despite his frequent protestations to the contrary), this was tantamount to the coup de grâce with which the bullfighters finish off their victims. However shaky my relationship with him, he was one of the three pillars of my life thus far, and to have this also pulled away from under me felt like the end of my life had come. I felt totally abandoned, totally alone, totally bereft. As ever, I said not a word to anyone; who was there to tell it to? Mary's response was to focus on getting me an outfit to wear to the wedding.

Pat wrote a nice little letter and sent a box of luxury soap, which I appreciated as a token gesture. I even kept the pretty box as a container for the lovely rice-paper Bible Grannie had given me, and which is even now my most prized possession. Grannie had inscribed it: "To Jean C. MacPhail: 'Strive hard to enter in at the straight gate.' (Luke 13.23). Wishing you many happy returns, with love from Grannie." She had given me it in nineteen fifty-four, the year of her death. It was her last bequest to me, which I have made the motto of my life, for I knew she wanted me to struggle as she had to "attain immortal life". The Bible had become very worn and needed protection. Somehow I felt that by using Pat's box as its container her relationship with me would be sanctified and might perhaps be happier than those I had had thus far with the other players in my father's life. As I cast my glance on the bookcase near me I can see the red, gold and white box with its precious contents, and simply say, "If at first you don't succeed, try, try, try again."

I went to the wedding, which was in April. I have no memory of it, other than that Daisy went with me and looked stunning. Her natural striking coloring—black wavy hair and the hazel-green eyes of the Celt, as well as her liking for bright, bold colors—made her a bird of paradise in the rather somber gathering that the Scots tend to present. She, as she always did, enjoyed herself immensely. My father was in kilt, of course, and Pat looked very happy; but what I felt I have no idea. I think I was just numb from the shock of being treated like a piece of furniture with no feelings of any sort. That both he and Mary would have treated me this way was particularly galling. In their defense I could hypothesize that my utter taciturnity about my mother may have made them think that I was abnormally insensitive and that they could, therefore, take such liberties with me. Mary, at least, was a deeply caring person and I feel sure she would have been sad to know how much she had hurt me.

I returned to the Sudan in December of nineteen fifty-eight, a year after the previous visit, looking forward to renewing my acquaintance with my African friends. I also hoped to get to know Pat better and try to build up a rather more normal relationship with my father than had been possible previously. From the start, however, it was clear that things were not going to go smoothly. My father was confrontational and drinking more than he had the previous year and Pat was sharp and unfriendly, which came as a surprise. She had seemed like a nice "Scots lassie" when I had had the few moments with her in Scotland; but this was not at all in keeping with that impression. She was not happy in the Sudan; she found it too hot, too uncivilized and had a much less tolerant attitude than my father to the Africans. I felt dimly that maybe all of this was making her fretful and tried to be soothing and friendly nevertheless. However, nothing seemed to work and I resigned myself to a long, hot visit. And, of course, my father had hurt me terribly in his handling of his engagement and marriage and it is entirely possible that I was being quite aggressive, which is the way I tend to behave when I am upset.

We were scheduled to go to the Egyptian border with my father and his students. They were on a field trip to the dispensaries that dotted the stark countryside and gave whatever meager medical care there was to the rural people. With his usual attitude of exposing others to "character-molding" experiences, my father took myself and Pat along. I found it quite fascinating and exciting, but poor Pat, I fear, was not enjoying it at all. The heat was tremendous: as we rattled over the desert in a huge truck I somehow found out that the temperature was in the hundred and thirties! The air, however, was bone dry and, though I was sweating profusely, I felt quite light and exhilarated. Then there were the men. As an official group from Khartoum University, we were received everywhere formally, which meant large numbers of men, with nary a woman in sight. By that time I was used to being in overwhelmingly male company, being in the science and math stream in a coed school; but Pat was extremely uncomfortable and out of her element.

The outer events were, however, absorbingly interesting. We went north through the desert to the Egyptian border, the first part of the journey by train—a thirty-hour journey, by far the longest I had taken—

and the remainder by truck. We stopped at innumerable dispensaries to inspect how clean and well stocked they were, and what sort of work they were doing. There were endless cases of trachoma, an eye infection leading to blindness, and schistosomiasis, an infection contracted from wading barefoot in infected water, which led to total organ failure and death over the course of time. It was truly pathetic to see child after child with his or her eyes all filmed over and adults with swollen bellies due to massive enlargement of the spleen. My father got quite excited, explaining that both conditions were preventable, provided the people were better fed and educated, and that trachoma, at least, was readily treated, provided the necessary antibiotic was available. As with female circumcision and all of the other plagues enervating this large country, the main issue was education. But how to communicate with these people, illiterate and at best living in a medieval mindset? How to communicate to them the rewards of simple changes of behavior patterns which had been established, more than likely, for millennia? It was clear that he felt himself in another net like that of the Roman Catholic mindset in Irish Glasgow, and that he was as involved in the struggle to change the situation as he had been there.

Another item that engaged me intensely and thrilled me through and through was seeing the pyramids and huge sculptures at what I think must have been Abu Simbel, though I cannot vouch for it. From my earliest years I had been fascinated by Egyptian culture and had read about it extensively. Now I was right in the middle of the pyramids, vaster than anything I had seen thus far and conveying a sense of enduring presence that was quite compelling. No matter that I was engaged in long discussions as to how these people managed to get the huge stones into the desert and fashion them into the iconic, monumental images before us. As soon as I stopped talking, I could feel the vastness, the commanding silence, the hypnotic connection with deep levels of human consciousness that were thus far unknown to me, but which had a clear and irresistible voice, speaking without words.

There were several memorable incidents, but one is most prominent in my mind. Somewhere in the north we were entertained in grand style by some very highly placed people. We had an outdoor banquet, at which I encountered okra for the first time, cooked into a huge slimy mass which I found rather intimidating, but nevertheless managed to eat without blanching. All eyes were on me, as they knew that Europeans were not keen on this particular delicacy; and my valiant efforts were met with grins and smiles of appreciation. After lunch we went inside and had coffee and sweets. This was a really beautiful house, large, roomy and cool, well-appointed in an oriental fashion, and our hosts were the picture of dignified Arab hospitality. They were more obviously of Arab blood than anyone we had met thus far: their skin was light, their hair wavy, and many of their eyes golden or hazel rather than dark brown. All of them men, of course, and some really handsome, with beautiful chiseled features and aquiline noses. They were dressed in the immaculately clean, flowing robes of the Arab in white or muted pastel shades, wearing Arab headdress and carrying themselves with the utmost poise and dignity. They spoke softly and with great refinement. I was simply transfixed by the elegance and beauty of it all. "This is what the patriarchs of the Bible were like", I thought. "I could be with Abraham or Isaac." My father was in one room with the older men and talking in English. Pat and I were in a smaller room with the younger men, most of whom spoke only Arabic. Dr. Anis, my father's Egyptian assistant, acted as interpreter for our rather simple, but nevertheless gracious conversation with these really impressive people.

But refinement and culture notwithstanding, nature will have its way. I had drunk quite a lot at dinner and now needed to go to the bathroom. Pat did not know where it was, and I was too shy to ask Dr. Anis. So I went into the other room and asked my father at a moment when our hosts' attention was on something else, maybe ordering more coffee. Instead of simply telling me, he stood up and started walking me to the door. Why he didn't realize how this action would affect the courteous Arab men I have no idea, but of course they all stood up respectfully and began to follow us to the door. It was about time for us to go, and they probably thought that he was leaving, though no doubt it was a bit sudden. And of course, courteous hospitality would simply move graciously with the honored guest. I felt a moment of panic. This was going to be terribly embarrassing! When we got to the door and my father pointed out the bathroom at the end of a long outdoor path, our hosts understood what was going on and began to laugh. I was surprised at how jolly it was, quite out of keeping with the low-key demeanor they had maintained up till then. As it was indeed about time for us to go, my father remained with them at the door, so they watched me make my way down the path and try to get into the bathroom.

But horror was added to horror—the door was locked! The large group of men watching me started to laugh, this time uproariously. I wanted to die a thousand deaths! Dr. Anis, kind soul that he was, realized my predicament and came down the path to help me. "There is someone in there. Please don't mind waiting a moment", he said. When the occupant came out—an elderly man, as I recall—he was as embarrassed as I was. Once I got in, I never wanted to come out again! But of course I had to, and by the time I rejoined the party, calm and dignified refinement had once more descended. I was rather annoyed with my father, who I felt should have been more aware of the situation. But no real harm was done and maybe I had added yet another layer of thickness to my skin! A good thing, on the whole. I am sure that all of these experiences were very broadening and character-molding.

In and through it all my personal drama with my parents was also unfolding. I discovered that when Pat and I were alone, we got along much better than when my father was there. Perhaps we had breakfast together before my father got up—whatever the circumstances, we found quite a bit of common ground and engaged in girl-talk. Perhaps she was lonely in this sea of foreign men; but perhaps she, like myself, really wanted to be friends. Whatever the reason, I was very glad and responded as fully as I could. What was really interesting was that when my father joined us or picked up on this friendly relationship beginning to grow between us, he would start reviling or attacking me. Why? Why? Why? And what was really upsetting to me is that Pat would fall in line and take up her previously hostile stance. It has never ceased to amaze me how women automatically take their cues from men—of course, they are so often dependent on them, and have to play their game. But what *was* my father's game? It seemed to me that he was determined to turn Pat against me. Who knows what he had already told her about me?

But what could my father possibly gain from destroying any relationship between Pat and myself? To this day I have no idea, but of course it could well have been yet another round of "punishing" me for my mother's "crimes". As I was to find out in short order, he was still burning with resentment against her and would stop at nothing to crush me with it. He seemed to want to deprive me of any happiness or natural relationship with anyone that was close to him—and of course, Pat at that moment was the most important. I was deeply saddened, but of course my main attention was on the trip and keeping up a cheery appearance, so I had to put the problem on hold for the time being.

One episode occurred in Khartoum during this visit. I think it was after we got back from the northern trip, but it may have been beforehand.

Certainly, it was Christmas Eve. Dr. Anis called up to say that one of his friends had had a birth in the family and would we like to see the celebrations? This would be a rather unusual opportunity for Europeans. We went, driving over the desert at night. As usual the evening sky was stunning. There were palm trees silhouetted against the skyline, just like the Christmas cards we would send in those days. "This is like going to Bethlehem to see Jesus!" I said. In some ways yes, but in other ways, no. We could hear the drumming as we got out of the jeep. This was Africa.

We were ushered into a large open-air compound where a large number of men were seated. As Europeans and guests of honor we were given three seats at the head of the group, me full of anticipation and Pat hating every minute of it. The drumming became more and more intense and then a group of women dressed in gorgeous robes stepped into the space at the center and began to dance. I had never seen anything like it. They arched their backs and held their hands out behind them. "Why are they dancing like that?" I whispered to Dr. Anis. That is the way female pigeons dance before mating," he said. Alright—this was a celebration of procreation, after all. But along with that, the rhythm was almost overwhelmingly intense. Everything began to blur. I think poor Pat, a respectably repressed Protestant from rural Scotland, was having a very difficult time. For the British these "native" doings were disagreeable, uncouth and threatening. In many ways I, too, was a respectable Protestant, but for some reason I was absorbed in what was going on. I did not find it offensive in the least and, indeed, was completely caught up in the rhythm. Perhaps I was feeling that way because of all the dancing I had done myself, from folk dances at the Girls' High to ballroom dancing at the Church Youth Club and on to South American and rock and roll at Dollar—one of the unusually "cool" aspects of that otherwise rather formal establishment.

The dance was reaching fever pitch. It seemed as if it would never end and was indeed in eternity. Suddenly one of the women came dancing up to where we were, and took my hand. As if hypnotized I got up and started dancing myself. As something of a performing artist, dance is another sphere in which I was quite good at expressing myself, and so I was off and running (or arching!) in no time. Who knows what deaths my parents were going through! Whatever they may have thought, however, I was a big hit with the Sudanese. My father told me that one sheikh had offered him two hundred camels and a hundred horses for me! "O Daddy! Why not?" Obviously the event had intoxicated me! But the other side was that I had become so used to thinking of myself as a dowd, a frump, someone that no one could ever love, that all of this was quite exhilarating. The attention I got in the Sudan definitely helped me see myself in a different way and built up my self-esteem considerably—though, of course, probably for all the wrong reasons. I was now a young woman, overweight, but not unattractive. And my "night at the dance" opened up a creative and expressive side that Scottish respectability had worked hard to suppress. Of course Jean Irwin and specially Miss Paterson had done a great deal for me, insisting that I learn to express myself directly and creatively, perhaps helping the bud to form. But on Christmas Eve, nineteen fifty-eight, the blossom opened, never to shut again.

But all this notwithstanding, my father was still in a difficult frame of mind, hassling and attacking me at every turn. The night before I was due to leave for England he asked me point blank what I intended to study at university. I was surprised, for I had already told him several times over the past few years that I wanted to be a doctor. He had been drinking heavily and was in a dark, confrontational mood. "I want to be a doctor." "You? You, stupid, hysterical bitch! You are incapable of being a doctor! You are emotionally incompetent, just like your bitch of a mother!" "But, Daddy, I am called to serve humanity. This is what Christ wants of me." His face turned livid and his lip curled derisively. "That is the kind of idiotic drivel I despise you so much for! You are weak-minded and incompetent. If you insist on studying medicine, I will not pay for it."

Here was a confrontation worthy of Stanley and Blanche in *A Streetcar Named Desire*. By that time I had had some years without my father's presence and had had time to work on myself. I believe I had indeed matured somewhat and learned how to negotiate around his outbursts. But this was the worst ever. What really upset me was his abusive attitude to my mother. This was the issue that hit me hardest, for I loved my mother intensely and any negatives about her simply undid me. Like Blanche with Stanley, I completely lost my self-possession and succumbed once again to helpless misery. People who are sane and balanced can perhaps be defined by how they refrain from using such lethal verbal weapons against others; but people as traumatized as my father have no such compunction. He had hit me right in the heart and there was no turning back.

The other thing that distressed me was that I might not be able to fulfill what I saw as my religious vocation, the calling that I felt I had. On this issue, however, I was quite adamant. I decided that I would get a basic arts degree, teach for some years and then put myself through

Christ Blessing (The Savior of the World) by El Greco.
With permission of the National Galleries of Scotland, Edinburgh.

medical school. But of course I said nothing to my parents. Pat had not been present at the showdown, and I did not mention it to her. This was something I had to work on personally.

Our houseboy, Abdul, was very solicitous of me the following morning. He went all-out with his meal preparations, offering the things he knew I liked the most. He had done the same thing after any sort of difficulties with my father during the previous visit, but this time he was the essence of a mother, his dark eyes looking at me with the utmost kindliness, sympathy and affection. I was grateful for this wonderful, silent support, for the atmosphere otherwise was, to say the least, frosty and strained. Dr. Anis, who picked us up to go the airport in the evening, also seemed to have intuitively understood the strain I was under and was kind and supportive in low-key and meaningful ways. At the airport my father was at his most jolly and exuberant, perhaps trying to cover over what was really going on. I found it excruciatingly tedious and turned my attention to the moon that was rising in the velvet darkness. A huge slice of watermelon!

I had left Khartoum wearing only a cotton dress, to which I added, as we approached London, the duster coat Mary had bought me for my father's wedding. London was in the grip of a severe winter, with ice everywhere and snow. I was totally inadequately dressed and by the time I reached Clipsham was coming down with a lollapalooza of a cold. As I had only three days before I had to leave for Dollar, Mary went into high nursing gear and, as was her way, made a princess out of me. She was a wonderful nurse, anticipating every need and making me feel like the center of the universe—which was what I was needing more than anything else at that moment. I let myself flow into the warmth and kindness at Clipsham, also under snow, and put aside my broodings for a few days. As was usual with me, I said nothing to Mary about what had happened; there was no appropriate moment to do so and besides, I simply could not talk about something that had wounded me so terribly.

The Easter term at Dollar, however, was deeply bruising. I was totally preoccupied with how I was going to work out my future without financial support, for somehow it never occurred to me that there might be alternatives. I was so personally shocked and traumatized that I was working on the problem strictly within the confines of my relationship with my father, I suppose. As ever, not a word crossed my lips about what was going on. I started to have vomiting spells, somewhat similar to attacks I had had when I was quite young. As had been the case at that time, the doctor could find no cause for them, nor could an Edinburgh surgeon, to whom I was sent for a consultation. I felt as if I was living in a dungeon, with no air, no light, no sound. Easter time, always intense for me, was almost overwhelming. As the light flooded in, heralding the light half of the year, I became exquisitely sensitive to light, which almost hurt my eyes, while spasm after spasm wracked my whole body. I felt as if I were being sucked into a whirlpool, suffocating in a dark vortex of energy that I was unable to control.

It was a relief to get back to Clipsham for the Easter holidays. One morning I was sewing in our huge, farmhouse kitchen, just before our coffee break. Mary was in the scullery, a room even bigger than the kitchen, working on laundry or something like that. She came into the kitchen, I thought to bring in the coffee. Her hands were empty, however, and she uncharacteristically took up her stance on the other side of the table. I could tell she was going to take me on in a big way.

"Jean!" she said, "Something terrible happened between you and your father when you were in Africa! Don't deny it—I can see it all over your face. I saw it when you got back, but you didn't tell me anything. I am not going to let you keep this to yourself. I will stand here till you tell me!" I looked at her in astonishment for a few minutes. I had gotten so used to brooding alone that the idea of telling anyone else was rather novel. But Mary was absolutely determined and I knew that it was in my best interests to confide in her. I gave her a brief rundown of what had happened and my own plans for the future. "Och, Colin is just full of all kinds of nonsense!" Mary said. "This is his latest ploy. He will come round and support you." "I don't think he will," I said solemnly. "It was awfully bruising and final." Mary said nothing more, but acted immediately. She contacted her sister Malina and her brother Willie, the two who were closest to my father. They contacted him and found him defiant and adamant that he would not support me, that I was an emotional incompetent, etc. etc. Mary lost no time whatsoever. Within a few days I was filling out a form for a grant from the government, Mary had signed up her husband George as one of my financial supporters, and my Uncle Willie had also chipped in to help. This last moved me deeply. Uncle Willie was not well off and now had four boys of his own to educate. The financial sacrifice he was willing to make was the most telling proof of his love for me.

All of this was balm to my soul. No matter that huge barriers had been raised against me—it now seemed as if things would work out and, secretly, I felt that this turn of events was a validation of my decision.

My father's verbal assault had reopened the huge inner struggle between the artistic and sides of my nature, as well as reinforcing my tendency to self-doubt; but the rest of my family saw in me a worthy candidate and by their willingness to support me gave me enough confidence to continue on. My acceptance for a grant from the British Government was also heartening, though not unexpected; I had been a top student all the way through my education thus far.

In the meantime, my girlish side was in play. There was the matter of applying to a particular medical school, and the application had to be submitted immediately. It was now April, and classes began in October. Glasgow University was the obvious choice, as all of our family had studied there and my cousin Jean was enrolled there in medical school. I would be near the family and in spending time with them would get out of the city. But I chose to apply to Edinburgh University. By this time I was used to the East and doubtless was hearing more about Edinburgh than Glasgow; Edinburgh was (or had been) a renowned medical school; I liked variety and new experiences; the Dunlops were now living in Edinburgh and were, as far as I was concerned, also family. Then there was Dizzy. I had conceived a total infatuation for one of my classmates, Dizzy, a teenage crush as intense as such crushes can be. Dizzy was from the Eastern farming county of Forfar, an intelligent boy, in the top stream like myself, and also a good sportsman, with considerable powers of persuasion, humorous and with a certain charm. He was tall and skinny, with a face only a mother could love. He was, unlike me, very gregarious and dependent on his support group (which he saw to it was a large one), interested in being in the "social flow". He was flattered by my feelings for him, but he had not the slightest intention of getting involved with me in any way. He preferred quiet, country girls with placid, pliable temperaments.

My misguided intuition of a space in Dizzy's soul was perhaps why I decided to go to Edinburgh University, where he was already enrolled to study medicine. It was, of course, ridiculous; and in fact I rarely saw him after I got there. When I did, we were ships passing in the night. He started a dance band, took to drinking heavily, dropped out of medical school, and finally died of lymphoma the year before I graduated. At this point in time, I feel that what attracted me in Dizzy were qualities similar to many of my father's: Intelligent, witty, charming—but also self-centered and at times self-serving. As with my father, there was a deep bond, but one that Dizzy kept denying, in his case because he was not strong enough to take on an emotional heavyweight like myself. From my side, I was trying to create a loving relationship with a personality like my father, in the hope of solving the many difficulties that thus far I had not been able to go beyond. Not surprisingly, this was a constantly recurring theme in my life, which was later to find a solution in a rather surprising way.

My childhood was coming to an end. In many ways I had been like a little animal, surviving many challenging situations through sheer luck and perhaps native survival skills. I had been born in a family that, although threatening in one way, was also nurturing and supportive, and had been fortunate enough to find shelter with those adults who could protect me and keep me afloat in the sometimes very dangerous currents I had to negotiate. My responses to everything in many ways had been more or less instinctual, though perhaps informed by whatever I had brought with me from previous life experiences. I do not remember much in the way of insight or understanding—things just happened, and I somehow reacted in a way that helped me survive, aided, as I remarked before, by empathetic adults.

What had emerged, however, was a pattern of inner experience that somehow seemed to be the framework holding up the tent of my life. At intervals of approximately every five years the outer world had stood still and something from within myself had spoken clearly and directly, lighting up my mind and pointing in the direction I was to go, giving me fresh energy and a sense of purpose and meaning. I had received these as given without any analysis or discussion, somewhat like little Samuel in the Bible, who received a direct command from God; or the boy Satyakama in the Upanishads, to whom truth was revealed in his camp fire and from the mouths of cattle and birds. These moments had come out of the blue, with no particular connection with events in my mind; but that had not decreased their impact. On the contrary, their suddenness and my unquestioning receptivity had perhaps made them all the more important as turning points in my life.

These moments had taken different forms, creating a pattern that was going to repeat itself in the course of the next forty years: at five had come a vivid, living dream (of Christ), which presaged the spiritual teacher (my grandmother) I was about to meet. When I was ten a powerful waking experience had lifted me from the depths of an almost overwhelming situation (the emotional turmoil with my father) to a much calmer and more stable plane. Around the age of fifteen my drawn-out struggle to decide on my career had opened my mind to a deeper understanding of the inner power that supported me and was guiding me forward. Now, approaching twenty and the official end of childhood, the tremendous force that was carrying me forward over all my father's objections was like the voice of God, permitting me to fulfill my aspirations and be true to how I saw myself. Outer events were—miraculously it seemed—beginning to fall into place (I was soon to be studying medicine in Edinburgh) and, at the same time, I was metamorphosing. I was leaving behind the egg of childhood and emerging as a caterpillar, perhaps: chubby, voracious, blind, emotional.

CHAPTER 9

AULD REEKIE: 1959-1960

The traditional nickname for Edinburgh, the next backdrop of my life, is Auld Reekie—Broad Scots for Old Smokey, no doubt referring to the smoke from the many fires "reeking" in the long-established capital city of Scotland. And, although only sixty miles apart in the rift valley that separates the Scottish Highlands from the undulating Lowlands, Glasgow and Edinburgh—the two cities in my early life—are two different worlds. Glasgow, although an ancient city, grew into its pre-eminent size (by Scottish standards) during the economic boom of the eighteenth and nineteenth centuries, when large numbers of workers came from the Western Highlands and Ireland to work in the industries springing up overnight, and were, as "industrial slavies", housed in mostly red sandstone tenements. Although Glasgow has some ancient monuments—such as its University and Cathedral—dating back to late medieval times, the main impression of the city, at least in my time, was of a sprawling, industrial pile, put up in haste and left to melt down under the incessant, acid rain. Edinburgh, by contrast, is much cleaner and full of surviving historic monuments, all cheek by jowl, particularly on the Royal Mile, where Saint Giles's Cathedral, John Knox's house and the royal palace of Holyrood House are maintained in all of their medieval or early modern splendor. The main street, Prince's Street, is quite a showcase, with the sunken gardens on one side and the high quality shops on the other. The buildings in Edinburgh, whether ancient or more modern, are made of gray granite, a durable stone unlike the Glasgow sandstone, so that the overall impression is of a hard-edged, permanent and determined city.

The climate of the two cities is also quite different, despite the small distance between them. Unlike quite unexpectedly mild Glasgow, Edinburgh is open to the winds from the North Sea, coming from Eastern Europe, and particularly Siberia. Standing at a windy bus stop of a winter day, one would fully appreciate just what that meant! Perhaps this geographical difference has something to do with the difference in character of the people from the two cities—as the Glaswegians would say of the people from Edinburgh, "East-windy and West-endy": the cuttingly cold wind comes from the East, and the demeanor of the burghers is definitely chilly and with pretensions to superiority toward the wild Celts of the West, the dirty industrial city of Glasgow, and indeed anything else coming out of the rest of Scotland. The Glaswegians would say, "The best thing that ever came out of Edinburgh is the train for Glasgow."

These are the stereotypes, which to some extent I found to be true. My move to Edinburgh was definitely a foray into another land, for which, however, I was by this time somewhat prepared by my sojourn at Dollar. When I contemplate what at that time was a quite radical change, I realize that it was not simply Dizzy that made me undertake it—that was a trivial reason, after all. What was moving me forward was a deep need to be independent, to create a new life for myself, as far away as possible from the darkness and pain I had felt throughout almost all of my childhood. I just needed to be alone, free to make my own decisions and follow my own inclinations. Nowadays, especially in America, such thinking is taken for granted, but in the milieu in which I grew up it was not so common. In those days it made far more sense to remain close to family and friends, protected in so many ways, and with on-tap companionship and support. Women, in particular, tended to remain in the family circle, to move about with people whom they already knew and always with a group of other women. Mary tried hard to get me to live in a hostel for women run by the university, but I was adamant that I had had enough of group living and of women and girls to last me for the rest of my life. She was full of apprehension about me, headstrong and unconventional as I was, but I steadfastly refused to listen to her—perhaps for the first time in my life—and finally she had to let me go ahead.

I now believe I am a rather independent person, but at that time I had no such notion about myself. My first inkling about this feature of my personality had come in a rather unexpected way, from Carol, the girl at Dollar whose friendship with Daisy I had rather cut into when I went there. Carol was from a prominent social family, a model of the type of person the school aimed to turn out: A team-player, a sportswoman, a leader, in that she accepted roles in the hierarchy and intended to play along with it. She was pleasant, accommodating and, although in the leadership stream, suitably feminine in her behavior. Her friendship with Daisy had been more one of convenience, I think, for Carol did not have the wacky intelligence and humor that Daisy and I shared, nor the tendency to rammy, as we called our shenanigans of one sort or another. However, we had remained a threesome, though I think Carol often felt a bit left out. Occasionally she would be a bit confrontational with me, hinting that I was an intruder, but on the whole we were friends, in a formal sort of way.

I always tried to be especially nice to Carol, but I did not ever confide in her or show her what was going on inside myself. Indeed, I was so used to being part of a cheery, upbeat, relentlessly maintained group spirit that I never expected any sort of close relationship or confidences from anyone. I was, therefore, rather taken aback when the day before she left the school for good, Carol asked me to go for a walk with her. This was something she had never done, and I sensed that she had something she wanted to say. I rather dreaded what it might be, because she was in the habit of upbraiding me for my nonconformity and general wackishness. Perhaps she was going to give me a last bromide, just to get me straight before she left. However, we chatted lightly and had a nice time for most of the walk, and I was wondering what it was all about by the time we started heading home. As we approached our boarding house, however, she suddenly became very emotional (a total no-no with someone like her!) and said to me in a choked voice, "I admire you so intensely!" She repeated it several times, much to my utter amazement. Carol admiring me, the most rumpled and volatile member of the group! I was speechless, but finally was able to say, "Good heavens! Me! Whatever for?" She could barely speak, she was so overcome with emotion, but finally blurted out, "You know who you are! You follow yourself! You are independent and free!"

I was dumbfounded. My first reaction was to reassure her, as she seemed to be in such distress. "Carol, why are you saying all this? You are one of our most respected and liked seniors, responsible, trusted, and popular! We are all going to miss you. The hockey team won't be the same without you. We need leaders like you. And look at me—I am nothing at all here, just a renegade from Glasgow, an egghead, a weirdo." She had calmed down by this time. "No!" she said. "You really know who you are and can follow it without letting anyone stop you. I just follow what other people are doing or tell me to. I really wish I was like you." I was so flabbergasted by this whole exchange that I simply did not know what to say. Carol, one of our most admired girls, making this confession to myself, perhaps the school's most desperate nonconformist! By this time we were almost at the door of the boarding house, so the conversation came to an end. It wouldn't do for others to overhear such a revelation!

This was the first time I had been told that I am a maverick, an independent and the object of admiration by others, more conformist and "normal" than I, but it certainly was not to be the last. The scene was to be repeated in a number of situations—some of them quite desperate—and would afford me a moment of validity in what was otherwise turmoil of the maximum kind. However, I have never cherished such ideas about myself or thought of myself as out of the ordinary. I have been forced to understand that there is something unusually independent about me by sheer force of circumstance. And it now seems to me that my move to Edinburgh and dogged refusal to fit in with more "molding" in the conformist, feminine mode was the first organized expression of this part of my character.

Fortunately, the Dunlops, who were now well-established in Edinburgh, stepped in to the situation. John was no longer working for the family tea-house business, but had started a company of his own and was living with his family at Randolph Crescent, one of the showpieces of Edinburgh's eighteenth-century Georgian architecture. There they had also purchased a large, three or four-story house which they had done up as apartments for rent, and for a nominal sum they were offering me a room, within a mile or two of the University. Anne, who looked on me as her own child, also invited me to have supper with her family at the weekends.

John and Anne Dunlop, probably in the nineteen thirties.

I believe this turn of events took a lot of pressure off Mary's mind. She had an extremely protective attitude toward me, and always seemed to think that I would get myself into trouble, probably understanding how headstrong and independent I was, and at the same time, so vulnerable. She was aware of the pitfalls of going up to university: the men lying in wait for innocent young girls, the alcohol (but not in those days, drugs) and the other traditional "snares of the devil". What she did not reckon with was my natural inclinations, which were quite in the opposite direction to the usual pattern. I never liked parties (I screamed my head off at the age of three when taken to my first party—I wanted my Mummy to come and take me home!); I had seen enough of the results of drinking alcohol to give it a wide berth (though, as ever, as wee glass of sherry on special occasions was quite in order); and I was intensely wary of men, after my experiences with Uncle Robert and my father. Of course, I was terribly thirsty for love, but was sufficiently alert (at least when I was in my right mind) to realize just how difficult it was to find and not to have too high expectations of anyone I met.

I was not sorry to leave Dollar behind. It had indeed been "character-molding", a slice of life which would stand me in good stead later on; but what made it tick was far from my own interests and aspirations. The summer I left I took my first job, determined to make every contribution I could to my expenses. I signed on as a kitchen maid at a shooting lodge in Glen Etive, one of the remote hunting areas in Argyllshire, the county northwest of Glasgow. The two months I spent there were an interesting mix of *Upstairs, Downstairs* and communing with the romantic myths of the Celts. My employers were rich English people whose houseguests included the famous and influential, while my cohorts were professional servants, conforming so totally to the stereotypes I had read of in the works of Dickens and so on that I never ceased to be entertained. The cook was fast-talking and heavy-drinking and with values quite different from my own. One day, noticing a pot, clean on the inside but with some oatmeal left on the outside, she solemnly told me that she would show me how to clean pans properly. After huffing and puffing over it for about fifteen minutes, she showed me a pot, shining on the outside, but still caked with oatmeal on the inside! I understood that what was all-important for her was to impress the bosses; while for me having a clean inner pot was what was important.

Then there was the serving maid. A middle aged woman with pretensions to gentility, she surprised me one day by pulling me down the corridor to the dining room door and making me peer through the keyhole at a banquet going on inside. "The gentleman with his back to us is Lord—," she whispered loudly. "Who?" "Don't you know? Lord—!!" I had no idea who Lord—was, nor which of the overweight diners he might be. But for her, this was important, so I pretended to be impressed. My other encounter with this woman was on the evening I decided to clean out the pantries, as the cook had been asking me to do for a couple of weeks. The pantries were kept locked, to keep out the dogs and any other strays who might take a fancy to their contents. Imagine my surprise, on entering the liquor pantry, to find the cook and the serving maid ensconced in a couple of chairs, downing the owner's Scotch, the serving maid with upraised pinkie as she did so! Their almost ferocious invitation to join them made me realize that I was caught in the crosshairs of inter-class struggle. I made it clear that not a word would cross my lips about the episode, and they let me go, perhaps taking into account that, as a middle class person, I did not have the same stake in the situation as they did.

Behind this drama lay the Glen, glorious in its fall colors, for when the heather blooms, Scotland becomes ablaze. In addition to its physical beauty, Glen Etive was associated with a very poignant episode in Celtic legend. This was where Deirdre of the Sorrows, the most beautiful woman in Ireland, had lived in exile with her husband Naoise and his brother. She had been banished from Ireland for choosing Naoise over the king, who had earmarked her as his own from her childhood. She lived in Argyll for several years, longing, as the Celts always do, for her homeland and its people; but at the same time loving Glen Etive and other beautiful spots she and her companions frequented. Finally the king called them back to Ireland, pretending to have extended a pardon. But as soon as the brothers put foot on Irish soil, their heads were struck off and Deirdre was abducted in order to force her to marry one of the king's court. Determined not to yield to this humiliation, she threw herself from the chariot carrying her off and died as her head struck a large rock on the path.

Such are the sad tales of the Celts. It had captured my imagination, perhaps because I felt that I, too, was the victim of an authoritative and arbitrary male. There is a beautiful song which Deirdre is supposed to have sung while leaving Glen Etive for Ireland, in her heart knowing what was about to happen to Naoise and herself:

> Farewell, Alba[10]! Land o'er yonder
> Thou dear land of wood and wave!
> Sore my heart that I must leave thee,
> But 'tis Naoise I may not leave.
>
> O Glen Eiche[11], O Glen Eiche,
> Where they builded my bridal hold;
> Beauteous glen in early morning,
> Flocks of sunbeams crowd thy fold.

---

[10]   Alba is the Gaelic name for Scotland.
[11]   Eiche is the Gaelic for Etive.

Glen da Ruad, Glen da Ruad[12]
My love to all whose mother thou.
From a cliff-tree called a cuckoo,
And I think I hear him now.
Glen da Ruad! Glen da Ruad!

This song was for me the twin of *Be Thou My Vision* in my life at that time. Its haunting melody was ever in my mind, and its theme, as I say, resonated with much of what I was feeling. Whenever I could get out (for the work hours were pretty stiff), I would walk in the glen and sing these songs to myself, reveling in their melancholy, timelessness, and deep wells of conviction. As I walked through the glorious landscape, reveling in the wondrous colors and shimmering light of the Scottish fall, these songs carried me aloft and I knew that what was in me was of inexhaustible power and would take me to freedom. In those days I still thought in terms of a Father God on whom I could rely totally, but what I was feeling then was my own inner energy radiating out toward the sun in ever-widening circles, touching and connecting with everything it met and ultimately spreading into the whole universe, into infinity.

Such was my mood on going up to University. Things were looking good: I had arrived where I wanted to be, I had the support of my family behind me and the hospitality and kindness of the Dunlops to look forward to. But, though I was then unaware of it, I was approaching the second phase of my life's spiral, in which the first turn is always one of overwhelming challenge, of things being thrown at you, willy-nilly, as my mother's anguish and death had hit me during the first five years of the "turn" I was currently in. However, the first couple of years in Edinburgh were essentially the end of the first spiral, a "grace period" during which I was familiarizing myself with a whole new way of life. This was the first time I had any control over what I ate, what I thought, what I did, and I went ahead with several new initiatives. I wanted to be normal, to put all my babyishness behind me.

The first year of medical school covered physics, chemistry and biology. Students who had passed those subjects in the Highers were allowed to skip first year, but as my father had vetoed my taking the full science course at high school, at university I had to go through two subjects I already knew—physics and chemistry—in order to pass in

---

[12]   Another glen in the same area.

biology. I was fascinated and repelled by biology, hating the dissections, maimings and killings we inflicted on innumerable leeches and frogs, but entranced by the information I was gaining about life processes and evolution. As I had more time on my hands than I expected, I signed up for a number of extracurricular activities, including the University Film Society, which screened the work of masters like Renoir, Truffaut, Zeffirelli, Bergman, and others, exposing me to serious movies in a way unprecedented thus far. I was hooked, but there was one problem—the screenings were on a Sunday afternoon. I was amused and annoyed to find that my Wee Free Presbyterian upbringing was creating scruples about spending Sunday on things as "worldly" as the movies. I tussled with the problem for a year and finally decided that my cultural life was more important than rote-following of rules. In many ways watching movies was a form of rest, which was the whole idea behind the observance of the Sabbath. And it was really my main form of diversion and relaxation, for I was not a partygoer at all: they were too fraught with alcohol and the ever-increasing pressures of sex, for even Scotland was now becoming "liberated" by the sexual revolution. Perhaps if my classmates had been more interesting, I would have been tempted to go to their revels, but for the most part they were loud, insensitive, bragging about their exploits and half-tiddly much of the time. Too reminiscent of my father at his worst, poor man. The Film Society had much more to offer and, though I did not realize it then, was to open an important door in my life.

I did fall in with a group of women who were ardent Christians and drew me into meetings at the Evangelical Society. I had no idea what *Evangelical* stood for, as I had grown up in the rather traditional, conservative Presbyterian world. I was not too keen on some of their emotional effusions, but I was seeking spiritual companionship and this was what was on offer. I also attended functions at the Chaplaincy Center, particularly weekly lunches at which we paid for a full meal but ate only bread and water, the money going to work overseas with the poor and uneducated people of the third world. These were extremely earnest and good people, but I never felt comfortable with them. There was a sanctimonious piousness, a whiff of self-righteousness and holier-than-thou-ness that did not sit well with me.

The inevitable showdown finally came: I was talked into going to a prayer meeting. Grannie used to attend prayer meetings regularly, but I had not had anything to do with them thus far. I felt a bit apprehensive about what might happen, but dutifully got on my knees and prepared for spiritual combat. The leader of the group started off the prayers and I realized to my horror that each person was supposed to offer a prayer out loud. Golly! I was not prepared for this! I was even less prepared for the prayers that were being offered: "God, have pity on the ignorant, dirty people of Africa/India, whatever; may we bring them light." I felt as I had felt when Mr. Meek was empathizing with the Indians for having to use twigs for toothbrushes—who do we think we are? And now, of course, I was much more able to express myself. As it happened, I was last "in line". When it came my turn, I could not speak at first. My heart was pounding and I thought everyone must be able to hear it. Finally I said, "God, please help us to understand that we do not know everything and may be completely wrong in our estimation of other people." There was dead silence for quite a long time. However, these were British people, so they were quite polite in offering me tea and cookies, which I somehow managed to choke down. But that was the absolute, total end of my Evangelical days.

As an earnest Christian and churchgoer I had started to attend the Presbyterian Church near my bed-sitter. This was in Georgian Edinburgh, where the well-heeled were living, and this was one of the largest, most well-known churches in the city. Our minister was young, dynamic and very, very earnest, pounding the pulpit every Sunday as he exhorted us to more and more involvement with the social problems all around us. Within a year or so of going to Edinburgh I decided to join the church and went to twelve special classes intended to prepare us for First Communion. I really wanted to respond to what the minister had to say, but the truth was that I came out of every class wondering what on earth it had all been about.

I had not a clue what communion—that central sacrament of Christianity—was supposed to mean, and intuitively felt that it would do no good to inquire any further. And I am sorry to say that my first communion left me no better off. Because the Presbyterian Church has communion very infrequently—maybe four times a year—it becomes a large social event. People come to communion whom we never see for the rest of the year; and of course, they are all dressed up to the nines. The whole proceeding takes place in utter silence, so that the squeaking of the elders' shoes as they solemnly walk round with the wine in tiny glasses, the chmmmpffhh as people choke down the dry bread and glug, glug, rumble, rumble as the wine goes down is what attracts attention—at least it did mine. The only thing that topped those experiences was the sight of a woman near me in a huge fur boa, entertaining herself by watching the light come off a large diamond ring, which she kept moving back and forth. Her face was total bliss, but not that of spiritual communion.

I was not impressed, either with the spectacle or with my own, errant thoughts. Why did I not feel the presence of Christ? Why did the communion service result in nothing but silly distracted thoughts? I vowed that I would do better next time, but unfortunately, no matter how often I went through communion (and I did keep trying for a number of years), the result was always the same. Obviously, there was a problem and, having been brought up to believe that there was much wrong with me, I tended to blame myself. I just was not connecting up with Christianity, and it hurt me. I loved Christ intensely, but I simply could not find meaning in the doings of his church.

Later, I signed on as a Sunday-school teacher. The children were from well-off families, privileged and, to my mind, spoiled. It was impossible to tell them anything—they had already seen it on TV. As I had grown up without TV, this was a new experience. No matter how hard I worked to prepare classes, I could not get their attention. They knew it all already—from a factual perspective, that is. I tried to talk about the deeper meaning of the stories, but that went nowhere. Finally, I got them started on art work and handicrafts, which did interest them, but they were not able to take any sort of suggestion and there were several otherwise avoidable accidents, which made it a lot less pleasant to undertake our work. Another saddening aspect of this work was dealing with children from homes where there had been divorce, a first for me, for divorce was unheard in our family or that of our friends. I had two children in my class whose parents were divorced—Charles, who was the quintessential angry and troublesome young man and Helen, outstandingly beautiful and intelligent, but deeply sad and withdrawn into herself. It broke my heart to see their suffering, and made me realize that, relatively speaking, I had had it easy. Thinking about it now, it seems likely that my parents would have divorced over the long run, but I had been spared the actual trauma of it by my mother's death, the reason for which I had not as yet fully fathomed—though I was beginning to have my suspicions.

With a view to modernizing our work, the church brought in Abe, an American minister—a move which met with mixed reviews. He was a go-getter with lots of ideas, most of which seemed superficial and not really related to religion as we understood it. We spent a lot of time on Abe's projects, but nothing seemed to get off the ground. Perhaps there was subconscious resistance on the part of the teachers—after all, who wants to be told what to do by someone who doesn't really have a clue about your culture? The Scots are a traditional, conservative people and American go-gettery was not what we warmed up to. The final blow as far as I was concerned was Abe's way of pitting the boys against the girls in everything that we did. No matter what the project, it was always: will the boys win, or will the girls? I spoke to Abe about this, pointing out that Christianity was about learning to love and cooperate with others, not whipping up competition, of which we had more than enough in the workplace; but he simply made fun of me and carried on regardless. Probably he saw me as a reactionary Scot with quaint old ideas about religion. And, although some of the teachers agreed with me privately, they saw fit to go along with Abe and his project and the competitiveness simply went on and on and got more and more difficult to put up with. I finally took stock of my priorities and called it quits with Abe and the Presbyterian Church.

However, the process of withdrawing from the church took me a number of years. During the same time I was trying to find a foothold socially, to define myself in terms of the medical milieu. Ruling out party-going, I also tried out the lunch scene, which, as far as those in the in-crowd were concerned, took place at a large cafe across the street from the medical school. There they would sit, loosely according to ethnic and cultural superiority, with English boarding school types dominating, of course. Though the discussion was ostensibly about our work, in fact it was about hierarchy, sex and dominance, just as at Dollar.

It definitely seemed that the world that had supported me thus far was beginning to recede from my life. What was coming up, with greater and greater insistence as time went by, was the emotional need that had been created in me by my difficult childhood. I believe this understanding was ushered into my life by a dream I had within a year of arriving in Edinburgh. I dreamt that I was walking at dawn in a field covered in daisies where I found, lying asleep, the most beautiful boy-man imaginable, embodying the powers of nature, principally the sun. He was golden-hued, with golden hair, completely at one with surrounding nature. His breathing was slow and steady and his whole being spoke of bliss. I instantly recognized him as "the dream that I am, and the soul of me." I gazed on him, enraptured. Something about my gaze seemed to have roused him, for he opened his eyes, sat up and looked at me. But, as I noticed ruefully,

> His was the fleeting foot when the world cried loud . . .
> For he was of the essence of living,
> Good to be sought for, but hard to find.

He was gone without looking back, and I was left, pondering what it all meant. I felt:

> I would live with him, bright drop of my being;
> But up with the sun he is,
> And away from the meadow.
> Up where the feet of me cannot follow,
> Gray dust as I am.

This was an unusually vivid dream, carrying a sense of reality and importance. As I turned it over in my mind, I understood, at least in principle, that I would never find real love if I pursued it too intently. I had felt so deprived of love by my parents that it had created an almost insatiable longing in my heart, making me very intense with people whom I cared for a lot, or felt might be able to love me the way I craved. I dimly realized that that was what had held Dizzy away—he could not cope with such intense emotion. And, sad to say, I was to be aware of it many, many times beyond that. This was an important lesson, though one that would be difficult to put into practice.

But there was another side to this dream, which was encouraging. I felt I had seen who I really am in a much deeper sense than anything I have talked about thus far. Androgynous—that is, beyond gender; closely linked to the energy of the sun; free from the bondages of the body, emotions and mind; and innately full of bliss. He was not at all shackled by emotional neediness and indeed flew from it. This was such a totally different way of seeing who I was, something not really "Christian", as I had understood the word to mean thus far, and yet so much truer to what I really am than anything I had experienced up till then. At that time I had felt it was some Celtic god whom I had seen, but being totally ignorant about the gods, even in a Celtic country, I could not be sure just what form had presented itself to me. I had seen it, and that was enough for now.

If only we could hold on to these glimpses and use them immediately to change our lives! But that is not how things seem to work. There was to be a whole lot of longing, of rebuff, of abuse, of even degradation before this dream re-emerged in a concrete form. However, to have had it all was a truly great blessing. It lay more or less dormant for nearly ten years, sending out an occasional glimmer of light in the almost unrelenting darkness I was working through as I worked through my third decade.

These were the explorations I made during the first years at university. I had started out, following much the same pattern as I had followed thus far in my life, but was discovering that in so many ways it was not really suiting me. Medical school was so focused on the material world (why should I have thought otherwise!) and was rather cruel; my classmates were not at all interesting; social life was a bore; and my hobbies were not bringing me the satisfaction I craved. What was worse, my religious activities were increasingly meaningless. I had tried so hard to get involved, but could find no sort of sustenance or inspiration whatever in any of what I had been doing. Part of this may have been the increasing depression that was creeping up on me, but it seems likely that there really was a dissociation going on between me and the life I had led thus far. Gone were my epiphanies, my moments of inspiration and uplift. Everything was becoming a grind without any relieving meaning. I would look out the window over Randolph Crescent, seeing the trees, the gray granite buildings, the sky, the birds wheeling about, and would feel that it was all totally without life or meaning. Not a very auspicious beginning for my life of service! But, of course, the more earnest you are, the more you are tried, it seems. There was no devotee of God greater than Job in the Old Testament, and he was tried beyond all decency, human or divine. The question was: Would I be able to hold on to my vision as he had, or would I be overcome by the crushing mass of problems that seemed to be besetting me?

SECOND TURN OF THE SPIRAL

MOTHER OF THE DAWN

1961-1980

FIRST QUARTER

GROUNDWORK, AGAIN

CHAPTER 10

TENNESSEE WILLIAMS RIDES AGAIN!
1961-1965

In the early sixties the medical course at the University of Edinburgh spanned six years. The first three years covered the basic science subjects, such as physics, chemistry, biology, human anatomy, physiology and biochemistry, while the remaining three years dealt with disease processes (pathology) clinical casework, and therapy. The first three years, covered in the previous chapter, concluded the first turn of my life's spiral and brought me up into my twenties. I had found the work interesting intellectually and had particularly enjoyed anatomy, which was more of a hands-on experience than the other subjects. I was particularly interested in the human brain, and would put in several hours on Saturday morning doing extra work with "my" brain. Many of my classmates were repelled and disgusted with this work, but I never gave it a thought. I was just fascinated with what I was discovering and, apparently, had little concern about dead bodies or anything of the sort. I became somewhat of an authority on the anatomy of the human brain, and toyed with the idea of taking off a couple of years to work on a Ph.D. on neuroanatomy.

But I learned more than mere facts in the anatomy class. One of our instructors was a lady who stood out from all the others, as far as I was concerned. She may have been the only female instructor—for there were very few in my medical course—but she was unusual for other reasons. She was obviously suffering from some fell disease, for she was painfully thin, with a sallow complexion, had had an arm amputated and wore a brace on one of her legs. She moved around slowly and carefully, going from one group of dissectors to the other, and one wondered just how she managed. If she was asked to help with a problem, she brought to bear on the subject an incredible intensity and depth which impressed me deeply, as did her extreme self-possession. Although almost distant, her eyes showed a great deal of kindness and insight, and sometimes she would talk a bit about her life, throwing light into her own career. One day she told us that at one point she had been totally confused in her medical studies. She could not at all see how it all fitted together, or where it was going. Consultation with her instructors was not helping, because they could not understand where her difficulties were coming from. Then one day she met an instructor who, as they say nowadays, "was on her page". He completely understood her approach and was able to throw light on her problem in terms she could use, not only then but also for the rest of her work. This had been a great blessing for her, finding someone who did not criticize her for thinking differently, but was able to see things through her eyes and give her the encouragement she needed so badly.

This story made a huge impression on my mind. At the time I was not fully aware of what was going on, but basically I was quite simply not meeting with anyone who could understand me. What was most bothering me was my inability to find real friends in the Christian establishment; I was just not able to say politically correct things or behave in ways that were considered "spiritual". Temperamentally unable to join the wine-women-and-song driven company of most of my classmates, I was basically retiring into the shell that my little bed-sitter afforded. I began to yearn for someone who could really understand me and speak to me from a position of strength, rather than these Christian "timorous itsters" (as the poet e. e. cummings would say), whose main impact on me was to increase my self-doubt.

As time went by, I slipped into a depression, at the weekends particularly sitting in my room for long hours and spiraling deeper and deeper into bottomless doubt and despair. By nature I am more or less cheerful and positive, but all that was hitting me at that time was pushing me down, down, down. The pain of my father's rejection of me was probably the most difficult to deal with—how could he throw me off like this? And, of course, the horrible thought that maybe he was right: I was not suited to medicine, after all. Thoughts of suicide began to flit through my mind, no doubt grounded in the example my mother had set. As often as not, they would be brought to an end by the arrival of dinnertime, when I was due at the Dunlops'. There is no doubt that their cheerful and affectionate company helped to keep me going. They loved me just as I was, and had no "Christian" scruples with which to torture me. I would linger in their home till bedtime, so grateful for their company.

One outlet was the Film Society, where I would immerse myself in another world than the rather dreary one I was then living in. But, as time went by, I began to feel that the movies were not exactly helping me, either, for I became aware of the same materialism and lack of love and compassion as I was experiencing in my daily grind. The movies of Ingmar Bergman, in particular, were dismal, dark and ultimately depressing. Nordic gloom enveloped me completely for at least a week after each screening, and I began to wonder if I would not be better off without the Film Society. But it was my only regular exposure to anything beyond the bricks and stones, blood and bones, that made up my life at the time. I was hungry for a more ideal image, something uplifting and inspiring—but where was I going to find it? I no longer felt any sort of divine presence, perhaps because I was now older, but maybe also because there just wasn't the love, the immediate awareness of Christ that I had basked in at Grant Street. Nothing like it for making your heart sing!

I mentally put the Film Society on notice. I would attend a few more screenings, and if they continued to depress me as much as they had the previous year, I would bring the whole thing to an end. As it happened, the next program was *World of Apu*, one of a trilogy made by the Indian movie-maker, Satyajit Roy. I had no knowledge of India or its culture, though I had seen Indians moving about in Glasgow. I had wondered why they kept on wearing turbans and saris, so impractical in our wet, foggy climate, but that was all. I had no great expectations of *World of Apu*. But it was important, because the Film Society was on notice, and this might either make it or break it.

What I saw was a rather slow, long drawn out tale about a young, impoverished man called Apu, living in a big Indian city, who attends the wedding ceremony of a friend in the country. The wedding tent collapses and kills the groom, and there is a hue and cry. It is very inauspicious for the bride to remain unmarried, and is there anyone who will volunteer to marry her? No one suitable can be found, except Apu, and so he returns to the city with a bride! I found this situation rather preposterous, but suspended judgment. Not much happens thereafter, except a slow, slow study of how the young couple comes to know and appreciate each other, building up a loving relationship through the small events of their restricted and impoverished life. This was so totally different from the action-packed Western movies that I was rather bemused by it. I left the Film Society almost as befuddled as with the other movies, but there was a difference. There had been no intentional violence, no cruelty, unlike the Western movies. On the whole, the effect had been uplifting and soothing, with a feeling that there really was love of a very meaningful kind.

The impact of this movie was slow in developing, but by the end of the following week I was thinking, "There has to be something in Indian culture that supports a much gentler and more loving way of life." To search further, I went to the Public Library and scanned the Indian Philosophy section. There I saw the *Complete Works* of an Indian swami, whose name of course I did not know; but the picture of him wearing a turban rather put me off—for me turbans stood for a failure to adapt and move on, a clinging to old forms that was not necessary. I therefore opted for *Hindu Dharma* by Mohandas Gandhi, as he was of course a well-known figure. I am, however, not at all sure how I got through *Hindu Dharma*, which deals with such arcane issues as untouchability, sacred cows, temples, and other exotica, so utterly remote from anything in my own life it had little intrinsic meaning for me. But I must have been hungry to learn about Indian culture, for I did in fact finish the book. Maybe, too, the Mahatma's way of writing conveyed something of the atmosphere that had attracted me. What was important and was to hold my attention, was the Mahatma's frequent comments on and quotes from *The Bhagavad Gita*, or the Gita, as I would call it. This ancient Hindu text had been his *vade mecum*, helping him work through many a stormy passage of his eventful life. I just loved what I read and made up my mind to take out a copy from the library.

The only version of the Gita that the Public Library had was that of Radhakrishnan, the well-known Indian scholar who had also made his name in leading universities in Britain. Radhakrishnan's work was scholarly, polished and intercultural, not at all like *Hindu Dharma*, which was a book written for Indians and their specific problems. Radhakrishnan was familiar with the Western spiritual and philosophical literature and had a wonderful way of relating the spiritual ideas of the Gita to the Western tradition. As by that time I had begun to read Western spiritual classics such as *The Imitation of Christ* and Saint Augustine's *Confessions*, as well as the books of C. S. Lewis, I appreciated the professor's informed commentary. But all that apart, the Gita spoke to me on its own terms. In the teachings of Krishna at the center of the Gita I found answers to some of the problems that were really tormenting me.

Perhaps the most urgent problem related to my desire to "Be ye therefore perfect, even as your Father in Heaven is perfect", Christ's message to his followers. The idea of "imitating" Christ and becoming Christ-like appealed to me immensely and I was certainly striving, as Grannie had asked me to do, to "enter in at the straight gate that leads to life". The Gospel tells us that there are very few who find this gate and walk along the narrow path to eternal life; but I knew that Grannie had done it and probably also my beloved Granpa, and it was certainly my earnest desire to follow in their footsteps. But it was also clear to me that I had such immense obstacles to surmount and so many weaknesses that beset me that I had grave doubts of ever getting to the door in this life, far less going through it. How could I ever hope to attain perfection, when all that was given me was one, short, and at the moment rather nasty life? I had become quite overwrought about this problem and, of course, there was nobody to turn to. Our minister, good soul that he was, was not concerned with such arcane issues and the rest of the world thought things like this were just nonsense. But I found in the Gita that the slow process of perfecting oneself takes place over a series of lives, building up gradually to more and more developed understanding and self-control. I found this idea very soothing and had no trouble in accepting the notion of reincarnation, though my whole upbringing thus far had not mentioned it, even remotely. Somehow it just made more sense; why would a spiritual teacher like Christ ask us to become perfect, when it is not possible in one lifetime? Was he crazy? No, Krishna's explanation was far more practical and I gladly accepted it.

Another subject on which I found a great deal of light in the Gita pertained to my efforts to "serve" Christ as a medical doctor. I was so terribly earnest about this idea, though I was finding the reality rather less appealing than I might have liked. I kept feeling that the effort involved to keep going was getting too much for me, that I was simply not performing well enough and that God would ultimately reject me. This was another problem that I could in no way talk about with anyone. But I found in the pages of the Gita the memorable sentiment, "I accept with gladness even leaves, flowers, fruits and water, whatever is offered with love." (Gita 9.26) Krishna, the spiritual teacher of the Gita, makes it clear that what is most important is the love with which one does anything, and that the actual gift itself is secondary. What balm this idea brought to my soul! There was no doubt whatever that I had made this offering with my whole heart; it was only the competitive and reductionistic way of thinking that I was falling into that had made me judge myself harshly and find fault with my efforts.

Finally, another idea that took root in my mind was that of the realized soul, someone who has transcended human failings completely and lives in the world as an exemplar of God. The Gita discusses such people from several standpoints, each of which is deeply impressive and convincing, the more so because the exemplars arrive at this exalted status through their own, steady efforts and practices, focused on the ideal. This seemed so much more democratic and psychologically realistic than the Christian idea of incarnation, which had created a barrier between us "ordinary" mortals and the supernatural, unattainable Son. Of course, reading the Gospels, Jesus came across as manifestly accessible and loveable; but what you heard in church and elsewhere did nothing but erect barriers to any sort of true imitation of Christ. Krishna's ideas appealed to me much, much more, and I began to wonder if perhaps I would one day meet such a realized soul. Perhaps, like the mentor of my anatomy tutor, he or she would be the one who could understand me fully and give me the direction that my soul craved so intensely. Perhaps he or she could help me get my own act together and give me practical instructions on how to get going on the path Grannie had pointed out to me.

My obsession with the Gita led me into another relationship of great importance. For two consecutive years I worked as a nurse in a mental hospital in Sussex during the summer vacation. I found it quite agreeable and of course made some pocket money. The second year I made friends with Vive, one of the nurses, originally from Singapore. His family was Hindu and hailed from Tamil Nadu in South India, but had moved to Singapore, where his father was a supervisor of mines. The family had been quite well off, but the Second World War had brought the Japanese invasion. When Vive was just eight or so, the Japanese had marched his father outside the house and executed him in full view of the family. Vive had wanted to become a doctor, but with his father gone there could be no question of paying for medical school. He somehow finished high school, but then had to face another tragedy: he developed tuberculosis of the spine. For over a year he lay in a cast in hospital, wondering what would become of himself and his family. Perhaps it was during that time that he developed his love for the Hindu scriptures, which had kept him going through his ordeal. Somehow he recovered from his serious illness and, in fulfillment of his desire to care for the sick as well as to take responsibility for his family he had taken up nursing, for which he was paid even while in training. The family survived, his siblings got their basic education and he himself seemed free of any further disease.

Vive was basically very serious, but not without a sense of humor. He was athletic and also responsible, being involved in many activities for the staff at the hospital, which was, like many old mental institutions, in the middle of the country far away from towns. In every way he was a fine young man, well-liked and hard-working. At that time I was so absorbed in the Gita that I would speak about it to anyone I met; and of course, Vive being Hindu, I brought up the subject early on in our friendship. He turned out to love it as intensely as I, and it was only natural that we would spend time reading it together and talking about what it meant, in and of itself and for our lives.

When we were off duty we would go for long walks in the lovely Sussex countryside and talk endlessly about Indian philosophy and culture, our own lives and our dreams for the future. We would sit in the woods reading out the Gita and making up our own commentaries on it. He loaned me some books about Indian spiritual life, one of which was *Common Sense about Yoga* by a Swami Pavitrananda. I had never heard the word yoga, but found this little book interesting, if only for the idea that spirituality is something you can cultivate rationally and systematically. I felt a freedom with Vive to speak of the things that really mattered to me and would be delighted to get intelligent, informed replies. This was the first time in my life that someone of my own age group had shown interest in and familiarity with spiritual life, and it was probably inevitable that we would fall in love. I felt the proverbial "floating on air" that I had heard was a sign of being in love; I existed only to see him at the end of a long workday, and so on. Naturally, it was very difficult to say goodbye at the end of the summer and return to chilly, gray Edinburgh. But we wrote to each other every week, long philosophical letters that for me brightened up an otherwise dreary existence. As time went by I realized that our friendship had not just been a "summer romance", but something much more lasting, and I began to wonder if there was any chance of making our relationship permanent—despite the fact that I still knew I did not want to marry.

As I worked over the events of the summer I had a difficult time finding a focus, I was so deeply impelled by my emotions. For the first time I had met a man who was a real man, athletic like the men in my own family; yet kind, gentle and interested in spiritual life. There was no question of the way he felt about me, he was so direct and honest. I was really fortunate to have met such an open person who offered me so much. It was, of course, too early to think of a permanent relationship, but there was one problem that worried me. The fact that he was Hindu, a person of color, didn't bother me at all—he spoke perfect English, was completely rational and thoroughly modern, not at all quaint or culty—such things would have been total obstacles for me. What bothered me was the discrepancy in our educational levels. He was intelligent—and of course, should have been a doctor, had it not been for circumstances beyond his control; but the fact was that he did not belong to the social and educational stratum that I did. I did not feel it when I was alone with him, but I did when we were mixing with his Indian friends. They treated me like a memsahib, a goddess, or some such thing, which I found very disconcerting. They seemed to look up to me and agree with all I said, for reasons that were quite other than anything I was actually saying. I began to realize that, although he seemed to be quite at ease in my world, he also belonged to a culture that I found uncomfortable and difficult.

I already knew from the results of "mixed" marriages (Catholic and Protestant) which I had seen from a distance at school, that family life where there are incompatible elements is extremely difficult. From direct experience I knew that marriage and raising a family were difficult in and of themselves, and had decided, in theory, that if I ever did get married, it would have to be to someone with whom I had a maximum of shared cultural values. Gender stereotypes were still important in those days and I was aware that discrepancies in income, education and social standing between partners could cause a lot of difficulties over the long haul—indeed, they may have played a role in the difficulties between my parents. I was putting all of this together in relationship to Vive, as well as the fact that I might have to go and live in Singapore, an Asian city about which I knew nothing.

After I met Vive, I would make a point of seeing him whenever I went from Clipsham to London, which was not far by train from the hospital in Sussex where he was working. The most memorable time was during a visit to Uncle Donald, who was now living in Chingford, London. I confided in him about Vive, whom I had not mentioned to Mary or anyone else. He was sympathetic and supportive, telling me to follow my own intuitions and was fully aware that I was spending the daytime with Vive. Whenever I met him, all my scruples disappeared or seemed ridiculous. There was a magical connection between us that could not be gainsaid, and it was obvious he still felt the same way about me. I made up my mind I would invite him to Clipsham to meet my family, a move that would bring him closer to me and make it easier to see him. When I got back to Clipsham after my London visit, I brought up the subject with Mary and Uncle George. Mary was sympathetic, herself quite cosmopolitan; but Uncle George, the quintessential Englishman whose home is his castle, minced no words. "I am not having any blacks in my house!" This was a man whose word was law and who would not brook anything other than what he himself thought was right. I knew it was useless to plead my case; in many ways he put up with me because of his love for Mary and often said he thought there was something wrong with me. Trying to argue with him would have annoyed him and maybe created difficulties between him and Mary.

One part of me was heartbroken, but another felt that this was a pointer for me. I believed then and still believe that marriage, particularly when there will be children, is a family issue and that it is not advisable to marry without the agreement and blessing of the family. Rifts and quarrels separate the family and shut off from the children associations with relatives and grandparents, which are vital to their psychological well-being. This sentence of doom was, I felt, something it would be inadvisable to try to work around. It only served to reinforce my own reservations about tying myself permanently to a man from a culture so different from my own.

Vive was philosophical about this turn of events. He continued to write to me, even after he moved from England not that long afterward. He subsequently returned to Singapore, married a Hindu girl and had three children; but his letters arrived nevertheless quite regularly. He would now tell me about his family and their concerns, but the old spiritual tone was still there, uplifting me and keeping me in touch with what was most important to me. Our correspondence lasted for a total of ten years, by which time I had moved to America and started out on a totally different path. But, as of nineteen sixty-two I had gone through a great deal of suffering and doubt, from which his loving letters would always help to lift me up and give me hope of better things to come. I will always think of him as a guardian angel, sent by some kindly providence to prove that human beings are not totally cruel and incapable of love.

When I returned to Edinburgh after that enchanted summer, our study program took up the specifically medical sciences: pathology, pharmacology and bacteriology. I found all of them interesting, but perhaps pathology the most. Pathology is the study of disease processes, which gave me insight into the how of sickness as also the key to finding ways to combat it. Among other things, pathology included attendance at post mortems, another gruesome hurdle we all had to jump over. Many of my classmates had to leave the autopsy room from time to time to throw up, but as with dissecting cadavers, I was oblivious of the what and totally focused on the how and why. I would become so interested in the case history, what was being discovered and how it was answering the questions raised while the patient had still been alive, that the blood, the smell and the sight of a human body being eviscerated had no effect on me at all. Furthermore, finding out the answers to such questions would not only solve the difficult issues raised in this particular case, but would also educate the doctors involved and most likely help to prevent a recurrence of whatever mistakes had been made. The information gained would quite likely also throw more light on the different ways disease processes can affect the human body and advance our general understanding of what can happen when the body malfunctions along certain disease pathways.

The study of pharmacology was also interesting to me, as it throws light on the actual chemistry and physical mechanisms of drugs interacting with living tissues. As chemistry had been one of my stronger subjects in science, it was perhaps not remarkable that I did well in pharmacology, which in some ways is just the study of one kind of chemistry (inorganic) interacting with another—the complex organic structures of the body— and precipitating complicated cascades of reactions which lead to healing and repair. As one of the better students I was asked at the end of the year if I might be interested in working for a Ph.D. in pharmacology. I was flattered, but as with neuroanatomy, I decided to finish my medical studies before I made any decisions to specialize. I could never lose sight of my goal to relieve suffering, which I was still envisioning as the actual care of patients.

I was definitely moving along the course I had set out for myself, not with anything like the distinction I had had at high school, but well enough to be considered a potential Ph.D. candidate. For me, at that time, that was good enough. My mind was much more involved with the struggle with my emotions, which were truly overwhelming. The separation from Vive caused me terrible anguish. For the whole of my fourth year of medical school I was really very depressed. I went nowhere but to the Dunlops', bless them, and would spend hours alone in my bed-sitter, spiraling into dark vortices of crying, self-doubt and at moments, despair. The idea of suicide, introduced so early into my life as one way of doing things, kept flitting on the edges of the vortex like a hungry, blood-sucking bat, sending out at time quite piercing screams. Again and again I would manage to pull myself out of these truly Faustian brushes with the dark side, mostly by reminding myself that I had a mission to serve humanity and that letting myself go like this was doing nothing but holding me back and wasting time. Good old Scotch common sense!

I had by this time more or less dropped out of the church, supporting myself with my readings of the *Bhagavad Gita* and ruminations over its meaning, which I suppose could qualify as meditations of a sort, which were beginning to replace the prayers I dutifully offered every day according to my grandmother's instructions. Over the years I had come to depend on experiences within myself to help me keep going through all of the problems that were always in the foreground; and in many ways what I had experienced within was independent of the religious content outside. Now in my early twenties, I was basically cut off from the sort of inspiration my grandmother had given me, and was associating with people who were formal Christians—good, earnest souls, but not on fire with the love of God. They thought in terms of rules and regulations, many of which I found life-and-love-denying, or just downright cruel, and I was quite simply not getting any inspiration.

There was one straw at which I was clutching at the time: psychiatry. I discovered that I had unusual rapport with the mentally disturbed, being able to draw out from them information that others could not get at, and also was deeply interested in our study of how the mind functions in health and in disease. I was concurrently doing electives in neurology, adding to my knowledge of the nervous system, and was beginning to feel "at home" with the brain and its functioning. I began to think that perhaps neurology or psychiatry might be where I could work most effectively, and applied myself with extra enthusiasm to those particular studies. But I found, on the whole, that the approach we were taking was altogether too reductionistic, a problem that had been besetting me all through my medical studies, if the truth be told. The problem came to a head one day in a tutorial on psychiatry, when we were introduced to the mental mechanisms that characterize the human mind, such as repression, projection, denial, introjection, sublimation, etc. It was interesting, but it struck me that all of them were ways of avoiding the need to face things *as they are*. We were being told that the human mind is hard-wired to evade reality, and I could not accept it. At the end of the tutorial I asked the tutor, "Are these mechanisms absolutely universal? Is there a stage at which we transcend them and can live with things as they are?" He looked at me for a while, probably in total disbelief. Then, in a patronizing tone he said, "Of course not. This is the way the mind is, and our job is to deal with it as it is." That was the end of psychiatry as a possibility for me, and an epiphany in which I realized how deeply the ideals of the Gita had gone into my system. I had internalized the ideal of transcending the mind in all of its manifestations and of living from a spiritual center which not only is not touched by the mind but actually is the source and controller of the mind itself.

Adding to my increasingly unhappy mood was the round of weddings that I was now being invited to. My old friends from Glasgow were getting married after graduating, which was the way we did things then. They looked radiantly happy and it was heartwarming to see them surrounded by their loving families and colleagues from work. But when I got back to my bed-sitter, I would feel rather lonely. I was now in my twenties, and where were my chances of marriage? I would remind myself that I had deliberately chosen not to walk that path; though sometimes I would console myself with the inconsistent idea that, after I had graduated and was working, I could think of finding a husband, though of course I would not have a family, as that would interfere with my work. But in reality the writing was on the wall: I was not going to marry, and this time it was not just an idea, but for real.

Suicidal thoughts became more and more insistent, and one dark winter day when I was really on the brink I realized that I had to deal with my rapidly increasing problem. My own doctor was very concerned about me and arranged for me to speak with the psychiatrist at the Students' Health Service. Like all the psychiatrists at our medical school, he was a model of Scottish common sense; getting results with the patients was the goal, and not proliferating all kinds of esoteric theories. He pointed out to me that medical students in their fifth year of study are notoriously prone to depression—too many years with too little to show for them—and in response to my weepy question: Did he think I am hysterical and emotionally incompetent? He replied, "Miss MacPhail, from what I hear about you from your own doctor, and from my own discussion with you,

I would not only say you are not weak, but rather that you are one of the most sturdy and stable personalities I have ever met. You have been through a lot of extremely difficult psychological trauma, with which you are coping very well."

Such a ringing and unhesitating response went a long way to calming me down, of course. I was not so enthusiastic about his prescription, however. He told me, "I think that part of your problem is that you are spending too much time alone. At least for a while I suggest you live in a hostel or at least in a boarding house with other students." I had come to love my hermit life in my bed-sitter, and was not keen on the idea of group life. In addition, I did not want to hurt the Dunlops' feelings; they were so good to me, and moving elsewhere might look as if I was not grateful. But I knew my problem had to be dealt with, and decided to follow the doctor's advice. And the Dunlops were wonderful. Their only concern was my well-being and they readily understood my problem. I went ahead and made arrangements to move to a boarding house when the summer term began in April.

But for the meantime I was in a bottomless vortex, whirling, whirling, whirling. All the self-doubt, self-dislike and self-disparagement that had ever been expressed in my life was now concentrated into one big, ugly monster that was devouring me. Everything that had supported me seemed to have vanished and I felt the same dread as I had felt during my mother's last year of life. Then I had no way of knowing clearly that something terrible would happen; I simply reacted to things as they took place. But now, I had had experience of just how bad things could be, and was consumed with dread of what was to come.

History was repeating itself, I dimly realized. I was going through the buildup to yet another terrible crisis—but what could it possibly be? I was too emotionally wrought-up to see that it was the emotion itself that was dragging me down. I had found nowhere to peg it so that it would hold steady, and so it was flapping about like a flag in a hurricane. Nearly three years ago I had had that wonderful dream about my golden, spiritual Self, but it had become so submerged under the tsunami of my crisis that it could no longer speak to me. Things were very, very bad. I was finding no consolation in Christianity and Christ seemed to have disappeared with it—where was I going to find my stability, the meaning of my life?

What has always been so amazing to me is how my inner self responds to these crises. As I prepared nearly twenty years ago for my mother's last, desperate act, Jesus himself had appeared in a dream, lifting me up and giving me the energy to come through the ordeal, essentially unscathed, but silent as a tomb. As I now surged about on the huge waves of my emotions, disconsolate on the dark, cold, cold, cold waters, where there were no longer blissful seals to play with or sea birds with which to fly, one night I had a most unexpected dream. I went to bed in my usual misery and coldness, expecting nothing whatsoever from life or from myself. During the night I felt I was walking in utter darkness with no idea where I was or where I was going. Everything was absolutely silent; the only sound was my mind telling me, "This is how it will be for the rest of your life." I felt a great resignation to my fate—I had no energy to do anything else. Then suddenly I noticed a tiny light a long distance away. Light! Where there is light there is warmth, there is understanding! I immediately started moving toward it.

The darkness and silence were really uncanny, but as I got nearer the light, which was spreading a huge corona, I realized that I was not alone. There were huge numbers of people, maybe millions, standing gazing at the light. I could not see who they were, or any details of their faces. But the fact that they were all so focused on the light told me that this was something of major importance. I plodded on, wondering how long it would take me to arrive. As I did so, I could see more and more clearly the vastness of the throng of people gazing intently at the light. Their faces were full of devotion and happiness, some had their hands folded in salutation, while others wept for joy. I was amazed that so many people could be all in one place and experiencing so much emotion, and yet create not a sound. The other thing that baffled me was that, though there were literally millions of people, there was a clear path for me to keep moving forward. It seemed strange that a path would remain, with everyone so intent on seeing the source of the light.

This was a very mysterious dream. What kept me plodding on I have no idea, other than, of course, the attraction of the light itself. Slowly I began to see that the source of the light was a young man seated on an ornate golden throne. He had his eyes closed or cast down, was serene, completely self-possessed, and blissfully at peace. In some ways this was my golden Self, but much more mature, much more established and of course much more responsive to human emotion, for this was the being absorbing the worship and adoration of these millions and millions of people. I felt a certain hesitation about coming nearer this venerable being; but as there was a clear path before me and the attraction was so intense,

I kept moving forward. Occasionally I wondered why no one was trying to stop me from approaching so close, but there was not a ripple in that vast ocean of humanity.

Finally I arrived. I stood before this glorious being, gazing at him in total wonderment. Who was this? What did he mean to me? Certainly, it was not Jesus, whom I knew so well by that time. And would he run away, as had my golden Self, oppressed by my turbulent emotion?

He slowly opened or raised his eyes and looked at me. It is impossible to explain what he conveyed, but it was something so real, so very, very real, so calm yet loving, gracious yet powerful and full of the radiant energy that had sent his light spreading out over the long distance I had walked to find him. I felt myself dissolving into wave upon wave of bliss, lifting me up from my body, my emotions, my intellect, any part of me that I can give a name to. And then I awoke. This was still my bed-sitter; this was still an Edinburgh winter; I still had to get up and go to classes; Vive was still far away; I still wondered who I really was—but somehow it was all saturated with bliss that penetrated to the very core of any sort of being. My mood was completely changed, and I felt that whatever I had to face, I would and could face it successfully and would come out on the other side, not only in one piece as I had after my mother's death, but a wiser, better and less tormented person.

When I had somewhat absorbed all of this, my regular mind kicked in with the inevitable question: Who was this being? I had no idea whom I had seen, at least not with my ordinary mind. But something within me answered, "That was Buddha." Buddha! I had no knowledge whatsoever of Buddha, although I had heard the name. How could I possibly have met Buddha in a dream? I was totally bamboozled. There obviously were indeed more things in heaven and earth than I was dreaming of in my philosophy. At the time I was just happy to have it and enjoy the lasting benefits it bestowed upon me, but now I think it possible that I had absorbed more about Buddha than I realized from my reading of Radhakrishnan's commentary on the Gita, which brought in informed references from many different religious traditions. I have never taken the time to check this hypothesis, but of course what is important for this story is that Buddha, like Christ some twenty years before, did indeed appear to me at a time of great darkness and suffering and give me the support I was going to need on the next, compelling act of my life's drama.

Parthasarathi [Krishna as the Teacher of the Bhagavad Gita]
by Nandalal Bose (1883-1966).

Another question that came to my mind was: Could this person have been Krishna? I had come to revere Krishna as a wise, loving and supremely balanced spiritual teacher, but I had given no thought as to his appearance. Certainly, in the window of an antique shop across the street I had seen an exquisite ivory statuette of the boy Krishna playing the flute, and fallen in love with it, but I knew that this was a different aspect of Krishna than the teacher of the Gita. Krishna the enlightened teacher was older, not only in years but also in history, for the teacher of the Gita spoke long before Indian imagination created the delightful myths of Krishna's youth. So the question remained: Had I seen Krishna, whose thoughts were so entraining my mind? Although I had absolutely no way of verifying my conviction, I still felt, contrary to all evidence, that I had seen Buddha, another great spiritual teacher who had come to the world long, long after Krishna. And, now that I know much more about it, I am still sure that is who it was.

I took stock of myself after this encouraging dream: I had now been studying medicine for four years and was, despite my inner struggles, making quite good progress. I was not considered a mental incompetent, a hysterical idiot, as my father had characterized me. I had had some wonderful friendships with men, which had helped to heal some of the insecurity I felt with men generally, and on the whole, felt better than at any time previous to my mother's death. I began to think that it was really ridiculous to be estranged from my father. By this time I had proved who I was and he simply must accept me on the basis of hard evidence. One side of him loved me intensely and that was the side I would make him emphasize. I decided that I would visit him and work toward a reconciliation.

By that time he and Pat were living in a northern English town, where he had a senior position in the Department of Preventive Medicine at the University. He was in touch with the family, mostly his older sister Malina and Uncle Willie, from whom Mary had heard that in many ways Pat was very good for him. A trained public health nurse and a sweet personality, she had taken a firm line with him on his drinking, and on the whole he was doing much better. I was encouraged: this was maybe the time to implement my plan. I told no one about it, neither my father, nor Mary, nor the Dunlops, as I did not want to hear anything against what I was planning to do. I just got on the train for the north of England at the beginning of one of my vacations and set out for my father's house.

I found my father sitting at the dining table (covered in an old-fashioned lace table cloth), reading. He didn't hear me at first, so I just stood where I was, waiting for him to see me. Finally he sensed something and looked up. When he saw me, tears came into his eyes and he said, very pathetically, "Jean! Jean! Jean! You came to see me!" It was obvious he was delighted to see me and also at a loss as to what to do. As, for some reason Pat was not there, the responsibility for the social niceties fell upon me, and I, also overwhelmed with emotion, struggled to keep control of myself. I was intensely aware of all that could go wrong, and had decided to play my part as coolly as possible, giving him nothing to catch hold of and use against me. But, as it turned out, I had caught him off guard and what he was expressing was unfeigned affection and even love. He conveyed to me that he was really proud of me and set about making me comfortable for the day and night I planned to stay.

We spent the time together in a pleasant, friendly way. I could see that he was drinking much, much less than previously and was altogether a different person: Pat and married life were obviously suiting him. I was extremely happy to see all of this and hope began to flicker once again. I had come prepared for anything, but principally drunken scenes with lots of abusive language. This was so utterly different from what I had anticipated that it was almost like being with a totally different person; but I did not let this wonderful discovery affect me too much. I responded to his effusiveness in a kindly way, but without dropping my guard. I had no idea what might suddenly swoop down on me and destroy everything all over again.

The visit of a few days passed agreeably, and as I left he invited me, begged me, to come again, which I did, I believe on my next vacation three months later. On that occasion I stayed a little longer and managed to come through without any unpleasant events. Pat was away on that occasion also, so my father and I were one-on-one, as with the previous visit. Once again he expressed nothing but affection for me and pride in my achievements, for which he kept assigning the credit to the MacPhail side of my family. He could never resist a swipe at the Laughland sisters-in-law, whom he regarded as hysterical women (with the honorable exception of Aunt Jane, who had been so kind to him). I did not care for this sort of thing, but held my tongue. Too much was at stake, and to squabble over family feuds at this juncture was simply inane. I left, still aware that my father had not just feet of clay, but a considerable part of his anatomy, but also with hope that somehow we could work through it and come out into the sunshine of a more normal relationship, which would of course include Pat.

I was invited to return, this time in April of nineteen sixty-four. I was still associated with the Sunday school work, and remember that the day before I left for my father's the teachers had had some sort of picnic, at which Abe's wife served American lemonade, which met with my sincere approval. We were all very jolly and on our way home went barreling through Georgian Edinburgh in Abe's coupé singing at the top of our lungs. I was enjoying every minute of it, but at the same time was afflicted with terrible dread. I knew that I was soon going to bow out of the church—I could go on no longer—and perhaps also had a premonition of what was in store at my father's. The first two visits had been so unexpectedly good and promising—but would this one turn out as well?

The first difference from the previous visits was that Pat was there. As I mentioned in connection with my second visit to the Sudan, Pat's presence seemed to bring something out of my father, an urge to strike at me and hurt me, which of course, as far as I knew, had nothing to do with Pat herself. Certainly, I could see at once that he was in an aggressive and confrontational mood, and I went on high alert, drawing in from showing my feelings and bracing for the worst. Pat was polite and non-committal, probably wanting to avoid a scene as much as I. By that time I had learned the ropes and was able to ignore the various taunts and jeers he kept hurling at me. I was mature enough to understand that he was sick and needed kindness and help more than anything else. Moreover, by that time I was financially independent of him, following my own path and with all kinds of collateral to help me in the event he went too far. I felt that he could not really hurt me anymore.

But it was excruciatingly unpleasant, and I had several days to get through. I tried to resist the temptation to answer back or to ask for help from Pat; she had so much invested in my father that it would be improper for me to drag her into my problem. The days went by in unmitigated misery, each one unfolding a new level of nastiness and abuse, going closer and closer to the core of what was bothering him and increasing the chances that he might push my buttons. I noticed that he was drinking more and more, no doubt to Pat's dismay, for she had worked very hard with him and attained quite a level of success. All her good work was unraveling because of me!

Finally the last day came. We negotiated through it somehow, and all that remained was the evening. He started drinking in the afternoon and by evening was besotted. Pat and I were suffering agony to see him in this condition, so unnecessary, so humiliating, so destructive! His barbs were becoming more and more biting and drawing more and more blood. I was losing my composure and beginning to fight back—a response natural to me but of no use in dealing with a person in his condition. I wondered if this would ever come to an end, whether I would maintain my sanity, whether I would get out of the house in one piece.

Then he started in on his litany of abuse about my mother. The same old stuff—a whore, a bitch, a hysterical incompetent, on and on and on. I had really worked at controlling myself though the whole visit; and when this began I told myself, "Don't react. Don't react. He wants to get you with this, but don't react." I stood still and quiet for what seemed an eternity, and then something happened, which I can only describe as supernatural.

He was using forbidden weapons forged from the rawest of raw emotions, terribly destructive and painful. From my side, ordinary weapons, such as reasoning, appeals and so on would not suffice—what was called for was what the Hindus call the *brahmastra*, the ultimately terrible celestial weapon against which nothing can prevail. Of course, at the time I knew nothing of Hinduism, supernatural weapons, nor even the psychology of what happened, but I can testify that I became possessed, as it were, by a higher power. I felt myself melting away and a huge, powerful spiral of energy rise up like a tornado, whirling away all of my rationality, "compassion", longing for resolution of the conflict. And I heard my voice, as if from a long distance and in a very strange way, say something utterly counterintuitive, something I had not actually thought or worked out at all, something that was as terrible a weapon as anything he had ever used. Pointing my right finger directly at him, I said, in a calm, slow and strange voice, "You are talking that way about my mother because you are responsible for her death."

Probably no one in the room was more surprised than I to hear this. I still did not know for sure that her death was a suicide, for I had never discussed it with anyone. And, reciprocally, no one had ever discussed it with me. But the evidence I had seen in the months before she died, and the condition she was in when she went out into the rain, naturally made me suspicious. With the passage of time, and with the increasing evidence of my father's irresponsibility and imperviousness to human emotions and ties, some connection had begun to form in my mind between her death and his behavior, though I had no idea what he might have done. And all of this had taken place in an intuitive space which never expressed itself in words; no doubt it was something even I did not care to go into too deeply, raising all sorts of horrible possibilities and further damaging my relationship with my father. To make such an accusation was a terrible, terrible thing, nothing that I would have dreamt of in my normal consciousness. And to have made it without any "real" evidence at all, was unbelievable. What was going on? This, I felt, was the stuff that writers like Tennessee Williams and Eugene O'Neill worked with. It was so contrary to "civilized" behavior as we understood it then, so startling and at the same time so interesting, bringing up issues that perhaps we had collectively not been facing for a long time. This was, no doubt, why *A Streetcar Named Desire* had been considered such an epochal cultural event.

But if my own behavior was impossible to fathom, my father's reaction was utterly devastating. In the state I was in, there was no room for calculation as to what he might do; I was totally invested in the factuality of what I was saying. Perhaps the more conditioned part of me feared he might attack me physically; we had gotten close to it when I was a child, but thank God he had always stopped in time. As I was to learn much later, physical violence takes these things to a totally different level, where finding solutions calls for a wholly different set of tools. What actually happened was, however, so utterly different from anything I had ever seen (or ever wish to see again!) or could possibly conceive of. He had attacked me with deep, subconscious weapons, with which he had succeeded in the past; but I was now capable of wielding my own weapons, which I was using for the first time—and, as it turned out, with devastating effect. I had hit him at the center of his being and he was showing it in a simply dreadful way.

He curled up in his chair in the fetal position and began to whimper like a little animal trapped by a large predator, from which there was no escape. This was the worst, the very worst thing I have ever seen—and as a medical doctor, I have seen a lot. To see your own father reduced to the lowest common denominator of animal life was a humiliation, a reduction of human decency and dignity that hit me like an avalanche. I stood there, silent, appalled—and at the same time thinking, "I was right! He *was* responsible for her death! I have to find out *how*!" This line of thought brought with it a certain elation, for finding the truth is always exhilarating—but at what a terrible cost! The conflicting emotions fixed me to the spot; and as he continued to whimper it looked as if we would be there for eternity.

"Colin! This is enough! I am not going to let you treat your daughter like this any more!" It was Pat, the silent and probably appalled witness of the whole sorry affair. Like the good, sensible woman she was, she stepped in at this cosmic moment and took charge. I was surprised that she did not attack me for what I had done to my father—for it was really traumatizing to see him like that. Instead, her inner witness, up till then holding its peace, seemed to be speaking. She turned to me and took my arm. "Jean, you come with me. I am going to see to it that your father has nothing more to do with you while you are here."

She took me to a sitting room at the back of the house, leaving my father to fend for himself. Sitting me down, she locked the door and said, with great emotion, "Jean, I have to apologize to you. Up till now I have thought you were just a troublesome, spoiled child, lashing out at people for no reason at all. But I see the whole thing now quite clearly. Your father has traumatized you terribly, and you are doing your best to cope with a very difficult situation." This was totally unexpected, of course. But what she said next was even more unexpected. "Will you forgive me?" Tears came to my eyes. Pat had a lot to lose by supporting me and what she was doing was coming from nothing but basic goodness of heart and ability to see the truth in a nasty situation. I replied, "Pat, you are not to blame for anything. You have not had a chance to really get to know me—I met you only at the wedding, and in Africa of course, it was impossible. My story is complicated and difficult. How could you understand what is going on? I don't even understand it myself. What I just said to my father took me totally by surprise. It was terrible, but there may be some truth in it, judging by how he responded." I began to get emotional and Pat said, "Don't let's talk about it any more. What you need is a good meal and rest. I will see to it that you get both and will take you to the train station myself tomorrow." At the railway station she gave me a big hug, settling once and for all any score that might have existed between us.

I have no idea what happened to my father on account of this momentous episode. He never got back to me, and also responded in a definite way the next time I proposed to come and see him. I can hardly believe that I did it, but I decided that I could not let this horrible situation go unresolved and wrote to him suggesting we meet again and try to reach an understanding. I received no reply to this proposal, but nevertheless made up my mind that I would arrive at the suggested time. I think I had been working somewhere, because I arrived at eleven at night, an awkward time. The lights of his flat were out, and I thought that my parents must have gone to bed, even though they knew I was coming. However, several rings of the doorbell elicited no response, and after about half an hour I had to accept that for some reason they were not home.

I was in a residential area of a city about which I knew absolutely nothing. I had no idea where I could spend the night, as it was far too late to catch a train to Mary's, which was my next destination. But as there were lights in the apartment above my parents', the next step seemed to be to inquire of the people upstairs where I could find a hotel that would put me up so late at night. I rang the doorbell and a gentleman appeared in his bath robe. I introduced myself as Professor MacPhail's daughter, at which he looked at me askance. At that moment, his wife appeared and said, "Oh, yes! I can see the family resemblance!" But he said, "Professor MacPhail never told us he had a daughter. He and Pat have gone away on a holiday." That hurt, badly. His wife changed the subject. "Love, you don't have anywhere to spend the night? Why don't you just spend it in our house." Thank God for women! The gentleman was a rather kindly soul, but with the usual male inability to understand situations. They put me up, gave me a wonderful supper and breakfast and saw me off the next day.

Clearly, my father did not want to see me ever again—not surprising, in view of what had happened on my previous visit. But to let me know it like this was very, very hard for me to take. Why couldn't he have told me in a letter? Perhaps I was to blame by showing up on his doorstep after he had disowned me. Then again, perhaps he did not get the letter. But I had sent several in order to get a response; and of course the lack of reply was actually speaking volumes.

I should have given up years ago. Why did I keep trying, trying, trying to communicate with him, when the reality was that he saw me as a hated ghost from his troubled past that he just wanted out his life forever, even at the cost of driving a stake through my heart? My rising up in another form that was capable of attacking him frontally had been the last straw. He was absolutely not going to face his ghosts, and that was that. That is how I interpret these last episodes in my relationship with my father. I have no idea what Pat went through, though of course I understand that, as his wife, she had to go along with him or risk estrangement. Much as she had helped me in my moment of crisis, her primary relationship was with him and now that a final severance was taking place, she had packed the bags and gone off wherever it was they had gone. Who knows what had gone through her mind? But that is her story, not mine.

CHAPTER 11

PICKING UP THE PIECES: 1966

The parting of the ways with my father was painful beyond anything I had experienced thus far. Now more aware of myself than I was when my mother left me, I felt a level of abandonment that was really devastating, and at the same time a guilt that I had not experienced in connection with her death. For there had indeed been a long tussle with my father before this terrible dénoument, while with her the problem had been entirely hers and I had played only the role of a bystander. I was too devastated to think clearly after the scene with my father, but in my own defense I would remember from time to time that from the start I had been at a terrible disadvantage with him, as my mother's tragic and unexplained death had left me very insecure. Then, of course, he himself was scarred emotionally and had really subjected me to a lot of pressure that children are not normally expected to absorb. Finally, Mary would remind me that almost all of the family—so kind and so forbearing, like Grannie herself—would no longer permit my father into their homes, his behavior was so disturbing and at times abusive. These considerations helped me to keep some kind of perspective, but nevertheless I could not help feeling overwhelmed by what I had done to my father. Over the years I had indeed burst out angrily at his taunts and jibes—though what could be expected of a young child? But now I was an adult, and expected better things of myself.

I certainly had had no intention of reducing him to the pathetic state I had seen; on the contrary, I had wanted to build up something positive and loving. Some terrible inner demon had made me say what I said, completely outwith my conscious intentions. Perhaps it was a result of my strange silence for such a long time. If during the last twenty years it had been possible for me to talk about my inner pain and to find out more about the circumstances of my mother's death, there would not have been that huge tsunami of emotion and premonition building up inside. It is, of course, a cliché to say *What if*; final answers will never be known. It was a terrible tragedy for me and that was it.

An illustration in ink on paper for a poem about the
Minotaur by a famous Latin American poet. Drawn in
1970, but expressing my feelings in 1966.

However, whatever the ultimate causes of the drama, the immediate sequelae were unmistakable and at the same time rather familiar. I went through a period of turmoil much worse than anything I had gone through thus far; I learned a great deal; and, as had happened after my mother's death, I moved to another world entirely and met a spiritual teacher who could help heal the wounds and move me in a completely different direction. But the first thing I did after I realized how totally and irrevocably my father had rejected me, was to get information about my mother's death. I made an appointment to visit the Medical Examiner in Dumbarton, where the inquest had been held after my mother's death, and arrived there one summer day on my way to a visit with Aunt Jane. I made the decision to go to the authorities before I spoke to the family because I wanted the bare facts without any emotional overlay. Moreover, there had been twenty years of silence on the issue and it seemed almost wrong to bring up the subject with the family now.

The Medical Examiner was able to tell me immediately that the cause of my mother's death was cold and exposure (suicide). By this time I had done the pathology course and was familiar with causes of death. "How exactly did she die?" I asked. "Did she actually injure herself?' "No", he said, "She seems just to have kept walking in the hills in the rain until she collapsed and died of the cold. She was found lying in a burn." That is exactly how I had seen it: Even as I lay under the gas mantle that night, I had been aware of her struggling along in the rain and the dark, and stumbling on the rough terrain. And I had seen her lying dead in the burn, with the water pulling her hair this way and that. All this was no news, really. But it was terrible to hear, nonetheless.

But there was a problem for me: "How can you call it a suicide, then? She didn't actively take her life, it seems." He replied, digging into the file, "Miss MacPhail, she left a note." He handed me a small piece of paper, on which I recognized her large, sloping, handwriting: "I have completely lost faith in human nature. There is nothing left to live for." To some this may perhaps seem a rather abstract reason for dying—but for me, all the more searing. She and her sisters were all intellectuals, all idealistic, and I had certainly inherited those tendencies. To think of my beautiful, joyful, childlike mother losing all faith in humanity and because of it throwing away her precious life all alone, cold and abandoned, was quite overwhelming.

The Medical Examiner was a model of tact and politely waited for me to recover. After a while I said, "There is one other thing I would like to know from the record of the inquest. Was there any discussion of my mother having an affair with a German prisoner of war?" He at once replied, "No. There was no suggestion that your mother was having an affair with a German prisoner of war or with anyone else. There was no suggestion of any misconduct whatsoever." This was valuable information, though of course it might have been partial. People were dying like flies in those days and who knows how thorough the inquests were. But, whoever had spread that rumor about her had obviously not spoken up at the inquest and, as far as the official record went, there were no black marks against her name. To some extent this was a relief, but I had already made up my mind that if she had indeed had an affair with that lovely German man we met on the railroad tracks she had a lot of good sense. She was living so alone, so forgotten, and he was so loving and sweet, that to my mind at the time, it would have been totally natural for her to fall in love with him.

I proceeded on to Aunt Jane's and had a nice weekend, enjoying her good cooking and wonderful company. But I said not a word about what I had just discovered. However, as soon as I got back to Edinburgh I made a point of speaking with Anne Dunlop, who had been closest to my mother just before her death. I went down to Randolph Crescent one day from my new lodgings and talked one on one with Anne, who had, of course, also given me a great meal. I told her what had happened with my father and also what I had just learned from the Dumbarton Medical Examiner. Could she fill in the blanks?

It took a while for Anne to reply. She, too, was deeply moved to hear what I told her, for I don't think she knew about the suicide note. We made a pot of tea and settled down for a long, long chat. "Jean," she said, "Your mother was very idealistic. She had so much faith in Germany, which she thought was the place that was going to give the solution to all of the problems of Europe. Certainly, they had worked out a wonderful philosophy and there was so much that was good going on, like the Froebel Institute, where she studied. But when Hitler came on the scene, she was horrified. And as the war went on and we all learned what Hitler was up to with the concentration camps, she was completely devastated. The same thing happened with the Communists. She had thought that they would liberate people and bring a new world of justice and decency into being. But as we learned more about Stalin, especially after the war was over, it turned out he was as bad as Hitler. Your mother took it very, very badly and we could not console her. She was intelligent, but also high strung and sometimes she just got carried away."

"Things got worse after you went to Hillview Road to live with your Uncle Robert and Aunt Eileen. Eileen was the sister closest to your mother; they had been best friends all along, and it seemed like a wonderful idea to share that house on Hillview Road. But Robert, as you know, has problems of his own, and made life hell for your mother. Then he finally kicked her out, despite your father's protests. Your father had paid for his part of the house, but of course was in Europe with the army and could not be in Scotland to confront Robert. It really was illegal, what Robert did. But your mother could stand it no longer and so the two of you went off to Shandon to live with the mother of one of your father's boon companions. After your mother died, that woman stole everything of value that your mother had."

This was terrible, but it was difficult to understand how it would push my mother over the edge. "Something else must have happened, Anne", I said. "What was my father's role in all of this? I suspect him of having done something very bad." Anne paused for quite a long time. Finally she said, "It wasn't so much what your father did—it was what he didn't do." She told me that she had gone to the station with my mother to meet my father on one occasion when he was coming home on leave. My mother was excited, maybe too excited, and was absolutely agog when the train pulled in. Many servicemen, also on leave, bundled out, so glad to be home, if even for just a bit. Slowly the crowd thinned and there was no Colin. Anne and my mother went up and down the platform, but there was absolutely no sign of my father. My mother became very upset, and started to cry. "This is what he does to me! He prefers to go drinking with his boon companions!" From this Anne understood that this was not the first time this had happened. She waited at the station with my mother until the last train of the day had arrived, but there was absolutely no sign of my father. Nor were there any telephone calls, any explanations that might have softened the blow.

Anne told me this in a flat, unemotional voice. She made no negative remarks about my father, just the plain facts as she had seen them. But for me it was easy to understand how he had rejected my mother, again and again turning away and leaving her to suffer, worrying about him being in the line of fire on the European battlefields all the time—hadn't he been wounded in the head twice, and even been decorated for bravery? I started to cry as I thought of my mother's agony and how I had known nothing about it though it was all happening while I was with her.

But I was determined to hear the whole story and asked Anne to go on. She was reluctant, but I insisted. Anne said, "In some ways the worst was at the end. Poor Nan was living in that God-forsaken place in the middle of nowhere with that terrible woman, no contact with her own family, your father being so unreliable and her all upset about Hitler and Stalin. She made friends with those German prisoners of war and wanted to do something for them. That is the way she was—so generous, kind-hearted, and in a way, silly. But of course the local people saw it differently. They saw it as collaborating with the enemy—and, of course, many of them had lost boys in the war. I suppose it was human nature that they told your mother that they would no longer serve her in the shops or speak with her at all. That is what finished her off." I immediately remembered the letter she had received a few days before her death and thought that that was probably the one the local people had written to her. It had indeed changed her mood drastically and made me fearful of what would happen.

I was shaken to the depths of my being. My poor mother had experienced such an unrelenting series of betrayals and rejections, for which she was not well-prepared by her atheistic outlook. All possible support had been taken away—most notably Aunt Jane, who was caring for her dying husband—and she had been forced to face her darkness completely alone. It had all been just too much and she had walked out into the night, scarcely knowing what was happening. What a terrible tragedy, and how much my father had contributed! How could he have understood the anguish his behavior caused her? I already knew that he didn't seem to care about my feelings at all. But then again, who knows what he was going through himself? I already knew that he was shell-shocked, or had what we now call PTSD, and was trying to anesthetize himself with alcohol. Hitler and Stalin and all that they represented had shattered his life as much as hers, it seemed to me. I felt that if there was a villain, it was the war itself, and the whole attitude to life from which it had sprung.

But there was one point I wanted to know more about. I asked Anne about the alleged affair with a German prisoner of war. She had not heard anything about it and was quite surprised when I mentioned it. "Where did you hear that?" she asked. I replied, "My father keeps bringing it up."

"Jean, I think your mother would have told me if there had been anything like that. She was very open, like a child. The only man I ever heard her talk about was your father. She was crazy over him. I can't believe there is any truth in it. But I will say one thing: her landlady was an old witch. She was a notorious gossip, everybody knew it. She may have made up some story to tell your father the day he came to pick you up and bring you over to our place.

All of this was, of course, valuable. There is no substitute for facts and information, and it was good that I now knew the story from the most reliable sources. But it was also terribly bruising, and I found myself crabby and bitter in my dealings with my classmates, who got on my nerves as they never had before. There was no church to turn to now, and indeed my own faith in human nature had been pretty badly shaken. I kept asking myself: how could people be so unrelentingly cruel? And I found no answer.

It is a measure of just how deeply shaken I was by the scene with my father and what I had learned from it that I took up with a man whom I would never have looked at twice before or after that time. I met him a few months after the event when I was working in Inverness at a summer job at Raigmore Hospital. He was an Egyptian doctor on the staff, smooth-talking and unscrupulous. He didn't really hide anything from me; I knew he was at least a petty criminal but, in the dreadful state of mind I was in, found it exciting rather than repellant. Although he told me he wanted to marry me, I knew I was being used, and was so utterly lacking in self-esteem that I allowed myself to go along with the whole thing. He bought me an engagement ring—the cheapest he could persuade me to accept—and a lot of other feminine things. I am not a person interested in gifts and flattery as a rule, but at that time I was totally without self-respect or any sense of perspective. He was filling a huge, aching, raw void and I went along with it. I took him to Fortrose on a visit with my Uncle Willie, who said nothing overtly. However, it was obvious from his face that he was utterly appalled, particularly at the idea of my committing myself to this man on a permanent basis. However, his silent reaction was very helpful, for it spoke to my own higher self and objectified my own inner, but up till then inexpressible, misgivings.

After my work at the hospital I was scheduled to go on a painting holiday in Spain. This was something Mary had cooked up long before this whole drama, trying to divert me from my growing depression by a combination of the Mediterranean and art. By the time I was to leave, however, she and the whole family were on red alert on account of my relationship with the Egyptian doctor, but nobody dared to say anything to me. I was in full rebellion mode, determined to destroy myself, as I had in my Shamrock Street days; and they all knew that trying to stand in my way would only make things worse. No doubt they were all praying on my behalf as I was gadding about England with this man right up to the time of my scheduled departure. He did not want me to go, no doubt because he sensed that I would break away from him if I managed to be on my own at all. But by that time my irreducible common sense was returning and I told him firmly that I would indeed go.

When I got back to London after three weeks of painting in the north of Spain, (including a visit to Barcelona, where the Gaudi buildings and a bullfight had been the more memorable events), I was brown as a berry, in a much better mood, and more in command of myself than I had been since my disaster some four months previously. The Egyptian doctor met me at the railway station, but as soon as I saw him I wanted nothing more to do with him. He deployed all of his persuasive powers—which were considerable—but I was adamant. I was getting on the first train for Clipsham, and that was that.

Mary met me at the station and drove me home. She was unusually solicitous of me, even for her. I had not really had time to talk to her about what was going on in my mind since the débacle with my father, but she had met the Egyptian and was in mortal fear I would marry him. She had at once contacted the police and found out he was trying to escape from Interpol, and forthwith engaged a detective to follow me wherever I went. I was mightily furious with Mary for having so little trust in me, but she said, "Jean, you are just not yourself. Even at the best of times you are prone to getting into all kinds of adventures and this one was really dangerous. If he had succeeded in marrying you, it would have much more difficult or even impossible to save you." We were silent for a bit, while I fumed and she got ready for her next salvo. "You have not told me what happened, but I know something very bad happened with your father when you visited him. You must understand that you cannot change him. What is happening is that he is injuring you, over and over and over. This time he has nearly killed you. That is why you got involved with this Egyptian man. You would not do anything like this when you are in your right mind."

I said nothing, but I knew she was right. I had not really thought it through, but I felt it in every cell of my body. This whole descent into hell had been triggered by my insane need for love from my father, who in this particular body and mind was incapable of giving me it in any way I could understand. I had been warned in my dream of the golden Self that craving for love could end in nothing but disaster, but here I was, boomeranging off my poor father and on to this pathetic Egyptian, running away from the police and thinking he could use me to fend them off! I realized quite profoundly that craving for love could drag me down to the depths, and that there would always be people only too glad to take advantage of me. This was all so far from my dreams of working with a soul-mate to contribute to the well-being of humankind! This was assuredly one of the many lessons we all have to go through in order to learn. Unfortunately, there was enough of my mother in me to lead me into a few more dead ends, such was my craving for love; but basically I had grasped the principle and would eventually understand that love is not something that you buy or pick off the trees. It is a gift, very rare and very precious, and anyone who offers you "a quick fix" is deceiving you.

Mary was, as ever, deeply supportive and loving, and mothered me without any further discussion, but Uncle George, who was upset at how much Mary had been suffering over my furious adventures, took me to task one day. We were sitting down to morning coffee when he—the most taciturn and reticent of people—began to speak in an angry tone. "You are a selfish, silly girl! How could you make your Aunt Mary suffer so much! You have no consideration for anybody!" I understood completely why he was so upset, but his tone was altogether too reminiscent of my father, and something snapped in my head. I lunged toward the window, just wanting to jump out and to bring the whole thing to an end. Mary, who understood me perfectly, caught me round the waist and said to my uncle, "George! She is very, very upset. What she needs is complete rest."

All of the emotion I had not expressed at my father's came welling up and I could not stop crying. Uncle George's face was a study; perhaps some of the difficulties he had gone through with his bipolar first wife were re-surfacing. He looked on silently as Mary calmed me down and took me upstairs to my room. She told me she was going to call the doctor; she felt I needed something to calm me down and let me rest. Her idea of "calm down" turned out to be sedation—I was asleep round the clock for a whole week. The first few days it was welcome, but after that I could feel part of me objecting strenuously: I don't need this! I want to get up and get on with my life!

I believe it was around this time that I had an important discussion with Mary. I was agonizing over how my father made it so impossible for me to relate to him; every effort I made to communicate he stomped all over and turned into something ugly and painful. And for all of this I blamed largely myself. It must surely be my self-assertiveness that had created this situation! Mary let me ramble for a while and then said, "Jean, there is something you need to know. I kept this from you while you were a child, but I think you should hear it now." She paused for a moment, perhaps to let me compose my mind. "When your mother died, your father's first response was to put you up for adoption." I stared at her in silence. "As soon as the family got wind of it, all of us told him in no uncertain terms that we would allow nothing of the kind. Somehow we would find a home for you with the family."

There was a long, long pause. After all I had been through with my father I had no difficulty in believing what Mary was telling me, but, as always, I wanted to know: Why, why, why? What had possessed my father to think of throwing me—just a tot—out to the wide world, when so many of my family would have been glad to have me? Was he just incurably irresponsible? Was he deranged mentally, which I was by then capable of believing?

I would, of course, never know; but there was an important item that applied to me in a meaningful way. At the time of my mother's death my father had seen me perhaps four or five times in all, on those short visits home he had made from the army. How could I possibly have offended him then, just a wee moppet and—they tell me—an enchanting little girl, just as my mother had been at my age? No, his rejection of me had stemmed, not from anything I had said or done, but from some deep-seated knot in his own heart. As my mother had in fact rejected me without any cause from my side, so had my father. The quarrels and arguments we had as I was growing up were not the real causes of his attitude to me. Although excruciatingly painful emotionally, this discovery afforded me some relief: most of this dreadful situation was not really and primarily my fault. In the highly relaxed state I was now in, I simply sighed, thanked my guardian angel for protecting me, laid my head on the pillow and fell back to sleep.

On September twenty-eighth I finally came off my "rest therapy" and reconnected with my life. My mood was cheerful as I lay in bed watching the rays of the sun play round my room, touching the various artifacts I had assembled on my dresser:

> A blowsy rose
> Her green mantilla throws
> At her double arched reflection in the mirror,
> Bending fussily to dominate the clock,
> The noisy victim of her piqued hauteur.

Contemplating the climbing roses nodding outside my window, listening to the birds joyfully calling to each other outside, I really did feel as if a load had been lifted off my shoulders:

> Now the past is purged,
> Now I lie in peace.
> There is no feeling that my soul is urged
> To eternal restlessness.
> My fresh eyes see the day
> Skipping and leaping around my room,
> Engaging even the dusty specks in play,
> And singing of happiness that is to come.

My upbeat mood was to quite a large extent due to the fact that I was going to spend the next term of three months in London, where I was to be an exchange student at the Middlesex Hospital. Mary, of course, kept me busy getting ready for departure, trying to make me "forget" the Egyptian. What she did not understand was that I had already made up my mind about him. He had been the first opportunity to self-destruct that I had met after the trauma with my father, and I now had no feelings for him at all. I regretted deeply that I had used another human being as an outlet for my feelings, but intended to atone for my mistake by not repeating it. I was much more interested in moving on with my life.

The most important part of my sojourn in London was the lady with whom I boarded, Mrs. Browne, who had traveled widely and was very cosmopolitan, open to any and all ideas. She was one of the most gracious people I ever met, a perfect lady in every sense of the term; extremely kind and understanding, she knew exactly how to put people, including myself, at ease and was exactly what I needed at that moment in time. Her quiet comments on my story helped me to get a perspective on my difficulties that was quite novel and ultimately connected with spiritual insight, though she was not a religious person outwardly. I felt that I had been guided to yet another wonderful "mother", and have been eternally grateful for the opportunity to meet her. And she had her own tragedy: her husband, an architect, was paranoid and no longer lived with her. On his occasional visits he would accuse her of the most dreadful things, which made my blood run cold in my veins. I realized that even the best of people, the really good, are not spared the kind of suffering I had been through, an insight of the greatest importance.

An important cultural discovery in London was what it is to be American. Up till then my sole experience with Americans was getting bars of chocolate and oranges from servicemen my mother and I ran into on some outing in Glasgow; and of course Abe, who lived in a domain beyond my ken. It was, therefore, a novel experience to work with the several Americans I met at the Middlesex. I enjoyed their company immensely—so open, enthusiastic and friendly, unlike the English, who tended on the whole to be a bit distant—but I couldn't help thinking that the American women were a lot more interesting than the men, who seemed a bit silly and childish at times, though nice people.

Far from the least of my really worthwhile experiences in London was my attendance at meetings with the Society of Friends, or Quakers as they are more popularly known. I loved the Quaker idea of the inner light, "that of God within", and the idea of drawing it out and making it manifest in daily life. It seemed so much more real, living and *practical* than the stories about crucifixion and atonement and things of that sort that had been dished up to me thus far by the Church. The meetings themselves were a wonderful demonstration of what the Quakers were talking about: an hour's silent meditation, during which anyone moved by the spirit could speak briefly about something that had moved her recently. Most of the time the first speaker was one of the lifetime Quakers who were the *de facto* "elders" of the group. The thought could be anything—some solution to a problem, seeing the first buds of spring—but given in a quiet and meditative way. There would be more silence for a while, and then, one by one, those who felt moved would also rise and share their inner thoughts with us. What was said was often simple, even simplistic, but very telling. Quaker meetings are not intended to be discussions; people could speak only once, briefly, and to the point—no answers or ripostes to something someone else had said. The idea was to share in a meditative space some of the deepest thoughts of your heart and soul.

In a good meeting the effect was simply amazing: bit by bit the original thought would grow into a vast, all-encompassing insight, containing all possibilities and embracing not only the group but the whole world. We would all feel the presence of Spirit, a shared oneness that was palpably living and loving.

As soon as I got back to Edinburgh I started to attend the Quakers regularly. It was a nice group, with the additional interest that several professors from the university were core members. I fitted in immediately, and became part of their social circle, where I felt so much more at home than I had with the Presbyterians, good souls that they are. There was one interesting event that made a big impression on my mind. The Quakers had organized a discussion between two distinguished professors from the university, John MacDougall, a Quaker and a well-known psychologist, and Ritichie Calder, a noted humanist. I looked forward eagerly to this event, as I had read Professor MacDougall's books and enjoyed their benign, insightful content. The subject for the evening discussion had been something like "What is the nature and purpose of a human being?"—the sort of thing I was interested in at the time. I was, therefore, bitterly disappointed to learn, on arriving for the meeting, that Professor MacDougall had taken ill and that Professor Calder alone would speak.

Professor Calder was a dark, masculine man with an assertive delivery. Honest and direct, he expatiated at length on how human beings, given correct environments, would inevitably develop into perfected beings and would transform the earth, and that things like religion were absolutely non-essential to such development. These were the sorts of ideas that my mother and her sisters had espoused, and at that moment in space and time, remembering what my mother had gone through and intuiting the suffering of my Aunt Eileen in the clutches of Uncle Robert, I was not receptive to them. At the question and answer period, therefore, I tackled Professor Calder with unusual forcefulness. I cannot remember my exact words or even thoughts, but my main point was that our experience thus far of "humans in favorable environments" had not been too inspiring. What of Hitler, Stalin and the rest, not only arising from the most privileged societies in the world, but carrying along with them the vast majority of their people, wading through seas of human blood and showing not the slightest flicker of any of the qualities we normally think of as "human"? I was rather taken aback at my own vehemence and doggedness, not accepting any of the professor's pat replies.

I rather think Professor Calder was quite glad to get out of the Quakers' that evening, for by the time I was finished I had really given him a pasting. It seems likely that the last thing he would expect from the gentle Quakers was such a harangue as I had given him. Although I did not really regret what I had said, I felt abashed and remorseful at having behaved so aggressively at an event organized by my new friends. As soon as the professor left, I made a public apology for my behavior. However, I was totally taken aback by their reaction. They unanimously told me that they were proud of me, that I had said exactly what they were feeling, only much better than they could have. Their eyes were shining and there was a mood of elation at this "victory", which they had hoped for from Professor MacDougall.

This was something radically new. Up till then I had always been the butt of criticism for my forthright disquisitions, particularly with my Evangelical friends. But the Quakers were of a different stamp. Though personally gentle and sweet, they had strong convictions bred of their vibrant sense of the indwelling presence of God. Those convictions had brought them through the terrible persecutions they had suffered after their founding in the seventeenth century and through all of the principled stands and various humanitarian works they had so nobly undertaken over the centuries. I realized how fortunate I was to have met and been accepted by these wonderful people. On the other side of the coin, the encounter with Professor Calder had brought me a deep insight into yet another aspect of my mother's death: her lack of religious conviction had made her heart-rendingly vulnerable to the unrelenting waves of abandonment and betrayal she had been subject to. No matter what non-religious people may say about religion being the opiate of the masses, the truth is that religious conviction does give an edge in the life-and-death battles we all seem to be called to fight at some point or another in our life. I said a silent prayer of thanks for my ability to see and hold on to the spiritual experiences I had had, and for the nearly ten years of exposure to a life as full of spiritual intensity as my grandmother's.

An important friend I made at the Quakers was Harold, an English medical student. He was older than I, having been in some other field, engineering or straight science, but having decided that he wanted to serve people more directly—a resume that resonated with me! He had a quick mind and incisive delivery, molding himself consciously on the eighteenth century savant, Dr. Johnson, whose *bon mots* and epigrams I enjoyed hugely. When I was younger I had rather liked the works of my distant ancestor, Lord MacAulay, an English litterateur and later lawgiver of the early nineteenth century, with a highly piquant and polished way of conveying his rapid-fire thinking, and found it easy to relate to Harold and his Dr. Johnson. Harold and I would spend hours fencing intellectually, and thoroughly enjoying it.

Harold was sincere about his religious convictions, but was not really in tune with the meditative and inward ways of the Quakers. His contributions at meetings tended to have a rather argumentative edge to them, and after meeting he would be haranguing one or other of the sweet "elders" on points of dogma—which, of course, the Quakers didn't really have. One weekend he invited me to join him on retreat with some Catholic brothers outside Edinburgh. This was the first time I had even so much as spoken to Catholics, but I was agreeably surprised that the brothers turned out to be gentle, kindly souls, not in the least hitting me with dogma or threats of hell.

On the Sunday afternoon Harold and I went for a walk on the frosty grounds, during which he told me that he had decided to give up his studies and become a monk, a turn of events which gave me pause. Harold was really quite brilliant—why would he want to become a monk? As a died-in-the-wool Protestant, monastic life was for me a non-existent entity. The only exposure I had had to it was seeing some nuns at a pig farm I had once passed on a walk in Dumbarton. Pigs are rather unusual in Scotland and so are women dressed in long dark garments with huge white headdresses reminiscent of a goose taking off from the ground. I had wondered for a moment what on earth they were thinking, and that was the end of it.

I had absolutely no concept of monastic life, but I did have an exalted ideal of marriage, which I thought of as a meeting of souls to work together for the betterment of themselves and society. I had eschewed marriage, at least in principle (though of course I was naturally attracted to intelligent and good men); but had no notion of submitting myself to an external rule and discipline decided upon by a religious hierarchy. If I had given the subject any thought at all, I had thought of myself as a servant of humanity, following my own inner light and spiritual inspiration. Harold's enthusiasm was, therefore, a quite novel experience for me. I questioned him about it, but could not make anything of his replies. Finally he gave me a copy of *The Golden String,* the autobiography of Father Bede Griffiths, a student of C. S. Lewis who had converted to Catholicism, become a monk and gone to work in India, at first as a missionary but later as a student of the spirituality of that country. Father Bede was a persuasive writer and apologist for monastic life. He made it clear that monastic life is intended to deepen religious faith and spiritual experience, a concept which struck me very forcibly. There is a way of life designed to deepen spiritual experience! Would it be better than serving humanity as a medical doctor, as I had been envisioning thus far?

I was intrigued that Father Bede had opted to go to India, a move which resonated with my own increasing interest in Vedanta, the philosophy at the root of the indigenous religions of India; but at that time he had only just been there a short time and it was much later that I learned what he had discovered there. But the conjunction of the deep religious conviction and commitment to which he bore witness with the spiritual ideals I was rapidly making my own, had made a big impression on my mind. I tried to follow through on some of these ideas with the Quakers, but they, of course, were resolutely Protestant and notions of monasticism were quite foreign to them. I was also reading mystical works such as the *Life* of Saint Teresa of Avila, and searched the Quaker library for similar literature, to no effect. I realized that in some respects they were deficient: they were deeply sincere, truly devoted to the inner life, but were not metaphysically developed. I felt a little disappointed, but also realized that these were such outstanding people, such a blessed oasis in my life, that I nevertheless kept coming regularly and participating in weekly meeting.

I graduated in the summer of nineteen sixty-five. Mary came up to Edinburgh for the ceremony, which should have been a happy and exalted moment in my life. In many ways I had managed to surmount my father's obstructiveness; I had proved that I was not a hysterical incompetent; and I was poised to move forward under my own steam in a worthwhile profession, for which I had proven myself more than merely prepared. For whatever reason, however, I was very depressed. I was assailed with a terrible bout of self-denigration and lack of confidence and a dread of going out into the world after my six years in an academic cocoon in Edinburgh. Mary tried her best to lift my spirits, but to no avail. She left for England, shrugging her shoulders: would I never be satisfied? I myself was rather puzzled by it all, but had perhaps a glimmer of insight into the fact that the unrelenting materialism and reductionism of my education for the last ten years was in serious conflict with another, much deeper longing in my soul—that of transcending myself and living in the world of spirit, the inner sanctum which ultimately controls all else. I was not at all sure that my medical work was going to support that agenda and indeed feared that it was going to prove an insurmountable obstacle.

My passport for the United States, 1965.

But there was not much time to brood. I was off almost immediately for America. The previous summer many of my classmates had fanned out over the world to do summer jobs in exotic locations. Many had gone to our ex- and still-existent colonies, but a large number had hit America, and come home raving about it. So much freedom! Such marvels of technology! I had been intrigued by it all and had decided that I would head out right after graduation. Arriving to work at St. Mary's Hospital in Grand Rapids, Michigan, I was mightily surprised to find two or three of my female classmates ensconced there when I arrived. Unfortunately, my black and angry mood of the previous year had turned some of these women against me and they afforded me a far from pleasant welcome; but I decided that I was putting the past behind me once and for all, and directed my energies into the work and into attendance at the local Quakers. As ever, the Quakers were wonderful, and being American, utterly generous and hospitable. I spent most of my time off in their homes, either in the city or by the Lake, simply bowled over by the luxury they lived in—though no doubt by American standards they were living simply, as do all of the Quakers.

In addition to the openness and friendliness of the Quakers I was happy to find so much graciousness and *esprit de corps* in the workplace. The hospital was run by Catholic nuns, giving it a tone and way of doing things which, I realized later, was rather unusual. There was a lot of respect for the patients, the staff was cooperative and pleasant and my colleagues treated me with a degree of respect and equality that simply intoxicated me. It was possible to get the attention of my male superiors and to discuss things in a way I could not have dreamed of in Britain. I began to revise the stereotypes that had been drummed into my head about Americans: rude, inconsiderate, worldly. In addition, I found that Catholicism was not necessarily synonymous with ignorance and superstition as it was in Glasgow, but could express its very good points within a totally contemporary context.

I wound up this visit to America with quick trips to Philadelphia, New York and Washington, D.C., where most memorably I had my first (and so far, only) encounter with bed bugs. On one of my sessions on the Greyhound bus by which I was getting from place to place I met a young Native American man, who struck me as the most sincere, honest and loveable person I had met in my entire visit. He wanted me to come and visit his reservation, but I was on an organized student tour and could not take the time. However, mentally I took a rain check, intending one day to get to know the Native Americans, up till then a completely unknown factor in my life. I pressed on with my visits to the metropolises, which were brief, but gave me a taste of American big cities—a mixed experience, as I saw there urban blight such as I could not have imagined, even taking into account Glasgow as I had known it. Of the three cities New York was the one that most appealed to me. I was entranced by the galleries, the museums, the theaters, and decided that, if I returned to work in America, it would be in the Big Apple.

When I returned to London after my stay in Michigan, it seemed as though I had arrived in Lilliput, the land of the tiny. The people seemed like black ants scurrying about, the streets so narrow and the cars so ludicrously small! America certainly was much larger, conceived of in a more generous and expansive way, with huge resources that made its people more relaxed and self-confident than the British—or so it seemed to me at that time. The difference between an older and a younger nation, I suppose; in its earlier days Britain had certainly worked to find abundant resources—unfortunately at the cost of other nations—but now was elderly, bereft of its former glory and anxiously worrying about the future.

After my pleasant experience in Michigan the thought was beginning to form in my mind that perhaps I might look for a second internship in America rather than in Britain. In order to register as a fully qualified medical doctor we had to complete a year's internship, six months in internal medicine and six months in a surgical specialty, and at that time work in America was accepted toward this requirement. I was lined up for six months as a medical intern in Edinburgh, but the surgical stint was not yet arranged. For the moment I put the issue aside, deciding to see how the first internship went before reaching a final decision.

The Royal Infirmary of Edinburgh—the next hospital I worked in, starting in October—was a venerable, gray granite pile rambling over a large area, with many a turret and tower rising up and proclaiming its glory. It was next door to the medical school, and I had walked past it innumerable times as well as gone there for classes and clinical training. It was originally founded in seventeen twenty-nine to care for the sick poor; but, supported by the citizens, had rapidly evolved, grown and moved two or three times until coming to rest in its then location in the eighteen-seventies. As Edinburgh medical school attained world-class status the Infirmary, as its flagship hospital, had acquired tremendous prestige, and visiting professors and clinicians from all over the world haunted its corridors and wards. All this produced a vibrant intellectual atmosphere, but it was an institution over two hundred years old and tradition ruled it with a heavy hand. Interns were two a penny, disposable and required to be on duty every alternate night—a grueling schedule, made bearable only by the professionalism of the nursing staff, who were capable of dealing with many of the crises—but not all!—which arose in the wee hours. Thus the interns got a little more rest than the system might otherwise have allowed. It was notorious that interns got sick and some were not even able to complete their tour of duty, a situation which to me seemed intolerable. However, whenever I would bring this up to senior doctors, they would only say, "Well, *we* went through it—why not you?" I found this an entirely unsatisfactory reply, particularly as I was aware that at least three of my patients had died because I was so utterly exhausted that I could not think straight at crucial moments. One of them had been a man with three young children, a fact which weighs on my conscience even now. I was just too exhausted, I simply could not think at the moment of his desperate emergency. I felt a system that supported something like that just wasn't good enough.

I loved the work and I adored my patients—so good, so long-suffering and so grateful for whatever we did for them. I received so many gifts I was almost embarrassed, but of course I also reveled in the love, which is what my work was all about as far as I was concerned. At the same time I had to run the gauntlet of the entrenched hierarchy, which got away with things I felt were really not acceptable. One day one of my immediate seniors, annoyed at my persistent questioning of something rather substandard he was doing, said to me, "Run along, dear, and do your knitting." This attitude was more or less entrenched, though the older men were too polite to say it out loud.

But my real nemesis was the registered nurse in charge of the ward I was working on for the first three months. We referred to such women as Sister, probably a throwback to the days when nuns ran hospitals. Sister was another of those women who had not married on account of World War I, and one who had chosen to become embittered. She had had ambitions to be a doctor, but in her youth that had been difficult for women to accomplish. She had therefore settled for nursing and a career of tormenting interns, for which she was famous. As she had reduced my immediate predecessor to tuberculosis, I wondered what my fate might be. It was notorious that women doctors were her favorite food, but I made up my mind that I would be as professional as I could with her and try to extend to her more signs of respect and dignity than perhaps otherwise. Just how successful my efforts were may be gathered from an episode toward the end of my tour of duty with her. Every day the intern went through the ritual of having mid-morning coffee in her office, a nice touch if both parties were in rapport, but also affording opportunities for outbursts such as she proffered me: "Dr. MacPhail, I hated you the minute I saw you; I hate you now—and I will always hate you!" I had no idea what had triggered this offering, but I did know that all I could do was say, in true British fashion; "The weather has not been good lately—but I gather it will improve at the weekend!" and get out as quickly as possible. I felt for the poor woman, so bitter and so lonely, but of course there was nothing I could do. I had committed the sin of being a woman doctor and there was no expiation for it. However, the other nurses on our team more than compensated for Sister. Much younger, without her disillusionment, they were a jolly and highly professional lot.

They understood perfectly what Sister was trying to do to me and went out of their way to be friendly and supportive, which I deeply admired and appreciated, in addition to their wonderful, reliable work.

The whole situation with Sister came to a head one day on formal ward rounds. This was a grand ritual we carried out for the benefit of visiting professors and students, an educational spectacle which took an unexpected turn that day. Our guests were from Scandinavia, all thirty of them, and we were all on our best behavior and performance. At one point an issue came up about the nursing care of one patient with a chronic condition. Sister was queried, as also her assistant. They gave various answers, but none were acceptable to the doctor in charge. He wanted to hear something more original, more innovative. Watching from the outside, I could see an obvious solution, which I ventured when it looked like the nurses could go no further. No sooner had I said it than Sister turned on me, right at the end of the patient's bed, right in front of our august gaggle of guests, and said, glaring at me over her half-glasses: "Doctor MacPhail! We have been doing things this way for two hundred years—and if you think we are going to change now for a wee whippersnapper like you, you can think again!"

From one standpoint this was comical, but from another it was just the final touch to an impression that had been growing steadily since I got back from America: Britain was too old, too formal, too stick-in-the-mud, too rigid altogether. Young people were seen and not heard, were taken for granted and dealt with on the principle: use it once and throw it away. I went to the Medical Library and started to look for hospitals in America where I might do the second half of my internship. This decision gave me a fresh burst of energy—there is nothing like the idea of getting out of a trap for bucking you up!

At the end of the first three months of our tour of duty, the interns rotated, one leaving behind the Dragon Sister and her ward of women and the other engaging with her for the next three months. I was the lucky one, moving on to Sister McMurtry and her ward of men. Sister McMurtry could not have been more different from the other sister if she had tried. A soft-spoken Irishwoman, she was a devout Christian, looking on her work as serving Christ himself. As she was deeply understanding of my ideals and also of the struggles I was going through, our morning coffee breaks in her office were moments of happiness and togetherness, so unlike the torture chamber of the other, deprived sister.

Working with male patients instead of women turned out to be much less interesting professionally, as practically fifty percent were suffering from the same disease—heart attacks—while the women had presented a much wider range of problems. However, halfway through the three months I realized that this otherwise uniform group was pointing up something very important. I observed that the ultimate outcome of their illnesses seemed to depend more on their mental attitude than on anything else. Men with minor heart attacks, if they worried and bucked the system, would go on to complications and even death, while men with massive cardiac damage who let themselves flow into events, would recover and leave in remarkably good condition. The other big factor was motivation: men with loving families and children would quite visibly brace themselves to tackle the situation and would, more often than not, pull through.

Another episode, highly amusing and in some ways illustrative of how attitude plays such an important role in how sickness works itself out, was in connection with an Italian restaurateur who was admitted one evening when I was off duty. He had come to the emergency room with hives all over his body and the diagnosis of a severe, acute allergy had been made. Right before the eyes of the emergency room staff he had progressed to the feared and deadly next stage: respiratory arrest. They had resuscitated him and admitted him to our ward for observation and diagnostic tests. I picked up his chart the next morning, familiarized myself with his story, and went in to see him. He was a quintessential Italian—excitable, voluble—and not about to have anything to do with a woman doctor! He answered my few questions, but when I proposed to examine him he vehemently protested and refused to permit me to proceed. I did not force the issue, but went to my office to write on his chart that he refused to cooperate. As the tests had all been lined up the night before and I more or less had little further responsibility for him, I put him out of my mind and went on with other, more pressing issues.

As I was sitting in my office doing paperwork the head nurse came in and said, "Dr. MacPhail, that Italian man is signing himself out. He says he will not tolerate a woman doctor!"

"He can't sign himself out—he has a dire allergy that could kill him, and it isn't safe for him to leave until we find out what is causing it."

"Well, he is determined. He is getting dressed and ready to leave as we speak."

"What an idiot! Why do these people have such ridiculous prejudices?

"Doctor MacPhail, you will have to speak with him! He is utterly determined!"

I got up, very annoyed. There were several really sick people on our ward and their needs were urgent. Why did this silly fellow have to burn up my time like this? I decided to deal with him very firmly. When I got to his room the curtains were pulled round his bed, as he was getting dressed and ready to go. I pulled them back briskly, all ready for the confrontation, and saw him pulling on the pants of a lurid brown striped suit, the likes of which no self-respecting Scot would ever wear. I also saw that his back, which was still bare, was breaking out in huge allergic hives, and realized that it was the pants that were causing the reaction. This was a man who had nearly died the night before from his allergic reaction and I realized that those pants had to come off immediately. There was no time for discussion or delay: he might stop breathing at any moment, and I had to get the pants off him myself, no matter what it took to do so!

Without a word I lunged at his pants and started ripping them off. He was much bigger than I, but I had the advantage of surprise and had him on the floor immediately. He started to scream, "Rape! Rape! Help! Murder!" as I wrastled his pants off determinedly. All of the ambulatory patients and the nurses rushed to the room to see what was going on and stood watching in amazement. Soon the head nurse, my jolly friend, arrived. She was more intelligent than the others and understood what was going on. She started to laugh hysterically, a response which was by that time appropriate, as I had succeeded in my quest: The pants were off and the hives were now going down. Then the others—including myself—started to laugh, too. What with his screaming and the staff laughing, it was quite an uproar, and more and more people started to arrive, including hospital administrators.

It took quite a while to explain the whole situation. There was some question as to my sanity, but when I got across what I had observed and why I was doing what I was doing, everyone smiled and went away, satisfied. Later I learned that tests conclusively demonstrated that he was highly allergic to chemicals left on his suit by the drycleaners, where it had just been processed. I don't remember the immediate reaction of the Italian man, but I do remember some months later when I went into his restaurant with a friend for a coffee. I did not know it was his restaurant, but when I went to pay at the counter, we recognized each other and he launched out into a long emotional outburst in Italian. Then, he spoke in English: "Please wait here—I want to bring my family to see the person who saved my life!" He brought them in from the back and introduced them, one by one. They all stood looking at me as though I was a goddess, much to my amusement (though I did not show it outwardly). He bowed down to my feet and started to cry, thanking me over and over for saving his life. My only reaction was relief that he had understood what had happened and was therefore more likely not to repeat his mistake and endanger his life again.

Returning to the insight that attitude plays an important role in the unfolding of a sickness, I went a bit further with my observations. One of my jobs was to write the discharge letter to the patients' family doctors, in our system the linchpins that held the whole thing together. I took these letters very seriously, knowing that these doctors would be responsible for the patients' ongoing care, and therefore included as much information as would be necessary to ensure the best results. I was routinely given a copy of each of the letters, which I preserved and later analyzed systematically to test my impression about the role of mental attitude in determining the outcome in cases of heart attack. I found that I had indeed been right and made a mental note: Perhaps it might be more effective to work with the patients' attitude to prevent the attacks, rather than with caring for people's bodies after the damage is done? If attitude makes such a difference, no doubt it has a lot to do with creating sickness in the first place. The question was: What would be the most effective form of intervention? This line of thought was to have significant consequences on the rest of my life.

I had one important epiphany during my internship, an indication of the direction I was heading in, and this time informed by intellect, which had not been the case in my previous experiences. It took place one January morning when I was off duty. I headed out to the Botanical Gardens, of which I had become very fond. It was quiet, open and beautiful at all times of year, and I had made rather a habit of going there when I needed to think. A hoar frost was sparkling in the winter sun and enchanting everything, lifting my spirits considerably. My more relaxed mind was able to discern that I had doubts about what I was doing, not fully articulated as yet, but nevertheless grumbling away in the basement; but I had neither the energy nor the inclination to look at them closely—rather uncharacteristic of me, but no doubt due to the exhaustion I lived in perpetually.

After walking for a while I realized that the sun was picking up a bit of heat, and decided to sit down on one of the garden seats situated directly in its path. I had brought along *Thus Spake Zarathustra* by Friedrich Nietzsche in the vague idea that I might just be able to read a page or two. I pulled it out of the pocket of my sheepskin jacket and began. Almost immediately I was caught up in a whirlwind of thought such as I had never encountered previously, imperious, forceful and irresistible. About three hours later I looked up and realized that my feet and hands were blocks of ice, that it was lunchtime and that I had just gone through an initiation, though at the time I was not really familiar with that word. I have no idea what others have made of this book, but for me it was an opening out into a world much more real and meaningful than anything I had encountered thus far, at least in Western literature. As I read it, it was a statement of the higher human faculties, of the imperative to transcend the lower and attain the higher and thus become supermen and women. I did not feel in the least threatened by the idea of superman, perhaps because I was so saturated in the ideas of the Gita, where the qualities of superconscious human beings are discussed again and again. Reading the Gita had aroused my interest in such beings, but perhaps had been rather "Oriental" and thus remote. However, *Thus Spake*, written by a Westerner and in such ringing and assertive terms, made me feel that attaining such a state was not an exception, but rather a rule, if we only understood things correctly. The whole idea of self-transcendence suddenly became a reality, something that I might try for myself, something I might look for in the world I was living in, flatfooted, unimaginative and pragmatic as it might be.

I felt tremendously energized and awakened, as if the direction I was to follow had been pointed out to me directly, and that it would be the only thing worth doing, when all is said and done. In a dim way it connected up with the plans I was forming to work in America, where I already knew things were so much more expansive, open and likely to give me the opportunities I needed to find out who I really was. I was determined to put behind me completely all of the darkness and pain I had suffered up till then, and felt that moving to another space was where I could do it best. Thus the stage was being set, as it had twenty years before when I moved to Glasgow after my mother's death. There was as yet no "Grannie" to guide me on my way in this new venture, but I intuitively felt that the energy of my project would somehow provide whatever it was I needed.

SECOND QUARTER

CLEAR RESPONSE

CHAPTER 12

MAKING A BREAK FOR FREEDOM
1966-1967

When I finished my internship at the Royal there were three months until I left for America, where I had organized my second internship. I took what we call a locum (a temporary job filling in an empty slot) in obstetrics at a hospital in the southeast of England. Delivering babies was not one of my primary interests, though I had acquired some proficiency during the compulsory stint I had done as a student; I took the job because it was near London and Clipsham, where I could visit with family and friends.

I worked at first with a Dr. Cox, a Christian missionary home on leave and also doing a locum. He was really wonderful—kind, friendly and interested in helping me learn the ropes of obstetrics. When he left and was replaced by an American, I felt the difference. The American was friendly and professional, but did not have the thoughtfulness and consideration of Dr. Cox. I took note, concluding that serious religious commitment really does add a different dimension to the way one approaches relationships with other people and to the quality of work.

The other side of the coin, perhaps, was a relationship I had with an Indian lady doctor who was also working on the obstetrics unit, as far as I remember the only Indian on the staff. I had no occasion to interact directly with her professionally, but I did notice in the doctors' dining room that she always sat alone and looked very miserable. I was usually eating with the doctors I was working with, and would have liked to ask her to join us, but her demeanor was distant and standoffish. One day, however, I came into the dining room alone and saw her sitting, as usual, by herself. Picking up my meal, I went to her table and asked her if I might join her. She said yes, but she seemed uncomfortable and rather put out. However, I sat down and tried to engage her in light, friendly conversation. She answered curtly, almost rudely, making me feel that I was intruding on her in an almost intolerable way. I was completely baffled, for the Indians I had met thus far had been very friendly and, of course, I was deeply interested in their spiritual culture. But this didn't seem to matter to Dr. Gupta, who apparently felt that we British were simply unbearable.

I did find out more about her from the nursing staff. One day I received a call from the staff nurse of the other obstetrics unit from my own. She asked me if I would write up some medications for the patients. This was Dr. Gupta's ward, as I pointed out to the nurse, and not my jurisdiction. The nurse asked me to come over anyway and, when I got there, told me that it was all but impossible to work with the Indian doctor. I asked, "Is her English not good?" "No, her English is fine." "Then what is the problem—is she incompetent?" "I think she may be competent, but the problem is she will not listen to what anyone tells her. She seems to think she knows everything and starts screaming if we try to suggest anything. It is as if she hates us, or something." This was the first time I encountered such behavior, but it was most assuredly not going to be the last; indeed, this would be a model for a large segment of my experience as an adult. I agreed to help the nurses out as and when I could, but also suggested that they report the situation to see if Dr. Gupta could get help; dysfunctional professional relationships could do nothing but hurt the patients, who to me were sacred.

I found a little park near the hospital I was working in, where several magnificent horse chestnut trees were in bloom, and made a point of spending as much of my off duty time there as possible. I would sit or lie "under the spreading chestnut tree", glorying in the canopy of huge, hand-like leaves and the candles of bloom, white, pink and red. The weather was delightfully warm and sunny and I felt myself relaxing as I had never done before. I would find phrases from *Thus Spake Zarathustra* coming to my mind, lofting me up into a growing sense of self-confidence and purpose. I would discover who I was, what the purpose of my life was, what I was born to do! Zarathustra had injected into my understanding of the Gita a zeal, an immediacy, a sense of intense purpose, which I felt bubbling up irrepressibly, and which I was sure was going to take me exactly where I needed to be.

The locum job was an auspicious and pleasant transition into my next big venture: working in America. I really needed more space, more freedom, more opportunity than I was finding in my native country; and negatively, one part of me wanted to put as much space between myself and the pain of all that had happened in the previous twenty years. By the time I made up my mind, the available jobs in America were narrowed down, but I did find five openings in hospitals affiliated with medical schools, though not the Ivy League ones, which had been snapped up long ago. I finally opted for the Jewish Hospital of Brooklyn (which we would refer to as "the Jewish"), a teaching hospital affiliated with Downstate Medical School in New York. I knew nothing about it other than what I saw on the listing of hospitals, but what attracted me was its address—555 Prospect Place, Brooklyn—which resonated with one of my enduring passions as a child: the series of *Little Women* stories, written in the mid-nineteenth century by Louisa May Alcott. The stories about the four March girls and their development over time had utterly engaged me as a young girl, and somehow in the narrative I had picked up on Prospect Park in Brooklyn, though the girls' home was in Massachusetts. I realize now that what had attracted me was the worldview of Louisa Alcott, the daughter of the Transcendentalist Bronson Alcott, like Emerson informed by the Indian scriptures and striving to live a more consciously spiritual life than was the norm at the beginning of the nineteenth century. That quality had permeated the books and imbued even the name of Prospect Park in Brooklyn with magic.

However, the minute I got off the plane I encountered a much less inviting reality: It was impossible to get a taxi to where I wanted to go in Brooklyn. The cabbies simply said, "Bedford Stuyvesant! You have to be joking!" and drove off, leaving me in the dust. I realized that Prospect Place was not perhaps quite so magical as I had envisioned! It was late at night, and I was tired, apprehensive and hungry. After being rebuffed by several cabbies—and wondering what sort of professional standards they had in America—I finally started to cry when I got perhaps my fifth refusal. The cabbie was Polish American, basically a nice Joe, and he relented. "Get in", he said, "I'll take you there. But the minute you get out of the taxi I am locking it and hightailing it out of there!" On the way over he explained to me that Bedford Stuyvesant was one of the most dangerous areas of New York, that I was crazy to think of working there, and on and on and on.

The lady who received me at the hospital was very welcoming and friendly, however, and I finally got to bed, feeling a tad better than I had for the previous couple of hours. But I was in for quite a baptism of fire nevertheless, for within a couple of days I was dispatched to Greenpoint

Hospital, an affiliate of Downstate Medical School and a non-private facility that cared for the indigent of that rough section of Brooklyn. My first problem was that New York was in the grip of a heat wave, with temperatures as high as one hundred and eight degrees, and no air conditioning at all. For a girl from the north that was quite an ordeal, compounded by the fact that I was on call for the July fourth weekend. I knew nothing of American methods or protocols, and even less about how to deal with cases of heat stroke, which were arriving one after the other. The nursing staff was not inclined to be cooperative on the whole, but fortunately they knew how to deal with cases of heatstroke, and so we were busy all night plunging patients into tubs of ice, where they remained until their temperatures came down. This was perhaps the first time I had seen ice in any setting other than icicles hanging from the eaves of our house in Clipsham! In America, ice is an all-pervading part of everyday life, but thus far I had had nothing to do with it, other than as a phenomenon of nature. As someone said on learning I was from Britain, "Oh yes! The land of warm beer!"

I got through the first ordeal of coping with the heat wave, no doubt on the strength of my basically tough physical stamina and rather determined will. But there were other factors working against me, not the least of which was the terrible lack of professionalism of the nursing staff. I was appalled to discover that cases of severe acute infection had not been given their antibiotics, or diabetics in coma their insulin. My Pakistani resident told me, "Dr. MacPhail, if it is something important, you have to do it yourself." I was used to the highly professional staff I had worked with in Britain, and simply could not believe what the doctor was saying. But finding maggots in a varicose ulcer that had not been dressed for days, and also being present when an old, infirm lady was hit over the head with a metal bed pan, I realized that the standards of nursing care I was dealing with were quite other than anything I could imagine.

I also had no inkling of the attitudes that underlay such gross neglect. Thinking that the staff was motivated, I took them to task for these derelictions of duty, only to be met with blank faces and no indication that anything would change. I slowly began to realize that I was dealing with people who had no self-respect, no motivation to serve, no concern about professionalism and, underneath all, a seething resentment and anger. I was utterly baffled by this to me completely new phenomenon. Some light was thrown on the matter on a few evenings when I was alone at the nurses' station with a younger man, some sort of a temporary worker, I think.

He was, like the rest of the nursing staff, African American, but unlike them he was quite articulate and communicative. He wore some kind of turban, and was perhaps a Muslim. I told him a little of my difficulties and he managed to communicate to me some of the rage and alienation the African Americans were feeling. "I can empathize with that", I said, "But I don't understand why they are taking it out on the patients, most of whom are African Americans like themselves. That doesn't help anyone. And, besides, if they want to be taken more seriously, developing a more professional attitude is the way to go. If they perform well, they will be more readily accepted." He understood what I was saying, but made it clear to me that it was impossible for most of these people to think that way. He himself was a competent and sensitive worker, and perhaps realized what was necessary to change the situation, but, like the rest of us, found it just too overwhelming to deal with.

The idea of reporting all of this to the hospital administration never crossed my mind. I was just too used to staff who could auto-correct when any deficiency was pointed out to them. I may have thought that because I was European, the nurses perhaps were not used to my accent and way of doing things, and would soon come round. However, one day I was to be rudely disabused of that line of thought. The hospital administrator, an extremely nice man whom I knew slightly, came down to the floor and asked to speak with me. His usually friendly face was quite troubled and it was obvious he was not comfortable. He began by saying how much my work was appreciated, that everyone was impressed by my professional integrity, etc. etc. I wondered where this might be going, but did not have to wonder long. It turned out that the nurses had reported *me*, stating that it was impossible to work with me, I was so demanding!

Again, this was something so far from any experience I had ever had, I was at a loss for words. I was simply blown away at the inability to adjust and bear with circumstances that all this represented, and for a few minutes just stared at the administrator, looking at me expectantly and also rather encouragingly. It was obvious that he wanted this to go away, but was compelled to go through with it. Then I realized that this was the way things are dealt with in America: don't try to adjust—report! I also realized that this was my opportunity to let off steam about the appallingly substandard work that was being done. I felt for the sufferings of the African Americans, but the work was more important than any of us. I said, "I am glad you have brought this up. It had not occurred to me to report this to the higher authorities, but perhaps it is good that this has happened." Then I told him about the many episodes of dereliction of duty that had occurred in the only three weeks I had been there. As I rattled on, the doctor's face relaxed and he began to smile. I felt that all of this was already known to him, that perhaps, because he had not previously had a sufficiently clear statement with which to work, he could do nothing about it and that my uncompromising statements were providing him with much needed information.

When I finished, he shook my hand and said, "Dr. MacPhail, thank you for telling me all of this. I felt sure that you were not to blame for this problem, and what you have told me has made the whole situation crystal clear." He apologized for having brought up the subject, dwelling on the fact that it was his duty to respond to complaints, etc. etc. For me, this was all in a day's work and I moved on. But the administration took it seriously and, a few days before I was due to finish my month's rotation at the hospital, a meeting of the entire nursing staff was called in order to assess the work at the hospital. I was not invited to attend, but I understand that a radical discussion took place, and new guidelines for nursing standards were introduced. Apparently, this led to some improvement for some time; but ultimately the situation proved too difficult and a year or so later the Greenpoint Hospital was permanently closed down.

This was my introduction to the practice of medicine in America, starting, you might say, at the lowest rung on the ladder. The stonewalling, prevarication, and general ill-feeling that I encountered from the nursing staff was almost as bad as the more-or-less universal looking in the other direction, the pretense that all was well and basic impotence of the authorities to make any difference. I realized that there was a hideous problem caused by racial discrimination in America, how it was paralyzing cooperation with the white authorities, simply making the plight of the African Americans worse and compromising their hopes of coming up in the world. But I could not understand why everyone, including even the colored doctors from Pakistan and other Asian countries, opted to avoid any direct solutions to the problem, working round the incompetence of the nurses rather than trying to help them improve. Maybe they had some degree of fear, which I myself had felt to some extent on hearing the incessant drumming going on in the streets during those long, hot nights. It had reminded me of the British movies and the line, "The natives are restless tonight!" I had not felt inclined to go out at all, taking into consideration the drumming and also the heat and the dirty streets, overshadowed by the El, the elevated train tracks which threw the homes and streets into perpetual darkness and of course, tremendous, continuous noise. But threat or no threat, from where I am now I rather think that my radical innocence of the problem made it possible for me to speak up as if we were dealing with something simple, and that my testimony was perhaps the first time the authorities had had anything substantial to work with.

Under the circumstances, the decision of the authorities to go ahead with a general meeting was most commendable. This was the other side of the coin, American practicality and can-doism, which I admired intensely. Outside of the problems with the African Americans, I found my coworkers wonderfully open, willing to listen and to implement change when necessary. Unlike the residents and senior staff in Edinburgh, who basically left me rather callously to my own devices, the residents and senior doctors in America were definitely a team, and always ready to consult and help me out. Although a woman, I was taken seriously as a medical professional and what I had to say was given the same weight as the statements of anyone else.

Having completed my one-month's rotation at Greenpoint, an obligation all of the interns and residents had to fulfill, I returned to the parent hospital on Prospect Place. There I encountered a quite different mix among the staff, which threw a lot of light on the difficulties I had had at the public facility in Greenpoint. The senior doctors, whom we referred to as "attendings" were all Jewish Americans, as were most of the staff nurses, while the junior doctors were a mix of Jewish and Philippino, with a handful of Asians and Europeans and one or two African Americans. Apart from the staff nurses, the nursing staff was a mix of Philippina, West Indian and African Americans. The Jewish staff was highly trained and very professional, the nurses almost formidable in their toughness, seeing to it that the goods were delivered, no matter what the grumblings from the "underlings". What was most instructive to me was my relationship with the West Indian and African American nurses. The West Indians, all of African origin, were as I had found them in Britain: friendly, competent and a whole lot of fun. They seemed to like me because I was British and indeed would make rather a pet out of me.

But the story with the African Americans was quite different. Although more subdued than at Greenpoint (no doubt on account of the bloody-minded Jewish staff nurses), there was the same sullen, angry and non-cooperative attitude, which stood out all the more starkly in comparison with the attitude of the rest of the nursing staff. It was crystal clear to me that their problem stemmed from their long history of slavery, the stigma of which had relegated them to an abusively low station in American life, which the Philippinos and West Indians, also "people of color" in official American parlance, had not had to endure, at least to the same extent. I felt for the African Americans and would from time to time have flashbacks to some of the really aggressive Irish people I had met on buses in Glasgow (for we did not associate with them socially at all): belligerent, as often as not drunk, and with an irremovable chip on their shoulders. The Irish, too, had had a long, dismal history of enslavement—in their case by the English—of social abasement and of course, educational backwardness, thanks to the Catholic Church. I had been puzzled by them, inclined to empathy—but of course I had not had to try to work with them!

I vividly realized what the long-term results of slavery are, and would never ever agree with a number of Americans who would try to tell me that people of African origin are radically inferior. From my visits to the Sudan and from friendship with my classmates at medical school I already knew several Africans of the finest character and professional competence—and, moreover, how to explain the difference between the African American and the West Indian nurses?

All this was one layer of my experience that year. Another was the Jewishness of the hospital I was working in. The Jewish presence there was so overwhelming that my colleagues had no inhibitions whatsoever about expressing themselves from a totally Jewish perspective on the issues of the day. I learned how much influence Jewish lobbyists were having on the American government, and marveled that America would permit itself to be so governed by the interests of only one section of its population. There were also strong Zionist feelings, which boiled over into almost hysterical jubilation during and after the Six Day War when, in a struggle for land and water against the combined forces of a number of Arab states, the Israelis won and took over strategic territory from them. I realized how heady all this must be to a people so long under subjection, but wondered just where it would all lead. The Palestinians had been living in Israel for two thousand years—what about *their* interests? At the same time, I remembered the awful images I had seen in a movie entitled *Mein Kampf*, which showed footage shot in the Nazi death camps and had caused even the stoic and dour Scottish audience to cry out loud.

The whole thing was so extreme, so utterly unimaginable, that I really could not make any sense of it.

I was invited to a seder—the Jewish Passover feast—which greatly impressed me. I enjoyed the deep commitment to family and tradition that the Jewish people cherished and realized how it had held them together through all the vicissitudes and struggles they had had to go through in their long history. At the same time I occasionally ran into Jewish fundamentalism, such as being requested at a party not to touch a bottle of kosher wine or its owner could not drink its contents, which would be polluted by the touch of a non-Jew. This was the first time I had encountered anything of the sort, and was absolutely stunned. I had thought things like that had gone, along with all else medieval; but no—here it was, in young, progressive America. Before I knew what I was saying, I blurted out, "Now I understand why the Jews are not liked!"

This was a party of my Jewish friends, who all fell silent and turned to look at me. It was an excruciating moment, brought about by my tactlessness. But I could not recant. I simply said, "If you tell people they are contaminating you, how can you expect them to like you?" Most of those present were liberal and fond of me. No doubt they disliked the fundamentalism of the chap who had made the remark and certainly they knew what it feels like to be told you are contaminating someone by simply being who you are. One by one they started to laugh and some chided the silly fellow, assuring me that they did not share his views. I only experienced this one episode, but it caused me a terrible shock of separation, of being inferior in a radical way that I could do nothing about, a sort of condemnation to a non-negotiable hell. If I had had to live with such an attitude over a long period of time, who knows how I would have reacted? This question, I am sad to say, was to be answered in a big way later in my life.

Most of my colleagues were liberal or secular Jews, who did not harbor such thoughts of superiority (or its pair, inferiority), and therefore I had no difficulty at all in enjoying their company and learning from them about their beliefs and culture. I rather relished their jolly approach to things, their wonderful sense of humor and their commitment to their tradition and families, all of which reminded me quite a lot of my days in Glasgow. Perhaps one small example of the general tone occurred one day when I was on ward rounds with my colleagues, Dr. Wissmer from Switzerland, Dr. Gnauck from Germany, and Dr. de Bella, an Italian-American, all of whom were blond and blue-eyed. Of the group, I was the darkest, with my reddish brown hair and sea-blue eyes. Dr. Lionel Deutsch, one of our young Jewish attendings, happened to come on the floor and, seeing us all together, clasped his head and cried, "O, my God! I can't stand it! All of these beautiful, blond Aryans, all in one place!"

Adjustment to ethnic and cultural difference was definitely one of the major themes of my year in Brooklyn, and perhaps it was most concentrated in my relationship with Dr. Saraswati Ganapathy, an Indian intern in pediatrics. We met outside an elevator a week or so after I got back to the Jewish from Greenpoint. She asked me a question and, on hearing my reply, burst out: "You speak actual English! What a relief! I am worn out trying to understand these Americans!" I was a bit taken aback, but Cookie (her pet name, by which we always called her) was so charming and so friendly that I was immediately drawn into her world, which I was to share with her very closely for the remainder of the year.

Cookie had been sent for her education to Christian nuns, who spoke only English, and had imbibed from them an attitude more British than the British. I realized this from an early exchange with her. I was talking about my schedule on a certain rotation, pronouncing the word as *skedule*, like an American. Cookie cried, "O no! Jean—you are letting the side down! The word is *shedule*, as they say it in Britain!" I was amazed to hear her say it and replied, "Cookie, I don't have sides! You are working with newborn babies and don't have to communicate through language, but I am working with adults, and absolutely must be able to communicate with the natives! No one will understand me if I say *shedule*."

This was the first time I had met an Indian who so totally identified with British culture, no doubt on account of the painful experiences with the caste system she had gone through as a child and young girl. Her English was flawless and cultured and she herself was a bottomless pit of Western culture—especially American, about which I knew nothing. She took an apartment in Greenwich Village and plunged herself and me along with her into the Village scene. We danced all night at the Fillmore East. We went to parties thrown by WBAI, the egghead and counterculture radio station, where we hung out with the Fugs, a rock group, Alan Ginsberg and Co., and other assorted celebrities. By that time I was totally into interpretive dancing and after one of my "performances" was offered a job interpreting through dance the music of a young composer who combined electronic sounds with matching colors projected on the walls of the discotheque. I was fascinated by the project, which was to affect my own thinking and work in a big way nearly thirty years later; but at that time, an intern on duty every second or third night, I simply did not have the time or energy to get involved in such demanding extracurricular work.

Cookie's life and mine were different in many ways; in a sense, she was the Western one and I the Indian. I liked to be quiet, reading or walking in Prospect Park (which *did* materialize!) or reveling in the Botanical Gardens, where I was entranced by the Japanese garden, the forsythia bloom in winter, and the sixty varieties of magnolia in the spring. Of the two of us I was the introvert, deeply interested in religion; and she was the extravert, without any real religious identity.

A small incident of the period throws light on where we both stood. I was at her Village pad one morning, reading the *Village Voice*. I noticed an invitation from the Hare Krishnas, who were just getting started in America, to join them in tea and chanting the name of the Lord. I had of course no idea who these people were, but the idea of chanting the name of Krishna appealed to me, for by this time I was totally devoted to the Gita and to Krishna, its central figure. I said to Cookie, "Look, these Indian people chant Krishna's name and are inviting us to their place, which is just near where we are in Brooklyn. Why don't we go and see what it is like?" Cookie's reply was extremely revealing: "How blasphemous! How can you associate with these ignorant people?" In a couple of sentences she revealed her lack of religious interest and also her aversion to her Hindu heritage.

Cookie and I were similar in that we had moved away from our birth cultures and were trying to identify with its opposite: she with the British and I with the Indian. I think that neither of us really belonged where we were born: I never really felt comfortable in mainstream British culture, being too "mystical" and fey, and she was altogether much too healthily self-assertive and proactive to ever identify with the more or less usual passivity and otherworldliness of Hinduism. Perhaps as a symbol of all of this, we got into the habit of wearing each other's clothes when we went out partying together: she was in my rather smashing little black dress which I had found in London, and I was in one of her gorgeous saris, with dangly earrings, a sort of tiara in my hair, and whatnot. We must have looked a sight! Anyway, we enjoyed it all and each other and she has remained a friend right up to the present, though her living in India has created barriers to us seeing very much of each other.

A final note about my cross-cultural explorations: One of the residents, Dr. Lustig, introduced me to the writing of the Irish author James Joyce, who was steeped in Indian thought, having learned Sanskrit in order to read the Indian texts in the original. His *Ulysses* was loaded with quotations from the Indian texts, as also of the Scandinavian sacred literature and others besides. This book was so utterly different from anything I had ever read—it was all but devoid of Judeo-Christian preoccupations (for me a refreshing experience) and it addressed issues of self-identity, of the possibility of attaining to higher levels of consciousness, which I had picked up in *Zarathustra*, but in a less subtle form. The world of *Ulysses* was peopled with beings of different levels of understanding and being—some of them rather scandalous for an ex-Sunday School teacher—but what I took away from it was the idea that the supreme question of a work of art is: from what kind of life does it spring? This resonated with me intensely, an echo of something I had heard Naum Gabo, the great sculptor, say when I was still in Glasgow: The best medium for a work of art is a human life. I loved the idea that one could live in such a way that one's life was a thing of beauty, something that conveyed the Real in and through the actions of every day, and thus inspired and encouraged others. I had seen it in my Grandmother's life, in Mrs. Browne, even in Mary, with all of her politics and strong talk. Their lives had really shown that human beings can be unselfish, loving and intensely supportive, giving others hope and the inspiration to "go and do likewise".

The year at the Brooklyn Jewish was, in so many ways, a whole new perspective on life, giving me a sense of my own worth, of my capability as a doctor, of my loveableness, all of which I had almost constantly doubted in my years at Edinburgh. I enjoyed the multicultural milieu I was living in and threw myself with gusto into all of the variegated experiences that came my way. I felt intensely the openness of America, the freedom to be oneself and to grow and be supported, provided one was honest, proactive and hardworking. The limitations I had felt as a woman in Scotland just did not seem to exist in this new environment: I turned in a good day's work and was appreciated and rewarded for it, which I cannot say I had felt was for the most part the case in Edinburgh.

Another cross-cultural take on this situation came from one of the surgical residents with whom I worked for a couple of months. This was John Kurien, a Christian from Kerala in South India. He was hardworking, honest and incredibly jolly, not a trait I would have associated with Indians as a group, at least as I knew them thus far. He was also open and frank and readily responded when I asked him why he had chosen to work in America rather than Britain, where most of the expatriate Indian graduates tended to gravitate at that time.

"Oh", he replied, "Britain is almost as bad as India. I want the freedom to be myself and do what I think is right. In Britain I would be treated as inferior, whereas here there isn't the discrimination against me because of my ethnic origin. In India, you get put down all the time because you are junior. You are not allowed even to ask a question for nearly thirty years. Then you are suddenly promoted and expected to lead. But by that time all of your initiative and ability to lead has been crushed out of you—you are totally unprepared. Here, on the other hand, you get to ask questions, do research, take responsibility, and you grow. It is very dynamic here—but in India it is absolutely dead. Everything is crushed under the dead weight of tradition." I could understand what he was saying because of my own experience in the Royal Infirmary: I knew what it was to be ignored because I was junior, or minimized because I am a woman, but there had been some relieving features, particularly the respect with which my seniormost colleague, Dr. Michael Oliver, had treated me. I could not fully comprehend what Dr. Kurien was speaking of, but I did make note of a downside to the Hindu religion—social hierarchy and stratification—which was to become such a suffocating reality for me about twenty years later.

For the meantime, I had to deal with the shadow side of America and the issue of just what I wanted to do with my life. No matter the jollity, the freedom, the opportunity I found in America, there was just no escaping the fact that poor people were most definitely second-class citizens and were being very badly treated. Greenpoint had been an initial descent into the hell in which African Americans lived, but I had been too exhausted and overwhelmed to analyze the situation. On returning to the Jewish I worked with private patients—almost all of whom were Jewish—and saw a totally different picture. They were pampered—mollycoddled, by the standards I was used to—always wielding the threat of malpractice suits, to avoid which endless unnecessary lab tests and X-rays were performed. They were vocal and often uncooperative, contrasting markedly with the wonderfully stoic patients I had had in Britain and also the patients in the "public" ward, most of whom were African Americans, with a smattering of Puerto Ricans and one or two poor Jewish people.

What was most troubling to me was the radical difference in the care the private and public patients received: it was the difference of night and day. The nursing care on the public floor was quite different, while the patients were, for the most part, at the mercy of the house staff. There were senior doctors in attendance, going on ward rounds with us maybe a couple of times a week, but the sort of intense attention private patients got was simply not available for the poor. I could also see quite clearly that the patients were being used as guinea pigs for the training of the junior staff: in the surgical department, the residents would undertake surgery that a more senior person most probably would not, while in the medical department, various forms of therapy were attempted that would never have passed muster upstairs on the private wards. I do not think that the Jewish was alone in this matter: I had seen similar things in Grand Rapids (though more under wraps), and was pretty sure that this was the norm. In America, the dollar is almighty, I realized, and could not help thinking of Dr. Oliver, my senior in Edinburgh, who most nobly insisted that all patients should scrupulously be treated alike. This was, for the most part, the norm in Britain, where nationalized medicine was available to all, even those with money, if they so chose. In my experience, cases received attention according to their seriousness medically, not according to the bank account of the patient.

I was deeply troubled by this glaring injustice, as I saw it; and was extremely upset as I came to understand the devastation such a system wreaks on the minds of the victims. So many of my ward patients just had no faith in the doctors; they knew they were being exploited in one way or another, and would either express themselves through bursts of foul-mouthed anger, episodes of non-cooperation, or deeply depressing hopelessness. I remember one case in particular, a fine, handsome African American man, who was in such deep depression that it seemed most unlikely he would survive his ailment. I kept trying to rally him, but it was impossible. He had no trust, no faith, no nothing. He felt the system was totally against him, devaluing him because he was black and poor, and that there was absolutely no way he could hope to move forward. He was one of the more articulate ones, of course; and I sensed that almost all of these people were basically in the same state as he. As the days went by, I began to become rather depressed myself. How could a nation treat such a large section of its people like this and expect to prosper? And, right now, what could I do to help? Apart from treating these people with respect, which I already did to the best of my ability, there was really nothing.

Along with these more general thoughts, my own preoccupation with the healing process kept surfacing. I had gotten into the medical profession to bring healing and relief of suffering, but overall, I was increasingly getting the impression that suffering and healing were outwith my purview. I began to see, more clearly than I had in Edinburgh—for there the overlay of "manners" and the "stiff British upper lip" had obscured in many ways what was going on at the gut level—that disease and suffering are products of the outlook of the individual, and that healing depends on self-respect and trust more than anything else. Fear, hopelessness, smoldering anger and despair are the breeding grounds of deep-seated disease; and without the ability to trust oneself there can be no trust of others, effectively shutting off the channels through which healing can flow.

Nor was my experience on the private wards much better. The all-pervasive threat of lawsuits against the doctors weighed on me terribly, the lack of attention to the testimony of the patient, including hasty physical examination (passed over in favor of endless lab tests), and the general "thingification" of all that we did oppressed me deeply. I would sometimes feel that I was dealing with machines rather than with people—something that had not been the case in Britain, where we were so much less advanced technologically. The sort of communion I had had with my patients in Edinburgh and Sussex just did not exist in America. For me, that had been perhaps the most important aspect of my work, and certainly I felt it was the basis of whatever success I had had in the healing process. All of this could well have sprung from my own idealization of my work rather than from any defect in the American system; but from time to time my growing impression that something was wrong in American society received some justification from the Americans themselves. I was asked on a few occasions to consult on difficult cases in areas outwith my regular assignments—me, a mere rotating intern! When I would point out my junior status, my colleagues would tell me, "No, you have skills we don't have. You seem to understand things much more deeply and can get to the bottom of things that we can't." I would be flabbergasted at first, but on thinking it over I realized that the training we had received in close observation of the patients, of trusting their testimony and our own intuition, was in many ways more valuable than all the lab tests and X-rays in the world.

I felt so strongly that healing comes from trust, mutual understanding, and self-respect, not readily available, for different reasons, in the community I was working with. The impression that what was all-important was the attitude of the sufferer was becoming overwhelming, and that my ability to do anything about it was nil. Such ruminations became very oppressive and I slipped into a sense of crisis. Did I want to live a life of pretense, doing little or nothing of any real substance for my patients? That was how I saw the results of my work thus far. Patching up human bodies uninformed by the spirit seemed more and more meaningless and I became rather depressed. What should I do, if I really meant to heal? I spent several months agonizing over the problem, struggling as all interns do with overwork and lack of sleep, and becoming darker and darker in mood.

The time had come to look for my next job, and in my case to decide in what direction to move. In many ways I had enjoyed my work at the Jewish and definitely had made a lot of progress in building up my self-confidence and skill; but the deep existential question remained: Am I accomplishing anything of meaning or value? On account of my observations about the role the attitude of the patients played in their healing process, I was convinced that I should seek to work in a realm more involved with the human mind, but of course already knew how reductionistic psychiatry was. In addition, psychiatry works with mental pathology, and I was interested in the normal human mind. What to do? What to do? In the midst of this battle, I suddenly remembered the offer I had been made a few years prior to work on a Ph.D. in neuropharmacology. I began to wonder if studying the brain and how it is affected by chemicals might not give a more effective way of solving some of the desperate problems I was seeing and which were so terribly resistant to change. In hindsight, this was an incredibly naive line of thought, every bit as materialistic and reductionistic as I believed were the sources of the problem itself. If I wished to solve behavioral problems generated by materialism (as I understood the problem to be), the last thing that was needed was more work in the materialistic paradigm! My thinking at the time was that basic research in almost any field always offers much more radical solutions to problems than merely "patching up", as I now saw my work to be; I almost certainly felt a need for more intellectually stimulating work, much as I liked working with the patients; I had an offer already before me.

I wrote to Professor Perry, the head of the pharmacology department at Edinburgh University. He responded by telling me he would be attending a conference in New York in a month or two and would be happy to meet with me then. We did meet, I enjoyed the seminar, he was cordial and welcoming, and I signed up there and then as a Ph.D. student. I was gratified, of course, but also went through several months of deep depression: I had gotten into this whole medical thing to relieve the suffering of patients—why was I abandoning them? Was I failing in my duty? Of course, this was irrational and silly, but perhaps understandable.

I had worked so hard, often very much against the grain, to get to where I was—and now I was waltzing away from my patients because I had found it too difficult to deal with their way of looking at the world! No doubt there were whispers in my mind: perhaps my father is right—perhaps I am not really fit for this kind of work! All this from my shadow; but slowly my common sense got the upper hand. Working on a Ph.D. was not abandoning the patients: it was serving them in a more radical and ultimately effective way! My father himself had also left clinical work and gone into research, thus rendering tremendous service to the suffering, especially from tuberculosis. So that was that.

CHAPTER 13

DOWN THE RABBIT HOLE REDUX
1967-1968

The academic year in Edinburgh began in October. I arranged through the university to take a room in the house of a landlady who specialized in postgraduate students, thinking to avoid the depression that had so beset me in the last couple of years at Randolph Crescent. But the truth of the matter was that I had moved beyond all of the self-abasement and despair that had been oppressing me so terribly at that time. As I had hoped, my hectic and jolly days at the Jewish and in the milieu of burgeoning America had effectively blown away many of the cobwebs that I had accumulated as an undergraduate in the somewhat Gothic environment of Auld Reekie. I could have probably lived alone now without too many problems, but the die was cast—and, as it turned out, very interestingly. My housemates were all postgraduate women: Muriel, a business graduate from French Canada; Margaret from Wales, doing Celtic studies; and Noreen from Norway, who was working to become an interpreter.

An interesting vignette with much significance for my future presented itself at the Christmas party of the Celtic department, thanks to an invitation from Margaret, my Welsh housemate. This was a meeting with a professor from India. On my expressing surprise at finding an Indian in a Celtic department, he informed me that Gaelic (the native tongue of my own grandparents) was, of the European languages, one of the most closely related to Sanskrit, the ancient language of India. This was an unexpected link between two strands of my own life, which I found most interesting. But at that time I was much too preoccupied with my own studies to follow through in any way; that was to occur some thirty years later.

Taking into account the fact that I had been away from academe for nearly three years, the pharmacology department had decided to assign me to work alongside the undergraduate B.Sc. students to begin with, in order to assess just where I was in relationship to taking up my proposed Ph.D. work. I therefore found myself with a group of about six students some eight years younger than I—as always in Edinburgh, a cosmopolitan group, from England and Holland among others. Although I did not know it at the time, this was my first exposure to what would later be called the baby boomers; but certainly I could feel that they belonged to a totally different world from mine, a difference much more than the small age difference would lead one to expect. One day I overheard them referring to me as "the old woman"—at age twenty-six! This was my first experience of ageism, which I found funny and at the same time rather ominous.

Another aspect of this way of life that was most unpleasant was the almost total lack of imagination and empathy I found in my scientific co-workers. Their minds were like stone or metal, rigidly focused on "fact" to the exclusion of feeling, insight, or self-identification with anything but matter. Even Ian, one of the B.Sc. students who was far and away the most human of them all, would sometimes disappoint me. I remember one spring morning sitting with him beside a pond round which the plants and trees were bursting their buds, the birds flitting about and singing merrily. I was feeling happy and peaceful, rejoicing in the new life rising and expressing itself with such zest, but Ian was obsessed with naming all the plants and birds and getting annoyed with me because I was so abstracted. I felt his words hitting me like hammer blows and wished he would be quiet. I can be pretty verbal myself on occasion, but at that moment I just wanted to *be*, to feel my identity with nature rather than slit it up, stretch it out and dissect it.

No doubt in response to episodes like this—which were all too common—I wrote in a notebook:

> Earth Goddess I—
> Does no one care?
> I'm so aware, I'm so aware.
> Each breath around me draws me in,
> Electrons continuous with air.
> My nitrogen falling in the leaves,
> My carbon dioxide nourishing the trees,
> Sun energy pushing out my hair.

I was also aware that these people had a total disdain of the ethical behavior I had grown up with, openly and blatantly sexual, for the most part, and uncaring about the sequelae of what they said and did. I began to understand how they could be so relentlessly cruel to the experimental animals we sacrificed on a daily basis, and so uncaring to each other as human beings. It was as if I was living in a realm of automatons, humans under a spell that made them see themselves more as machines than as living beings. In a dim way, I connected all of this with the incredible callousness I had encountered in America, and began to realize that I was living in a world much, much different from the enchantment of my childhood.

Another issue that bothered me intensely was more intellectual than the others: just exactly what were we measuring in our experiments? I would look at the guinea-pig gut contracting in its bath of isotonic electrolytes and glucose, the measuring equipment, the graph that was appearing as we injected various chemicals into the system, and wonder: What does all of this have to do with what is actually going on, either in this little piece of gut or in a living guinea pig? I realized that there was practical value in our results: they were reproducible, they could be used to predict, and of course from work such as this medications were being developed that could definitely affect the course of human sickness. But what riveted my attention was: This experimental system is a superimposition on what is actually going on in the tissue; it is interfering with its natural function, and for all I know distorting it to the point of being irrelevant. I would feel that the little piece of gut contained a mystery that was actually laughing at us and our self-important interventions in its day. I would become so absorbed in these issues that the tutors who were circulating to help us with our work would be quite bemused, or would launch into gales of laughter or diatribes against my "mysticism". I took to reading books on the scientific method in an attempt to get to the bottom of this issue, but did not find much consolation, though A.N. Whitehead's book *Process and Reality*, dealing with the issue of how ongoing, organic, dynamic reality can be related to the intellectual constructs we superimpose on it cracked the door enough for a faint ray of light to enter. It was to be forty years until I got an answer that more or less satisfied me.

Within a short period of beginning my studies, Professor Perry told me that the department was satisfied with my work and felt it appropriate for me to proceed on to the materials for my Ph.D. My tutor would be Dr. Henry Adams, one of the senior members of the department, who was studying the metabolism and function of histamine in the brain. I was pleased with the assignment to Dr. Adams, who was by far the most humane of the staff, taking a kindly interest in me and not sneering at me because of my "otherworldly" thinking; but I was not so much interested in the subject matter. In addition to the course reading, I had been branching out on my own and was developing my interests in the field of studies of the mind-body connection. After all, it was how emotional attitude gave rise to sickness and affected the course of it that had led me into this work. However, at the time I said nothing, deciding to go with the flow and find out in more detail what the potential of Dr. Adams's work was for my own interests.

I was determined to make my own decisions without permitting myself to be crushed by what other people think, a goal which at that time I found embodied in one of my longstanding heroines, Marie Curie, whose biography I read at this time. Born in Poland at a time when the occupying Russians would not even let the Polish people speak their own language (shades of the fate of Gaelic in Scotland!), she nevertheless spoke her language and also became so proficient in science that she and her French husband, Pierre Curie, went on to win the Nobel prize for their pioneering work with radioactivity. Her one-pointed dedication, her utter devotion to her husband and the work they shared, and her personal simplicity and unassuming nature were icons for me. I found a full-page photo of her in *Life* magazine, which I cut out, framed and hung where I could see her the moment I woke up every morning.

But all of this notwithstanding, I was not really connecting up with the work I was doing. More and more I realized that I could not continue to work with whole animals; their suffering was impossible to bear. I read avidly about the technique of tissue culture and about work in the field of mind-body connection. I had been formally introduced to this subject about four years previously on reading *Raja Yoga* by Ernest Wood, an English interpreter of the ancient Indian science of mind-control and its influence on the functions of the body. My interest in the subject continued, and as far back as nineteen sixty-four, three years previous to my work in the pharmacology department, I had jotted in a notebook a sketchy outline of an experiment to tie together the function of the brain, the balance of hormones, particularly the adrenal steroids, and the cells of the immune system. As time went by, my mind kept returning to this idea and slowly I began to conceive of work with incubated immune cells as markers for the amounts, types, and patterns of hormones released in various emotional states.

I finally made up my mind that this was what I wanted to do; it had far more relevance to my interests than what was going on in the pharmacology department. So I found myself in Professor Perry's office outlining my ideas for my Ph.D. He looked at me kindly, but with a degree of near-disbelief. Doubtless he shared to some extent the prevailing opinion that I was out to lunch scientifically. But he confined his comments to purely practical considerations. "You see," he said, "We are not doing cell culture here; and the field you are talking about is controversial and perhaps not valid." The big N-word! I was disappointed, but not surprised. If only I had been in Los Angeles, where some ten years later the Cousins Center of Psycho-immuno-neurology would be founded! My life-story might have been utterly different.

Once again I felt the weight of materialistic reductionism pressing me down. I was fascinated and thrilled by the process of scientific inquiry and experimentation, but repelled by the hideous, unrelenting identification with the material world with which it seemed uneluctably to be associated. I began to realize that this was what had been crushing, crushing, crushing me throughout my childhood: the dead weight of my mother's Communism; my father's withering disdain for religion and lack of faith in human decency; and the lack of empathy at Dollar had been the roadblocks which had derailed me in so many ways. And of course the hideous injustice and cruelty in America, which I felt sprang from the vision of human beings as primarily bodies had brought it all to a head, bringing me into direct confrontation with it in the pharmacology department. Had I made a big mistake in committing myself to such a materialistic profession and did I really want to spend my days in what had turned out to be such soulless activity? And if not, what would I do with myself?

One subset of my difficulties was the lack of creative activity in my life, which caused me a lot of anguish. On going back to academic work I took advantage of the less demanding hours to enroll in classes in the Edinburgh School of Art, where I learned oil painting, much to my joy. There again I felt a certain dead weight of literalness and stodge, but nevertheless it was wonderful to be working once again with color, form and imagination. I produced quite a bit of work and my teacher was very encouraging. On my visits to the Glasgow area I connected up from time to time with Jean Irwin, my art teacher of twenty years before, always enjoying her kindly, imaginative company. Somewhere in the spring of nineteen sixty-eight she came over to Edinburgh on some project and had tea with me at my flat. I showed her the work I had done at the Art

School and she turned to me seriously. "Jean", she said, "I see you have lost none of your touch. If you wanted to, you could still be the best artist in Scotland." This hit me like a bombshell. I had just taken it for granted that I had lost my ability to create—that had perhaps been part of why I was feeling so badly—and given up on art entirely as a career. This ringing endorsement at a moment of intense crisis started up a whole new line of thought which was soon to take me to a radical decision.

In addition to my increasing understanding of the limitations of medicine, I was now beginning to appreciate more deeply the meaning of art, which I was delighted to find my Quaker friends shared with me wholeheartedly. Art was not just a sort of decoration, an afterthought to the main business of life, but a window out of the world of matter into something much deeper, more meaningful and for me more fulfilling, and suffused with a light that no amount of materialistic activity or success could bring. In a way, all of this I had dimly grasped previously; what I was now beginning to see was that the light that streamed in through the windows of artistic creativity was also deeply healing. Just the few daubs I was putting on canvas at the Art School had gone a long way to soothe my soul and give me a degree of consolation that nothing else I had done for nearly fifteen years had offered. It dawned on me that art, far from being useless, was actually a powerful means of healing, a means of conveying spiritual energy with tremendous capacity to uplift the soul and transform lives. But of course, in order to heal and transform art had to come from a life of utter dedication to truth, of one-pointed purity of purpose and action and complete honesty of methods. Was my life of that caliber? I could not answer that question, of course, but I was intensely attracted by this new vision, which seemed to promise so much more ability to heal, to uplift, than what I had been doing thus far.

One morning I found myself going to Dr. Adams's office, something I seldom did. He greeted me courteously and asked me what was up. "Dr Adams", I began, "I have come to understand that it is going to take me at least twenty years to begin to grasp the subject of histamine metabolism in the brain." "You are extremely perceptive", he said. "Most students don't realize how long it takes to master a subject like this." I went on, "Dr. Adams, the fact is: I don't really care about it enough to spend twenty years on it. I don't think that this kind of work is what I am suited for." His kindly face broke into a smile. "Jean, I am glad you are telling me this. I have always felt that your talents lie more in the creative and philosophical fields, and that you would do very well in either."

This was a turning point. I overcame my last scruples about turning my back on medicine and going forward into the world of art. I was convinced that devoting myself to art would be a much better way of contributing to human well-being than merely patching up bodies in which there was no light of understanding of higher values; or even of doing basic research, which operated entirely in the world of matter which was engulfing us.

Despite the great relief I felt, I had no money. With giving up my Ph.D. work I lost my grant, and I had very little in my savings account. But I was determined to do this alone; I would not ask my family for anything more. In their minds, I felt sure, I was being irresponsible (though none of them ever said so), and I had to manage the transition by myself. I also realized that I would have to continue working in the medical profession for a few more years in order to get together money for fees for art school, and furthermore, by working in America where I could live frugally—Scottish style—without feeling any problem, I could put savings together more rapidly than in Britain.

I no sooner did this calculation than I was in the library looking for a position in the States, having opted to work at pathology, a specialty which combines features of both clinical work and the research, laboratory approach, and also would have less demanding hours than I had been working thus far. My main goal was to have time and energy to attend art classes, to keep myself in practice while I trod water in my profession. In addition, I was determined to work in Manhattan, in order to be near all the art colleges, galleries and other cultural activity New York had to offer, but of course positions there were in demand and I was applying late in the working year. I finally settled for the Polyclinic Hospital and Medical School, located in the west fifties, which in its heyday had indeed been some sort of medical school, though it was no longer recognized as such. I realized that, despite its title, this was not a really great hospital, but I was so determined to be in the heart of the New York cultural scene that I settled for it anyway.

I was in for another long, dreary haul in America, preparing myself for a new, yet old career in art, the one that was really closest to my heart. In view of what I felt lay ahead, I decided to take a couple of months off, enjoying the nice apartment I was sharing with my Norwegian friend Noreen, and also the unusually good weather. April and May of nineteen sixty-eight were, as I recall them, almost uniformly sunny and mild and I took the opportunity to go for long walks around Edinburgh, particularly the residential area near us where there was a large park. I would take my sketchpad with me and capture many of the scenes unfolding before me, all of which seemed unusually "bathed in celestial light", as the poet Wordsworth said of his experiences as a young boy. One particularly elevating sight took place in the early morning, when everything was suffused in a rosy light and the dew was still glistening. I saw a swan presiding over the birth of her cygnet, which tapped inside its shell for quite some time and finally emerged, all wet and bedraggled. It was, like all newborns, not a particularly lovely sight, but its mother stood over it, her neck arched, the picture of motherly love in a halo of golden light. This was such an archetypal moment that I almost stopped breathing. Would I be able to capture such moments of ecstasy in my artwork? This was the big question. If I could convey even a fraction of what I experienced that morning, I would be giving the world something of the greatest value.

I spent a lot of time with my wonderful Quaker friends and read voraciously about the lives and works of the major European philosophers and artists, as also a huge number of novels, which I had had to eschew while I was working so hard at my medical studies. A recipe for bliss, one might think. But bliss is never unqualified. As Noreen and I ate our meals together, we would hear on the radio about revolt at the Sorbonne in Paris and other European universities. The students wanted Greek and Latin abolished from the curriculum, something that neither of us could understand. We both valued classical languages and understood that they were the links to our past. But the students wanted to sweep them away, along with the authority of the teachers and the European tradition. In America things were even worse. There was intense unrest over the Vietnam war, the young people were living in communes, high on drugs, with communal sex and apparently no concern for any of the values we had been brought up to cherish. In view of the intense materialism I had encountered in the States, I could empathize with the idea of a radical change in American culture, but had serious reservations about the lifestyle being embraced by these youngsters, the result, in many ways of the cultural meltdown after the Second World War.

I began to have classical migraine headaches—the flashing lights, headache and vomiting—and realized that this is what I had had previously in a less characteristic form when I was under stress—at Dollar, at Randolph Crescent when I was in combat with my father, and also when I was working in the emergency room at the Jewish. Then and during my break that spring they were a minor nuisance, but once back in America they were to assume the character of an avenging angel, shaping my life in significant ways. They were, in fact, my body telling me that things were badly out of kilter with my inner life, though I could not understand it then.

But what did surface was a return of my longing for someone who could really understand me and guide me as I needed to be guided. In many ways I was lost, the main problem being how to direct my life to achieve my goal of serving humanity while expressing my inner convictions. I found some consolation with my Quaker friends, but they were, for the most part, uncomplicated people without the sort of intellectual questions which racked me on and off, not the least of which was: Which spiritual culture do I belong in? I had left mainstream Christianity behind, but had not really settled in to Quakerism, much as I admired and liked it. I still read the Gita every day and meditated on it, bringing it up in any conversation that could tolerate it; but in some ways it had created problems for me. The vision of the God-realized soul that occurs throughout the Gita was intensely inspiring, a goal to be aimed for—but where were examples of such people? Everything I saw, particularly in America, pointed in quite the other direction, almost to a demoniacal world; and what was now emerging—this chaotic, self-righteous, undisciplined mob of young people, rejecting the old and not really with a clear idea of the new—did not seem promising soil for the production of truly great spiritual human beings.

I began to fear that the Gita was talking nonsense, that the realized soul was a figment of the overheated brains of the Indians. I felt sure that Grannie had been such a being, but she of course belonged to a generation of an entirely different type. Could it be that our present circumstances had snuffed out the possibility of humanity reaching up and realizing its spiritual potential? This was for me a dark thought, deeply disturbing. If it was not going to be possible to realize and express the spirituality at my core, why bother to go on?

I was in crisis, as bad as what I had gone through a little over twenty years before when my mother left me alone in the world. At that time it had been largely an issue of survival: would I find a home where I would be properly taken care of? But now it was more complicated. All of the cruelty and brutality I had witnessed and begun to understand over the past few years had led me to despair, despite the hopes I cherished and fed from my reading of the Gita. Was I totally deluded? Was this harsh environment where survival of the fittest seemed to be the motto actually reality—and all that had seemed so real to me just a figment of my imagination?

Something inside me was seeking with all of its might and main to find the source of light, of love, that I had been privileged to glimpse at Grant Street. Had the lights all gone out? Was I to live in the dark for the rest of my life? And I was to understand that this was not just my cry—there was a cosmic groan going up, as it were, from large numbers of people all over the world. I understood this from a small event that happened around that time. A young mother in our Quaker group, finding out that I had been working in pharmacology, asked me if I would speak to the parents' group about drug addiction. At that time I was unaware of the growing problem of drug addiction in young people, but I soon found out when I went to the medical library to prepare my talk. The British had always accepted that there would be some people who were chronically addicted and followed an official policy of providing them their drugs in order to avoid criminalization. But this had been a matter of a few hundred people; what was happening, especially in America, was nothing short of a pandemic, involving a large percentage of young people. America had gone the way of making drug-taking a criminal offense, and was facing the inevitable consequences.

At that point, the problem had not hit Britain to any extent, but it was clearly a matter of time, as the larger European countries were already infected with it. The Quaker parents were justifiably concerned, and we had an earnest discussion on that sunny summer day. Moving on from the purely pharmacological issues, we explored the question of why were we having this sudden epidemic. We decided that assuredly there was a terrible loss of faith, that people—all people, not just the young—were no longer finding joy in the inner life, but seeking satisfaction almost entirely in the physical world. The deep-seated craving of the human soul for meaning and for love was no longer going inward, but rushing out to gratification in drugs and (though we did not discuss it) sex and indiscriminate violence, which was becoming more and more visible in the movies, those harbingers of what was to come.

We decided that Western culture was in a state of crisis, shaken to its foundations by deep economic depression and the horrors of two world wars, which in many ways sprang from the failing energies of the modern worldview. It gave us some satisfaction to have pinpointed the problem—but in the meantime, what were the parents to do about their children? We all agreed that to love from the depths of the heart was the only way; given that, the rest would work itself out. If a child knows that she is truly loved, she herself can work through many of the difficulties she has to face. I knew this, of course, from my own experience, but silently wondered: what if the energy runs out?

As with all of my encounters with the Quakers—by definition, living from within—this was extremely valuable input for my own life, clarifying and encouraging. Somehow I had managed to escape the lure of chemical ecstasy, either from cigarettes, alcohol or drugs, but had had a more difficult time with relationships with men, where I sought to rediscover the kind of spiritual love I had found with Grannie. But of course, that is not the way it is. Although I had made up my mind not to marry, I somehow attracted men and had always someone or other dancing attendance on me, particularly older and more mature men. After my terrible experiences in the wake of my final break with my father, I had come to understand that relationships based only on human love could never satisfy me and did not permit myself to get involved in the slightest with any of these men. I remembered what had happened in my dream of the Golden Soul, some six to seven years previously: craving for satisfaction destroys the possibility of having it. But the question still remained: Would I live the rest of my life without love that could really support me and help me to grow? That was what I needed, that is what would protect me from the addictions so many around me were succumbing to, and that is what I still hoped for, despite all appearances that it was impossible.

Nevertheless, as I prepared to leave Edinburgh, uncharacteristically still sunny and attractive, I had moments of feeling that there was hope, that somehow I would find what I was looking for in America, though I was not in any way sure what it might be. I had faint premonitions that I would meet that someone I had been dreaming of who really understood me and could help me get over all of the traumas of my childhood. It had been an intermittent daydream since that day in the dissection room some seven years previously, but what I was feeling as I prepared to leave for America was more definite, more real, more *possible*, than mere daydreaming. It was a hopeful background to the difficulty of leaving Scotland—as I knew it would be—forever. I understood that I had reached the end of the line there and that whatever I was going to do would be in the States. Mary cried when I told her this; I was sorry, but I knew that that was the way it was going to be.

Within a few weeks after my arrival at the New York Polyclinic Hospital, located in the West fifties of Manhattan, I was reminded of just how bad things could be in America. Dirty—my room was infested with battalions of cockroaches, which would march in columns across my apartment, even over my bed as I was sleeping, and no amount of poisons seemed able to hold back—disorganized, and dysfunctional. The last pejorative applied as much to my department head as to the hospital itself, though it had plenty of its own dysfunction. This was the first time I had worked under a man whom I regarded as weak and ineffectual; I had met a few such women—my headmistress at Dollar, the Indian lady doctor in Sussex, and one or two Philippina doctors at the Jewish—but somehow I had never expected to meet a man who could not stand his ground and work according to principle, not emotion. Even to say good morning to this man was to see him cringe away; and as for the conferences we would have with him in his office, all questions were met with ridicule or put-downs. I rapidly became quite disgusted and made every effort to avoid him and any work he was related to. I realized that his behavior was affecting the rest of the staff, for though as individuals they were nice people, there was no *esprit de corps* in our group, quite unlike the teams I had worked with elsewhere in America. There was endless quarrelling and bickering, most unbecoming in a group of professionals. I made a mental note that the quality of the leadership is the most defining element in any situation, and resolved not to take any job without first seeing and testing the head of any department I would be working in.

I would remind myself that this job was merely a way of making a living and that, as I had signed a contract for a year, I would just have to make the best of it. I was much more interested in attending art classes, which I did two or three times a week at the Art Students' League. I attended drawing, painting and graphic design classes, making quite a bit of progress. My drawing and graphic design teachers were particularly encouraging, saying that they would support any application I would make to become a full-time student and also that they felt I could certainly get a full scholarship, such was the quality of my work. This was of course hopeful, but I was stuck at the Polyclinic for the rest of the working year and would have to tread water until I was finished there.

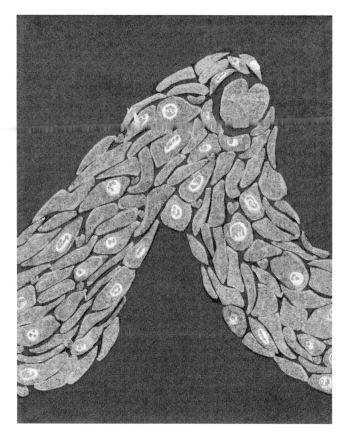

Appliqué: Tissue paper on red paper, 1970.

My graphics design teacher was a rather striking man whose deportment and appearance taught me an important lesson. Darkly handsome, he was the first man I met with a totally shaven head. I had seen Yul Brynner shaven in *The King and I*, but had not expected to see this striking "hair do" on anyone but a movie star. I wondered why my teacher had taken this drastic step and began to examine his head more closely. I realized that, though a young man, he was basically quite bald and that he had taken the logical step of simply shaving it all off. This struck me as the sensible thing to do. Baldness, especially central baldness such as he had, tended to make a man seem wimpy and unattractive, and most men like this would grow some hair longer on one side and comb it over their bald pates, always living in terror in case the wind blew and divulged their "secret". My father used to call them "greyhounds"—they make a little hair (hare) go a long way! But to simply shave it all off—what a good idea! It enhanced this man's native good looks and in addition made him seem mysterious and alluring. I felt that I should learn from him to rise above my weak spots and boldly take a stand in anything I did, maximizing my strengths.

Meanwhile, I had taken up again with the Quakers. I attended the meeting in Washington Square, quaint and in some ways a bit Gothic. These were colorful characters, not the low-key, self-effacing souls I had been associating with in Edinburgh. There was, in particular, Maeve, who told me with great pride that her name was that of an old Celtic queen of great prowess—and she herself, perhaps inspired by her name, was somewhat of a valkyrie. But she, like the others, was a good soul, and I soon fitted in quite comfortably, finding in their company what was lacking at my work and in the social circles I mixed with. The Quakers had a nice little yard with plants and trees, a lovely oasis in the summer heat, where they would serve refreshments after meeting and we could all get to know each other. There I met Lou Stuart, who would come more or less regularly with one or two of his friends. He was not a Quaker, but was interested in spiritual life and he and his friends would engage with a group of us in earnest discussion about the topic that had come up at meeting or about spiritual life in general.

Gradually he and I would have lunch, go for walks or visit Cookie, endlessly turning over various religious or spiritual topics as we did so. Lou was always asking leading questions, then cross-questioning me as I spun out long-winded disquisitions in response. He knew quite a bit about the literature and had met and spoken with a number of distinguished religious leaders and thinkers in America, whose ideas he would throw up to challenge or clarify mine. He had a mischievous sense of humor, and would often deflect me, if I got too serious or intense, with some riotous aside which would reduce me to helpless laughter.

Lou's family had immigrated from Russia after the Revolution, when he was eight years old. He had grown up in Baltimore, where he had become a captain in the merchant marine, but he had spent most of his working life in New York City, which he knew like the back of his hand. At the time I met him, he was semi-retired from the merchant marine, spending a lot of time dealing in antiques, particularly Asian ivories and jades, and he knew all the art and dealers galleries, art stores, and so on, throughout the city. He and I would go on long tours of discovery through the various sections of the city, look at art exhibits, attend auctions at a Park Bernet on Lexington Avenue (where we would see celebrities such as Paul McCartney and Andy Warhol), and generally culture-vulture. I had signed up for art appreciation classes at the Museum of Modern Art, to which he came with me, as well as to the Lincoln Center programs, for which I had a subscription. I particularly loved dance programs, as to me they were the most complete art, combining story, music, color and movement.

Lou lived in one of the towers at the top of the Dakota, the prestigious dwelling place of the rich and famous on Central Park West. It was a totally illegal rental, of course, but what a view over the city! And just a hop and a skip into Central Park, which became my home from home. Lou and I would spend the hot summer days in the shady parts of the park, pursuing our metaphysical discussions while watching the world go by in all of its variety. Slowly the impression began to form in my mind that Lou was the person I had dreamt about as a sad little preteen in Grant Street. I had seen an older man from Eastern Europe, kind and humorous, who was engaged in some kind of art dealing and was unusually understanding of me and my preoccupations. I wondered if indeed it was possible—my Scotch "common sense" was still not inclined to give credence to the occult or paranormal—but it was undeniable that this man was really fulfilling the longing that I had some fifteen years previously.

A flower study, pencil and wax crayon on paper, 1969-1970.

Granted, he was actually an American—and indeed I got my grounding in what America was all about from Lou, finding out that aristocratic ideas of any sort would not be tolerated, nor would the idea of God. "Don't use that word!" he would say with vehemence. "Why not? I thought you were interested in religion." "Yes, but religion doesn't have to talk about God!" I was amazed. "Isn't religion about something beyond the mere human mind? You have to call it something—and what is wrong with God? We have been doing it for millennia. Granted, it has gotten a bit tarnished by the way religious people have behaved, but all that is needed is to go back to basics and rediscover what the word means from your own experience." After a number of these Alice-in-Wonderland exchanges I realized that Lou was merely repeating a prejudice he had picked up from the American mainstream, because when he answered my questions seriously, he was not denying God in the sense of atheism: he just had a knee-jerk aversion to the actual word *God*. I was to run into this prejudice many more times, sometimes in the most unexpected places—including a convent.

Despite some drawbacks, I was in a favorable position. I was developing my art portfolio and doing well at art school, I was putting quite a bit of money in my savings account, I was moving forward with the Quakers, I was making compatible new friends and living an interesting cultural life in the most dynamic city in the world, or so it seemed. Dirt and noise notwithstanding, New York was always for me exciting and invigorating; I just loved being there, and through Lou I was discovering the most attractive and interesting places: the parks, the exquisite museums—such as the Frick, where I fell deeply in love with a Madonna and child that seemed to express not only the love and compassion, but also the deep joy I had felt in my ongoing relationship with the Divine Mother—and various quiet little hideaways where I could eat and think quietly. But all was not well. Although Lou was one of the few people I had met with whom I could talk about spiritual and intellectual things, I realized that he was beginning to find my intellect a bit overpowering and was behaving in a rather odd way, moody and excitable. Talking with his friends I came to know that he suffered from bipolar disease, which was quite a setback for me; I kept reminding myself that I could not invest myself totally in human relationships, and tried to go deeper within myself to calm down.

But, though I had silenced my various cravings on the outside, something inside was very out of alignment. What drew my attention to the problem was the onset, in October, of the most devastating migraine headaches, which would incapacitate me for as many as three days at a stretch. The flickering lights, the headache, and above all the vomiting would lay me low, unable to eat or swallow any medicine, barely able to drink and utterly miserable. I was missing quite a bit of time at work, but fortunately, because I was able to catch up quickly, there were no complaints from my employers. I remembered that I had had unexplained vomiting attacks as a child and by this time knew that that was part of the way migraines develop in a life cycle—vomiting in childhood, classic migraines in adult life and dizzy spells when older. I also knew from my medical training that their cause is usually psychosomatic, a response to stress, and realized that something of major import was going on with me, though at the moment I could not think what it might be.

Lou was very concerned and suggested that I should go visit "the swamis". "What is a swami?" I asked him. "Swamis are holy men from India." "Are they Hindus?" "Yes." "Lou", I said, "I am not a Hindu. I am interested in the Gita and get a lot of inspiration from it, but that is not the same as being a Hindu." He responded, "You don't have to be a Hindu to get the benefit of meeting holy people. These are the genuine article, and I think meeting them will help you figure out what is going on."

However, although I initially rejected Lou's "prescription" for my ailment, I did feel that his intuition that my problem had spiritual roots might be correct and decided that, rather than get mixed up with mysterious swamis, I would go ahead and become an actual member of the Quakers. I had benefited so much from the nearly four years of my association with them and admired their wonderfully unselfish, focused work with all manner of afflicted people that it seemed time to throw my lot in with them, despite my problems with their lack of clear intellectual belief statements. However, one does not just "join" the Quakers—one has to work one's way in slowly from the first rung—monthly meeting, if I remember right. The Quakers hold themselves together by a series of regular meetings: the weekly meeting for meditative worship, monthly to deal with local issues, quarterly to deal with regional matters and so on up to big convocations, held I do not remember how frequently. As I had attended weekly meetings regularly and had been deemed a suitable person to join the group, I was inducted into monthly meeting.

The first one I went to was a study in the most unusual dynamics of the Quaker faith. Held in a draughty hall in the Village, the meeting dealt, among other things, with the problem of a rather large leak in the roof, apparent from the continuous dripping of icy water into an enameled bucket on the floor beside us. To anyone else, dealing with this issue would have been a rather obvious matter; but the Quakers do things by consensus, meaning that they wait until everyone is in complete agreement before taking a step. For some inscrutable reason, there was one older man holding out against getting the roof fixed, the onset of winter or no. He was a typical grouch, probably from New England (which in my experience tends to specialize in gents of the sort) and implacably refused to cooperate with the reasonable requests of the group. I could see how the consensus method could lend itself to manipulation by anyone with a negative agenda, and wondered how the group was going to solve the problem. Finally the leader (who I believe was Maeve) said, "Alright, brothers and sisters. Brother John cannot see his way to consensus. We will now have a period of silent contemplation, just to give us all space to think this through and, God willing, reach a happy solution." Whereupon we all closed our eyes and stilled our minds, calling on the light within to convince Brother John before the winter became much more severe. As a total novice, I could not help peeking at John to see how he was responding to this. He was bent over, but not in meditation. Muttering under his breath, he was casting alternately angry and anxious looks at the group, obviously feeling the unspoken pressure and the implied threat of alienation if he did not come round to a more reasonable point of view.

I found this utterly fascinating—would the group succeed in bringing round this difficult man? What if he were senile and unable to really understand what was going on? How long would it take to get a solution, and how could they possibly get anything done? Of course, because I already knew how effective the Quakers are in so many ways, I knew that consensus can and does work, but obviously it is something that requires tremendous patience and self-denial, of an order most of us cannot conceive of, far less develop.

But I was not finding a solution to the deep anguish that seemed to be troubling me. As Christmas approached I agonized over the direction my life was taking; I felt that there was within me a precious gift of understanding, joy and happiness that transcended most common experience, but the question was: How to express it? Although I rejoiced inwardly, my friends were so oblivious to what I was seeing and experiencing. I was beginning to realize that I would really have to let go of most of my current friends, who simply could not understand what was motivating me. I placed before myself two alternatives: 1. To devote myself totally to being happy with people, a project I realized would take up an entire lifetime; 2. To forget people and discipline my energies into *work*. This appealed to me more, for I really wanted to leave even *one* single idea for others. I wrote in my diary, "I don't believe *happiness* is the measure of life. To me, following one's destiny, the unfolding of one's own true self, is more important. Already I have found that this can bring JOY."

All of this was coming to a tremendous crisis. I came down with a massive migraine, which lasted for nearly ten days. I tried to keep going, but collapsed at my work and ended up a patient in the hospital. The doctor who admitted me to the hospital was a colleague who, I was aware, was trying to get involved with me romantically. I had, however, remained aloof; I dimly realized as they put me on a gurney to wheel me off that he would use his control over me as a patient to browbeat me into submission. And that is how it was. He kept trying to prove that I had a brain tumor that was causing the almost non-stop vomiting, despite my protestations that I simply had an extremely severe migraine attack. I finally had to refuse to cooperate, rejecting invasive diagnostic procedures such as a spinal tap and cerebral angiogram and ended up signing myself out, although I was very weak from not eating for nearly a week.

During my stay in the hospital I had felt a little better one day and tried to do some reading. At that time I read all sorts of things and the current book—*Naked Lunch* by William Burroughs—was an ugly number with no reason to exist but to be disgusting. As soon as I had read a couple of paragraphs I could feel the vomiting beginning again and realized quite clearly that what was making me sick was the hideous, materialistic world I kept immersing myself in. I felt totally, totally alone. Was there nowhere where I could find the sort of understanding and love that my soul was craving? Was I going to have to spend my life standing in an ivory tower, calling and calling and calling, with no response? I wrote in my diary, "To *work* constantly, to be detached from people—to observe them, but not *need* them. That is my desire! For needing people is destroying me."

But as has always happened in my life, this cry of anguish was immediately met with a rejoinder from within. I wrote, "O, the day of self-discovery shines like an imminent dawn! The bursting of the sun, the searing and flaming in the sky! The wild rising of the whale from the unfathomable depths! I wait, wait, wait! The waiting is so long." It was now over three years since the final end of the drama with my father and the pain was still expressing itself in my relationship with other people, no matter how hard I tried to rise above it. Over twenty years before, the agony of my mother's death had been alleviated by going to live with my grandmother, who had given me a love of a totally different kind. Now twenty-seven years old and going on twenty-eight, I was craving from the depths of my being to find another soul who could help me find my way and give me the energy to stay on the path. It was quite obviously not Lou, much as I enjoyed his company; what I needed was a person of spiritual stature, someone like the realized souls I had read about in the Gita and cherished in my mind as my own ideal. But, though I had been familiar with this ideal for nearly eight years, I had met not one single person who even remotely measured up to it. Though I had known some wonderful people, none had the kind of insight and love I was craving—and, indeed, most people were quite the opposite, seeking to take advantage of me in one way or another, materialistic, and with no higher ideals whatsoever.

Finally, Lou said, "Now you absolutely must go and see the swami."
I was so desperate that this time I could not resist. Lou seemed so
convinced that a swami could help, and from my side, what else did I
have? So we went. It was Sunday, January fourth, nineteen sixty-nine.
The Vedanta Center was on West Seventy-First Street, round the
corner from Lou's apartment and twenty blocks or so uptown from
where I was living. The chapel was in a brownstone building, one
of these narrow, vertical buildings characteristic of New York, and
was reached at the top of a steep flight of stairs. There were large
windows on to the street, but the rest of the long, narrow chapel was
lit only by electric light. The decor was muted, with grayish curtains
behind the altar, itself simple and with only one item on it—a black
and white picture of an Indian man with a very indrawn look on his
face. The chapel seemed very quiet, dark and somewhat reminiscent
of a movie theater, what with the lighting and the low-key decor.
It was so different from any religious building I had been in, I was
rather intrigued. There was no sign of an organ, or any of the other
paraphernalia I was used to associating with places of worship. I
wondered what on earth would take place.

The swami entered silently, with no fanfare of any sort. He was tall for an Indian, extremely thin, with pure white hair and rather staccato movements, which were nevertheless quite graceful and gentle. He was dressed in a regular suit, with an orange shawl over his shoulders, a mix of East and West. What was most striking was the incredibly serene atmosphere that enveloped him as he stood for a moment before the altar with folded hands, communing with the being in the picture; when he sat down and remained immobile during his short invocation; and as he spoke—for a full hour and without any notes!—in a slightly hesitant manner, with long pauses and with somewhat of a speech impediment. This was not a glamorous or handsome person; if anything, rather awkward, physically speaking; but what he said and how he said it seemed to be so utterly sincere and true I was transfixed. I have no recollection of what the subject was or what he actually said, but I do know that I felt, quite profoundly, "This is one of those realized people I have read about in the Gita! This person is a genuinely spiritual person. This is the one I have been looking for!"

And after that I went three times a week to hear him speak—Tuesday, Friday and Sunday—without so much as a backward look at the Quakers.

CHAPTER 14

ROSY GLOW: 1969-1970

Swami Pavitrananda was an East Indian man in his early seventies, who headed up the Vedanta Society of New York. The Center had

been founded in eighteen ninety-four by Swami Vivekananda, who the previous year had been an Indian delegate to the World's Parliament of Religions at the Columbian Exposition in Chicago. He had gone on to found a monastic order which, in addition to educational and social work in India, also sent swamis or monks to the West to teach the ancient Indian philosophy and religion of Vedanta and to train Westerners in spiritual life, including meditation. These men had attracted a small but select following, including Western intellectuals such as Gerald Heard, Aldous Huxley, Christopher Isherwood, Joseph Campbell, J.D. Salinger and Huston Smith, as well as the socially prominent. As a case in point, the brownstone in which the New York Vedanta society was housed had been donated to Swami Pavitrananda's predecessor by Helen Morton, the daughter of Levi P. Morton, Vice President of the United States from eighteen eighty-nine to eighteen ninety-three.

When I started going to the Center, Swami's health was in decline and the previously quite burgeoning society was beginning to contract, leaving a core of dedicated Vedantists who would stick with him to the last as well as a few younger people like myself, attracted less by any "Oriental glamour" the swami might have had than by the intensity of his spirituality. Although I was not to know it for some time, Swami was a trustee of the order in India and had been quite high on the hierarchy there before coming to the United States, where he had been sent in nineteen fifty-one on account of his delicate health. As a monk, he had no money of his own and depended on the membership of the society for his board and maintenance, which was gladly provided by the generally quite well-heeled members. Two of his closest followers were French Canadian women who had come from a wealthy and distinguished family and were utterly dedicated to caring for the aging swami. He was, therefore, dressed in elegant clothes of top quality and distinction and everything at the Center was done in a quiet, tasteful and artistic way.

At that time all I knew was that what he was teaching spoke directly to my soul. It seemed so self-evident, so practical, so *real*, unlike the various dogmas I had been asked to accept in Christianity. He was asking us to stand on our own inner Self, to discover the strength and blessedness of it and to learn how to express it in our day-to-day life, ideas I had read about in the book on yoga Vive had lent me seven years prior, and had also encountered in my dream of the Golden Self. Only later did I realize that Swami was its author and therefore in some ways a bringing into fulfillment of my deep relationship with Vive. Rather than making me feel inadequate and guilty—as mainstream Christianity had rather tended to do—I felt empowered, uplifted, and very hopeful by all that the swami had to say. The Quakers, of course, emphasized the inner light, making it the central focus and depending on it to guide every aspect of their lives. They were, I felt, the Christian equivalent of what I was now hearing—but there was a big difference. The Quakers were really lovely people, sincere and honest; but I felt that the swami was a living embodiment of everything he taught, a blazing fire of spirituality, speaking with compelling conviction and, as I was to learn later, not compromising in the slightest with any sort of loose thinking or behavior.

But that did not mean that he was aggressive or intimidating. On the contrary, he was extremely gentle, sweet and kind. The first real experience I had of his melting kindness and love was one evening when I asked a question after the Tuesday evening Bhagavad Gita class. I had been attending his classes for nearly three months, I believe, and had asked questions on several occasions, but had not felt free to touch on anything of personal importance. I was, in fact, rather in awe of the swami's magisterial presence and radiant spirituality and perhaps was holding back, afraid of being disappointed and hurt yet again by someone who seemed to be so important to me. Be that as it may, on the particular evening I am speaking of now the swami had mentioned in the course of his class that people who felt that material objects were of significance in their spiritual life were usually mistaken. Spirituality came from within, from inner work, and not from anything outside. This troubled me. I could not forget the silver birch tree through which I had had the amazing experience—the "out-of-the-body" experience—up at Fortrose some eighteen years previously. I wanted to ask him about it, but did not want to divulge publicly anything of what I had experienced. I therefore waited and waited to bring up the subject, mentioning it just as the swami was getting ready to wind up the class.

My voice was unusually high-pitched, quavering and stumbling as I tried to couch my question in a way that would not make me vulnerable to a crushing rejoinder. By this time I knew from hearing his responses to questions after his classes that the swami was capable of being quite sarcastic, though I had not realized that he was that way only with people who were not sincere or were just trying to "show off". I quavered, "What about trees? Cannot they be part of a spiritual experience? Cannot anything in the material world be part of our spiritual growth?" Then I waited for the thunderbolt to fall, but it didn't. The swami looked at me with the most melting affection and said, his voice dripping honey,

"Yes, of course. But it is a matter of the attitude of the person." It was not what he said so much as the way he said it. Rather than criticism I felt I was receiving the strongest validation, support and blessing I could ever imagine—the complete opposite of almost everything that had happened to me thus far. I felt that he understood what I was talking about, although I had not really told him anything; that he accepted me as a genuine spiritual seeker and loved me just as I was.

This was the kind of love I had experienced with Grannie, not based on anything but recognition of the spirit within me, no matter how I might deform or diffuse it with my various muddlements. Like her, he could see deep within me and respond to what I was really trying to say rather than to the nonsense I was babbling on the surface. She and he both *recognized* me for what I really am, a truly exhilarating experience after the bruising anguish I had been going through. Both Grannie and Swami had come into my life at a moment of desperate crisis—she after my mother's death and he at a moment when I was totally losing faith in the world and myself, an ominous echo of the events which had led up to my mother's suicide. Grannie had come when I was six and Swami when I was twenty-seven, approximately twenty years apart. Naturally, there was a huge difference in how their advent had affected me. Just a tot of five when my mother died, I barely understood what was going on and accepted more or less as a matter of course that I was living with my Grannie. I was then incapable of understanding what a great spiritual personality she was and indeed had taken it more or less for granted as it unfolded for me its unusual beauty. But when I met Swami I had experienced, as a more or less conscious adult, just how insensitive and cruel the world can be and was painfully aware of how I craved spiritual love and understanding, for which I had been seeking fruitlessly and with the maximum of anguish.

That I had met someone like Swami was a grace beyond my most overreaching imagination. At the time I felt it was an act of God, but now I can see it as part of a pattern repeating itself in what I had lived of the second twenty years of my life. As with my tothood, the first five years had been nothing but gathering thunderclouds, with the inevitable storm hitting me with the maximum force and leaving me bereft. I had now lost my mother and my father in the most agonizing of circumstances and had gone through a period of intense bereavement in which I had felt that the end of the world had come. But in both situations I had been given great moments of assurance in the form of a dream or dreams which inspired and supported me before the final event. As a tot I had accepted the dream without question, but having more understanding of their import and importance as a young adult, had relied on them more consciously to interpret what was happening to me and to replenish my energy for the seemingly unending battle. As a tot and as a young adult I had been led to a spiritual being who offered me a haven, which in the case of my grandmother had stood firm and given me a base from which to work. Would this Indian holy man, who seemed to be able to give me what my heart craved, prove as reliable as she had?

That question was to trouble me for some time; it is hard to get over the impression caused by the rebuffs and rejections one inevitably suffers in ordinary human relationships. But in March of nineteen sixty-nine, what was uppermost was a sense of the most intense happiness, of joy that I had met such a being. Later I learned that this stage is known as "rosy glow", the happiness and excitement of meeting your spiritual teacher. I felt as if I could do anything at all, fly over all obstacles and go and come back from the moon in the blink of an eye. I think it was that year that the first astronauts landed on the moon. Lou and I went to Central Park to see movies of it happening, projected on a huge outdoor screen. Naturally everyone was awestruck—but inwardly I felt that I had already been on the "moon" that it is within myself and that it was far more important. It also occurred to me that if the West generally focused a bit more on such interior "moon landings", our culture might be a bit more humane and decent in its dealings with the rest of the world.

Buoyed up like this, I began to feel that Swami was a person who could help me with my ongoing struggles, the most difficult of which at that time was my relationship to my work. I was beginning to realize that, even if I was working primarily to make money for my art career, I simply could not settle for the sort of half-baked way we were doing things at the Polyclinic. I still had some years more to work in order to achieve my goal of putting myself through art school in London, and would simply have to upgrade where I worked or I would go cuckoo. But upgrading to a teaching hospital, I knew, would mean much more demanding hours and work schedule, and I really wanted time to work on my art.

I kept turning all of this over and over in my mind, not sure if this was the sort of thing one discussed with someone so exalted as the swami seemed to be. I hesitated to approach him, but I was getting nowhere on my own. In addition, I did want to ask him more about the significance of the episode with the silver birch tree, for he had raised a doubt in my mind about an experience that had been so important and meaningful to me. On April twenty-fourth, nineteen sixty-nine I finally went to the Vedanta Society and met with Swami. He lived on the floor above the chapel, sleeping and working in the back room and using the large room in the front for interviews. As with the rest of the house, everything was old-fashioned, but kept with immaculate care; the room had the quality of a shrine, it was so clean, orderly and quiet. As I sat on the sofa waiting for Swami to come in I could feel myself relaxing and calming down. Always extremely punctual, Swami appeared at exactly the moment scheduled for our interview and showed the utmost warmth and even joy at seeing me. I felt more than welcome and any lack of self-confidence that I might have had simply evaporated. After a few pleasant remarks he sat down and turned to me, his face expectant and his whole being completely open to whatever I might say. I felt as if I were the only person in the whole world and that whatever I might say was the most precious utterance ever.

I quickly discovered just how powerful Swami was spiritually. It was obvious he was distressed to hear my tale of woe, but it took him no time to tell me, "Don't give up your medical work; you have spent so much time preparing to be a doctor and to change now will burn up so much energy. What you need now is to discover who you really are; put your energy there and then you will be able to answer all of these questions and make a correct decision." Although this was far from what I had expected or hoped to hear, it struck me as sensible and by far the best thing to do. In that light, the next step was simply to upgrade where I was working and to get to grips with the issue of my real identity—a project that seemed obvious then, but has proven excruciatingly difficult over the long run!

There remained the issue about the tree. Rather hesitantly I opened up the subject and told him that my question in the class a few weeks prior had arisen from an experience I had had. For the first time I felt I was with a person who would not misunderstand or mock me if I spoke about my inner life. And indeed, as I recounted my tale—for the very first time to another person—Swami remained quite calm and detached, showing no sign of reaction, good or bad. As I spoke of what had happened, it was natural that I should feel some of the exaltation of the moment, and I realized once again just how important a turning point the whole event had been. Swami, however, did not seem to be much affected by what I was telling him—a relief in many ways, for I was in mortal dread of the type of rejection I had suffered at the hands of my father and co-workers, even when speaking of things a lot less intimate and deep than this experience. When I finished speaking, he looked at me coolly and said, "You see, many people have experiences like this. What is important is development of character, of steadfastness, self-reliance, faith and understanding. Did this experience make any difference in that respect? That is the question."

From one standpoint this, too, was a rejection. Swami had not been impressed by my experience, it seemed, nor had he offered any interpretation of it, at least in any way I could have imagined. But he had made an important point about the main significance of spiritual life: The acid test of all spirituality was what kind of human being it produced. However, his remarks did not strike me as a putdown, but rather as a very practical approach to the question I had asked. I was, therefore, not in the least put out, but rather enthusiastic about getting on with becoming a better human being, whether that involved supernormal experiences or not.

However, Swami's Socratic question had started up something that was to be of great importance over the long haul: an ever-increasing examination and understanding of just how much my various experiences had molded my life. It took me nearly fifteen years to grasp just how important the "silver birch experience" had been: it had, in fact, given me something much deeper to hold on to at a time when the ground was slipping away from under my feet. If I had not had it, I could well have gone on to being a chronic rebel and malcontent, constantly angry and bitter and, like a number of other women whom I later met whose fathers had been alcoholic and abusive, an alcoholic or abusive person myself. The profound sense of shelter and protection I had found in the experience had kept me going through the darkness I had felt at Dollar, taking the half-seen form of a deeply supportive Dark Mother, whose face was hidden at the time. Yes, it had been a most important event of deep spiritual significance, as measured by how it had molded me as a human being. That Swami had challenged me on this subject was one of the best things that happened to me, for it set up a line of self-examination and inquiry which has radically formed my view of spiritual life and helped me to work through the overall view I am presenting in this very memoir.

In order to help me with my difficulties at work Swami suggested I read *The Practice of the Presence of God* by Brother Lawrence, a seventeenth century lay brother in a French Carmelite monastery. Brother Lawrence was a simple-hearted man of the people with a bad limp and a fervent heart. He had not found scholarly or contemplative pursuits to his taste, but reveled in his work in the monastery kitchen. He found in time that every movement and gesture he made as he toiled over the pots and pans was one of the uttermost joy, of communion with the divine. This wonderful man had learned, quite spontaneously, the art of spiritualizing work, of seeing the divine in what other people would consider mundane things and of infusing everything he did with the presence of God. His brother Carmelites, including those at the top of the hierarchy, saw him as an extremely wise and loving saint and revered him as such, though he himself had no notion of anything but the blissful presence of God.

Within a day or two of talking with Swami I set out to find this little book and thus to enter an almost entirely different world from what I had been living in. I had read Saint Augustine's *Confessions* and Saint Thomas à Kempis's *The Imitation of Christ*, but neither of them had struck me so forcefully as this unpretentious, simple-hearted testimony from an almost unknown saint. I naturally tried to follow it in practice, even through those excruciating meetings in my boss's office; with what success I have no idea. What was so important to me was the idea that it was possible to actually *experience* God directly, even in and through all of one's daily chores, no matter how arduous or difficult. I had felt the truth of this while talking to Swami, and engaging with Brother Lawrence merely served to reinforce this wonderful new discovery. Although not physically prepossessing, low key and sparing of words, Swami exerted a tremendous influence over me. I felt, for the first time in my life and without it having actually been said in so many words, that I was a genuinely spiritual being, that I would succeed in realizing my inner spiritual nature, and that following Swami's advice and guidance was the best way to do it. Without flickering a muscle I moved on to sign a contract for the following year with the Roosevelt Hospital, an affiliate of Columbia Presbyterian Medical School, where I knew full well I would have to work to a higher standard and therefore have less spare time for my art work. I continued on with my art classes for the rest of the semester, but already knew that I would not become a professional artist. Swami had made me understand that even my medical work was a way to progress spiritually and that it was not necessary to go through the effort to change my profession. Somehow that question had been resolved in the much bigger one: How to progress spiritually and thereby get beyond all of the conflicts that were besetting me.

My life had now taken a radically different turn, similar to what had happened on my move to Grant Street some twenty years prior. There the spirituality of my grandmother had taken me to "a safe place", where I could grow out of the pain and anger my early childhood experiences had engendered in me. But, of course, that did not mean that there would be no further struggle. When one moves forward spiritually, I believe, there is an almost automatic reaction from what the professionals call "the shadow", the dark, difficult side of the psyche, where lurk all the unresolved conflicts, not only of this particular life but of previous lives as well. In Grant Street I had had to face the sense of rejection and abandonment my mother's death had created in me, as well as the growing understanding that my father's attitude toward me was not much different from my mother's. Twenty years further on, the reaction from the depths took the form of continuing, truly blinding migraines, which not only continued unabated, but seemed to have me in a death-grip. The doctors were helpless, because vomiting was such a prominent feature of the attacks that I simply could not keep down any medicines they prescribed. I would lie in my darkened room, not eating, drinking, or thinking—in a sort of estevation or suspension of life. My mind was quite blank, lying helpless in the clutches of these "visitations".

Now a medical doctor and facing a severe handicap to both my professional and private life, I realized that I was going to have to deal with the situation myself. I knew that migraine attacks often have a psychosomatic basis and that keeping an accurate record of what I had eaten, done or thought before an attack would help me to get a handle on the situation. I therefore began a record that was to go on for twenty years, gradually understanding what was happening and what I had to do to solve the problem. It did not take me long to discover that lack of sleep, drinking coffee, tea and too much wine were potent triggers of the attacks. From there I went on to discover that my mad culture-vulturing, gadding all over New York every evening of the week except Tuesday (which was stay-home, cut-your-nails-and-clean-up night), was going to have to stop. These were painful discoveries, but it was inescapable that giving up the triggers definitely improved the situation: I had fewer attacks and much less devastating when I did have them. However, they did still continue, apparently playing the role of a "nanny", though even at the time I realized that it was a deeper level of myself that was speaking to me in language so direct that I simply had to obey it.

By the end of June I had become sufficiently close to the Vedanta Society to be invited to attend the annual seeing-off of Swami, who spent every summer in Southern California with his brother monk from India.

The California swami's large, bustling centers in Hollywood, Santa Barbara and Orange County could support guest swamis, unlike our own, small and low-key operation. We all went to the airport and had lunch there with Swami, many of the women teary-eyed, though smiling. I realized just how central Swami had become to the lives of these people, but of course in connection with the Vedanta Society I was still just a happy camper and my mind was busy with my plans for the summer. I enjoyed being with Swami's group, whom I was beginning to know a little bit, but was still quite definitely an outsider, for all intents and purposes.

Lou and I went on a perfectly blissful vacation to Pennsylvania. The weather was dry and sunny, the landscape picture-postcard and I was totally immersed in reading *The Gospel of Sri Ramakrishna*. This was one of the core texts of the Vedanta Society, the life and teachings of Ramakrishna, the man with the indrawn look on his face whose picture I had first seen on the altar at the Center. He was the

Ramakrishna: from a painting by Frank Dvorak.

spiritual inspiration for the movement behind our Center, a holy man who had lived in Bengal, India, in the nineteenth century. Such was the influence of his teachings that his disciple Swami Vivekananda had come to America at the end of the nineteenth century and had met with considerable success, being able to found our Center, which had subsequently been kept in operation by monks from the order the swami had founded in India.

The *Gospel* is actually a diary which one of Ramakrishna's disciples, Mahendranath Gupta, had kept during Ramakrishna's lifetime. Mahendranath had made a habit, as soon as he got home from his visits with the Master, of writing down all that Ramakrishna had said and done that day. It is, therefore, an extremely accurate and fresh account of the doings and sayings of a very spontaneous teacher, whose infinitely varied utterances would most likely have eluded the grasp of a less dedicated biographer. What made it even more interesting to me at that time was that the English translation of this book had come out in America in nineteen forty-two, in the depths of World War II, when it had seemed as if all lights of any sort had gone out, far less spiritual ones; and also the fact that the well-known scholar of myth, Joseph Campbell, had been involved in editing it. Its steady sales worldwide have only proven how relevant and valuable its contents are to spiritual seekers everywhere.

In the summer of nineteen sixty-nine, of course, I was more or less oblivious of all of the background to the book. Probably Swami had suggested I read it, and I was fulfilling a behest more than anything else. However, it was intriguing that Aldous Huxley, one of my literary heroes, had written the foreword. At Dollar I had read large numbers of his darkly satirical and even saturnine novels, and to now find him eulogizing this Hindu saint came as rather a surprise. This was naturally an incentive to keep going—there must be something worthwhile if Aldous Huxley had gotten involved! I soldiered on, perhaps struggling with my subconscious British disdain for the Hindus—not consciously fostered, but simply inherited, as it were. The opening paragraphs rather fed into this attitude, as they were the author's eulogy of the temple where Ramakrishna lived, and of his first impressions of the Master, with whom he "fell in love" at first sight. Mahendranath was bowled over by the simplicity, purity and affection of Ramakrishna, one of the most unassuming of people, despite his reputation as a very great holy man.

This was all well and good, but it reminded me of some of the devotional stuff I had read in some Catholic texts. "These Hindus are so sentimental!" I thought. "I am not sure I can read this book at all!" But Swami had asked me to do it, so I persevered. A few pages further on, I was amazed to find that Ramakrishna quite openly and overtly worshiped God as Mother Kali, the Black One. This was something utterly new! Unconsciously, the part of me that had felt as if I were being protected by an unseen, Dark Mother, responded. I realized just how much I had been longing to find a spiritual Mother to whom I could talk and with whom I could be completely free and open, unlike the Father-in-the-Sky Christianity offered me. And now here was a Mother—and how she made Ramakrishna laugh! Here was an almost unbelievably childlike soul, overflowing with happiness and spontaneity, responding to poor Mahendranath and his terrible domestic troubles with the utmost affection and empathy, just like a mother himself. This was more like what I had been so inchoately looking for! And, when a few pages later, Ramakrishna began to dance in ecstasy, overflowing with spiritual bliss, I was done for. Here was someone after my own heart—laughing, dancing and rejoicing in the divine, as I had felt in my visions of swimming in the Atlantic like a happy, free seal.

I could not put the book down and spoke of nothing but it. Lou had read it and knew it quite well, and our long walks we would discuss it endlessly, he asking me pointed questions and I elaborating on the ideas and theories that it was giving rise to in my receptive mind. Lou particularly dwelt on the idea of God as Mother, asking me over and over if it wasn't something a bit primitive. But I already had a strong feeling for Mother, as I was sure it was she who had been sustaining me through all of my struggles in Scotland. Whether or not she was "primitive" I had no idea and also could not care less about. She was what had supported me and that was enough. When I got back to New York I did a drawing of her, flying through the sky with her hair streaming in the wind and carrying a big sword. I knew that in certain forms this Dark Mother was represented as an old hag—perhaps evoking Grannie, though of course the last thing she was was a hag. At any rate, my Kali had a rather gaunt face and a masculine appearance, which satisfied me, though not any Hindu I showed it to. They preferred the feminine, prettified images of India—but for me Mother was not a pretty girl, but a strong, powerful woman with infinite ability to keep me moving forward and rising above anything the turning world could bring against me.

Painting by an unknown artist of the image of Kali
worshipped in Kolkata by Ramakrishna.

Maybe there were unconscious echoes of the images of the North Wind I had seen in the George MacDonald book (though even she was too feminine for my taste)—or, deeper still and as yet unknown, the formidable Celtic goddesses that lay in my own cultural inheritance.

My view of Kali, pencil on paper, New York, 1970.

A whole new life was opening out for me. In September, the beginning of the working year in America, I applied for membership at the Vedanta Society and was graciously accepted. Bill Conrad and John Schlenck, the two brothers whom I had gotten to know through friendly chats at the back of the chapel after classes and Sunday lectures, told me it was unusual for Swami to accept people so quickly and that I must have taken his fancy. Even more unusual was the invitation shortly thereafter to attend Swami's library classes, held on the nights when there was no public function. The library class, I learned, was by invitation only and very few were invited. I wondered how could Swami impose such a selective format on usually fiercely "democratic" Americans and at the same time realized I was involved with something out of the usual for America—or Britain, for that matter. Where could I find a person of such spiritual stature as Swami in the length and breadth of my native land?

I went to the class, which I found to be like nothing I had experienced thus far. It was held in the library amid the large number of potted plants John Schlenck maintained there. There were perhaps ten to fourteen "chosen" attendees, all of whom, other than myself, were "veterans". Someone would read a short passage from one of the texts of our movement, selected by Swami. These were books about the practical aspects of spiritual life, intimate and to the point in ways that any Christian groups with which I had been associated most certainly were not. After the reading, Swami would ask each person present what they had found of value, interest or whatnot. To my surprise, everyone came up with amazingly percipient contributions, mentioning things in the text which had completely escaped my notice. What the person selected reflected very much his or her own personality, and sometimes also the preoccupations particularly taking them up at any given moment. It occurred to me that in this class Swami was getting a clear window into the minds of his followers, an immediate "spot check" on where they were at that moment of time. He himself said very little, merely observing us closely and taking in all that was going on. But I did not feel that there was anything threatening or underhand in what we were doing. On the contrary, Swami's silent and serene presence was creating a background on which we were all feeling free to "paint" ourselves in the most frank and open way, discovering in this unusual situation not only a great deal about ourselves that would not otherwise be visible, but also about the others as well. The self-revelatory nature of this class made me realize why Swami had opted to make it selective; if anyone had been there of an antagonistic or contrary nature, it would not have been possible for us to be so open and so self-revealing. I understood that I was highly privileged to have been invited to participate, and never ever missed one of these unique evenings.

Occasionally, one of the group would blurt out some problem that had been troubling recently—usually one of the men. And sometimes it was quite close to the bone, dealing with sex or competitiveness or greed. At that time Swami would get involved, engaging the student in a Socratic dialog, sometimes upbraiding him, or actually giving an impromptu talk, explaining the principle involved. But whether Swami addressed our issues in words or with his more usual silence, I always felt as if my tank had been filled to the brim, giving me strength to go out and face the next day in a much more calm and recollected spirit. In our library classes we were seated at the center of the universe, I felt; directly in connection with the source of energy that animates everything. And in addition, I was being welded to Swami and his close group in a way that nothing else could have done.

In the medical world of America, junior posts change on the first of July, and that year I moved to a job as a second year resident at the Roosevelt Hospital, a nice little facility in midtown Manhattan, which served as a community hospital and also was affiliated with the Columbia Presbyterian Medical School. In many ways, it was the best of many worlds: with high standards of work and teaching, big enough to see quite a variety of material, but small enough and community-centered enough to be very friendly.

Once again my life and career seemed to be moving upwards; but, as always, there was a downside. As I grew closer and closer to Swami and Vedanta, Lou began to show signs of resentment and bipolar destabilization. During the first year he had come with me three times a week to attend the public classes and services at the Vedanta Society, but after I started to attend there every evening he dropped out, and for the first time since I had known him he began to show his negative side seriously. I would find him in strange and disturbing frames of mind, in which he did not accuse me of anything or explain what the problem was; he just simply was "funny". I did not realize what was going on at the time, but I see now that he was jealous and that that had triggered his bipolar disorder.

I was extremely fond of Lou and in addition owed him a tremendous debt for giving me so much happiness and for introducing me to Vedanta. I did everything I could to soothe him and assuage his troubled mood. But of course it was hopeless. He just quite simply did not have the same interest as I and, in addition, was suffering from mental imbalance which would respond only to medication—and that he quite simply would not take. There were many difficult episodes which left me feeling bereft and almost hopeless—though, of course, that was silly, for I had a whole new group to which I belonged, as well as many other professional friends.

All this exacerbated my migraines, which assailed me once again with renewed vigor. I would be prostrate once again for up to three days, sometimes almost wishing to die, I felt so sick. By that time I had begun to speak directly to Kali, the Dark Mother whom I had met through *The Gospel of Sri Ramakrishna*. Through that medium the Mother who had supported me all along had now taken a form and had a name, to which I would now turn in my prayers and call on when I was in distress. One day, as I was lying in the deepest agony, in terrible pain and vomiting as though there could be no end to it, I felt her presence above me and looked up with the eyes of the spirit. I saw her, not in any particular form, but radiant, powerful, and profoundly loving. "Mother! Mother!" I cried feebly. I felt her bending down toward me and then she lifted me up in her arms and held me very close to her heart. I could hear it beating and felt that I was at the center of the cosmos, where all that exists was being generated. Time stood still, for how long I do not know. I was lying in the dark, enveloped by the Dark and in utter darkness of mind. When I became aware of myself again, my pain was still there but was not touching me in the slightest. It was possible to get through the remainder of the attack, standing back, as it were, and observing it. Even in the incredibly primal state I was in, I could understand that I had tapped into a part of me that transcended my body and was looking at it as something other than what I really am.

In some ways this was similar to the experience with the tree—but this time it was much less a visitation from outside and more something that came from within. I had called on her consciously and she had responded. I had understood more fully what was happening, and had been able to see what it meant in terms of my inner experience. In addition, it was something that was "mine", not so much something that happened to me. I had several more bad migraine attacks over the next year and in all of them she came and held me, taking me to a deeper and more peaceful place, where the emotional anguish could no longer touch me.

I had not the slightest doubt that this "upgrading" of my inner experience was due to the influence Swami had on me and to the Vedanta I was now studying. There I was learning that it is possible to transcend the body through systematic practice and meditation and even to go beyond the realm of emotion, intellect and more, beyond which you discover the very core of who you are. At the first library class I had attended I had heard the word *Self* mentioned several times in the reading, and wondered what it meant. From the context, it was clear that it did not mean what we usually mean by *self*—our bodies, for the most part. I therefore asked Swami toward the end of the class, "Swami, I keep hearing this word *Self*. What does it mean?" He looked at me closely for a moment and then said, "It means what you think it means. Try to find out what it means *right now*, as you are. Then live it, live *in* it, find out all that it is. If you keep asking and trying to find out, you will discover deeper and deeper meaning." From one standpoint, this answer could be seen as Oriental evasion; but for me at that moment, it was an open sesame. I had real interest in knowing who I am on deeper and deeper levels and here was Swami giving me a formula through which to arrive at the answer. He did not give pat definitions, dogmas or anything of the sort, but an invitation to explore and find out for myself, which was exactly how I wanted to hear the answer—I wanted to discover for myself.

On Fridays Swami would have the library class read and ponder the works of Swami Vivekananda, Ramakrishna's "emissary to the West", who had worked in America in the eighteen-nineties. As this young man had been educated in Western mode, and had also

A poster of Swami Vivekananda at the World's
Parliament of Religions, Chicago, 1893.

experienced the spiritual depths of Vedanta under the tutelage of
Ramakrishna, his presentation of Vedanta was an integration of both. He
conveyed profound experiences in the language of the West, particularly
of the perennial philosophy and German Idealism, itself a product of the
Western search for Vedantic truth. Vivekananda had an utterly brilliant,
diamond-sharp mind which penetrated to the depths of anything he spoke
of. I was dazzled by his brilliance and found his exposition of raja yoga,
the yoga of meditation (which he called the most "scientific" of the yogas)
absorbingly interesting. There he discussed the various levels of consciousness
which can be accessed through rational, systematic practice, at the same
time using the language of the kundalini with its chakras symbolizing the
different levels. I think that part of the fascination was because I myself
had tapped into levels of consciousness that were not only so different from
"normal", but also so very, very healing and transformative. Where else was
I finding an explanation of what was going on, and so accessible? I had
the deepest admiration for and loyalty to the scientific method, though I
had utterly rejected the materialism of science as it was being practiced,

and it seemed to me that in Vivekananda I was finding scientific method brought to bear on human consciousness, a wonderful integration of two areas I was engaged with. The result was very stimulating; and, in addition, it carried me beyond my previous, superficial feelings about the turban the swami was depicted as wearing, for I had by now realized that this was the spiritual teacher whose works I had rejected some seven years previously in the Edinburgh Public Library on account of his Indian garb.

I had always spent some time in the morning and evening "praying", as Grannie had asked me to do. Such praying was more or less rumination over how my life was going forward and attempts to touch an inner base that would help to stabilize me and help me to keep steady. Reading Vivekananda's *Raja Yoga* I came to understand that in addition to such exercises, it was of the utmost importance to lead a disciplined life, not giving in to excesses nor skimping on what was absolutely necessary. I began to understand that the direction my migraines were pushing me in was precisely that of more control and balance, regular eating, sleeping and habits of work, along with avoidance of artificial stimulants, rather than the rather wild and overloaded way I had been rushing around, spreading my energy in many different directions.

All this was extremely helpful and gave me a deeper and deeper feeling of worth and meaningfulness. But, along with that, I began to chafe against Vivekananda's magisterial intellectuality. Raja yoga was valuable, but what I really needed was love—and at that moment in time, I was not able to see how love and intellect were compatible, nor was I fully aware of how much my own intellectuality was making it difficult to find love, particularly with men. Even before meeting Swami made him jealous, Lou's increasingly dark mood was, I now see, due to some extent to his resentment of my intellectual dominance—and, I now suspect, my ability to more than hold my own intellectually with my father may well have contributed to the difficulties I had had with him. Women are supposed to be soft, gentle and pliable, not self-assertive and capable of carrying on an in-depth analysis of anything. But such was my interest in ideas and their development that I would never hold back on a promising discussion, even if it meant ruffling the feathers of whatever man I was speaking with.

On this dark background drone, a new note was introduced in the library classes. We began to read a little book of conversations of Sarada Devi, the spiritual consort of Ramakrishna. She had been quite a bit younger than he, and after his death had become for over thirty years the *de facto* guide of the movement begun by Vivekananda on his return to India from the West. Although lacking in formal education, she was a woman of the most profound intelligence, unerring in her wise judgments and generosity of heart. Her decisions became, quite naturally and without any coercion, absolute law to the group of brilliant, spiritually advanced disciples Ramakrishna left to carry on his work. One example of her way of thinking referred to the celebration of Durga Puja, the fall festival of the Divine Mother, a major event in the

lives of the people of Bengal. Swami Vivekananda, a warrior at heart, had felt that it would be appropriate to leave in place the animal sacrifice that traditionally was part of this festival; his ideas on Vedanta themselves were revolutionary and he perhaps wished to avoid further friction with the Hindu fundamentalists, who already had caused him considerable grief since his return from the West. But Sarada Devi, speaking with the utmost gentleness and tender persuasion, quietly said no. She herself had also suffered at the hands of fundamentalists, but nevertheless could see that it was time to do away with the lingering barbarism of some of the ancient Hindu festivals. Such was her presence and spiritual authority that Vivekananda, along with all of his followers, obeyed her implicitly, and there was no further animal sacrifice or discussion about it.

Entering her world through the pages of the book we were studying in the class, I found that this woman was the most self-effacing person imaginable. She followed the traditional purdah system of India, remaining indoors with her group of women companions and hiding her face behind a veil when talking with men. However, when it came to responding to the needs of others, she was quite fearless and self-giving. She gave her love and blessings to people whom the stringent Indian caste system pronounced untouchable, or hated foreigners, such as the Muslims or Westerners. She would talk with such people, feed them, and get involved in their ongoing struggles and problems, herself risking outcasting. Anyone in need, whether of the body, emotions, intellect, or spirit, she would make her very own and care for like a mother, following their progress with affectionate concern and giving, giving, giving way beyond what most of us would consider reasonable. And the recipient would find in short order that his or her life had been radically transformed, moving to deeper and deeper levels of spiritual experience and the capacity to love and give. She became known to all as Mother, the embodiment of spiritual motherhood.

Mother summarized her whole attitude to the world on her deathbed, when she said, "Learn to make the whole world your own. No one is a stranger. Do not look into the faults of others: rather, look into your own. The whole world is your own." How she herself made everyone her own was dramatically illustrated in the pages of the little book we pondered evening after evening at the Vedanta Society. Gently, quietly, lovingly, she responded to situation after situation, behaving like a simple-hearted and infinitely affectionate mother, although she was, in fact, brilliantly intelligent and wielded spiritual power of a magnitude we as yet have not understood in its fullness. Like everyone else who has come to know of her, she exerted a profound influence on me and I began to see that intelligence and creativity can be utilized in many ways, even that of a seemingly humble housewife. But despite this persona, Mother was not petty-minded like so many housewives I had known. She understood and supported brilliant, gifted women like Ramakrishna's niece, her own companion Yogin Ma, and Sister Nivedita, Vivekananda's Anglo-Irish disciple whose task it was to uplift and educate the women of India. Mother put her huge spiritual authority behind them, while behaving toward them as a loving mother, always ready to soothe and inspire them.

A word which came up a great deal in Vedanta was *purity*. It was not part of my existing religious vocabulary, and indeed it sounded a bit ominous, in a way, fraught with possibilities for holier-than-thou-ness, one of the scourges of religious people. One day it occurred to me that purity is a word used in chemistry; when isolating any compound, purification is a vital step in the process of identification. Purification there means removing anything that is not the compound being isolated. By analogy, it came to me in a flash that spiritual purity is the state where there is absolutely nothing but awareness of the divine, uncontaminated with any base or selfish alloy. And just what it meant in practice had been made crystal clear, first by Swami's behavior, which was so utterly focused on spirit (his name Pavitrananda meant the *bliss of purity*), and now by the life and teachings of Mother Sarada, so transparently a manifestation of spiritual motherhood, with its utter unselfishness and giving. It seemed almost impossible that such people could exist at all, but there it was—and right before me. I began to feel what the word *blessed* means.

In the fall that year I decided to take a short vacation in upstate New York. I had decided to read another large work on Ramakrishna—*The Great Master*, written by Swami Saradananda, one of his close disciples, himself a very developed spiritual person and familiar, not only with the Indian tradition, but also with Western ways of thinking. Almost as soon as I opened the book, I found it utterly fascinating, an enthralling blend of explanation of the different levels of consciousness that Ramakrishna had passed through and made his own and also of Western-style historical biography. As soon as I had finished breakfast and my morning walk, I would settle into a hammock with my tome and be oblivious to the world until lunchtime. I lived, moved and had my being in the world of consciousness beyond the mundane—and mundane it certainly was. One day at tea time some of my fundamentalist Christian host and hostess's visitors were extolling the Reverend Ian Paisley, a Protestant fundamentalist in Northern Ireland, whose hatred of the Catholics was proverbial and whose curmudgeonly opposition to a solution to the "Irish question" was effcctively preventing it from ever happening. It took me all of my self-control to remain silent, but finally I could keep quiet no longer. "That man should be hanged!" was my sensitive contribution to the conversation! My hostess liked me a lot and was unaffected, but her husband did not speak to me again, as I recall.

But by that time such things had no effect on me. I was utterly absorbed in the knowledge that a human being can attain to levels of consciousness indistinguishable from the divine and also live in our world, to all intents and purposes like an "ordinary" person. I knew the Christian notions of divine incarnation, but they had seemed so remote, so *calculating*, that I could not really get involved with them. They seemed to turn the beautiful Christ into a dreary, pompous, self-righteous Presbyterian meenister with no attraction whatsoever. The witness to Ramakrishna that I was now reading was quite different. Ramakrishna was such an accessible, loveable and contemporary person, speaking so directly to the exact problems I was struggling with, that he himself was irresistible; and the interpretations that the learned author of the book was offering made so much sense in terms of psychology that I accepted them effortlessly. I was not being asked to accept some myth based on old notions of animal sacrifice (the atonement) or cannibalism as in the Christian communion, but was being offered a systematic, believable explanation of levels of consciousness innate in human makeup and susceptible to cultivation through time-tested methods of self-transformation. It was possible for me to accept these ideas, at least provisionally, because I myself had experienced some of what I read in the book, and in addition I had seen the life of my grandmother and now Swami, both of whom were quite palpably living in spheres of consciousness way beyond the round of materialism, selfishness, competitiveness, and hatred that passes for "normal" in our culture.

But again, the course of true love never does run smooth, as they say. At some point during nineteen-seventy—I think near the beginning—Swami became sick, with recurrent fevers and prostration. Never of robust health, he was laid low by this enigmatic sickness and he was unable to conduct the classes and lectures. As the Center had recorded all of his talks, there was no dearth of materials to play at the various slots on the public schedule, but it meant, of course, that we were deprived of his actual presence. Worse, for me, was the end of the library classes and opportunities to talk with him at interviews. I desperately missed the inspiration of being in his company and began to pine for him. Lou and I still went out on expeditions in and around the city, but the life had gone out of our relationship and indeed Lou tended to give me a rather hard time. I was not happy.

At my work I had become quite friendly with Dr. Sanford Farrar, one of the staff members in the pathology department. Although the standard of work at the Roosevelt was high, Sandy was outstanding and set the bar of performance very high indeed. Working with him was not just business as usual—it was always a memorable learning experience, which I deeply appreciated. From his side, he was appreciative of my own efforts and would involve me in little research projects, which deepened my understanding of pathology and how to "do" it well. One day, when we were looking at slides together, Sandy suddenly said, "Jean, you are wasting your time here. A person of your caliber should be working at Harvard University." As he himself was a Harvard man, he knew whereof he spoke. I was extremely taken aback and replied, "Sandy, I have no plans to leave New York. I like the Roosevelt and I think it is pretty good. Thanks for the suggestion, but it is a no-starter." But one of Sandy's characteristics was tenacity. He would never take no for an answer, and was known as a bit of a holy terror in the lab, of which he was the supervisor. Having once broached the subject with me, he never let it go. Again and again and again the subject of Harvard came up, me protesting and he insisting.

When he first brought up the subject Lou and I were still best friends and I was getting close to Swami. New York seemed like the center of the world and I had absolutely no desire to leave. But as the months passed, as Lou became funny and Swami disappeared into his room upstairs, I began to weaken. Maybe Sandy was right. Swami had asked me to concentrate on my medical work, and where would that be possible if not at Harvard? I was really quite happy at the Roosevelt, but maybe I would be better off in a more high-powered place. I had, of course, doubts about my ability to perform at such an august institution, but Sandy was adamant that that was not a question at all. I began to wonder if perhaps going to Harvard was what Swami would want of me—but of course he was not available for comment. I was becoming more and more interested in my work and Harvard would indeed give me experience and training second to none. It would perhaps be better if I moved on, getting away from my difficulties with Lou and those friends whose lifestyle, involving drugs, was becoming increasingly difficult for me to live with. And again, there was a Vedanta Society in Boston, whose swami I had met and liked instantly.

This indecision went on for months. I was seriously torn between New York and Boston, and just could not make up my mind. Sandy must have sensed my indecision and mounted an aggressive attack on me. "You are just wasting your life, working at this level! You have the capacity to be really great! You are just cut out for Harvard!" To my thoughts that my credentials were not good enough for Harvard he always would shout, "I will give you credentials that no one can turn down! They know me very well there and will listen to me!" Finally, somewhere in the early fall of nineteen-seventy I caved in and agreed to go to Boston for an interview at the Peter Bent Brigham Hospital, Sandy's old *alma mater*. To my utter amazement I met with the most cordial reception and was offered a job as a senior resident in pathology.

Now I was in a pickle. I was facing the reality of leaving New York. Suddenly my relationship with Lou seemed very important and in addition, Swami's health had improved after his annual summer visit to Hollywood, where the doctors had gotten to the bottom of his problem and resolved it. Classes and lectures had resumed as before, along with the library classes. The idea of leaving seemed impossible; my willingness to contemplate it had perhaps been driven by the loss of Swami from my life, and now that he was back again the prospect of leaving was terrible. I agonized over the problem for a month or so, but never once thought of asking Swami about it. Certainly, now that I had decided to remain in the medical profession I felt that it would be foolish to pass up an opportunity for advancement like this, no matter what the personal cost. From another side, it may have been that I had gotten so used to making my own decisions that it did not occur to me to confer with anyone; or, perhaps, there was one side of me—contrary and defiant—that was not about to be told what to do, even by such a wonderful, spiritual man as Swami. It would have been difficult to see at that time when I was totally immersed in the rosy glow, but all unbeknownst to me there was, at the center of what seemed like a beautiful, perfect apple, the worm that seems to be inevitable in the human condition.

CHAPTER 15

OUT OF THE FRYING PAN: 1971-73

I started work at the Peter Bent Brigham Hospital, Boston, on July first, nineteen seventy-one. Almost immediately I realized that I had jumped from the frying pan of my emotions in New York into a fire of a ruthlessness and competition that burned beyond all understanding. For the first time in my life I was with people whose main interest was in trying to win a Nobel Prize and who were willing to do anything to get it, including sleeping overnight in their labs and seeing their families only occasionally. We house-staff had tiny little cubicles to work in, exposed to all the noise and bustle of other staff coming and going and seemingly endlessly talking. I yearned for the Roosevelt, with its nice, clean and well-appointed facilities and low-key staff! There seemed to be no concern for our working conditions at the Brigham, though of course the crush may have partially been due to antiquated facilities and lack of space. We worked ferocious hours, from eight to five and half days Saturday, with the expectation that we do independent research and paper-writing in our own time. As I remember it, we were on call every second night and weekend, and when on call would almost always be called to perform autopsies, even during the night. I used to wonder what constituted an emergency in the case of autopsies—being carried out on patients who were already quite dead!

Shortly after going to Boston I started going out with one of our staff members, Chris, an American who had two Ph.D.s—not that unusual in that environment. He was a nice man, but I quickly realized that we were living in two utterly different worlds. This situation vividly illustrated for me one day when we went for a hike in the countryside.

I was blissed-out at getting out of the concrete, noisy city and into the quiet, soothing presence of the forest and hills, but he was obsessed with his gear. There just seemed to be no end to the adjustments he had to make to his boots, his backpack, whatever; and as we moved forward I realized that he was all but oblivious to nature around us. I suddenly realized that most Americans lived mentally in concrete, glass and metal boxes (with lights eternally burning, energy was so cheap), with no windows or doors to nature, its processes, its silent transformations and its beauty. No matter how hard I tried to get the subject off his equipment and theories, we never got more than a few inches further out into what was around us.

This was of course in the days before the ecological movement had really gotten underway; the degree to which the Americans I was meeting were dissociated from natural processes was nothing but dumbfounding, I must say. They had no idea of where the sun and moon were, of the seasons, of the subtle and beautiful transformations eternally going on. Nor, for that matter, of their own bodies and how they worked. They tended to be overweight, gulping down foods that to me were nothing but textured plastic, and endlessly taking painkillers, antacids and nowadays mood enhancers. I realized that the technological sophistication of Americans had actually trapped them in a cocoon (made, of course, of the latest "wonder fiber") from which it was going to be difficult to escape, and was rather grateful for my own, exceedingly "low tech" upbringing, which had kept me close to the land, the sea and the myths associated with them, some of which I had created myself. I felt the same gritty, materialistic "dust" settling on me as I had at Dollar, Edinburgh, and New York, the this-worldly, to-hell-with-people attitude that characterized everything we did. What mattered was how the equipment was working, what results were being got, whether one was a step nearer the Nobel, or at least promotion in the hierarchy. Everything else was simply grist for the mill, throw it all in, willy-nilly, and grind it to a pulp. In such an environment it was very difficult for me to make friends of any sort, other than Chris, who seems to have had more emotional content than the others.

I naturally sought the companionship of the people at the Vedanta Center, located not far from where I lived. The swami there, Swami Sarvagatananda, was an unusually lovely man with much of the same

spiritual quality as Swami Pavitrananda. I made a point of attending all of the Sunday lectures that I could get to, but was disappointed to find that there was no program at the Center from Sunday afternoon through Wednesday evening. Swami Sarvagatananda followed a grueling schedule of running two centers, one in Boston and the other in Providence, splitting his time equally between them. He would leave for Providence after lunch on Sunday and return to Boston on Wednesday evening, thus living up to his name, Sarvagata-nanda, which means the bliss of that which goes everywhere. This is a name of the divine, indicating its omnipresence—but in his case, it also meant, quite literally, moving like a shuttle every single week.

Early on, somewhere in the fall, I went to the Center to talk with Swami privately. Reaching the top of the many steps leading to the door of the large mansion by the Charles River, I rang the bell and waited. I was expecting, as in New York, that one of the devotees would answer—usually, in New York, Miss Jeanne Genet, one of the ladies in residence at the Center. She was always perfectly groomed, a professional receptionist who ushered us in with the maximum of genteel formality. Swami himself never answered the door, almost certainly because Jeanne and her mother (as I later learned) insisted on waiting on him hand and foot. I was, therefore, surprised when Swami Sarvagatananda opened the door, and the more so because he was dressed so informally, wearing an apron and with an oven mitt on his free hand. "Come in!" he said warmly. "I have some cookies in the oven, nearly ready. We'll make some tea and we can have cookies." This was so utterly different from New York I was really quite speechless. But who can resist freshly baked cookies, particularly when offered with so much cordiality and affection? I felt at once that if Swami Pavitrananda in New York was my spiritual father, Swami Sarvagatananda of Boston was my spiritual mother.

I never felt with Swami Sarvagatananda the awe that I had felt with Swami Pavitrananda. He was so very accessible, so very down to earth that I felt he was my best and closest friend. I was able to talk with him freely and he, for his part, included me at once in what he was doing and the work of the Center. He invited me to join the group on Saturday mornings which convened to clean the Center and participate in a class together and then have lunch.

Although I was deeply grateful for this all-too-brief oasis on Saturday mornings, it was nowhere near as concentrated and intense as the New York library group, for which I began to feel quite a strong nostalgia. Not long after I moved to Boston I got into the habit of going down to New York whenever I had a weekend off, which was once or twice a month. In many ways, I had never really left New York, for I was on the phone with Lou hours at a stretch and more than once a week. This, for me, was something quite new. As with other technologies, I was no fan of the telephone and regarded it as merely an instrument for getting things done. But the loneliness and isolation I felt in Boston led me to spend huge sums of money on endless talks with Lou, who was still one of my best friends and hearing whose voice brought me a degree of consolation. I quickly worked out a plan: somehow I would get out of work at three on Friday, beat the rush by a hairsbreadth to the Greyhound bus depot and settle in for the four-hour ride to New York with my *Atlantic Monthly*.

But, although my visits were ostensibly to visit Lou, in actual fact I dropped off my bag at his place and immediately went over to the Center for the Friday night class. Saturday morning and afternoon Lou and I would go for one of our long rambles, but come the evening I was there at the library group, feeling as if I had finally come home and was really myself. Sunday, right after the lecture at the Center, I would grab a bite to eat and jump on the bus to keep ahead of the huge crowds which seemed to commute every weekend between Boston and New York. But, although these "immersions" at the New York Center brought me back to life, as it were, I did not consciously focus on that fact. I just mechanically and without fail made the trip, month after month, not in the least analyzing what I was doing. The next time I would see Swami Sarvagatananda he would invariably inquire about

Swami Pavitrananda, showing the utmost reverence and affection for him. So complete was his focus on Swami that I was rather impressed. I had such tremendous regard for the accessible Boston swami that I had rather tended to minimize Swami Pavitrananda, who seemed rather remote, not only in place but also psychologically—and all this despite the fact that I was buzzing down to New York and going out of my way to be in his presence at every possible opportunity! As this scenario repeated itself month after month it slowly began to dawn on me that Swami Pavitrananda was something more than out of the usual. To be held in such unfailing esteem by the Boston Swami made me realize that he was very, very special—and, despite myself, I had to admit that there was a strong attraction that made me undertake the rather grueling trip every second weekend or so.

I now see quite clearly what a huge influence Swami Pavitrananda had on me from the moment I met him. When I was with him it seemed as if I really was who I was in every sense; but away from him there was a restlessness and unhappiness that was really quite devastating, and was making my stay in Boston far more difficult than it would otherwise have been. What was strange was that I practically never thought about him—but whenever I had the chance, I made a beeline back. Somehow part of me was suppressing what I felt, partially my usual pulling-back from people I loved. But I think that with Swami Pavitrananda there was something more. This was a blazing fire of spirituality, not sweet and comforting like Swami Sarvagatananda, but challenging me to come forward and be totally transformed in its intensity. Subconsciously I was running away from it, fearing that I would once again be mangled; and this time, perhaps, even destroyed. Talking with others about this situation, I have subsequently discovered that quite a number of people "ran away" to some degree from the power of the guru, and also that several people were particularly in awe of Swami, who was so uncompromising and spiritually powerful. I was not alone in my situation—but I was perhaps unique in my utter oblivion as to what was going on; and certainly very thorough in my "running away", putting several hundred miles of eastern seaboard between myself and him. I felt tremendously empty and many a night would cry myself to sleep, not really knowing what I was crying about and feeling thoroughly silly.

In I believe September or October of that year Mary came to visit me for about three weeks. Uncle George had died shortly after I had gone to Boston and she had moved from the Clipsham farm to the local town, Stamford. It had all been exhausting and difficult, and I had suggested she come to America for a change. I meant well, but of course, with the hours I was working I could not really be as available for her as I wanted. And Mary and I were not at all in sync. She was obsessed with how my career was going and whether I had plans to marry and settle down—concerns that could not have been further from my mind. She was delighted to meet Chris, with whom she had far more in common than she did with me. Among other things, Chris took us out to a lobster dinner, which tickled Mary pink as she donned her bib and dealt with the butter and claws and whatnot. She and Chris were as thick as thieves, with me looking on in silent misery.

I felt, once again, that I simply was not meant for this world; and when Mary began to pressure me over marrying Chris, I really thought my head would split open. How could she understand how men and women related to each other at that time? Marriage for her had worked out wonderfully, coming after decades of waiting by a man who was most unusual in his one-pointed devotion to her. Did such things exist any more? I felt that, romantic as it was, it was a thing of the past, as indeed was my intense craving to find someone who was as dedicated as I to the world of the spirit. I now felt that the idea of partnership which I longed for was not on the cards, and I had basically given up any notion of ever finding a man who could even conceive of such a thing. Chris was a nice man, but living in a world which not only had no interest for me, but also was rapidly becoming something I really detested. As Mary rattled on, I felt every word like a hammer blow; I loved her and wanted to make her happy, but what she was looking for was totally out of the question. Over and above even that, I had now tasted a relationship that was so utterly beyond all of this that I was becoming very impatient with what I increasingly regarded as mere silliness. I could not of course tell Mary any of this, for she would not have understood a word of it and have been hurt and angered by it; and besides, I could barely put it into words myself. What I did say, with my usual pungency, was: "Mary, you and Chris get along so well—why don't the two of you get married! I think it would be a much better match than him and me."

Tremendous pressure was building in my head, what with my reservations about my work, my struggles with my feelings for Lou and Chris, my unacknowledged longing for Swami, and Mary's well-meaning interrogations. I realized more clearly than I ever had how different were the worlds she and I lived in. She was an extremely good person who loved me intensely, but she could never understand the interest in and longing for the inner world of spiritual experience and knowledge that was moving to center stage of my life at that time. It was inevitable that a migraine would hit—and hit it did, in one of the worst attacks ever, just a couple of days before she was to leave. I had had migraines with more pain, but the vomiting this time was just terrible. I felt as if I was going to die, and kept wondering where it all came from. I knew I must be terribly dehydrated, as I could not keep even water down.

Poor Mary was very distressed. There was really nothing she could do to help. I wouldn't let her call a doctor, as I knew that this thing would resolve itself in due time. But it was extremely unpleasant for her in my one room apartment, watching me in such agony. Finally, she got up and put on her coat. "Jean, I am going out for a walk," she said. "The fresh air will do me good." I felt bad at the idea of her out in the Fenway in the cold fall weather by herself, but I was helpless to do anything about it. I just had to lie there, wishing I was dead. My one and only consolation was that she was such a pro-active person she would make of the situation not only the very best, but probably come home with some new friend she had made.

I lay there in the dark, spiraling downward and downward into some huge black, unnamed hole that threatened to obliterate me completely. Suddenly the scene shifted and I saw that I was immersed in a huge, black, rapidly flowing river that threatened to carry me off to heaven knows where. I had somehow managed to catch hold of a rock jutting out of the water near the bank of the river and was clinging on to it for dear life. But the strategy was not really helping me: the impact of the current kept throwing me against the bank, banging, banging, banging me mercilessly. I was all bruised and battered and wondered if I was going to survive at all. Something from within myself was crying and crying, but in utter silence, which seemed to permeate the whole scene, for I could not hear the rushing of the river any more.

This was a desperate situation which seemed to go on for an eternity. Then suddenly I heard a voice saying, "Why are you clinging on like this? Let go and you will be all right." It was a woman's voice, sweet, gentle and at the same time authoritative—not in a masculine way, but out of love. This, I felt dimly, is Mother herself telling me what I need to do because she understands me and knows what will really help. I did not see any form, but was quite sure it was Mother Sarada Devi who was speaking to me. "Mother!" I cried, "Mother, I want to let go but I can't! I'm afraid of what the river will do to me!" Then I fell asleep, or passed into some sort of state where the whole thing disappeared. What woke me up was Mary coming back in. I sat up in bed and said, "Mary, would you like a cup of tea?" Her look of worry changed into a smile. "Can you take some tea?" she asked. Yes, I could—and did. And probably a cookie or two.

As Mary was leaving a couple of days later, I put all my attention on helping her get ready and to keeping her happy. Which I am glad to say I succeeded in doing. She had been distressed by my obvious anguish—and of course her inability to understand what was going on—but my sudden recovery lifted her spirits considerably. I had returned to my usual rather jolly self, humoring her and paying great attention to her needs. And of course I had felt badly about my previous behavior, over which I had no control.

Some deep shadow had been speaking, confronting her and what she stood for, possibly giving her a message of what was to come. This was a widow in mourning, whom I had invited to travel a long, long way—and here was I acting up and out, just as I had as a little girl some twenty years before. Then I had been enraged by my parents' behavior and was in total rebellion, what with my Irish chums and gutter language. As a trained psychiatric nurse, Mary had been able to understand and support me then; but what she was facing now was much more subtle and very difficult for her to understand. I myself was hard put to understand it, and of course had no time to work on the matter while she was still with me. That would take time—quite a lot of time, in fact.

I was glad I had "done right" by her by having her visit; but at the same time I had realized that the gulf between us was rapidly widening and that I was now completely "on my own". She was not going to be the one to help me out of my present tailspin, as she had twenty years before. I had moved into a completely new space and, repeating the same sequence as I had previously, was going to have to work it all out according to the new ground rules of my life. That I had somehow made a direct connection with Mother Sarada was clear. In the same way, I had connected up with the Dark Mother (whom I now knew as Kali) twenty years previously when facing the terrible anger that was raging in my heart and leading me to defy my family and its social conventions. As I had with the Dark Mother, I found Mother Sarada's presence extremely calming and soothing, which was of course the primary need at that moment. But what exactly did the experience mean? What was she trying to tell me? What did the river signify, what the rock and what the need to let go my hold of what seemed on the surface to be the means of survival? At that particular moment I did not have a clue. But whoever sets the stage for these dramas was busy in the wings getting me set up to find an answer.

What was clear was that my ability to understand what was going on was considerably developed. When I was ten years old, all I knew was a sense of defiance and not *why* I felt it, nor how my big experience with the tree was connected with it in any way. Now, twenty years later, I was not really clear what was going on, but there was an awareness of the conflict between the "outer" world of work and family, which relentlessly emphasized the external and material, and the "inner" world which was beckoning me through my adherence to Vedanta and to the two wonderful swamis who were leading me deeper into it. In some ways I already knew where I was heading, away from efforts to make an impression in the "ordinary" world and to establish myself once and for all in the "inner worlds" which as yet I only knew about sketchily.

THIRD QUARTER

ANOTHER BIG DECISION

CHAPTER 16

TACKLING THE PROBLEM: 1971-1973

One thing was clear: I had just come through another major turning point, in which, almost like a stage drama, the clouds billowing around me had cleared and I had seen into the depths of my own soul. I have never understood why the deeper levels of one's being always speak in parables and don't just make it clear in so many words what is going on. Perhaps the rational mind puts some sort of filter on the soul which makes it so difficult to understand. Certainly the episode with the tree, while it uplifted me tremendously, was a total surprise and left me not a lot the wiser, though of course it radically changed my behavior. Which was, of course, what was most important at that moment of time. That said, it is also true that my new encounter with my inner self—which had taken the form of a much better-known, historical Mother figure than the archetypal Black Mother of my childhood—did leave me with a distinct impression that the time had come to face a big issue and make radical changes in myself. I was definitely more aware than after my experience with the tree—but then I was twenty years older.

But just exactly where I was to turn was not clear at all. Swami had asked me to continue on in medicine and here I was, working at the top of the profession. Why wasn't it working out? On his account I had turned my back finally on art and was giving my work all I had—why was I so dissatisfied? Just what was it I was craving? And so insistently? That was the burning issue which I had to work out and face, in this the third turn of the second spiral of my life.

But, even as I thrashed about, events were falling into place that were to make me face the issue frontally, which seems to happen at this juncture in each phase of my development. The catalyst of this extremely intense process was Dr. Bill, whom I encountered one day in the residents' room. Over the babble of talking that seemed to go on eternally I could hear his rather penetrating, Ohio drawl and peeped over the top of my tiny cubicle to see who the newcomer was. He was talking with Dave Walker, our chief resident, trying to get something out of him, it seemed. This was a man only a few years older than myself, of medium height, with unusually large, staring, yellowish-green eyes and black hair that kept falling over his left eye. As my head appeared over the cubicle, his eyes met mine and I felt as if I had had a mark put on me that I was not going to be able to get rid of very easily.

After he had gone I asked Dave who he was. Dave explained that he was the new guy brought in to start a sub-department of neuropathology. He had been a Harvard man, and was thought to be the best person to get something going in our extremely dense, overcrowded and competitive department. I got the impression that Dr. Bill was "talent-hunting", trying to earmark one of the residents for his own. And, as time went by, I felt he was homing in on me in particular. He would sidle up to me in a friendly way, but with a degree of concentration and focus that made me realize that the only thing on his mind was business—a constant feature of Sir William. It did not take long for him to proposition me about becoming his resident in neuropathology, to which I said no. There was something about him that did not attract me at all, and my intuition told me to keep back. But Bill was not one to be put off at all. He offered me a higher salary and kept mentioning that I would be working in an office of my own, with far more control over my work than I presently had.

At that time I was actually negotiating to go back to the Roosevelt, where I had been so much happier—and of course, closer to Swami. I really did not identify with the horrendously competitive milieu at Harvard and just wanted to do a good job of work without all the hassle and compulsion of being at a top institution. However, it soon occurred to me that it might be a good idea to get out of the main drag at the Brigham for the remainder of the year I had signed up for, and have that quiet place Bill promised where I could get on with my work. Again, it was true that my main interest was in the neurosciences, and it might be good to have the experience in neuropathology while I was at Harvard. It would enhance my resume and might even be the specialty that was best for me in the long run. Perhaps exploring this opportunity was the way to solve this crisis that just never seemed to go away . . . .

Bill's "department" was located in a temporary building at the back of the main hospital, in which he had a personal office, a lab and an office for the residents. It was small but it was quiet, one of the main draws for me. Most of the time I worked alone, with an occasional neurology or pathology resident passing through on an elective. And I did find, almost immediately, that working with the nervous system really held my attention in a way the general work had not. On the whole, I was quite happy with the new arrangement. I no longer had to listen to the other residents bragging and hassling for rank—or as a mostly male group, telling dirty stories.

So far, so good. What I had not reckoned with was my role as Bill's guide, philosopher, and friend. He was trying to start a new department in an already terribly overcrowded situation, where competition and turf wars were the order of the day. In addition, he was a young man with a powerful, driving personality, and I rather think raised many a hackle. Certainly he ran into almost unbelievable opposition and obstruction, which he got into the habit of coming and telling me about. Just as I would be getting ready to leave for the day, he would make a dramatic entrance, plop himself down in a chair and launch out into his latest tale of perfidy and subterfuge trying to ensnare him. As I have never been good at pushing people aside, I would listen to all of this and give him my opinion and advice. Whatever I said seemed to be helpful and in no time we had gotten into the habit of hashing over his "battle-plans" to deal with the in-house opposition, over pasta at Joyce Chen's, lobster and Indian pudding at Durgin Park, or simply divine seafood with the fishermen and wharf workers at the No-Name restaurant on the wharf.

Bill was a very, very focused individual, not at all laid back like most Americans. I attributed this to the fact that he was a first generation American, his parents being immigrants from Germany. Bill himself spoke fluent German and went to Germany on his vacations. And, although he was thoroughly American in one way, like all other first generation Americans I have known, he had enough of the European in him to be much closer to my own wavelength than "regular" Americans, who, even after forty years still strike me as belonging to a different world than my own. He was just that much more obsessive, I might say, that we could connect up with each other in a big way.

It did not take long for us "Europeans" to get into a regular schedule in our new "department". However, I found that Bill was as chaotic in work as I am methodical. He was endlessly throwing a monkey wrench into all that I was doing, bursting in with one "emergency" or another. I found this exasperating, and on account of our close personal relationship would tell him so. He didn't mind, of course, as long as he got what he wanted done. On Tuesdays he spent the whole day at the V.A., leaving me in blissful peace and quiet, catching up with my backlog, eating quiet meals by myself and getting home in time to read, take a leisurely bath and an early bed.

It seemed as if things were settling down; but of course my life is not about peace and quiet. Bill started to work on me, telling me about his dedication to neuropathology and how he wanted to be the best neuropathologist in the world. He dreamed of making our department the world-center for neuropathology and would spend hours laying out his plans in detail, for decades into the future. Slowly it dawned on me that I was being told all of this because he was envisioning me as part and parcel of it. As time went by, he openly spoke of my staying with him as his permanent associate and told me that if I continued to work with him he would see to it that I became a full professor within ten years. I had my doubts about that; but I already knew how driving he was and how he seemed to be able to get things done, by sheer force of will and/or pulling strings with his influential contacts. It was not entirely impossible that working with him would really take me to the top of my profession in as short a time as was humanly possible.

For most people all this would have been exciting, but inexplicably it depressed me very much. I realized I was under the spell of my ever-recurring dream of being in partnership with someone who was totally dedicated to what he was doing; for the first time I was working with someone who was utterly absorbed in his career and was willing and even eager to include me in it. And this was no ordinary career—we were talking professorship at Harvard University, one of the most prestigious institutions in the world! As they say, the world was at my feet. But at the same time, I had reservations. Yes, he was dedicated—but to what? I could not help thinking that it was his own advancement that was uppermost in his mind. Somehow that was not what I was dreaming of. What inspired me was the dedication of a Ramon y Cajal, the Spanish pioneer neuroanatomist, or a Madame Curie, both of whom worked tirelessly for pure love of the knowledge they were seeking. Again, I was beginning to fall in love with Bill and at the same time understood intuitively that he could never ever respond to me. And over and above—or perhaps under and below—there was something else that was trying to make its voice heard, a muffled cry that I was not able to attend to because of the sound and fury of my outer life.

Bill was not one to wait for an answer. He was pressurizing, pressurizing me without a moment's respite. I finally gave in to the extent that I agreed to work with him for at least one more year. I passed the American Board of Pathologists exam in the winter of nineteen seventy-two and was therefore fully qualified to get myself a job wherever I might want to go—nice to have a feeling of some independence! In addition, I was finding neuropathology interesting enough to be willing to work another year with Bill. There was no doubt that working there would make a huge difference to my resume, and at the same time Bill was indeed making headway with his department so that the work was really rather interesting and fun. His secret weapon, however—what actually held me in its grip—was his repeated assertions that he could never have gotten as far as he could without me: it was my help, support and hard, reliable work that had kept him afloat and made it possible to get the department off the ground and in working condition. What woman—what human being—could resist feeling that they were so invaluable, so important? I was all but mesmerized by this crazy "German", and at the same time utterly frustrated by his inability to respond to me as a person. In my own way, I was a "crazy Celt", with my own intense aspirations, which he was quite unable to factor in to his ever-spiraling plans.

If anything was helping me find my focus, it was Vedanta, and I never missed a class or lecture unless I had to work at the hospital. That meant that on Thursday and Friday nights, when Swami Sarvagatananda gave classes, I would not eat with Bill, or that he would have to drive me over to the Center after a hurried meal. It also meant that on the Saturdays I was in Boston (for I still kept up my bi-monthly trips to New York) I was at the Center and not available for endless talks with Bill. He was always quite nice about all this—he had the polite, even courtly manners of a European rather than an American—but I understood from his occasional swipe at "Vedanty" that he was not keen on my being involved with it. This is a feature of men that I always found oppressive: they want a woman to be totally and exclusively committed to their interests, and resent her having independent activities.

As they say, what was in it for me? There was much that was interesting, even absorbingly interesting, and certainly glamorous. But did I really want it? Was I really ready to pay the price for it? Was I really prepared to be the giver all the time, without any hope of receiving the sort of love my heart craved? And, if not, what was it that I really wanted? I became dimly aware that I was embarking on a reprise of the struggle that had played itself out at Dollar twenty years before. I was going to have to make a decision—but between what, exactly? Then it was between a career in art or in science;

now, it was between my medical career and—what? The whole situation was thrown into a bright spotlight one Saturday morning as Bill and I sat in his car at a gas station. I remember Bill drawling, "I simply cannot understand you. You have everything anyone could want: Youth, good health, intelligence, talents galore, many friends, some of whom love you deeply, and the prospects of a stellar career—yet you are never happy. You are not satisfied, even with all of this. Just what is it you want?"

My first response was to note mentally that "some of my friends loved me deeply", which I think really was a statement of how he felt about me, though I am quite sure the relationship would most likely never have taken any form that would satisfy me. But more importantly, when I was finally alone and going through my daily meditation, his words hit me like a bombshell: "Just what do you want?" Yes! What was it that my heart was craving? Why couldn't I settle down and be happy with all that had been given me? I remembered my father's tirades in the same vein: "You have enough to eat and a roof over your head—what more do you want?" At that time what I had thought—but not said—was (quoting the Bible), "Man shall not live by bread alone, but by every word that proceedeth out of the mouth of God." Turning this over in my mind, I wondered if perhaps it was something like that which was beneath my present state of intense disquiet. My recent experience with Mother came to my mind and I wondered if the reason why I was suffering so much was because I was holding on to the "rock" of my career, which I had thought would save me from the destructive elements of the powerful current of my life. In view of my present distress, I wondered, was I meant to "let go", as Mother had asked me to, and permit myself to be carried forward by the river to a destination about which I as yet knew nothing? This was all very dark and a bit muddled, but I felt it was pointing in the right direction. Although I felt I was being asked to put my present security behind me and surrender to a force I as yet did not understand—what was the "river", after all?—it seemed more "right" than anything else I could think of. But, even with that much to work with, I had no idea what I was meant to do, if anything.

Bill and I continued on, getting busier and busier as he became more appreciated and in demand. I was now chief resident (over the one or two residents who straggled in from neurology or general pathology), and was more and more involved in decisions about how the department was to be run and organized, details for which Bill did not have much of a head. I lived for the times when I was alone in my office, poring over cases or doing background reading. We had a few particularly interesting cases, none more so than a Mr. Wright, whose brain biopsy yielded slides that totally baffled us. This was not a tumor, nor was it an infection—just what was it? Mr. Wright was increasingly disabled and his physicians totally stumped as to what to do for him. Suddenly I realized that this was most likely a case of progressive multifocal leukoencephalopathy or PML, about which I had just read an article in the *New England Journal of Medicine*. This was a debilitating, fatal disease that struck the brains of individuals whose immune systems were impaired, most often by therapeutic steroids (which Mr. Wright was on). It seemed to be a strange virus infection which induced the cells of the brain to take on forms similar to cancer, raising the interesting possibility that some cancers at least might be caused by viruses in people with compromised immune systems.

I rushed into Bill's office with the slides shouting, "He's got PML! I think. Take a look at this!" Bill was particularly interested in these odd virus infections in immune-compromised patients—a class of cases even now not fully understood—and responded eagerly. We went over all the features of the slides and realized that indeed PML is what we were looking at. "You know what this means?" Bill shouted excitedly. "It is very unusual to make this diagnosis while the patient is still alive. This is a golden opportunity to study this case and do a super autopsy. We must get permission to perform an autopsy as soon after death as possible, so we can document as no one else has just what the details of these cases are." He was beside himself with excitement, conveniently forgetting that it is illegal to ask for permission to do an autopsy while the patient is still alive. After he calmed down, he told me: "You will have to keep close tabs on this patient and see to it that we get autopsy permission the moment he dies—and have everything set up in advance to do all the special tests that need to be done."

Thus began my hovering around the neurology floor, asking the residents in an appropriately sepulchral voice, "How is Mr. Wright doing today?" They knew why I was doing this, and would have a good laugh. As I used to wear a cape in those days—indeed I had a snazzy navy trouser suit with pea green lining on the cape—they took to calling me *The Cape Woman*, in addition to my already existing nickname, *The Tigress*. One side of me was amused, and another rather disgusted that Bill was making use of me like this; but again, this was in the service of science—or was it? Was it simply his ambition to get into print an article on this interesting disease and thus jack up his reputation?

In hindsight I was casting about for reasons to distance myself from Bill, but not in a clear-cut way. Like a see-saw, things were going up and down. As time went by I was making friends with the neurology residents who rotated through our department in order to better understand the disease process in their patients. They invited me to give presentations on neuropathology to the neurologists, which I geared to increasing their understanding of disease processes in general and in particular in the nervous system, as I had understood from talking with the residents who came through that they had really no concept of what was actually taking place in the tissues of their patients. I put this down to the tendency in America to specialize early on in the training process and not to give sufficient emphasis on other skills that were pertinent to the work on hand. My little presentations were in some way rather simple-minded; no lofty discussion of physics or quantum theory—just demonstrations of what actually happens in the brain in various diseases and how various methods of treatment affect what goes on. One or two "hotrods" thought it was pretty dumb, but the rest appreciated it, and even senior staff attended, much to my surprise. I learned that they had gotten more out of my presentations than from any other source, because I addressed the issues that they had as clinicians trying to understand the problems they were dealing with. All this was of course gratifying; it was very meaningful to think that I was contributing to the understanding of colleagues who were actively involved in the care of the patients. In some ways, this got closest to fulfilling my motives for going into medicine in the first place.

But there was the other side. One Saturday morning when I was working alone in my office, I could hear the bellowing of a calf someone was doing experiments on. It got louder and louder and more and more agonized until it suddenly stopped, much to my relief. Then I saw the carcass being trundled by my window—they had cut it open; its severed ribs were jutting out from the flesh and it looked as if they had disemboweled it. I couldn't believe such utter cruelty. How could they do something like this to an anaesthetized animal? This was how the Elizabethans had executed criminals four hundred years ago, intended to be maximally painful and cruel. I was utterly appalled and felt quite sick to my stomach. It occurred to me that they had done it early Saturday morning in order not to be heard, not counting in early birds like myself. I wanted to know who had done it, but was not sure exactly where the sound or the sickening carcass had come from. I went outside to see if I could get a better idea, but I really was not familiar with the other facilities in the area, nor could I see lights on anywhere or signs of any activity. I felt frustrated, knowing that pushing an inquiry any further without any actual facts would take up a huge amount of time and almost certainly get me into deep trouble without any constructive result. I made up my mind that if I ever heard anything like that again I would immediately get up and trace the sound to its source, so that I could confidently make a case against the perpetrators. On this occasion I had succumbed to a psychology I was later to see in a big way in others: denial of something unpleasant that was happening in my own space. It had taken the sight of the carcass to galvanize me into action, but by then it was too late.

This event pushed me once again into the negative mode. Although my work was in many ways satisfying, it was all based on a philosophy that was innately inhuman, cruel and callous, not giving humans or their close relatives, animals, proper respect and love. Bill had helped me immensely, but his demand to take over my life was forcing me to ask the question: Where is the love? What guarantee do I have that I will be treated right or that I will be happy at the end of the day? I had seen just too much of "man's inhumanity to man", as my father used to quote from the Scottish poet, Robert Burns—and now man's inhumanity to animals. And I also knew of the tremendous lack of respect for the earth and all that grows and lives on it, creating an imbalance that in the long run might prove dangerous. Bill and I started to disagree and even quarrel, tussling over cases as if our lives depended on it, much to the entertainment of the lady who ran the lab next door.

As I tended to do when younger, I started to write poetry in order to express what I felt, this time addressing it to Mother, in whose arms I was now sure I was lying:

> My dear love,
> Take me in your arms
> And may I find my nothingness
> Between the beatings of your heart.
>
> O, warm, quiet stillness,
> In which life flows;
> Loving diastole,
> Flooding the empty chamber of my life,
> Feeding the aching substance of my soul—

Moment of knowledge!
Heart of my heart—
O, let me rest for a space,
Bathed in your soul-blood's
Gathering power.
Into the Eternal
Eye of the Storm:
O, unchanged point
Where all is still!
Let me become,
For a moment's eternity,
That which feeds and is fed.

O, it will come—
The beat, the ejection—
The turbulent flow
That empties the One,
Shattering into the many—

My dear love,
Hold me in your arms,
And may I find my nothingness
Between the beatings of your heart.

The drumbeats were getting louder and louder. How was I going to resolve the increasing crisis I was living in? I had by then heard that the swamis initiate, something that was never mentioned in the New York Center. It at first struck me as strange—Jesus had had disciples, but afterwards, did anyone else? And of course Ramakrishna had had them, too—it was they who had brought Vedanta to the West. It all seemed very exotic, and I had the impression that only the really great spiritual teachers had disciples. The rest of us just had to manage on our own, or so it seemed. Once I got over this rather stereotypical reaction to the news, my curiosity was aroused: Would it be possible to be initiated, and would it do me any good? In the condition I was at that time, it seemed worthwhile to look into it, and certainly seeking someone who could help me move forward spiritually had been—and still was, now that I thought of it—one of my goals.

I took to going to see any Indian spiritual teacher of note who passed through Boston, including Guru Maharaji, the teenage sensation, and Sri Chinmoy, the adult miracle-worker. I think there was some vague idea in my mind that one of these well-known figures might be the "teacher" I was looking for. But both of them left me utterly unaffected and even disillusioned. They, too, seemed to have been touched by the same brush as my day-to-day contacts. A visit to the Hare Krishnas on one of their festival days left me, not cold and disillusioned, but toweringly angry. After an ecstatic ritual, a young American convert gave us a talk in which he berated Ramakrishna as a fraud, a womanizer and alcoholic. I could not believe my ears. What did these people have against Ramakrishna? I suspected some sort of rivalry between the increasingly numerous Indian teachers in America, and was quite disgusted at the vulgar methods being used to discredit the angelic Ramakrishna. On the way home I launched into a rip-roaring migraine that was with me for several days.

These experiences made me understand that the kind of love I was looking for was not necessarily related to being Indian; it was easy to misunderstand their motives in view of the exotic, formalized and at times florid devotionalism many of them exhibited. Indians could be as venal and insensitive as Westerners, in a perhaps more subtle way. More importantly, it made me understand just how urgent it was to find that person I had been longing for since my days in the anatomy department in Edinburgh, now over ten years ago. Would I never meet the spiritual teacher my heart was craving so intensely? It seemed likely that it would be someone from the Ramakrishna lineage, but who, Oh who, would it be? And when would I meet him?

The pressure within me was rising to maximum. It was a Saturday morning in April, that time of ecstatic new life, fragrance of freshly opened blooms, over which hung the bitter-sweetness of Easter. Bill and I attended a seminar at the Massachusetts General Hospital and then decided to whoop it up at a posh Italian restaurant. We did ourselves proud, dispatching a bottle of fine Italian wine between us. I had never felt closer to Bill, who was uncharacteristically very sweet and low key. I could palpably feel the love he had for me—though never expressed directly—and it seemed as if we really were meant to be together for good; what we felt for each other would unfold over time. I had drunk a fair amount of wine, but what really intoxicated me was the feeling I had for Bill that morning. I was, quite simply, in what more prosaic people were beginning to call "an altered state of consciousness", which sounds exciting and is, but at least in my case carrying with it subterranean depth charges.

Without consciously thinking about what I was saying I found myself launching into a rhapsody about the Atman, the inner Self of the Vedanta, which is one with the impersonal Godhead. This was the Self I had asked Swami Pavitrananda about at the first library class, and which somehow I had come to understand more fully, without being conscious I was doing so; for this outburst, like many others before and after, took me completely by surprise. Gazing out at the wisteria hanging on the trellis of the restaurant, and gliding, as it were, along the shafts of spring sunshine crisscrossing the dining room, I intoned, almost in ecstasy, "I am He! I am He!"—a mantra asserting the identity of the human individual with the Divine Ground. As I did so, I felt myself rising higher and higher, leaving the world behind and passing into a place of exquisite happiness and peace. This was my way of expressing how I felt. Vedanta had obviously gone much deeper into my soul than I had realized.

Then I looked at Bill. The sweet smile on his face was gone and his mouth was set in a thin, grim line. His face was actually black, quite obviously expressing the utmost disgust, anger and loathing. I suddenly understood why cartoonists depict this state with a black cloud over the head, and wanted to laugh. I felt utterly detached at that moment, but it was obvious that he detested what I was saying. I felt enveloped in a thick, negative, entropic cloud of emotion, which, however, could not affect me in my inner being. He got up suddenly without a word, and I meekly followed him. We drove home in utter silence, me still floating on a pink cloud and he sullen and angry.

After the glow had subsided and I had returned to "normal" consciousness, two things were perfectly clear: 1) Vedanta meant more to me than anything else; 2) I had cooked my goose with Bill. And it seemed likely that the two were interrelated. My deep resistance to him was due to Vedanta tugging me in another direction. He would never understand the yearning to transcend myself that had taken me over as I studied Vedanta, and indeed had been part of my life all along. In comparison to Vedanta his status, achievements, promises, even his (presumed) love, seemed unimportant. I understood where the conflict was now: between success in my career and the irresistible urge to go deeper into myself and discover the divine. This was the new "mode" of a similar struggle I had gone through twenty years before: between the seemingly prosaic world of science and the imaginative, creative world of art.

This was the core discovery. Along with it went a sense of despair, of anguish at the loss of Bill and all that he stood for. For a brief moment I lost my hard-won equilibrium and gave way to the old, bitter sense of rejection, bringing in its wake thoughts of suicide. But by then such thoughts had become quite foreign and, after a brief tussle, I put them behind me. This also made me realize how much I had changed, how much I had left behind, and how much I was now aiming for. From one point of view, I had lost very badly, but from another I had cleared the field and was now in a position to take stock of my life with a lot more clarity than I had had during the turbulent emotional period since the showdown with my father. Something within myself insisted that there was still more to move on to, though I could not at that moment see what it might be. And yet another side recognized, though rather hazily, that once again my inner "truth" had asserted itself to disengage me from what had been, in reality, a sort of mesmerism by a forceful and dominant person who somehow had been tapping into the myth that was driving me. Bringing it to an end had been imperative if I was to see my way more clearly—and so it had had to be, no matter how painful. I was thankful for and also rather in awe of that part of me that would rise up at moments of crisis and assert what I felt most deeply to be true. It seemed to operate completely independently of "me", the socially conditioned persona which, according to my generation, made me seek to please others, specially men, even if I was compromising my own best interests.

But, all that apart, what was I to do now? The idea had been forming in my mind for quite some time to take a year's leave of absence in order to stand back from my life and reach a final conclusion as to where its energy would be directed. I was now thirty-two years old and it was becoming urgent to decide upon a definite career. I had by then saved enough money to take up art work, if I still felt inclined to do so. In addition, I wanted to see more of America and, having benefitted so much from Vedanta, felt I would like to visit the various centers scattered all over the United States. There were about twelve of them at that time, distributed largely on the two seaboards, but with one or two in the Midwest. And I had at that time a friend from Oklahoma, who was pressing me to visit her there and see the Native American reservations, with which she had been involved. There were other friends from around the States who had issued me cordial invitations to visit and now seemed the right time—I would see the natural beauty of the country and connect up with all those people, both inside and outside Vedanta, who were meaningful to me.

By the next time I saw Bill I had made up my mind. However, much to my surprise he greeted me with the utmost cordiality and warmth and showed every sign of caring for me more than ever. This unexpected turn of events naturally took me by surprise. I took a few days to re-examine my position and jack myself up for the impact, but the die was definitely cast. When I did break the news to Bill, his body language conveyed his disappointment, but verbally, he—always the consummate operator—took it quite philosophically. Perhaps even for him the struggles between us had been a bit too much. What was most interesting was that now I had made up my mind and no longer needed anything from Bill, we returned to our old cordiality and closeness. I made a mental note of this: if you don't want or need something from someone, things are OK. What causes problems is neediness, expectation, demands. So far so good—but how to avoid being needy? That was the sixty-four thousand dollar question.

Only a few more weeks were left at the Brigham. Despite some regrets, my outlook was mostly one of hope and expectation, a longing to move on to further discovery and hopefully to finding a more satisfying goal to work toward. I was encouraged by the response of several of my workmates, who confided in me that they wished they could do what I was doing, that they, too, would love to take stock of their lives and, if possible, strike out in a different direction. Several confided in me that they felt trapped at Harvard and would love to see a radical change in the ways things were done. But these were married men with children, who could not lightly pick up and move on. I realized how fortunate I was to be unmarried and have the freedom to "follow my bliss" as Joseph Campbell said. What had seemed to me to be a lack in my life suddenly became an asset.

However, there were still a few more hurdles to get over. A few weeks before I left I received a call from Floyd, the head of neuropathology at the Children's Hospital across the street from the Brigham. We knew each other quite well, both professionally and socially, and I rather liked him. Unlike Bill, he was quiet and thoughtful, the type of man which has always appealed to me. He asked me to come over and speak with him for a few minutes. I was puzzled as to what this might be, but went over anyway. To my utter amazement, Floyd asked me if I would be interested in heading up a huge research project funded by the Government. At this point in time I cannot remember exactly what it was about, but I do recall that the funding was six million dollars, in those days an astronomical sum. The work would involve moving between Washington, DC, New York and Boston, with headquarters in Floyd's department at Children's. I was utterly speechless. Why was I being teased like this? Was I not meant to move away from all of this, after all? I am seldom unable to answer immediately, but this turn of events certainly caught me short. I looked at Floyd for what seemed an eternity and finally said, "Floyd, I am taking a year's leave of absence." "We will hold the project till you get back", was his laconic answer. So he really meant that I should do this! Another eternity, and: "I don't think I am coming back." Even for me this last was a revelation; I had made up my mind even more decisively than my outer self had realized.

I couldn't believe that this was happening: so much recognition and possibility of major promotion, just as I was about to leave—as I now fully understood, forever. I later learned the story from the Upanishads, the canonical texts of Vedanta, in which a young boy, Nachiketas, goes to the house of Death and seeks to know the secret of immortality. Death is reluctant to give out "trade secrets" and tries to distract Nachiketas with offers of long life, health, beautiful wives and concubines, livestock, chariots and all of the other paraphernalia of worldly success. But Nachiketas has made up his mind: he seeks the secret of immortality and nothing else. Death is very impressed and now gladly tells his young postulant what he seeks to know. In many ways my case was the same, though I did not know for sure what it was I was seeking. I was quite clear what I did not want—and by that time I certainly had had a chance to see what was on offer—but just what was it that I craved? Even then I had a faint idea that it had to do with love, which was at that time the Holy Grail of my life. But just what kind of love was not crystal clear. If you had asked me then, I would have said, "spiritual love", but just what that meant was not precisely clear.

It did not take long for me to feel a tremendous vacuum the half-week when I could not go to the Center, and I made the amazing decision to attend mass in the local Roman Catholic church, just to keep in touch with a spiritual group. This was the first time I had done any such thing, and as I stood in the congregation the thought occurred to me, "My family would lay an egg if they knew I was doing this." But any qualms I might have had were completely dispersed as I saw the faithful come back to their seats from the communion rail. This was a working class congregation at midday, a time when none but the really devout were able to come to mass, no doubt accounting for their remarkable fervor. I was surprised, actually, to find the church quite full even at that odd hour; but what really spoke to me was the beatific expressions on the faces of the faithful as they turned from receiving communion. It was clear that this meant the world to them, lifting them above the humdrum world. What a contrast to my experience of communion in the Presbyterian Church in Edinburgh! This simple experience made me understand why Catholicism has endured as long as it has: it gives its people an experience that really means something to them.

I believe I went to mass every single day from then onwards, living vicariously in the rapture of the communicants. But my primary interest was still Vedanta, and whenever I could I went over to the Center and participated in the work, which at that time was painting the kitchen. I was exposed for the first time to the down-to-earth American do-it-yourself outlook on life and, in a big way, also to ice cream, an item I had not much cared for before. But by the time I was finished, I was consuming a whole half-gallon along with the other no-nonsense New England types who were the mainstay of the Center. What really interested me was having lunch with Swami, whose conversations were always quite enthralling, lifting me up with as much energy as those simple-hearted Catholics on the other side of the Fenway. I was amazed to see him eat beef without batting an eyelid. I knew that no Hindu even so much as thinks of eating beef, it is so utterly taboo; but here was this palpably holy man eating it and enjoying it with his American devotees. Later I was to learn how he consciously trained himself to get over the taboo and how in so many other ways he had adapted to the American way of life, in order not to foster any sense of difference between himself and Americans. This was a first sign of what real love can do: sacrifice its shibboleths and taboos for the sake of others.

One day, a few weeks before leaving for New York, the first leg of my sabbatical journey I went to talk with Swami. He met me in the library, a lovely, airy room in a house that was quite impressive architecturally, with a sweeping staircase and beautiful sculptured wooden fireplaces. He started by asking me about my sabbatical. I told him my plans and he inquired, "What will you do, besides travel? Will you be reading?"

"Yes, Swami."

"What do you plan to read?" I paused for a moment; I had not really been paying much attention to that subject. "Well, the Gita, for one thing . . ."

"Will you read the works of Swami Vivekananda?" I did not hesitate on that one: "Heavens, no!"

"Why not? What is wrong with him?"

"O, Swami! He is so disgustingly intellectual! I want to put that sort of thing behind me. I have had enough to do with the intellect to last me a lifetime! What I need in my life is love!"

That was pretty definitive. Swami remained silent for a moment and then he said, "Do you see that book up there on the shelf, the small one?" I followed his pointing finger and got up to pull the book off the shelf—*Poems* of Swami Vivekananda. Swami found a poem in it and handed the book to me. "Can you read this out to me?" The poem was entitled *To a Friend*, an innocuous enough title. Totally unsuspecting, I sat down to read, mustering up my best Miss Paterson voice and style. I flipped through it before I began and noticed that it was fairly long. Like a long-distance runner, I prepared myself for the project, beginning slowly and deliberately and planning to pick up steam later.

The poem began with Swami Vivekananda describing his own search for knowledge that he expected would take him beyond the human condition of ignorance and suffering. In this period of struggle he had fully understood the hollowness of rituals, austerities, renunciation, which he regarded as delusions of the mind, even though in India they were considered the *sine qua non* of religious life. But he had found out one thing, the sole treasure: Love, the one thing needful. At this I mentally sat up. The brilliant Vivekananda saying this! And of course, it was for me nothing but an echo of the words of another hero of mine, Saint Paul: "If I speak with the tongues of men and of angels, and have not love, it profits me nothing."

But the love of which these spiritual giants speak is not ordinary human love. Vivekananda goes on to say that this love lives in the hearts of all living beings, urging them to sacrifice for each other, bringing consolation in the deepest suffering and thereby drawing the fangs of the relentless pairs of opposites the world torments us with: creation and destruction, good and bad, and so on. Everything we do—good or bad—is, whether we know it or not, "*Its* worship in manifold modes."

The tone of the poem then becomes that of exhortation: If you want true happiness, seek nothing for yourself:

> Let go your vain reliance on knowledge,
> Let go your prayers, offerings, and strength,
> For selfless love is the only resource;
> Look, the insects teach, embracing the flame!

Had I not been investing myself in all sorts of intellectual pursuits, austerities, and so on? And of course I had not been at all at peace or in the least happy. The image of the moths going to their death for love of the flame spoke to me powerfully, an echo of how I had felt when under Grannie's direct influence.

All of this had begun to work on me. As I turned the page and moved into the last three verses I could feel tears welling up, but clamped into place my well-trained, British stiff upper lip and continued on:

> Aye, you are born heir to the Infinite;
> Within your heart is the ocean of Love.
> "Give, Give away"—whoever asks for return,
> His ocean dwindles down to a drop.

> From highest Brahman[13] to the yonder worm,
> And to the very minutest atom—
> Everywhere is the same God, the All-love;
> Friend, offer mind, soul, body at their feet.

> These are His manifold forms before you;
> Rejecting them, where do you seek for God?
> Who loves all beings without distinction,
> He indeed is worshipping best his God.

I have no idea how I got to the end of this, but I did, profoundly moved and changed irrevocably. I had finally had a glimpse of the emotional depths of a man I had thought to be a brittle intellectual like myself. At that time I did not know the story of how he had given his very

---

13   The divine, impersonal Ground.

life to uplift both India and the West, dying of exhaustion at the early age of thirty-nine. But I could hear and respond to the call of spiritual Love, grounded in a Reality that was beyond comprehending, but which spoke to us through this universal language of giving, sacrificing love.

It took me a few minutes to calm down and finally raise my eyes to look at the swami. During the reading he had been totally quiet. It was as if I were reading to myself, or to some empty space. And when I looked at him, I understood why. He was sitting absolutely still, with his eyes closed, looking like a beautiful, dark Buddha. He was completely absorbed in the thoughts I had just read out, and in the Love of which they spoke. This I could grasp; but when I noticed that tears were slowly trickling down from the outer corners of his eyes, I was devastated. Men crying was not something that one usually saw—and this, of course, was for something so uplifting, so sublime, that I understood just how deeply the poem spoke to him. I sat there with him in total silence for quite some time before he returned to his normal self. Then came the tea and cookies—and my signing out from the library the *Complete Works of Swami Vivekananda*! This was something I was never to look back from. From that day on studying and trying to follow Vivekananda was the polestar of my life, which was to take me through some tumultuous adventures and even life-threatening experiences. My path was open before me and all that remained was to walk along it.

CHAPTER 17

IN DEEPER: 1973

New York was my first port of call on my proposed journey, which had now assumed the character of a pilgrimage. I was definitely on a journey of discovery, a search for a Holy Grail of which I had only the faintest idea, but enough to make me give up my work at Harvard and strike out into untested waters. A couple of years prior—in the intense vision of Mother—I had reached a turning point in which I had understood that there was something I had to relinquish in order to enter a fuller, stronger current that was flowing within me, but had had no idea what that might be. Now, divested of my responsibilities at Harvard, I felt much freer and more purposeful: perhaps giving up my medical work was what was required of me. But it was very difficult. Had I not been following the inspiration given me by my grandmother, the main light of the first twenty years of my life? Had I not been seeking to serve humankind? What had gone so wrong? Why had I felt such a strong impulse to leave it behind, particularly when I was doing so well and could have stepped forward into a great career? Just where was I going, and how?

Swami Sarvagatananda had been tremendously helpful and supportive as I went through all of this. As a long-time counselor at both MIT and Harvard, he well knew the problems of both students and staff, and was in a position to help me keep a perspective. As I unveiled to him the various struggles on the way, my doubts and anxieties, he would tell me that he had been hearing so much of this from everyone at these prestigious institutions. No one, it seemed, was happy. Everyone was asking *why*? He told me, "The professors have an idea of what the problem is, but it is too late for them to do anything about it. The students are deeply unhappy, but it will take them decades to find out why. You are fortunate that you have begun to understand what is going on and are able to take action while you are still young. You will find the answer." This was all highly mysterious, but at the same time encouraging. He had helped me see that this was a process I was working through and that my reactions were quite acceptable in the light of a broader perspective.

At the same time, I felt a strong need to talk with Swami Pavitrananda in New York before setting off on my journey. Although I had been attending his classes and lectures at every chance I got to get out of Boston, I do not recall speaking with him one-on-one during my sojourn in the city of beans. I had, however, written him one or two letters during my last year at Harvard, to which he had replied tersely, but giving me great encouragement as to my ability to succeed in spiritual life.

It was now September, and Swami had just returned from his annual visit to Southern California. I therefore planned to spend a week or so in the Big Apple before setting off for Michigan, my first port of call. I would, I thought, base myself at Lou's, just round the corner from the Vedanta Society, and spend my time at the Center. But things are never as one plans. Swami was not well. Ever since his debilitating illness in nineteen-seventy, his always delicate health had become extremely fragile, and it took him quite some time to recoup his strength after the long journey from Los Angeles. I therefore had to wait several weeks before I could hope to see him. In the meantime, there was the diversion of attending some of the programs in connection with the passing of Swami Nikhilananda from the center on the East Side. A brilliant intellectual, Swami Nikhilananda had done great work translating and expounding several of the most basic and important texts of Vedanta, and had attracted a number of distinguished intellectuals, such as the writer J.D. Salinger, the scholar Joseph Campbell and the poet John Moffit, of whom the last two had helped him substantially with his literary work. In particular, Joseph Campbell had helped him with his epochal English translation of *The Gospel of Sri Ramakrishna*, which had had such an impact on my own life.

Swami Nikhilananda's funeral services had attracted almost all of the swamis then working in America, including Swami Aseshananda, a disciple of Mother Sarada who worked in Portland, Oregon, as also Swami Shraddhananda, a disciple of another of Ramakrishna's disciples, and stationed in Sacramento. I was rather overawed to think that these were men so close to the source of my inspiration, and found them quite angelic, inspiring, and also very humorous, a quality which has always appealed to me. They seemed to be joyous children playing unselfconsciously in the lap of the divine. There were other, more junior swamis, whom I found brilliant and engaging, but somehow less interesting. Among these were the head of the center in Northern California and the assistant swami from Southern California. Little did I know what was to lie in store for me with these men!

But for the moment my attention was focused on the other side of Central Park, where Swami Pavitrananda was recuperating from his trip to Southern California. As I waited to see him, I made myself available to help out at the Center, as I had done at the Center in Boston. My happy experiences there had helped me to mentally break the ice of the formality of the New York Center, and in no time I was installed as the chief dish-and-bottle-washer—several notches down the scale of employment from Harvard, no doubt, but nevertheless a source of great satisfaction and joy. I got to know the in-residence Genets—Maman, the nonagerian matriarch and her daughter Jeanne—who so uncomplainingly lived in the rather dark and cramped quarters in the basement. They had come from a wealthy French Canadian background and had been drawn into Vedanta by Jeanne's sister Rolande, a vital, beautiful, talented dancer who in the nineteen-thirties had fallen in love with Vedanta and the elderly swami who had preceded Swami Pavitrananda. This wonderful old swami had been quite uncompromising in his mission and had spurned money from anyone who attached strings to it. He was, therefore, living in the utmost penury, eating at the automat and managing somehow to survive. Rolande had made it her job to cook for him and finally moved into the Center in order to take care of it and his needs. She was a dynamo and in no time had things running smoothly. Her mother and sister, who had never been separated from her, followed her into Vedanta and also, after some hesitation, into the Center. Rolande had passed away in the early sixties, but the old lady and Jeanne had stayed on at the Center, faithfully caring for it and the swami and pouring their considerable wealth into helping it to keep going.

Then there was Courtenaye, who did most of Swami's cooking and lived just a block uptown. She had known Swami since nineteen fifty-two, the year after he had come to America, and had become steadfastly devoted to him. Although she was very beautiful, having been a professional model and movie star, she was also cultured, dignified, sincere and good hearted,

and we were to become best friends and close co-workers as time went by.

John Schlenck, a musical composer and professional pianist who lived on the floor above Swami and was essentially a monk, was friendly and helpful. As he had lived at the Center since the early sixties and was Swami's personal attendant and secretary, he was well-informed about everything that was going on and kept me in the picture as I made my first steps at the Center. Bill Conrad, another "lay monk" who had been associated with the Center since the early sixties lived next door to the Center and ate his meals with John. He was a biophysicist, but

on account of ill health was out of work as often as not. Like John, he helped to keep the work at the Center going, doing odd jobs and also manning the recording that was made of Swami's lectures.

It was nearly six weeks before Swami was well enough to take up lectures and classes again. In the meantime I had built up quite a little routine at the Center, working there in the morning, going back home for lunch and a nap and arriving mid-afternoon to wash the dishes and work in the pocket-handkerchief of a garden at the back of the Center. I tried as much as possible to find things to do outside of Lou's place, among which was attending the public presentations of Sri Chinmoy, the guru whom I had seen in Boston. It all seemed quite strange—public ecstasies and other unusual phenomena—but it was better than having Lou haranguing me. I had by this time got it thoroughly into my head that I must find a spiritual teacher, and was ready to go anywhere and do just about anything to find one. Perhaps, too, there was also some pique with Swami Pavitrananda, who was keeping me waiting like this without any explanation. Finally, the ladies at the Center told me that Swami would be taking the library class that evening—a more than welcome piece of news.

When Swami entered the library that evening, he noticed me at once and said gruffly as he sat down, "Why are you still here? I thought you were going on a tour of America." Before I knew what I was saying, I heard myself: "Swami, I am not going anywhere. I am staying here." I was absolutely dumbfounded—what was I saying? Where had this idea come from? I had not, as far as I knew, had any such thought whatsoever.

When Swami heard this, his face broke out into a huge, toothy grin and he positively wriggled in his chair with delight. He said not a word, but it was obvious that he was thrilled to hear what I had said. For all I know, he had shed a few tears over my hegira to Boston—as I understand now, my attempt to escape from his compelling influence. It had not worked, of course, and he must have understood the whole situation by my dogged appearances at the library class every second weekend or so. But at the same time he knew by this time how independent I was and also that I had it in me to disappear forever into some other "spiritual" pursuit. He knew, for example, that I was planning to conclude my trip with a visit the convent in Santa Barbara, with special permission from the head of the Southern Californian centers.

Part of Swami's charisma was that he seldom spoke about his feelings. What with his slanty eyes (he was from East Bengal, next to Assam, and from there, Tibet) and his taciturnity, he was in many ways the very picture of the inscrutable Oriental. However, as I got to know him better, he began to share things with me which quite took me by surprise and were always profoundly illuminating. One day, maybe a year after I got back from Boston, he suddenly asked me, apropos of nothing we had been speaking about, "Why did you go to Boston?" I had not told him anything about my motivations or plans before I went, partially because he was so unwell and partially because I did not want to have any opposition to what I had in mind. I was rather taken aback by the question so long after the fact and had to cast about to remember what it was that had made me set off on my hegira. I dredged up my memories of feeling that I had to do better medical work than I had been doing, that I wanted to leave my previous lifestyle and friends behind, and . . . Not a word that I had been trying to run away from him. I still was not able to see that. "But", I said, "I was miserable. I cried myself to sleep almost every night." He looked at me for a while and then he said, looking extremely unhappy: "I knew you would be miserable." Then, drawing himself up to his full height, he added, dropping his voice and speaking with the utmost intensity, "But I also knew you would come back!' That was it. In a few words he conveyed just what he had been through—knowing I was suffering, feeling for me, and perhaps wondering if something would come in the way of my eventual return. He had just had to wait while I worked the whole thing out. So it was settled: I would stay in New York and work at the Center. And the first item of business was to find somewhere to stay. I simply had to move on from Lou, who by this time was quite manic and uncontrollable. As if by magic, Stanley Quinn, one of our members, told me that Jan, who came to Sunday lectures at the Center, was looking for a roommate. She lived on West Eighty-Sixth Street, some fifteen blocks or over a mile from the Center.

My main duties were during the week, when Courtenaye cooked Swami's lunches and took the role of "house mother" for me. The Genets were polite but distant for the most part, but Courtenaye, perhaps herself a little in need of less rarefied companionship than the two aristocratic French Canadian ladies, soon became best friends and shared with me all she knew of the history of the New York Center and Swami. Courtenaye was one of the mainstays of the Center, not only cooking for Swami, but also doing the accounts, and taking care of the Genets, whom she called "the elves", on account of their dissociation from anything anyone else regarded as normal. The two elderly ladies had never known want of any sort, and lived in a hyper-refined cocoon, assiduously cultivating their image as holy women. Jeanne, the daughter, was a simple-minded but good, innocuous soul, who had lived her entire life in the rigorous company of her mother and therefore had never known personal independence of any sort and had perspectives not much wider than the room she stood in. Maman, the matriarch, had adjusted herself to her role as dowager holy woman, but was in fact a woman of strong appetites, as became a wealthy person of French lineage. She brooked no opposition to her will and could be quite destructive emotionally toward anyone who differed with her in any way. She was, in fact, a holy terror and made the lives of any younger woman who wished to work at the Center interesting, to say the very least. But she was indeed old, being in her early nineties at that time, and so she was pandered to, in order to keep the peace.

Courtenaye had the job of caring for these ladies, cooking for them during the week and taking them out for a ride in her car on Saturdays, when a different crew cooked for Swami. The Genets were gracious to her, of course—as only the French know how—but, like everyone else, she was also made to feel inferior—as only the French know how! But she never complained, and I would marvel at her forbearance and goodness of heart. Courtenaye had worked out where her boundaries were with this situation and rigidly stuck to them. I was at first a bit taken aback by her unwillingness to bend, but later understood that this was how she coped with the situation. She told me herself that she was determined to fulfill the tasks Swami had given her, and that she was not going to let herself fail him, even one single day. She pointed out how Jeanne, who never said no to any request of Swami, would work insanely "on demand", and then collapse and be out of commission for a week, while others picked up the pieces. Courtenaye had vowed never to fail like that and had built up her defenses accordingly. I was struck by the difference in the way these two wonderful women worked—one impulsively and the other with great circumspection and mindfulness. Though Jeanne was the one that everyone called a saint, I knew I was the Courtenaye type and admired her immensely for taking this unpopular, but principled, stand.

On Saturdays, when the older ladies were out on a toot (usually to a New Jersey shopping mall) a crew of younger women "took over" the basement floor. The most dedicated was Pat Walker, an ex-ballerina who aspired to become a nun and was just a few years older than I. She worked full time for a well-known publishing company in New York and dedicated her weekday early mornings and evenings and all day Saturday and Sunday to cooking for Swami. At the weekend she was joined by a group of women—Luz, somewhat older than the rest and a long-time member; Sandi, a relative new comer; and Janet, like myself almost brand new. Being "off-duty" on Saturday and with nothing else to occupy myself, I went a few times on Saturday to see if I could help out. I quickly discovered, however, that I really did not fit in with the group, whom I now realize were dominated by baby-boomer values, in which I had no share or even understood. Pat was a kind, rather jolly, good-natured woman of my own generation, whose company I enjoyed very much, and Luz—who was there rather infrequently—was an entertaining and independent character; but the conversation almost always was focused on the various tribulations of the two younger women, including their relationships with men. As I was beginning to think of myself as a nun, I was not too keen to become extensively involved in such matters; Pat, bless her, was putting all her energy helping the girls work things out in a spiritual way, and I basically felt quite peripheral to the group. I therefore was at a loose end, as I had irrevocably made up my mind to have nothing more to do with my erstwhile New York friends, now taking drugs.

Which brings me to Stanley. Stanley was probably twenty years older than I, or even more. He was an honest, straightforward man of very genuine character, who had come to Vedanta maybe ten years prior, devastated by the death of his wife. Swami had given him consolation and refuge and made him part and parcel of the life at the Center. Although intelligent, Stanley was not as well-educated as most of the rest of the group, but his good-heartedness and willingness to help had endeared him to all of us. He worked full time as a composer, but nevertheless did a lot of work for the Center, specifically going down to the flower market before dawn on Friday mornings to purchase flowers for the Sunday lecture altar. On Saturdays he would actually do the flower arranging, which he had learned from Erik, another member who was a professional interior decorator.

When Stanley realized that I was going to be around for some time, he asked me to help him with the Saturday flower-arranging, with a view perhaps to taking over the job. I agreed, relishing the prospect of doing something artistic; and in no time Stanley and I were in business together, doing up the vases for the altar the next day. The job also entailed keeping the flowers alive and looking half-way decent through the following Friday evening class, which I took over *in toto* immediately. As the Center was seldom less than eighty degrees warm at any given time—Jeanne kept the heating up to help Swami, who suffered from malaria—keeping any flowers alive and decent for even two days was quite a challenge, and I believe Stanley was vastly relieved to pass the job on. Prior to my arrival, he had had to take care of the flowers every evening, pulling out the ones falling by the wayside and propping up the others to look as if they might survive. The very epitome of this task took place one night as Stanley and I arrived at the Center together for the library class. Before starting up the stairs to the library, Stanley popped his head through the auditorium door and intoned in a sepulchral voice: "Boy, those gladioli sure look sadioli!"

Stanley and I worked together for perhaps a few months, by which time it was clear that I could manage the job quite easily by myself. I had never done flower arranging before, but found it totally to my liking, and rejoiced to be working with something creative and beautiful, after the long grind in medicine. After we finished, Stanley would ask me if I wanted lunch, which he would then provide in his bed-sitter next door to the Center. We enjoyed each other's company and soon fell into a pattern of doing lunch and then going for a long walk, usually in Central Park, which was at the end of the block, but sometimes Riverside Park, through which I used to walk on my way down to the Center from West Eighty-Sixth Street. Stanley's direct and simple-hearted, though very wise companionship was a breath of fresh air after the claustrophobic atmosphere with the French Canadian ladies. He had a wonderful sense of humor and we laughed a great deal, something I always enjoy. One small specimen of his humor: One day I picked up his notebook where he kept notes of the swami's lectures. It was a school notebook, with a space on the front for the student's name and so on. Under *Name* Stanley had written: Stanley Quinn; under *Class*: Vedanta; and under *School*: Of Hard Knocks.

Another friend who had entered my life since arriving in New York, was Daya, a Swiss woman of about my own age, who was living the life of a Franciscan third-order nun, and was, to put it mildly, rather unusual. I had met her at the Center, where she came occasionally, drawn by Swami, of whom she was very fond. We hit it off together immediately; and despite my tight schedule we contrived to spend quite a bit of time together. Daya's unusual resume included the fact that by day she studied for a postgraduate degree in special education and at night she worked full time as an attendant in a mental hospital on Staten Island. In effect, she never slept. She meditated a lot and was prone to quite spectacular ecstasies—once she had been locked by mistake into a catacomb in Jerusalem for three days until she was found in an ecstasy, utterly oblivious to the world.

Daya was a free spirit, moving at will between the worlds of Christianity and Vedanta. She invited me out to various religious gatherings, including a weekend at an ashrama of Swami Satchitananda, the teacher of meditation with the long hair, beard, and charismatic manner. Twenty years previously, Daya had known him in Sri Lanka, where she had found him welcoming and friendly; but that was before he had come to the States and had created his large, successful movement. We at once realized, on being asked to fill out a five page questionnaire before we could be admitted, that we were dealing with a highly American, commercialized enterprise. Even by American standards, the questionnaire was remarkable. "Daya, they are asking for our medical history", I said. "They even want to know if we have had venereal disease." Daya replied in true Vedantic fashion, "I am not the body! I am the Spirit! I am writing that over this whole thing, and they will have to live with it!" We got admitted anyway, but were rather taken aback at every turn, where a sign would greet us: "Do not touch these plants—they are Swami's", "Leave the cat alone—she is Swami's", "Do not enter here—this place is Swami's", and on and on and on. I recall there even was a sign on the bathroom faucet in the same vein. "What sort of place is this, Daya?" I asked. Daya looked grim. "This is not what I experienced in Sri Lanka!" she said. "Something has gone terribly wrong. I understand he is in residence and tomorrow I am going to see him and ask him what has happened." "I don't think you'll get a satisfactory answer", I replied, for by now I was beginning to see how the meeting of East and West was working itself out: The Westerners were focusing on minutiae, and the Easterners were obsessed with organization and control.

As I expected, our request to see him privately was denied. Swami was in retreat, it seemed. Retreat from what? I wondered. But Daya was not going to take no for an answer. After breakfast we resolutely set out for his compound, some distance from the ashrama. As we marched forward I noticed a group of young American men dressed in Indian garb coming purposefully over the hill to our right. "Who d'you think that is, Daya?" She did not answer or even look to see, but strode on, her jaw set. I noticed they were moving along the hill in parallel with us and felt pretty sure that they had to do with us in a big way. Then they disappeared over the hill as we got close to the gate of the swami's compound. We finally came round the hill, ready to take the swami by storm—and there they were, blocking our way.

They wasted no time at all. "You are to leave this property within fifteen minutes, or else! What you are doing is illegal." Daya snorted. "I have known Swami Satchitananda for twenty years! Is this any way to treat visitors?" "You are illegal. Get off the property!" Daya started to move forward and the young men froze. "Get off the property!!" I looked to see if they were armed, but they didn't seem to be. They were probably in their early twenties, nice-looking young people, but strange. I thought of brainwashed characters I had seen in the movies or of some of the patients in the mental hospitals I had worked in as a student. I observed that, while their leader was obviously quite convinced about what he was doing, some of the others were very uncomfortable. All this was so unspiritual, so un-American—if, indeed, these two problems had any connection with each other! "This is America! This is supposed to be an ashrama!" I ventured. "You can't do this!"

"GET OFF THE PROPERTY!!!"

Daya was ready to put up a fight, but gradually I persuaded her to desist and we returned to the main house. Our bags were outside; they had been packed for us and thrown out, in order to help us get off the property in the stipulated fifteen minutes.

This was so utterly different from my experiences at Marshfield, Swami Sarvagatananda's ashrama in Massachusetts, that it really got me thinking. What made the difference between this mechanical, almost Nazi-like experience and the quiet warmth and friendliness at Marshfield? Clearly, big, commercial operations run by Orientals lacked not only the finesse, but also the usually redeeming decency of Americans. What was going on? How on earth could so many decent, educated American youngsters get themselves behind the horrors we had just experienced? What had happened to them? They seemed to have permitted themselves to lose their identity in a huge, crushing machine that lacked any of the characteristic features of spirituality, at least as we understood it in the

West. Although I did not know it then, this was a sign of things to come in my own personal future.

As of late nineteen seventy-three and early seventy-four, however, my main concern was to figure out what my personal path and destiny were to be. Rattling around with various Asian "gurus" was making the Ramakrishna swamis look very, very good, but there were still questions in my mind: There was a sort of reserve at the Center which bothered me. It was perhaps due to the fact that most of the close membership were what are known as "third order" monks and nuns; that is, earning a living, but living celibate lives devoted to supporting their religion, and therefore cultivating a more than usual degree of reserve. In a sense the Center was a monastery, and so it was inevitable that our self-expression was rather subdued. Swami himself was not readily available personally, though when he was his acceptance and love were nothing short of stunning. And certainly the Genets, though gracious, managed to convey a sense of distance and Gallic superiority, a trait I have noticed in almost all the French people I have encountered.

That bothered me, for my Scots-Irish upbringing had made me a rather roistering, jolly type, enjoying singing and dancing and general merry-making. Courtenaye and Stanley would respond enthusiastically, but I felt that some of the others, the Genets in particular, were not at all appreciative. In this situation it so happened that Daya took me around this time to a meeting of charismatic Catholics. Here there was an openness, a transparency, an emotional way of communicating which appealed to me immensely. I got to know some of the regulars, among whom was a nice American couple. The husband, in particular, was an outgoing sort and up for anything. He played the bagpipes—the way to any Scotsman's heart—and I had seen him performing *Las Cucarachas* on them at a block party, a combination of cultures that tickled my funny-bone. I began to cut class at the Vedanta Society and attend the meetings and social events of these charismatics, including a Christmas party at the home of the bagpiper.

It seemed that I was really trying to get away from Vedanta, no matter how strong the pull. At the time I thought that perhaps the emotional warmth of the charismatics would do me far more good. And so I began to attend the charismatic meetings regularly. I was a bit taken aback when the bagpiper began to speak in tongues, I must say—somehow when I read about such things in the Bible I had visualized it differently. I felt that the bagpiper was expressing something deeply emotional, for which he could not find appropriate words in any already established language. I learned to go with that particular flow, and somehow make it a part of my experience; but one day something happened which affected me in a much more serious way. That particular evening a young woman showed up whom I had not seen before. Everyone seemed on edge and all were apparently avoiding her. She seemed OK to me, and I talked with her a bit before the meeting. But when the meeting began, no one would sit near her and the meeting itself was very subdued and edgy. I believe she said something which on the surface seemed fine to me, but I could feel the whole group drawing away from her mentally. It was obvious she was being "shunned", although I had no idea why. It certainly was an unpleasant experience, and I sought out the wife of the bagpiper, with whom I was by that time quite friendly. "What happened?" I asked. "Something was terribly wrong at this meeting."

"It was that girl being there", she said.

"Why, what was that all about?"

She obviously did not want to talk to me about it, but she did say, "Something very bad happened. She betrayed the group and she is really a bad woman. We don't want her here."

This episode left a bad taste in my mouth. I began to see that bypassing the intellect and relying exclusively on emotion to communicate could be very dangerous. I had no idea what had happened with the group, but it had obviously been traumatic, and I did not particularly want to align myself with something so prone to nasty fallout like this. The following morning I realized that much of my motivation in getting involved in the charismatic group had been to re-identify with my Christian roots, and to soothe myself I went to mass on my way to Vedanta. As it turned out, a funeral was in progress, which struck me as a bad omen, but I settled in for it anyhow. The ritual went entirely over my head, but when the priest gave his homily I knew, once and for all, where I stood. It was so trite, so limited intellectually, so smug and so silly, that I just laughed at myself for thinking, even for a moment, that I could find in Christianity what I was being offered in Vedanta. That was my last attempt to connect up with anything Christian, charismatic or otherwise.

I went to the Vedanta Society, this time utterly grateful for the dignified control and deep spiritual motivation that characterized everything there. I nearly burst into tears that evening when I saw Swami, the very epitome of a wise and loving holy man, so utterly superior to the business-as-usual Catholic priests. I was so grateful to have found him and all that he stood for. But at the same time there was a lot of conflict going on in my soul. Vedanta, with its emphasis on the inner divinity and the necessity to evolve oneself Godward, even with the possibility of becoming a great spiritual being oneself, is very different from the Christianity I had grown up with. The Vedantic emphasis on self-effort and self-transcendence that had attracted me left me looking back nostalgically at the self-surrender and finding refuge in Jesus that had supported me as a youngster. Of course, as I was to find out later on, Vedanta also contains a yoga of love, in which surrender to and dependence on a loving God is the accepted path; but at that time I was focused on the other elements of this wide-ranging worldview. I had, perhaps, forgotten the Dark Mother who had brought me through my migraines and Sarada Devi who had ushered me into my present turn of the spiral—they were the essence of the Divine, accepting love and giving refuge and healing.

From time to time I felt I was betraying Jesus, the one aspect of Christianity which really mattered to me. Was taking up this exotic Indian religion not a denial of Jesus and all that he stood for in my life? However, I was reading the *Gospel of Sri Ramakrishna* and *The Great Master* every day now, as well as the *Complete Works of Swami Vivekananda*, going deeper into Vedanta and all that it contains, and was learning that one of Sri Ramakrishna's special features was that he embraced and validated other religions besides Vedanta—such as Buddhism, Sikhism, Christianity and Islam—and pronounced all of them equally valid paths to God. A highly visual mystic, he had actually seen, embraced and merged with the form of Jesus as well as of the prophet of Islam, merging himself in them and they in him. I held on to this image in my mind, forgetting the priests, the mass, the charismatics, and I began to realize that much of what I had thought was coldness at the Center was actually the calm and balance that regular meditation brings to our personality, and wished that I, too, might acquire some of it.

Around this time I had what I considered at the time one of the most important spiritual experiences of my life. I was lying on my bed in my dark little room, feeling utterly confused, angry and worthless. Possibly the ultra-refinement of the ladies at the Center was making me feel unworthy, maybe I was just too prone to feeling the underdog—but whatever the cause, I was crying bitterly, feeling quite, quite, quite worthless. But my own inner self-awareness, as ever, was not going to let me go on like this. Suddenly I was lifted totally out of myself into a realm of light and clarity, totally beyond any awareness of the world. Everything came to a total stop and I felt as if I were living in and utterly blissful eternity. I felt that Ramakrishna himself had taken me up in his arms and carried me back to the realm where Mother had taken me at Fortrose some twenty-three years prior, and Sarada Devi only a couple of years before. No sooner had this thought occurred to me than another one came: "How can I be so close to Ramakrishna? I am impure, I am not fit to be near him!" Immediately I felt myself beginning to fall, tumbling, tumbling, tumbling through cold, dark space, whirling past stars and planets in what felt like a huge vacuum. It felt like an eternity, though of course it was probably only a few seconds. Then there was a bump! And there I was, lying on my bed. I lay there, dazed, for quite some time. As my mind started to work "normally" it dawned on me how powerfully the way you think affects you. If you think of yourself as pure, you are pure and live in the land of the blessed; and if you think of yourself as impure or as a sinner, that is exactly what you will be and you will indeed live in a hell of darkness, cold, and emptiness. Although I did not understand it at that moment, this was actually a demonstration of the difference between Vedanta, which asserts that all beings are intrinsically divine and therefore blessed; and Christianity, which emphasizes sin and darkness. In Vedanta you can reach your inner divinity through conscious, directed effort, while in Christianity you have to rely on the church, a priest, or the atonement of Jesus, none of which really had any appeal for me by that time.

By that time I had learned that the swamis initiate, and had understood that Swami was the person I wanted as a spiritual teacher. But Swami was notoriously difficult to snag as a teacher: In order to speak with him privately, an appointment had to be made through Jeanne—and appointments were not so readily available. His health had never been strong, and now he was elderly and ailing, while Jeanne made it her business to screen him as much as possible from anything she perceived as troublesome or difficult. Then again, I was shy and still a taciturn Scot, and so I ended up seeing Swami only two or three times a year. But when I did, he gave me his full attention and somehow managed, without a word being spoken, to lift me up beyond all that was troubling me, while conveying to me a deep impression of my own spiritual worth and lovability. And, of course, being with him at class every evening was also an opportunity to learn and grow, of which I made the very most.

I later understood that Swami was not prepared to spend time on anyone who was not dead serious and willing to learn from him. He would play hard to get with anyone who was a "floater", mentally confused or disturbed, or just mildly curious, or simply an Indian national seeking familiar cultural events where he or she could feel comfortable. Perhaps to establish my credentials and thus get closer to him, I had to go through some rather difficult stuff, mostly related to my status as a medical doctor. Not long after I had started working at the Center Jeanne came into the kitchen where I was working on the dishes and told me her mother's leg had suddenly become numb. I rather reluctantly left the kitchen and approached the ornery old lady. I already knew that she had an irregular heartbeat, which was being treated by the doctor, and therefore knew that there was a possibility of her blowing a clot into her legs. As soon as I saw the leg—absolutely white—I felt that that is what must have happened. A major artery must be blocked and no blood was getting to the leg. Hesitantly and after asking permission, I put my hand on her leg and found it cold and without a pulse. Yes, indeed, she had blown a clot—and a big one at that! If something was not done at once she would lose the leg completely and would no longer be ambulatory.

I explained to her that she might have to have surgery, about which she was most unenthusiastic; but knowing that there was no time to lose, I went ahead. Maman was used to being pandered to, coaxed and cajoled. But I knew there wasn't time for that and got on the phone to a vascular surgeon I had worked with at the Roosevelt, which was just a little way downtown from the Center. Fortunately he was available and responded immediately to my request to see Maman. Within a few minutes she was in his office and within the hour was on the operating table, where the clot was removed and her leg was saved. Maman presented me with my own set of the *Complete Works of Swami Vivekananda*, and Jeanne worked me over something ferocious.

But the course of true work/love never does run smooth—or so they say, and I have lived to confirm innumerable times. For whatever reason, Maman conceived an intense dislike of me. Certainly, I was not "refined" in her Gallic way, certainly I was "invading" her cramped space in that tiny basement room (even though rendering continuous service), and then there is the phenomenon that the more you do for someone the more they hate you. Saving her life, apparently, had been a crime of the first magnitude—but why? No doubt she did not like to be beholden to anyone—she certainly preferred to be the Queen Bee—and perhaps she resented that I had some kind of "control" over her (though I went out of my way to keep a low profile once I understood what was going on). Whatever it was, it was there and there to stay; and in no time Swami suggested that I come to the Center only after lunch to do the dishes and other work. It was clear the Genets had put him up to this and I felt very, very bad. These were spiritual people—and still there was this rejection? I began to understand how difficult it is to be good, far less spiritual. A Ramakrishna or a Sarada Devi could have people around them all the time and make them welcome and happy—but such is divine behavior. For ordinary mortals things are not so easy; and mine was to accept the limitations of the ladies at the Center.

Swami softened the blow by encouraging me to use my morning time to study. Only a week after I had taken up this regime I saw how beneficial it was, and that it was exactly what I had been needing. I continued to devour the *Complete Works of Swami Vivekananda*, getting more and more out of them, and also systematically read the literature of the Ramakrishna tradition—the biographies of Ramakrishna, Sarada Devi, Swami Vivekananda and their disciples, as well as their teachings and the traditional scriptures of Vedanta. This lifted me up into a totally different realm of being, in which the petty jealousies and struggles in the basement of the Vedanta Society basically ceased to exist. I had moments of missing human company, especially as I walked the mile downtown to the Center after lunch, but had actually found something more meaningful in the realm of ideas and spiritual principles. This was the first hint as to how I was going to transcend the emotion that still plagued me intensely.

I believe it was around this time that I had a huge spiritual dream. That morning I had read in Swami Vivekananda's *Works* an account of him exhorting his monastic followers to live with the utmost intensity and to dedicate themselves to the welfare of others. This was toward the end of his tragically short life, when he felt tremendous pressure to get the order he had founded on the most stable and deeply spiritual footing before he himself passed on. The intensity of his exhortations may have had an effect on my mind, of which I was not fully aware at the time.

Be that as it may, that night I dreamt I was in Madison Square Garden, attending a big religious meeting. I was sitting in the last row, but could see that the speaker was Swami Vivekananda, a tiny orange spot on the podium. His talk was inspiring, though I have no recollection of what it was. What was remarkable was what he said at the end of the evening. He took out a list from his pocket and said, "After the meeting I would like to speak with these people." I began to get ready to leave, ahead of the huge crush that takes place when Madison Square Garden is emptying. As I was getting up, Swami Vivekananda was reading out the names—about ten of them. Almost at the exit, I was riveted to hear, at the end of the list, my own name: *Jean C. MacPhail*. How did he know my name? I had never met him. Nor was I absolutely sure I wanted to meet him. It was all so overpowering and unexpected. However, I waited till the hall cleared and went down to the podium, where the swami was talking quietly with each of the people he had asked to stay back. I was the last on the list, so I had to wait, seated on a small chair at the far end of the platform from the swami. My mind was a complete blank. I had nothing to say and no idea what on earth he could say, either. We did not know each other! What was this about?

Finally, my turn came. I got up and walked over toward the swami. He was smiling at me, a strong, masculine figure in radiant orange robes and matching turban. He seemed very friendly and benign and I felt quite at ease, not at all nervous. But as I got closer to him I could feel a vast field of energy enveloping me and I realized this was not simply a beautiful man—he was a huge power. Without a thought or a word I fell to my knees—the last thing a self-respecting, free-thinking Presbyterian would do! There we were in the huge darkness of Madison Square Garden after the show, and me acting like a Catholic, or something! He smiled at me with the utmost love and brought out a huge, radiant diamond-like stone—much bigger than the Koh-i-Noor, of which I had seen a replica in Glasgow Art Galleries. As I kneeled there, he leant over and put the stone on my forehead, where it remained, like a jewel hanging from a headdress. As it touched my forehead I felt the light and energy it contained flooding my whole being, lighting up my head and expanding my awareness, step by step, beyond the world, myself, or anything I could imagine. My head was like a huge light radiating over the universe. Everything came to a stop and there was the utmost silence, peace and knowledge, not the kind that talks, the kind that *is*.

Then I woke up. I had not the slightest idea what it meant, though I could relate it dimly to the effect that reading the swami's works was having on me. Perhaps, too, it helped me see why Swami emphasized my study of Vivekananda so much—there was some kind of connection between myself and the founder of our order that went far beyond mere intellectual assent. Maybe, behind that, I understood—but very, very dimly—that the swami was showing me my true nature and my ultimate destiny; but that, at that time, was a far cry. I had far too much baggage in my mind to be able to go with such exalted notions. I had a lot of other business to conduct in the here and now, and so I shelved this dream. Because of Swami's "veto" on talking about such experiences, I did not mention it to anyone at all. Indeed, I promptly forgot it. It remained in my attic for nearly twenty-five years, when it would come back to me at a time of terrible decision.

I finally got up the courage to ask Swami to initiate me. I had heard so many stories about how he would make people wait for years, how some people never got accepted, and so on. I expected a tussle, or even an outright rejection—something it was difficult for me to face, with all of my past history of abandonment. But when I asked he immediately said yes and that he would give me a mantra on the next auspicious day, which happened to be Ramakrishna's birthday. However, I had to go through a fiery baptism before I could finally be accepted. Just a few days before Ramakrishna's birthday I learned that Swami had passed blood in his urine, that his regular doctor was on vacation, and would I come over to the Center? Knowing that he had had prostate surgery in Hollywood that terrible year when he was so sick, I was alert—was this bleeding due to cancer recurring or some complication of his previous surgery? When I spoke with him personally it turned out that he was not able to pass much urine and I realized that this was an emergency. He wanted to wait till his personal physician returned in about a week or so, but I knew that wouldn't do—there had to be intervention before infection started and made him really sick once again. Accordingly, I set out on a voyage of discovery on the telephone and finally managed to find a urologist who was affiliated with Swami's doctor.

Swami had scar tissue from his previous surgery that required immediate surgery if he was going to be able to urinate. He was quite unwilling to go through with it without his doctor's presence—he had an almost childlike faith in his doctor, who had endeared himself to Swami by bringing him ice cream and behaving more like a devotee than a medical professional. For Swami, love and devotion were what mattered; but I was a beady-eyed professional myself, who saw what was on the table and therefore had the unenviable task of jawboning him into undergoing the surgery. If he waited for his doctor, he would be as sick as he had been in nineteen-seventy, when he nearly died from urinary obstruction. I prevailed at last, and Swami was admitted to hospital. He was to be there for only a few days, but there was quite a to-do about it. The Genets and anyone who would listen to them were all a-flutter, suggesting that I was unnecessarily subjecting Swami to surgery, that I should have waited for the doctor, and so on and on (no doubt building on some fable they were generating about Maman's surgery); while the men were trying to find someone who could be with Swami at the hospital.

As I was to learn over time, spiritual life is often built on a series of disciplines, some of them physical—certain patterns of doing things which conserve energy and make it easier to meditate, concentrate, keep centered, and so on. As Swami had always had delicate health, he had worked hard to build up patterns of doing things that kept him focused and able to shoulder the heavy spiritual burdens of others. It was important that he be able to maintain his routines—and for that he needed the help of one of our men. Accordingly, the first two days of the stay would be covered by Erik Johns, one of our longstanding members whose special calling was to tend Swami when he was ill. Erik always took him to the doctor and was a past master at humoring both him and the doctor to get things done as smoothly as possible. Although much in demand as an artist and businessman, Erik would drop whatever he was doing and come to help Swami whenever needed. But on this particular occasion, which of course had come up unexpectedly, he was unable to be with Swami on the third day, as he had a previous business appointment of the utmost urgency. The question now was: which of the men could fill in for that one, last day? John, who attended Swami's minute-to-minute needs at the Center, was the obvious choice; but he, too, had commitments that he could not drop without more notice. Stanley was working full-time, Bill was not really suited to the job, and any other close men that might have been suitable were simply unable to take up the responsibility.

The evening that Swami was admitted to hospital, the whole library group was standing round his bed. Courtenaye, much concerned, asked Swami outright: "Who will help you the third day? The men are all tied up with previous commitments." Without missing a beat Swami pointed at me and said in a strong voice: "She will do it. She is a medical doctor, and she can do it." There was a stunned silence and they all turned to look at me. Swami, a monk, was utterly scrupulous about his deportment with women. He followed strict monastic protocol: he was not in the company of a woman alone for any longer than was strictly necessary; he never traveled with women; and certainly his attendants were always men. At the time I used to think it was a bit exaggerated, but in the light of the revelations coming from the Catholic Church nowadays (and even some of the rumors going about the Ramakrishna Order) I now understand how wise he was. But now, here it was. Completely out of the usual—I was to be his attendant for a day! The men heaved a sigh of relief; but the women, I doubt not, were all a-twitter.

My only concern was to do a good job, and to that end I spent the next two days in the hospital working alongside Erik, learning the ropes of Swami's routines. I was simply flabbergasted at the way Erik worked—so quietly, so surely, so accurately. He seemed to understand Swami intuitively and to be able to anticipate his every need. To some extent, of course, it came from experience, but I also felt that there was a degree of love and commitment that went far beyond the usual. Erik had a charming personality, gentle, sweet and humorous. But he was not a milquetoast, as quickly became evident. For the first day or two, particularly after the (fairly minor) surgery, Swami was very quiet, silent and indrawn. I would stand hour after hour at the end of his bed, watching his serene face which, like his body, barely moved at all. It was difficult to get him to eat, to take interest in anything. To my mind, he was simply in a meditative state, concentrating his energy; but to the others, he might be preparing to die, and there was considerable disquiet. Erik, however, was his usual, cheerful self and he and I, having little to do, took the opportunity to get to know each other. We talked about all sorts of ideas and experiences, Erik telling me of how he had wanted to become a monk, how Swami had discouraged him and how he had gotten help from Swami Nitya-swarupa-nanda, one of the shakers and movers in the order, who had encouraged Erik to go into a business partnership with his friend Jack. The business—Party Decorators—had worked out extremely well (catering to the likes of Jackie Kennedy), and Erik felt that it was all for the good. However, what impressed me most about Erik was his unflappable equanimity, his assurance about himself, and his ability to create an atmosphere of the utmost grace and ease. I could see why Swami liked to have this wonderful man in attendance. He was what the Vedantins call *sattwika*, serene, gentle, utterly concerned with others—what is usually considered "spiritual".

On the afternoon of the second day, Swami was a bit perkier. He began to sit up and pay attention to what was going on. At one point he expressed annoyance about some item that had not been properly taken care of—if I remember rightly, the way he had been treated in X-Ray. I had complained to the department head about the rough way the technicians had handled him, but he was still rather disgusted with what had happened. Erik's eyes lit up. "Swami! That is utterly disgraceful! You should sue the hospital!" I couldn't believe I was hearing such fighting words from the gentle Erik! These words galvanized Swami, who sat up in bed, his face animated, and launched into a long harangue about how Americans had a lot to learn about how to behave properly with other people. He got so excited that I began to worry about him. But Erik was smiling serenely, consoling Swami, but also encouraging him to let off steam.

Afterwards, when Swami had fallen asleep, I asked Erik about this incident. "Why did you prod him into that tirade?" I asked. "You could injure his health, which is very delicate." Erik smiled like the Cheshire cat and said, "It does him good to let off steam. He lives so intensely he needs outlets like this. When he tends to go within too much I do this all the time—get him going on one of his hobbyhorses. It does him a world of good. Look, he is sleeping perfectly serenely. He has gotten his stuff off his chest and is perfectly all right. If we let him, he will just disappear, drift off into another world, from where we can't get him back." I stared at Erik, completely at a loss. This was such a radically different way of thinking about Swami! The ladies in the basement always spoke of him as an omniscient god, kissied up to and babied him and pandered to his every perceived need, whether it existed or not. But Erik saw him as a human being, with certain needs—albeit unusual, belonging to a realm that most of us do not live in—and responded to him in a direct, human way. It did not take me long to decide that I much preferred Erik's way (as, apparently, did Swami), and that what the men called the women's "swami-swooning" was not for me. I felt a tremendous closeness to Brother Erik, for whom I now had the utmost respect and affection.

All of this came into play the next day with Swami, when I was for one day his "attendant". He didn't ask much of me, for the most part; and, of course, I had gotten a lot down from my couple of days working with Erik. But there was one episode which was particularly significant. Swami was in a rather listless mood and not willing to move about or take initiatives. Suddenly he asked me for a bedpan, with a slight degree of hesitation, as if it was a bit much to ask of me. "Swami!" I said briskly, "You are perfectly capable of going to the toilet. You cannot lie in bed indefinitely, you know. You will lose energy—and besides, you are going home tomorrow and will have to manage to go to the bathroom there. You have to start training right now." He looked at me in disbelief. His lassitude was all gone and he was in a fighting mood. "I am too weak!" he said animatedly. "You will be even weaker if you don't get going now!" I insisted. "I will help you to get up and over to the toilet. You will have a much better result than you would on a bedpan. It is difficult to sit on those things and 'perform'". He looked at me pathetically. "How will I manage this?" he said, pointing to his intravenous line. "Swami, it is quite easy. You just push the stand—it has rollers."

After a little more discussion, he finally sat up and got out of bed, a little shaky on his pins. I helped him over to the toilet, showing him how to push the i.v. stand. I got him on to the toilet, closed the door and stood outside, wondering what would happen. I knew that medically I was completely correct, but had no idea what the psychology of this unusual being was. I wondered if Jeanne or some other sweet butterfly would have done this. They would have felt that bringing him a bedpan was a moment of glorious self-abasement and joyously rushed forward to comply. However, I knew that it would weaken him and prolong his recovery—but did he fully understand that? Perhaps he felt I was bossy, lacking in a spirit of service.

As I stood there ruminating, I heard the toilet flush and, before I could go in to help him out, he appeared at the door, pushing the i.v. stand. "You were perfectly right!" he said with great animation. "This was much more satisfactory! I am so glad you insisted! That is because you are a medical doctor and understand what needs to be done." I came forward to help him with the i.v. stand, but he was already halfway to his bed, managing it perfectly well. I had to help him a little getting into bed, but basically he was completely energized, out of his lassitude for good, and very cheerful and animated. The rest of the day we had a wonderful conversation about spiritual things, laughing a lot and teasing each other. This was heaven on earth, if it exists at all. That he was able to appreciate and accept where I was coming from and not push me back into tweetie-pie-ism was a huge, huge relief. The thought occurred to me that perhaps he, too, had his moments of weariness with it all; when faced with something more bracing, he was ready for it and able to comply completely. "What an unusual human being," I thought.

That evening almost the whole library group showed up to see Swami, now that he was so much better. Jeanne, too, had come—something most unusual, as she could never leave Maman for a moment; only *she* was capable of caring for her. She didn't even come to the library class, so urgent and essential was it for her to be with her mother at all times. But there she was, and happy to be so. As the group was chatting with Swami, he suddenly took out his dental plate and handed it to me. "Clean this, please!" he said. I was rather taken aback. Swami had cleaned it after lunch and had eaten nothing since. Why this sudden need? But I just took it anyway and headed off to the bathroom. As

I turned to do so, I saw Jeanne looking at me very strangely, her eyes glittering in the subdued light. What was in her mind? Why this intense stare? As I did the chore in the bathroom it suddenly dawned on me what was happening. Swami was going through this pantomime to make a point with Jeanne—and maybe others, as well, of course. Jeanne was a long-standing attendant on Swami—she served his breakfasts, kept his room clean and neat and generally looked out for him, following in the footsteps of her adored sister Rolande, whose service of Swami had been legendary. Perhaps she had begun to feel that she was especially important, that she was more "spiritual" than others—I do not know; but certainly she was backing her mother in the old lady's "mission" against me, and tending to make out that somehow the two of them were so much "above" me, whatever that means. This strange gesture of Swami's, so unexpected and so abrupt, was nothing less than a lesson for Jeanne, demonstrating to her that she was not the only one who was close to Swami and capable of serving him. It was also, perhaps, a message to her to make room for me, who was just as much of a devotee as she.

This was not the last such episode; Swami would go through something similar with me and another devotee at least two more times. It was very strange to me, but it certainly seemed to work, for Jeanne was a lot less hostile after this episode, although her mother continued to give me a hard time. In such circumstances, why didn't Swami just say something? That was not his way, apparently. By acting something out he seemed to be able to change the minds of people much more radically and permanently than with words. It was a lesson I took to heart and used later in my own life, though I still had to learn that such methods work only with people who basically love each other or are deeply committed to the same or similar ideals.

Step by step I was coming closer, but was not yet initiated. This whole hospital drama had taken place in the time space in which I was supposed to have had my initiation. I didn't really mind, however—it was more important to take care of what was immediately before me. And somehow the ongoing way was to be rather difficult and challenging. Despite all the pleasantness and "promotion" in the hospital, Swami and I started to fall out in a big way after he was discharged. I felt it was important for him to follow through on some health issues with his doctor, but he was adamant that he was not going to spend any more time on such matters.

Perhaps I got too big an idea of my influence on him; and certainly he was notorious for not wanting to bother with his health. Erik kept warning me, but I knew that action now would help prevent a lot of trouble later. Swami and I had fallen out badly within a few weeks of his discharge and I was quite disgruntled.

The climax of the drama came on the afternoon of Friday, April first. I was in the scullery, working away on the pots and pans. It was an overcast day, with rumbles of thunder, if I recall correctly. My own mood was thunderous, to say the least, and, as it was also rather warm, I was hot and sweaty. Suddenly the intercom buzzed and Jeanne came into the scullery. "Swami wants to speak with you", she said. "Immediately." I was a little put out, as Swami was seldom so urgent. Normally I would change out of my dirty work clothes on the few occasions that he needed to see me; but Jeanne would take no nay and so I had to go upstairs, hot, sweaty, dirty and in a really foul mood.

As I entered Swami's spacious room it was obvious that he was going to have it out with me. He was seated in his chair, sitting unusually straight, with his eyes flashing and his whole deportment one of challenge. His slim, erect, light figure with the pure white hair, the pale blue cashmere sweater, was quite a contrast to the dark, heavy, lowering sky outside, bearing down oppressively. He started in at once on the subject of how his medical problems were going to be handled. I was in a fighting mood, ready like a bulldog to hold on to the end and prevail. The interview did not go well: I got my grip and he his magical "white wizard" routine, and it seemed as if we could go on indefinitely, me holding and him transcending, holding and transcending . . . .

In the midst of this tussle, he suddenly took a totally different turn. Becoming low key and sweet, he told me endearingly, "You see, all of this medical business is of no importance to me. You are not here to get involved in my medical problems—you are here to grow spiritually." As I took this in, like a Neanderthal clubman contemplating a sudden change in behavior of his prey, Swami upped the ante even further. "Did I give you a name to repeat?" he asked sweetly. This was his way of discussing initiation, a subject he did not like to bring up. He disliked being called a guru or teacher, and always kept the whole initiation-disciple thing under tight wraps.

This was the ultimate change of subject. I realized that I was totally outflanked and had better throw in the towel. Which I did, of course.

He was perfectly right that my main interest was to deepen my spiritual life—the medical business was just a ruse to give me my own "space" in a tightly knit and sometimes competitive group. I suddenly became as tame as a lamb, a rather funny contrast to my bulldog demeanor of just a moment before. "No, Swami. You were in hospital the day it was supposed to take place." "I see. Well, today is Rama's birthday . . . an auspicious day. There is never any time better than the present." I couldn't believe this. Here I was, dirty, sweaty and angry and he was going to initiate me, on a day I understood nothing about. Who, in heaven's name was Rama? It obviously meant something to him, but for me was a total blank. I remembered the fancy skirt and blouse in my closet, specially purchased for my "big day", my plans for the fruit and flowers to be offered after initiation, and smiled to myself. And the ultimate laugh was—this was April Fools' Day! But, instead of seeming incongruous, it all seemed perfectly appropriate. I just was not a "regular" person, someone who does things in a conventional or conformist way—and neither, obviously, was he. I realized that we were two oddballs, playing out a drama against the rumblings, howlings and increasing patterings of rain outside. Later I learned that his initiations would usually take place early in the morning when no one was about. He really wanted to keep down any discussion or glorification about it, it seems. On such occasions, Jeanne, who was the resident genius of the place, would preside over the entry of the candidates, wafting them upstairs in an elf-like, confidential and whispery way, with incense no doubt burning on the altar.

For me, there had been no such gossamer, no such ritual, no such holiness. On the field of battle, in the midst of a thunderstorm, I was given a name to repeat, Swami saying it so softly and serenely that I could barely hear it. Looking back on it, it was so utterly appropriate, such a perfect conclusion to all the previous battles and such an auspicious beginning to all that were to come. And there were, as one might have expected, plenty in store.

CHAPTER 18

SPIRITUAL COMBAT AND
FLASHES OF LIGHT: 1974

Even as a child I would have my doubts about happy endings. After so much struggle, danger, and often misunderstanding, the hero and heroine would get married and "live happily ever after". I would think, "If they misunderstood each other beforehand, why not afterwards? If there were problems before, why would they suddenly go away?" Whether I was right about this or whether thinking this way made me stir up troubles, I was in for the tussle of my life after I was initiated. You would think that, in a spiritual biography, initiation would be the turning point after which the heroine "lived happily ever after". But the actual fact was that my troubles began only after that moment, so deliciously incongruous and unconventional as it was.

On the surface, of course, all was well. I was now a fully accepted member of the group, playing a role (and that is exactly what it was!) as Swami's "medical advisor", and being at least tolerated by the Genets in the domestic area. Swami had discovered my enthusiasm for Swami Vivekananda and had confided to me that one of the things that had most mattered to him when he was head of one of the order's premiere publishing houses in India was the publication, in the early nineteen-forties, of the great swami's collected poems. Swami had graduated with an MA in English literature and was, like myself, a great lover of poetry. One of the nicest things was quoting poems to him and enjoying his happiness at hearing them spoken out. He would ask me, "Do you know that one?" and would be like a child when I could repeat some verses for him. He had been so thrilled to put together Swami Vivekananda's poems, which previously had been published in bits and pieces, and to have done some background research as to the circumstances in which they were written. "I thought everyone would be so happy to have the poems published together", he said. "But everyone told me—as they had about my publication of his collected letters—that they would not be of interest to the public." I was amazed to hear this, but later understood that in the eyes of many Indians, Vivekananda was primarily a national and even a political leader, rather than a spiritual teacher and philosopher, which is how I personally saw him. Swami smiled sweetly: "But they were best-sellers. So many people were interested in Swami Vivekananda's inner life that we sold large numbers of the books."

Then he said, "Why don't you memorize Vivekananda's poems? It will do you good." I don't think I had told Swami about my epiphany in Boston on reading out *To a Friend* to Swami Sarvagatananda, but I had a hunch that he had tapped into whatever had given me the epiphany: Certainly my love for poetry, my attraction to Vivekananda, and particularly his amazing combination of a penetrating, all-rounded intellect with a deeply emotional and intuitive nature.

Then there was my proclivity for memorization. At school memorization was a normal part of our education, a fact for which I was intensely grateful. And on occasion I had gone beyond the formal requirements of school. If something appealed to me, I would commit it to memory forthwith. The most outstanding example was my reaction to Lord MacAulay's *Horatius*, a six-hundred line saga about a Roman hero who single-handedly held an enemy Etruscan army at bay until the city he was defending could muster its defenses. I have no idea why this longwinded tale in verse appealed to me so much—unless, of course, it was the theme of an individual struggling against overwhelming odds. And again, although I did not know it fully at the time, Lord MacAulay and I had a relationship to each other that was much deeper than met the eye. By the time I had met Swami I had come to know, from my Uncle Ian's compilation of the MacPhail family tree that MacAulay was, in fact, a distant relative on Grannie's side of the family, though that was a tiny tip of the iceberg. Since reading *The Great Master*, I also knew that MacAulay was responsible for the Indian education Bill of eighteen thirty-six, in which the British quite consciously set out to denationalize the Indians and turn them into "Europeans with dark skins". An unconscionable piece of Western imperialism; but as the author of *The Great Master* pointed out, Ramakrishna was born that very year, Indian's quiet response to the British, which in the end checkmated them and worked to neutralize the tremendous problems they had caused in the Indian psyche. This was a titillating little morsel, the full impact of which I was not to understand until over thirty years later.

But in the meantime all of this, combined with my respect for Swami, led me to start at once on Vivekananda's poetry, and within a few months I had the whole thing committed to memory. Some of his poems were written in English, some were translations from the Bengali, and the quality varied considerably. All of it was meaningful to me, but one or two passages struck me very forcibly. Among these was one from the long poem translated from Bengali, *And Let Shyama Dance There*—a poem about surrender to Shyama or Kali, the Black Goddess. This is a poem which calls spiritual heroes to face the dark and terrible side of life, to eschew the easy and pleasant and to take up the burdens of the world. The poem concludes with the lines:

> Awake, O hero! Shake off your vain dreams.
> Death stands at your head—does fear become you?
> A load of misery, true though it is—
> This Becoming[14]—know this to be your God!
> His temple the burning ground among corpses
> And funeral pyres; unending battle—
> That verily is his sacred worship.
> Constant defeat—let that not unnerve you;
> Shattered be little self, hope, name and fame.
> Set up a pyre of them and make your heart
> A burning-ground.
> And let Shyama dance there.

Somehow this seemed to epitomize my own life, with so many dark episodes and so much struggle, combined with the longing to give light and joy to others. That is what I had picked up in *To a Friend* in Boston, and which had affected me so profoundly. Now, here it was again, spelling out all of the difficulties and obstacles that had to be faced and overcome in an authentically spiritual life. This passage became a sort of unofficial personal motto, something I held on to when the darkness descended—which it was to and did, to a degree as yet unknown in my life.

Another, deeply meaningful note at this juncture before I descended into hell was a dream I had a few days after I was initiated. For some reason,

---

[14]   The aspect of constant change, of the wheel of birth and death, otherwise known as *the world*.

every day after my initiation Swami kept asking me to come and see him. He seemed to be expecting something, though he did not say so explicitly. It was certainly out of the usual, as I seldom saw Swami formally. At any rate, I did have the dream and it concerned my going on a long, difficult journey. I had been traveling a long, long time, carrying two huge, heavy bags, which most likely contained books—my whole life I have dragged heavy bags full of them. In the dream I arrived on the bank of a large body of water, perhaps an ocean, or maybe an inlet, for the water was eerily still. Ahead of me was a beautiful island, shining in the sun, and I somehow knew that that was where I had to go. But the water, I could see, was very, very deep; and, in addition, it looked dark, cold, forbidding, and who knows, either carried some terrible disease or perhaps a lurking sea-monster or crocodiles, of which I had always had a horror. I put down my bags and sat on them, feeling I could go on no further.

Yet, something in me told me I had to reach the island. That was the goal of my journey. What to do? I felt quite despondent, but was too tired and dejected to think of how I could get over to the island. At that juncture a small boy appeared beside me. He was perhaps six or seven years old, well-built, even muscular, with dark skin, a huge mass of rather fuzzy black hair, dimples in his cheeks and a dazzling, happy smile. He was speaking to me animatedly, but I couldn't understand what he was saying. He seemed to be encouraging me to move forward, but I couldn't see beyond the obstacles I was so oppressed by. Suddenly, he plunged into the water and began to swim over to the island. I was amazed at how strongly he swam—he all but flew through the water. In no time he reached the island and, standing on its beach, turned toward me and waved cheerfully, beckoning me to follow him.

I was bedazzled and at the same time found a clarity that I had not had before. "If he can get through the water, so can I", I thought. "Obviously there aren't any diseases or monsters in the water—he has demonstrated that. There is no reason whatsoever to hesitate." And with that, I plunged in, leaving my two heavy bags behind. I woke up, feeling light and happy. Writing this now, I see quite clearly that the boy was Swami, though at the time I thought it might be Ramakrishna, whose nature was definitely that of a happy, self-reliant boy.

The following day, when Swami spoke with me, I told him about this dream. He went into some kind of spiritual state, exclaiming, "Ah, ah, ah!" He could obviously see what the meaning of the dream was and had found it very important. It may have been a sign of how I envisioned the relationship between us, of what my path and future was going to be: in short, of who I am spiritually and what my destiny was to be. Whatever he saw, it was obviously that which he had been expecting, for after I told him about the dream he stopped asking me to come to see him.

All very happy and auspicious, no doubt, and the real core of the relationship between us. But along with such epiphanies comes all the baggage that we insist on dragging about with us. It was going to be some time before I managed to leave it behind—at least, the particular baggage I was working with then. About two weeks later, Swami and I commenced our "crucifixion battle". I think it must have arisen from my reaction to his Easter Sunday sermon, which would have occurred around then. The monks of the Ramakrishna Order make a point of observing the main festivals of whatever other religions are in force wherever they are posted, because Ramakrishna himself had followed the observances of both Christianity and Islam, as well as many, many of the different observances within Hinduism. His followers, therefore, made a point of cultivating religious pluralism, the recognition of the validity of all religions, and a respectful observance of the special days within whatever religion was most prevalent in their area of work. We therefore celebrated Christmas and Easter at the Center—in our own way, of course.

Christmas was always a happy time, a time of warmth and cheer, perhaps because we so needed to light up the dark and cold of winter, both in Scotland and in New York. But Easter had always been for me a time of conflict—and in my migraine period, of severe and frequent migraines. It had been a time of struggle against forces that seemed to be sucking me down, forces of darkness—perhaps what was symbolized in the Easter festival. In and through such times I had often found myself touching the Light, finding a source of affirmation and consolation within myself—again, reflecting the festival. Which came first, the Easter story or the gut reaction to the time of year, I do not know. But nineteen seventy-four was certainly an Easter to be remembered. Swami's sermon had a crushingly negative effect on me. I don't remember exactly what he said, but I had felt that it was a rather negative criticism of the Christian emphasis on suffering and atonement. Swami was an extremely rational person, and I rather think he might have also tended to minimize the resurrection theme, damning it with faint praise. On previous such occasions I had thought to myself, "He is, after all, an Indian. No doubt he suffered terribly at the hands of the missionaries, who, I doubt not, were as dogmatic and overbearing as some of the Christians I tried to work with in Scotland. I can understand why he is not keen on some of this dogmatic stuff." But sometimes I would also think, "Why does he get into Easter at all? If he doesn't agree, why not just leave it alone? We can live without it."

But that year, just newly initiated—and facing, though I did not fully understand it, a big showdown between Vedanta and Christianity—I expected more of him. Why did he have to be so negative? No matter what the Christians might have said or done to him, why couldn't he put it behind him? He was supposed to be a holy man! I became very, very agitated and disgusted.

Exactly how we began to argue about it, I do not recall. Most likely I started it, as Swami was not prone to bringing up negatives with us individually. But start we did, and with a vengeance. And, whatever the genesis of our quarrel, we both went at it with gusto. Swami made it clear, early on, that he would never approve of any religion based on a glorification of suffering, that the crucifixion and all that went with it was an ugly, degrading way of thinking. No matter that I kept saying that Christianity was about transcending suffering and that the way of the cross was a voluntary method of helping individuals to do so; he kept telling me to concentrate on the teachings of Jesus and not to glorify something that was a mere historical accident. This I could not accept: the crucifixion was part and parcel of Jesus and the culture he came from—he was executed precisely because of what he was and taught. I saw the whole row as a showdown between Vedanta and Christianity, a struggle that had already announced itself by my forays into charismatic Christianity.

Swami was coming from an uncompromising position, characteristic of Vedanta: There are several layers of consciousness, each succeeding one being more inclusive, more integral, than the one before. The goal of spiritual life is to enter into the deeper, more integral levels and live in, through and from them. His purpose as a spiritual teacher was to show us these deeper levels and help us work toward them ourselves. His temperament—or, perhaps, the level he lived on or the culture he came from—did not incline him to explain all this intellectually. Perhaps he knew that, with my intellectual baggage, I might simply turn these insights into something to play around with, and thus get distracted from the hard work of actually going deeper. For, as anyone who has read the mystical literature of any tradition knows, entering deeply into the divine is no child's play. Great self-denial is called for, hard work to move forward, great surrender to the deeper, more integral, and more loving levels, of which the lesser levels are afraid and do everything in their power to keep away from.

The only hint of all of this that Swami gave me was his remark: "All this business of suffering—how can there be suffering when you are one with that 'from which the universe comes into being, in which it is sustained, and unto which it returns'?" Although I did not know it then, this is a quotation from the Upanishads, the most basic scriptures of Vedanta, going back some four thousand years. In the Upanishads the key idea is that the divine permeates the entire universe and can be discovered and seen anywhere, provided one has the eyes to see. Most importantly for an individual life, the divine is what you really are; and moreover, you can realize that and live from that truth. And when you do so, the whole universe changes. Suffering and delusion can no longer affect you radically—you *know* who you are and cannot be touched by anything of the world. Swami did not explain all this—he simply quoted the verse.

For a moment I paused: It was a beautiful thought, and resonated within me. It struck me as somehow being perfectly in tune with the teachings of Jesus, who would talk of treasures in heaven, which moths can't corrupt nor rust destroy. Then again, I had a faint recall of how the vision of Kali had taken me beyond the excruciating pain of my migraines and lifted me into a realm of happiness that made the pain seem trivial. And, finally, I thought of Ramakrishna, who died of cancer of the throat—a terrible death, in which he could not eat or breathe and suffered terrible pain from the cancer boring into the bones of his neck as well as terrifying bleeding, and all this in the days before anything could be done about it. However, despite this slow, painful "crucifixion", the Master was never seen to be unhappy or cast down in any way. On the contrary, his face was always shining with happiness and he would make merry with his dejected followers, while looking out for their spiritual needs with a watchful eye and unbounded affection.

All of this rose up from within me as "Exhibit A", calling for my verdict—but no matter how powerful the experiences I had had might be, the force of my dogmatic Christian convictions, the pique from the behavior of the devotees—who seemed not much better than my father in some ways—and most likely a deep resistance to accepting Swami's authority, prevented me from accepting what Swami was saying. I might have been quiet outwardly, but inwardly I regarded this as merely round one in the struggle. There were certainly to be many more. For the following year, up through Easter of nineteen seventy-five, Swami and I were to skirmish on and off, sparring at his meal table and also particularly at the library class. Even the remotest echo of the Christian doctrine of suffering would set me off and would get Swami going with his strong assertions of human divinity and the impossibility of suffering for one who is truly spiritual. Things got so bad that the devotees would actually groan whenever anything came up in the reading about Christianity or anything remotely related to it. And Swami himself would leap at the slightest echo of Christianity in anything we read to get going with me again. It was obvious he wanted to thrash this whole thing out.

The men at the Center didn't seem to mind all this—they themselves had their intellectual run-ins with Swami—but the women disliked it intensely. Courtenaye, who was utterly devoted to Swami and believed everything he said at face value, would get very upset when he and I would argue in the library class and sometimes would go so far as to cry, "You can't talk to Swami like this! Do you know who he is?" But I was going to get to the bottom of this and nothing would stop me, I was such a bulldog.

The other side of this situation was my feelings of "lacking devotion". Although Swami was extremely intelligent and intellectual, as well as rational, he also emphasized devotion—devotion to the ideal, devotion to ideal characters such as Ramakrishna and Sarada Devi, and devotion to the work done in their name. He would praise anyone who showed devotion to work or a devotional attitude in general. This was something new for me. Although Christianity is primarily a religion of love and devotion, somehow no one ever talked about devotion or asked us to cultivate it. To have our performance commented on like this was unusual, and suggested a whole different approach than what I was used to. It seemed that the Vedantins made a more overt project out of spiritual life.

Be that as it may, the women in particular vied with each other to be "devotional", trying to be sweet, kind and actually devotional—a totally admirable effort, I must say; but, as I later realized, often motivated more by getting attention from Swami than by anything else. I definitely had my difficulties with it, though I never said anything. One day Swami invited me to come to his lunch on Sunday after the lecture. This was a little ritual he went through with the close ladies, making himself available to the women (most of whom had regular jobs) at a time when they could come and he himself was in a relaxed mood after giving his weekly Sunday lecture. And his meals were indeed a sight to behold. The

Genets had set him up at a table with damask linen, the best German bone china, and several layers of forks, spoons and other gewgaws, many from Hammacher Schlemmer, the expensive New York store—and, of course, a bouquet of fresh flowers, which Stanley or I would do up with whatever was left over from the altar work.

By decree of, I think, Rolande, who had set up the whole show at the Center in the nineteen fifties, Swami always ate alone, except when a distinguished guest came through. Rolande had always waited hand and foot on Swami, standing all the way through his meal and making attention to his every need the equivalent of High Mass or the mysteries in an Egyptian temple. Jeanne and Maman had continued this tradition, though it was the cook who now attended on him and sat through the proceedings. But Swami was not a recluse, really, nor an aristocrat. He loved people; and they would come to talk with him while he was eating. The Genets had decreed that Swami ate alone; but he attracted us and we would happily sit through his meal, chatting with him and getting all sorts of impromptu pearls of wisdom. And the Sunday "meeting" was, of course, the equivalent of what we called in Scotland "the gathering of the clans", for all of the close women workers would converge on the dining room after the Sunday lecture—Pat, who was, of course, the cook, Courtenaye, Susan (a professional musician whose work kept her away from the Center much of the time, but was extremely devoted to Swami), Janet and Sandy. Jeanne would be there at the beginning, but would always have to leave in order to attend on her mother. It was a select group, and I guess it was an honor to be invited. But my first attendance was enough—I simply could not stand the syrupy, tweetie-pie devotionalism, which for me was pure, unrelieved sentimentalism and even honest-to-goodness baloney.

I was a Scot. The Scots are famous for their understatement, their stoicism, their duodenal ulcers from repressed emotion—I guess what is meant by *dour* (pronounced to rhyme with *poor*, not *sour*). We had total disdain for the English with their "dahlings!", their hugs and kisses. "Sassenachs!" we would hiss, and that would say it all. I was simply revolted at what I saw as babying, toadying, putting on a show. How could they treat this intelligent, highly spiritual being like a mental retard at worst, or a child needing potty training at best? Then again, how could he put up with it? Was he, after all, a sucker for this sort of thing? I almost wanted to throw up—and needless to say, I did not come back for more. I was aware that Swami was watching me closely, but he said nothing—and neither did I.

I kept my counsel, as I had learned to do in the kitchen with the ladies. My brand of rather masculine, edgy, critical thinking was not appreciated by the ladies—they were altogether too refined, too "sattwic", too utterly, utterly . . . . And now, of course, it was not easy to talk with Swami, who previously had always been very appreciative of me and my trenchant way of thinking. For nearly a year I was shut up in a pressure cooker, in which I stewed mightily. I began to feel that perhaps I was just altogether too tough, too hardened by the world. I could not be "devotional'—and perhaps had no devotion. I didn't care about notions of "devotion", but *having* devotion did matter; I, too, had intense feelings toward the divine—was that not devotion? But wimp I could not. And would not. Come hell or high water.

Things continued to deteriorate with the Genets, no doubt fueled by my disquiet and soul-searching. In May Maman and I had a big row—about what I have no idea, but perhaps because of my taking initiatives in the garden—and Swami was rather annoyed at me. He reprimanded me privately, which of course did not help at all. As a sort of "consolation prize", however, he began to comment to myself and to others on "how concentrated MacPhail's mind is". In those days he always called me MacPhail, possibly a step up from "Miss MacPhail", which had been his form of address before I started working at the Center. I never did find out why he did this, though I figured it was related to the British custom of calling pupils by their last names at boarding school. But even in Britain, it usually applied only to boys, the "tough guys" (though we girls, perhaps in an attempt at "equality" used to address each other in this fashion). I got the dim impression that Swami was singling me out for this dubious distinction on account of my British background, my rather assertive manner (acquired, I may say, as a means of survival at boarding school) and also my ineradicably masculine cast of mind. Certainly, this way of addressing me rather blunted any gratification I might have gotten from his appreciation of my mental concentration—though certainly, in the situation I was in, any sort of appreciation was welcome.

As soon as Swami had left for California that summer, the Genets made it clear that I was not welcome at the Center. I was, therefore, left entirely to my own devices for the entire day, with no particular jobs or responsibilities. I did go down to the Center in the afternoons and do work with the men, usually John, who gave me work with the books in the library or tending the seventy plus houseplants he had gathered there. And, of course, I spent the morning reading and studying, as Swami had asked me to. But, even for someone as self-sufficient as I basically am, it was not possible to live totally like a hermit. I would talk at length with my roommate Jan, of whom I was very fond, though I did find she had somewhat similar tendencies to the ladies at the Center. "There has to be complete, unquestioning obedience to the guru!" she would tell me, to which I would respond, "What if he is asking you to do something unethical?" I started seeing Daya again, and going out with her as before, but not to the charismatics. Daya had lived in India and Japan for nearly two years, where she contrived to spend most of her time in meditation. She, too, was initiated by a Vedantic swami and I picked her brains on the subject of the relationship with the guru. Daya was entirely her own self, and I do not recall any response other than a smile, or at the most a twinkle and "You have to be yourself!"

I definitely needed more focused work, but that was not available until Swami returned from California in September. At that time the Genets simply had to let me in, partially because of the increased workload, which was too much for Jeanne alone; and partially because Swami would not permit them to keep me out. The basement was indeed the Genets' home, but it was also the place where the other workers and devotees had a chance to practice their spirituality—and for Swami that was a top priority. I would tiptoe in after lunch, seal myself into the scullery and clean every pot, pan, dish, spoon that had been used since daybreak—which was a lot, for Jeanne had no concept of economy or efficiency. Then I would move to the dining room to do some of the accounting work for Courtenaye or transcribe lectures; the flower room to resuscitate the vases on the altar; the garden to relax with my beloved plants; or go upstairs to work in the library on books or the ever-increasing house plants draped all round it. "John's jungle", I called it.

I began to blame Swami for my difficulties at the Center. I would rail at him mentally and even went so far as to write down a list of his faults, among which was his perceived standoffishness. At the same time I also began so see more and more clearly that my inveterate tendency to expect people to give me something was at the bottom of my problems. No one, not even a spiritual giant like Swami, could solve my problems and ultimately make me happy—I had to find the strength and resources for that within myself. I had to get over looking for someone to "save" me, and find my salvation, the love I sought, from within.

In this very introspective mood I also wrote down what I called the *Cyclical Function of the Mind*. My enforced solitude, the need to get to the bottom of my mental upheavals, and, no doubt, the direction my mind was turning to, finally began to come up with systematic ideas which pointed toward what was to come in my life. Briefly, I noted that the mind seemed to work in a fourfold pattern: First, a period of calm, purposeful openness in which whatever goal is being pursued is quite clear. In the second stage there is the beginning of struggle, in which the orderliness and clarity of the first stage starts to break down and there is excitement, flashes of inspiration and feelings of self-achievement. In the third stage, whatever is causing the difficulties in stage two comes into the foreground and conflict breaks out externally, along with negativity, heightened tendency to analyze, disillusionment, helplessness, despair and awareness of one's limitations. At the fourth stage, however, acceptance takes over and one is aware that one is adjusting, making more progress than was visible previously. The disciplines which were disrupted in stages two and three return, strengthened and deepened, creating a sense of greater self-reliance, while at the same time readying for the next cycle to start.

I arrived at all of this from looking at the patterns of my thirty-three years of life thus far, getting the information, not only from memory but also the fairly copious diaries I had kept for most of my life. And what was interesting is that I noticed this fourfold pattern in the way each day worked itself out, as well as each week, each month, each year. I noticed that the cycle seemed to begin in August of every year, when, at the end of summer, I was in a relaxed and fairly serene frame of mind. Around the beginning of November what I called "the Scorpio effect" begins to take over: flashes of insight and inspiration, along with which went my psychic experiences, discombobulated emotions and general destabilization. In February, self-analysis begins in earnest, with March bringing conflict, sparks of excitement, negativity and foreboding. April is always an intellectual month, while May is cheery, and the summer generally is a time of slowing down, of taking stock and of getting back in touch with the goals which direct one's life and which the efforts of the previous year were all about. By the time August comes round again, things have settled down and one is reorganized for another year of effort.

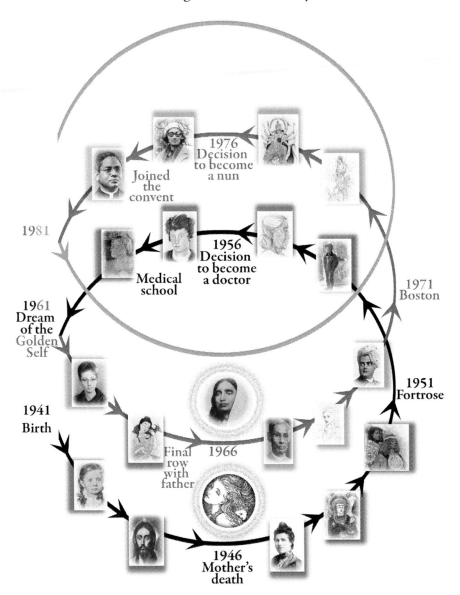

This is a pictorial representation in the form of two turns of a spiral of the events of my life recorded in this book, up to 1981. I also have added a third turn to indicate that the pattern continues on in time.

By that time I already had had enough experience to also notice that the same patterns seemed to apply to each group of four to five years. I documented the evidence I had for this conclusion and the facts certainly seemed persuasive. The first five years in a sort of calm with my mother seemed to correspond with the years after my twentieth birthday, when a relative calm and sense of purpose had supervened after getting established at medical school following the ugly showdown in Khartoum with my father. Then second, the terrible years of discombobulation after my mother's death fitted rather well with the anguish after the final row with my father. In both cases, despite the advent of my spiritual teachers—Grannie and now Swami—I had then "gone under" to something quite overwhelming, which I couldn't fully understand, and had been in an angry, rebellious mood. Perhaps because of their intervention both situations had ended in a deep spiritual encounter (my out-of-the-body experience at Fortrose and my experience of Mother Sarada in Boston) in which I had felt myself moved on in a radical way, leading me to a more focused inner state, but still beset by serious intellectual struggles; at Dollar on the subject of the choice between art and medicine and now—for I was certainly in the "third" part of the second cycle—between going back to my work as a medical doctor or (perhaps!) joining a convent. I was beginning to see in a dim way, in and through all the tussles with Swami and the devotees, that this was the choice I was beginning to formulate.

It seemed as if I there was a definite pattern to my life, working itself through all that I did and which I could see quite clearly on the micro-scale. On the bigger scale I had not put in enough time to be sure, but I certainly felt that it was likely that I was going through twenty-year cycles, in which the same fourfold pattern held good, with the psychic experiences I was prone to marking some of the major turning-points. Of course, only more experience could confirm this impression; but for the time being it seemed suggestive and certainly interesting. I had been attracted to the idea of levels of consciousness after reading about them in Swami Vivekananda's *Raja-Yoga*, and my ruminations in December of nineteen seventy-four concluded with the hypothesis that each cycle I had gone through might correspond to one of the classic levels of consciousness. It seemed that the first cycle had related to issues of physical survival and establishing patterns of organizing my life-processes in response to the quite desperate things that had impacted me. I hypothesized that all of that was tied in with the three lower chakras of the kundalini, which basically relate to issues of survival, reproduction and food, all of which had fallen into place in and through those four intense and very charged segments that characterized my first twenty years of life. If I was indeed now in a second cycle, it was most assuredly one of dealing with emotion, associated with the heart chakra, which was charging everything I thought, said, or did. I had been thrashing about since my twentieth birthday trying to find love, going into all sorts of nooks and crannies to do so, and learning, as I went along, that love does not grow on trees for the taking; it is something that comes only after long struggle and self-control. I was sufficiently aware to understand that Swami was, at long last, a worthy object of my love, but of course, I had to work hard to clarify the relationship and place it in a proper perspective; this "third" quadrant I was currently in was where I had to thrash through the intellectual questions and barriers that were currently in my way.

Finally, having arrived at the view of this possible structure to my life-experiences—I felt like a builder standing on a plank over half-built walls, looking at the mere foundations of a life—I had a further intuition: "If these cycles, seen so obviously in the material world, are correlated with levels of consciousness, there must be a fifth period corresponding to Enlightenment. One is not readily aware of this, but perhaps there is a period, infinitesimal at present, when the mind disappears into That; perhaps this is the time when the 'circuit' is completed." From the evidence I had then I was pretty clear that there were only four parts to each cycle and that, if there was a "fifth", it must be in and through all the others. In sum, I felt that I was looking at the first turn and a half of a spiral system that was unfolding in my life in twenty-year "turns", and that was sufficient evidence to suggest that I was moving upward in consciousness in a spiral fashion.

Seeing and documenting this was an important moment in my life. It was, of course, the outcome of the native tendency of my mind, which had been molded by a succession of psychic events as well as episodes in physical history, between which I could now see correspondences and in and through which an emerging overall pattern. My training in science had made it possible for me to make and record the observations with as much accuracy and immediacy as I could, while the intense psychic dynamo within me kept sending out "flares" or perhaps coded messages that had moved me on through the "system". But what had brought this new, much more organized insight was, of course, Vedanta, particularly the teachings of Swami Vivekananda, who combined within himself psychic experience of magisterial intensity with the discipline of a highly trained mind of genius level. He had brought to bear on his experiences the immemorial findings of the Indian sages, which supplied explanations and symbolic patterns that just seemed to fit perfectly with what I was going through. And, of course, it was all accessible to me because the swami had presented all of this in the easiest, most rational and scientifically acceptable way. The levels of consciousness of which he spoke were no longer merely fascinating ideas; I felt now that I was actually immersed in them, working through them along a highly coherent path that could be explained rationally and thus tie together the two major strands of my life, the scientific or rational and the intuitive or mystical. And, finally, though it was at that time not my major focus, my glimpse of the fifth dimension was of the utmost importance, investing the whole story with an ever-present dimension that only time would make clearer to me—and perhaps more immediate to me as experience.

And, coming back to that moment in time, it was all consistent with my intuition that "the third segment" within the second turn of the spiral in which I found myself is essentially about resolving crisis, of finding the answer in and through terrific outer battle and conflict. It was going through this segment at Dollar that had helped me to see what career choice I had to make, and no doubt was going to open up the way to me now. There was no doubt that the idea of joining a convent had been occurring to me, though not as an immediate option. As long as Swami was alive, I would stay with him, I was absolutely sure. Where would I find someone with the insight he had, the gift of seeing me as I am and appreciating what was best in me, as well as the meltingly sweet love that he showered on me? But Swami was old and not well and, of course, my money would not last forever. This was the categorical imperative looming over me and helping me to focus.

This moment of blessed clarity was of primary importance—but of course, there was the business of the world to attend to, and the immediate future had plenty in store. I was getting more and more frustrated with Swami, and my mind would start ranting on about him, that he was too old, perhaps senile; and, in the context of my conflict with him over Christianity, a bigot. Why couldn't he see where I was coming from? Why couldn't he see that there were other ways besides his own?

One evening in the library Swami got on to the Christian business—particularly the issue of sin, which he, like many Vedantins, thought was a negative and unhelpful concept. Vedanta offers instead the notion of ignorance, which leads us into all sorts of errors, which can and must be corrected, of course. Vivekananda had said that this was a much better idea than sin, because it puts the burden of responsibility on the perpetrator, rather than on an extraterrestrial God, or an object of vicarious atonement. As human beings, he said, we must take responsibility for our own lives and rectify the "mistakes" we have made through wrong information or just plain ignorance. That idea was fine with me—I much preferred it to the vicarious atonement theory of Christianity—why should the divine Jesus have to bear my burdens and suffer on my account? But I had my agenda with Swami, and my alarm system went on as he launched into his latest sally against Christianity.

As he went on and on I was fairly fuming, but said nothing. Finally he said that the whole emphasis on sin in Christianity was due to Saint Paul, that the idea is not emphasized by Saint John at all, that he was a "much more spiritual" person than Paul. In Christian circles I had heard the idea that Paul was responsible for cementing Christianity into its obsession with sin, but not that John was free of it, and did not have at that moment any evidence of my own to prove or disprove the theory. Even as the words came from Swami's lips, I made up my mind to look into the situation for myself and reach a final conclusion. I left the class in a black mood, with grim determination to clarify Swami's statement and, if possible, remove the "accusation" from one whom I revered, though did not know as well as I would have liked.

I would particularly fume and boil over all of this on my way down for the class in the evenings, working myself into a frenzy, which I steadfastly refused to express to anyone. One evening, the pressure in my head was overwhelming. I was striding down West End Avenue in what Mary used to call a stitherrum, completely oblivious of anything but my frustration and anger—and, for all I know, talking to out loud to myself like the poor, demented street people I was whizzing past. Suddenly I thought: "This is intolerable! I can't go on spending my energy like this! It has to come to an end!" The thought then occurred to me: Why don't you ask Mother Sarada about this? You have been going on and on for months and never once asked her about it. This insight immediately calmed me down. The Christians say, "Take it to the Lord in prayer", and there is a lot of truth to it. I felt a little sheepish, but I did say, "I am sorry I have not thought of speaking to you. You see the mess I am in. Can you help me?"

This was the moment when I learned beyond any doubt of the efficacy of prayer. Almost immediately I was aware of Ramakrishna's presence and distinctly heard his voice, very affectionate and endearing: "This—Swami—is how I am manifesting myself to you." I realized that Swami was the form through which I was to communicate with Ramakrishna, a live, breathing and loving form which responded to me—not always as I would like—but nevertheless a living God, not just something in a book or a received dogma. This revelation had the most amazing effect on me. I felt a huge mass of light all around me: West End Avenue was, as it were, illuminated. I was flying about three feet above the ground, carried forward by the energy of what I had just understood, and I wondered if the folks standing around could see me levitating. However, the light was so strong that I could see nothing distinctly. And by the time I got to the class I was back to normal and the evening passed uneventfully.

However, I still continued to pursue the issue of sin in the New Testament. I had gone through the texts counting the number of times *sin* was mentioned; and to my surprise, had found that Saint John scored way more times than Paul. Moreover, Paul's attitude to sin was much more pro-active, insisting that, though sin was a fact, it was possible and necessary to go beyond it, particularly relying on the strength of Jesus, the model and archetype for that age. That, at least, is how I interpreted my findings. Now saturated with my reading of Swami Vivekananda, I could see that Paul was, in many ways, very much like Vivekananda—strong, intellectual, fearlessly outspoken, and a powerful integrator of two quite different cultures. In Paul's case it had been Judaism and the Hellenic-Roman cultures and in Vivekananda's Vedanta and the scientific Western culture I myself had grown up in. I was thrilled by this discovery and was now able to think of myself and my name (*MacPhail*, in Gaelic meaning "daughter of Paul"), with a content and meaning that the phrase had not had previously. And, though I did not put it into so many words, I was beginning to see my own destiny as one of witnessing to truth in and through all manner of obstacles and attacks, just like my prophetic, Jewish "father" who, in turn, was pointing me (all unknowingly as yet) toward my Vedantic role model, Vivekananda.

CHAPTER 19

BURSTING THE ABSCESS: 1975

The various emotions bubbling in my cauldron resulted in ten days in bed with a dose of flu, at the end of which I was in a very defiant mood. I had proved to my own satisfaction that Swami was wrong about Saint Paul and I was ready to fight to the death. I finally showed up for the library class one evening, when the reading happened to be less about Vedantic principles and more about orthodox Hindu practices, which appealed to me a lot less. In the mood I was in, I was not about to mince words, and when my turn came to make a contribution I said, "I never heard such nonsense in my entire life! This was a huge waste of time!" There was a suppressed gasp around the room—no one ever spoke to Swami like this, at least not in the class. Swami, however, said nothing and simply passed on to the next person. He did look at me closely, however.

I believe John and Bill, who had had a number of arguments with Swami in the past, engaged me in discussion after Swami had left the library. All the sweet, dutiful women had gone downstairs, no doubt to tittle-tattle about me, but the men, I think, were trying to help me and to forge some solidarity. I was, therefore, the last to leave the library and start to come downstairs. At the top of the landing I could see Swami standing in his interview room, peeking through the cracked door. As soon as I arrived on the landing he came out vigorously and accosted me. "Come in and talk with me!" He said it animatedly, but not without affection and concern. I could easily have refused, but something about his demeanor made me go in anyway. He obviously was extremely concerned about me and wanted to know what was troubling me, but by that time I had gotten myself into such a state of fury with him that I would not say anything in response to his affectionate inquiries. I, however, told him that I did not feel free to say anything. He responded, "All right. Come to the evening classes—we shall communicate that way." Before I left he added, "Don't let what others say or do affect the way you see me."

This mollified me somewhat, but I still continued to rant on internally against him and to fill up my meditation time with intellectual lines of thought that did nothing to soothe me at all. I began to see that I was resisting, with all the power at my command, the authority that Swami so patently wielded. There may also have been deep resentment that, under his watch, so much rejection could take place—that is no doubt why he had told me not to let the behavior of the ladies in the basement affect me. By the beginning of February I was exhausted with all of this and finally went to see Swami. He made no attempt to find out specifically what was on my mind. Rather—and very typically, as I was to learn later—he asked me about my meditation. I told him that trying to meditate overheated my brain and he at once told me to study Vivekananda more. This was interesting, to my liking, and also made a deep impression on my mind that Vivekananda's teaching was the way to control and direct my formidable mental energies. This was something that was to prove true over and over and over again: There was the deepest connection between my spiritual well-being and the bracing, masculine, and strengthening message of Vedanta that Vivekananda had given the world.

I also asked Swami about the "obedience to the guru" business that had been exerting me so much. What it really was, of course, was a struggle between the attitude of the women who preferred to "swoon", to agree with all that Swami said, and to make endless rules and regulations to enforce what they perceived as Swami's "will", and my own, highly independent and self-reliant attitude, which preferred to get information from Swami himself and act upon that. As soon as I asked the question (without, of course, all of the explanation about the women), Swami smiled in recognition; I felt as if he had had some personal experience of this problem and that he was very empathetic to me. "It is very good to have a will of your own!" he said. "You are lucky to have such a strong will. Rely on it and do not let what others say and do affect you."

As time went by, I began to glimpse through the suffocating darkness that what was going on was a replay of my responses to my father. I had let his diatribes unnerve me, frighten me, cow me down and undermine my self-confidence. In many ways, the tremendous emotionalism I was prone to then was the outcome of that whole, unfortunate affair. My father had had dark, inchoate and highly emotional motives for his behavior, which I would never fathom—but destructive they were, beyond doubt. My mother and I could both bear witness to that! The question now was: Did Swami have similar motives? Was he as destructive, was he trying to drag me down and minimize me? No sooner had the question popped up than the overwhelming evidence began to pile up: Swami was the sole reason I had been able to pull myself up as far as I had come, I was improving day by day, thanks to him. He had given me a sweet, but very powerful love and several votes of confidence in my essential rightness, which were for me the pearl beyond price. So much in my past had contributed to a sense of worthlessness, to the extent of undermining me completely—and here was someone who, like Grannie, had the power to "put me together again", like some latter-day Humpty Dumpty. Where was I going to find such a spiritual powerhouse, so much faith in me, and so much love? I began to grin. I had to face that he was not as perfect as I naturally longed for; but he was head and shoulders above anyone else I knew; and, if I had any sense at all, I would accept him as he was and get on with developing my spiritual life. He was the best thing I had, and I was very lucky.

So was it. I returned to my routines at the Center and spoke with Swami occasionally. By way of explanation of my behavior, I tried to tell him about the bruising history with my father, but he showed no interest at all and rather turned the conversation to Rolande, Jeanne's legendary sister, whose whole life was one of dedication, self-forgetfulness and service, in which she showed a tremendous spirit of self-reliance and determination to get things done, even against great opposition. I realized that he was showing me a model of what he expected of me, and literally took note: I began to type up all of my conversations with him, now realizing how precious they were. He was definitely molding me and pointing me in the direction I was to go. But there was still unfinished business. Easter was upon us, and with it his Sunday sermon. Despite our battles during the year, he went right ahead and gave his denunciation of sin and the whole Christian thing of suffering. I was fuming unto total blackness. I saw Courtenaye, who was always looking out for me, glance at me from the other side of the aisle, and took it for a moment of empathy. After lunch I could not contain myself and began a diatribe about how I felt about Swami and his anti-Christianity. This was a first for me—I never said anything negative about Swami to Courtenaye, because of her child-like faith in him. But by now I had perhaps become more self-confident, or perhaps a bit more reckless. I saw her shocked face, but could not stop myself. As I ranted on, my inner Self rose up, as it so often did at moments of crisis, and spoke to me unequivocally. I saw, clearly and distinctly, first Swami standing before me smiling affectionately, and then my father, standing beside him. My father was sneering, showing his "fangs"—his prominent dog teeth, of which he was very proud—and slashing at me with cruel words, which I could not understand. As this was going on, my father moved in front of Swami and completely obscured him. It was like a big, black cloud covering the sun and obliterating its light.

I immediately understood what this meant. I stopped my diatribe and changed my tone completely. "Courtenaye", I said, "I have just understood what is going on. I keep superimposing my father's darkness and cruelty on to Swami and then beating up on Swami to punish him for it." Courtenaye was a mother, someone who had suffered a great deal, and a spiritual woman. She began to smile and put her arms round me. "Come on! Let's have tea and some of that wonderful Russian Easter cheesecake!"

This was a huge step forward. It had given me a direct line to understanding what was going on, finally breaking through the shield of anger I had been holding between myself and Swami. There had been several moments when I had understood dimly what was going on, but somehow I had not wanted to listen to reason and finally my inner voice had to project "a movie" to make me understand. This, if course, was the way my "system" seemed to work—and thank God it delivered at that moment, for otherwise I might really have upped and flown the coop.

And of course things changed externally, too. I finally was able to go to Swami's Sunday lunches with the ladies and sit through them without feeling too put out. Early on in this venture Swami put on one of his "demonstrations", which clarified things to my satisfaction. The ladies were ooohing and aahing over the lecture he had just given.

"Oh, Swaaaaaaami! It was soooo wooonderfuuuuul!" they were saying over and over, with their eyes shining. He was sitting there, smiling gently, perhaps with a sardonic touch. It seemed as if the ladies would never stop swooning and gushing, and I began to feel a little nauseous. Then he suddenly said, pointing to one of the most fulsome, "Can you tell me what I said in the lecture?" There was dead silence—what did he *say*? Actually? "But Swami, it was sooooooo wooonderfuuuuul!" was all that could be said. Swami, however, was in a certain mood. He went round the little circle, asking all of them to repeat anything he said in the lecture, drawing embarrassed smiles and blank stares. It was rather amusing, but I of course said nothing. These ladies spent the entire lecture scribbling down what he said, never so much as looking up to see him; whereas I, knowing that all that he was saying was in the books, or could be retrieved from the tape recording, felt my time better spent just trying to "be" in his presence, looking at his serene face, so focused on what he was saying and projecting the very essence of purity and concentration.

Having extracted not a bead from his little group of admirers, Swami suddenly turned to me. "What does *she* say?" he almost barked out. Somehow I had not expected to be included in this little melodrama, which I was thoroughly enjoying; but anyway I emerged from spectator mode in order to respond. And even I was rather surprised at my almost total recall. I was able to reproduce the gist of the lecture without any difficulty. The ladies all stared at me in silence, with their mouths open and blank incomprehension writ large on their faces, while Swami sat back, folded his arms and smiled an inscrutable smile like that on the face of the Cheshire cat.

In a way, this was a rather cruel little incident, but I realized that Swami had done it for a definite purpose—to help me see myself in a different light. I had been falling into a mood of self-abasement, feeling that I had no devotion, that these ladies were so much better than I, so full of love and devotion. Sometimes I would even cry at home because I felt so cold

Buddha: Painting by Nandalal Bose (1883-1966).

and unfeeling. But after the lunchtime episode I realized that without a word from me Swami had understood all this and was taking steps to show me that "devotion" can take more than one form. I had a formidable and highly trained mind, and to be able to get it behind what Swami was trying to convey to us was, in terms of my life, devotion and love.

This was one of many times that Swami managed to convey so much to me without being didactic. He had a genius for outflanking my emotional and intellectual tangles and moving me beyond them to much safer, sounder ground. And this was just the beginning. By the time he was through with me he had established me in a totally different way of evaluating myself and dealing with my problems. I was so impressed by this quality in him that I used to call him a Zen Swami, a term the others did not like, but I felt was quite appropriate. For me, he spoke in koans and his methods were nothing short of the bashing on the head the Zen masters used to bring their disciples to their senses—or perhaps more appropriately, to their spiritual selves. And in this latter quality I felt that he was the embodiment of Buddha, whom by this time I had come to know intimately and love intensely, no doubt inspired by my wonderful dream of over ten years before. Had Buddha not asked his disciples with his dying breath, "Be lamps unto yourselves"? Was this not what Swami, too, was requiring of me, kicking and screaming as I tried to be so?

Things were definitely looking up. I was back to my usual routines, my study was in place, and most important, I was in harmony with Swami again. But, as always, there is no rest for the wicked. Somehow, from January through April was excruciatingly hectic. My roommate was becoming more and more overwrought and talking my ear off compulsively, while several people showed up from my past, stirring up mixed emotions. And then an episode on the subway also added to my disquiet. My gadding about included trips to the Brooklyn Botanical Garden—still a place I loved to go—which of course involved long subway journeys. One day I was so busy reading that I did not notice that the carriage had completely emptied. I looked up to find a young black man standing over me with a penknife open and pointed at my throat. "Give me your money!" he said, in a rather shaky voice. I took stock of him. He was ridiculously young, skinny, and weak-looking; and I guessed he was just trying his luck. This was not a hardened criminal, but a kid, probably on his first attempt at a hold-up. "I have precisely three dollars and enough cents to get me back from Brooklyn", I said. "I can give you the three dollars, but I am telling you—is it worth it? Doing this sort of thing will get you into deep trouble. Do you really want to live that way? Get yourself a job and make something of your life." As I was saying this—him looking at me incredulously—the train was pulling into the station. There were cops standing on the platform. "Look!" I said, "There's the cops! I can call them right now. Do you want that? I'll let you go this time, but learn your lesson. Do you want to live this way?" He grinned and started to move toward the door. Then he stopped and looked back: "You wouldn't like to come with me?" "Get outta here!" I snapped. Saved by the subway stop! Not a pleasant experience, but somehow something that fitted in with the trend of my life, which seemed to be hurtling toward a very disagreeable destination.

I was pretty stressed by the time early April arrived, what with all of the drama that was building and exploding in my life. To add to the brew, Maman got sick again and had to be admitted to hospital. Whenever that happened I was drafted to live in the basement with Jeanne, who could not be left alone under any circumstances. But my mind was in an excited condition and I simply did not feel comfortable in the domain of the Genets. So, though I slept overnight and helped Jeanne with her morning chores and had lunch with her, in the afternoons I made a point of going back to my own room on West Eighty-Sixth street for a nap and a chance to be quiet.

I think it was about the second day of this rather hectic routine that I received a letter from my Aunt Malina. In it she informed me that my father had cancer of the tongue, which had been treated, but that there were now hard nodules in the neck. She said he was cheerful and optimistic; but as a medical doctor I knew the outlook was dismal and realized he was going to die. I was on the verge of a migraine when I read the letter and could not think straight at all. I lay down for a nap, but could not sleep in the slightest. My father about to die!! What should I do? The idea of his dying without my reconciling with him was very, very hard, but so was the vision of my going over there and the high likelihood of him savaging me again. I realized just how much remedial work Swami had done with me; although I was on an emotional roller-coaster of sorts, it was constructive, taking me somewhere I wanted to go, building up my self-confidence and giving me a sense of real purpose in life. I had the deep feeling that meeting with my father could be nothing but traumatic, unraveling all that Swami had done for me and taking me back to the state of jelly-like quivering my father had reduced me to.

What was I going to do? I could not at all see my way in this unexpected situation. I did feel, with somewhat of a wry smile, that it fitted in perfectly with all that had just been happening: My "exorcism" of my father at Easter, when I put him aside in favor of Swami, had perhaps drawn this response from him, a challenge to me to enter once more into his "lair". By this time I had had enough positive and encouraging experience to feel that I really did not want to try again with my father. Was it worth blasting away all the gains I had made, particularly with Swami? I was terribly torn, and incapable of seeing any light, a situation rather unlike me. And a decision had to be made quickly, if I were to be able to arrange a trip to England on time.

There was only one way to find an answer—Swami. It was a dark, thundery Saturday afternoon, a time when Swami was totally absorbed in preparing his meticulous, thoughtful Sunday sermon and was not to be disturbed. Very few people had his personal number, but I was one of the "elect". I hesitated for a few moments—I had never actually taken advantage of having the number to call him. But this was an emergency, the weight of which I knew would make it impossible to continue on with Jeanne in any sort of civilized way.

"I was wondering if I could come to see you, Swami."

"Is it something that can wait?" he asked sweetly. "I am working on tomorrow's sermon."

"My father is dying of cancer."

"Come at once!" he said in a strong, determined voice. When I had made clear the situation with my father's health, he began asking me about my past and my family, something he had never done before—in fact, he had actively discouraged such discussions. I was surprised that he asked me, not just about my immediate family, but all the way out through my aunts and uncles and cousins as well. Of course, they were significant, as they constituted, in many ways, "my parents" and "brothers and sisters"—but how did he know all of that? It took us over an hour to cover all of this ground, and I was beginning to worry about his sermon. But he was not about to rush or leave any stone unturned. He sat looking at me in silence, very indrawn and, I felt, deeply processing all I had told him.

"Swami, the question is—should I go over there to be with him when he dies? I am ready to do that, if you think it is the best thing to do." Swami continued to look at me in a meditative mood, going deep into himself to find an answer. Finally, it came; "No, don't go. It will not help him, it will not help you." Then he drew himself up strongly: "This is your home now, and these are your family!" My first reaction was intense relief. I really had no desire to go back to what, from one point of view was my father's bone-strewn and blood-soaked lair, and Swami's support for my feeling that I wanted to put the past behind me once and for all was very strengthening. I left, feeling much lighter and able to continue on with Jeanne without bursting a blood vessel. This was my family now, for better or for worse—and it gave me a wonderful sense of belonging, which, on account of my father's behavior, I had never been able to feel at Grant Street, the love of Grannie and Mary notwithstanding.

Despite all of this, however, I did feel for my father, facing death at the relatively young age of sixty-one, and the bleak fact that I had disappeared completely from his life. I couldn't help thinking that his cancer—on the tongue—was the outcome of his lifestyle: heavy drinking, which suppresses the immune system, and smoking a pipe, which is carcinogenic. As far as I knew no one else in the family had had cancer, and so it seemed that his was certainly brought on by his lifestyle decisions. I also could not avoid the thought that Ramakrishna, too, had had cancer of the same area; but his was of the vocal cords, brought on by speaking so incessantly to those who needed his help and blessings. What a difference! I thought. One was due to self-destructive behavior and the other due to self-forgetting and self-giving. This line of thought served to clarify where I stood and also, of course, to soothe my seriously ruffled emotions. The death of a father, especially with so much unfinished business, is not easy to face.

After this episode Swami changed his demeanor with me considerably. He stopped calling me *MacPhail* and began to call me *Jean*, a welcome change, for which of course he offered no explanation. But it was a clear indication that we had passed a milestone, and I felt much relieved to note it. He also started to tell me that I had the ability to make great progress spiritually, if I would turn my mind to God—which I took to mean that

I should be more focused on approaching my life as conscious spiritual practice. One day he surprised me by telling me, "You will have to face terrible trouble with your mind as you get close to realizing God." I was completely taken aback by his assumption that I would make so much spiritual progress. By that time I was avidly reading the spiritual classics, including Evelyn Underhill's *Mysticism*, and was becoming familiar with the patterns of spiritual development; I knew that many saints had had to go through desperate "dark nights", particularly before attaining illumination. But I had not had the slightest notion that I could possibly be anywhere near illumination and therefore have to think in terms of facing anything like what the saints had gone through. I was inclined to think that the difficulties I was facing right then were plenty for one life! But Swami's remarks did give me pause and filled me with a sense of awe and also a clearer awareness of my pride, which was scooping up all the mud it could from my subconscious and hurling it at him. In the light of his magisterial detachment from my nonsense, his capacity to penetrate through to what was true and real, and his unwavering focus on the progress of my self-transformation, I suddenly felt much humbler and more ready to submit to him.

One aspect of that project came up almost immediately. Swami began to show anxiety about my going home alone at night after the library class. I, of course, walked the two or so miles up West End Avenue, and gave no thought to it. But Swami was concerned about me and began to show it. "She is walking home alone!" he would say over and over at the end of the class. But I was adamant that I would not go on the bus or the subway. I felt much more secure on the open street, where I could make a getaway, if necessary. My recent experience on the subway had made me realize the dangers of being shut up in a closed carriage with minimal space for maneuver, and I much preferred the street. Tension was building—the women, in particular, were angry at me for not obeying Swami without question.

One evening one of our members, a lovely rabbi from Long Island, started coming to the library class with his wife. He was totally devoted to Swami and having just retired from his synagogue, was delighted to be free to attend Swami's class. When he heard Swami worrying over me, he at once volunteered to take me home in his car, much as I protested. I did not want to take him and his wife in the complete opposite direction from Long Island at ten o'clock at night! But I had to go—Rabbi was adamant, adamant, adamant. Though always utterly sweet and gracious. The next evening, to avoid the embarrassment of tying him up, I took the Broadway bus. Sure enough, a brawl broke out, with bottles flying and violence escalating. I was utterly terrified and got out several blocks before Eighty-Sixth Street. See! I knew I was right! After ten o'clock, New York is a jungle! I was much safer on West End, which is a nice, residential street!

I was in a pickle. Rabbi was not going to let me off his hook, and I was not prepared to get on the public transit hook, either. And Swami was not going to let up on me, while the ladies, like a Greek chorus, kept repeating over and over, "Do what Swami says! Do what Swami says!" Devotional people say that the Lord comes to the help of his or her devotees, especially if they are sincere, and I think that must have been the case with me. A few days after this crisis developed, Stanley informed me that a room was vacant in the rent-controlled house he lived in, only two doors away from the Center. It was, from almost every point of view, the perfect solution to my problem. It definitely seemed that a new chapter was opening in my life and it was time to move.

I moved to thirty-four West Seventy-First Street on June first, nineteen seventy-five. I realized that it meant I was "giving into" Swami and moving closer to him in every way, a situation I was both happy and a little anxious about. It was going to take time to trust him completely. As if to confirm the significance of what I had just done, I received a letter from Aunt Malina a few days later informing me of my father's death on the very day I had moved. This struck me hard. Now the file was closed; there was absolutely no possibility of ever resolving anything with him. Of course, I had consciously made the decision to stay aloof, but nevertheless I felt a lot of pain. From another side I understood that an era had definitively come to an end and that I was embarking on a whole new life, leaving behind the emotional darkness and defeat that always seemed to dog me under my father's influence.

Once again shut out from the Center after Swami left for California, I was at a loose end. That summer—and how long, hot, and sticky New York summers are!—I again went into a tailspin of pushing myself too hard with meditation, gadding about, yammering with the men at the Center, and, of course, coming down with the inevitable, blinding migraines. I realized just how much my decision not to go to my father was bothering me. To make things worse, Courtenaye, my usual confidante, had suddenly become indrawn and incommunicative. It was obvious that she had some terrible problem she was working with, but I was not party to it, nor could I have dreamt how serious it was.

I went to Marshfield in August, to find there Swami A., recently come from the center in Southern California, where he had been an assistant. He was apparently being considered as an assistant to Swami Sarvagatananda, and that was all I knew about him. I wondered why he had left Southern California. He was fairly young—just about ten years older than myself—energetic, even charismatic. Extremely devotional, he was also a good singer, and seemed to get along easily with people. This was such a contrast to Swami—who was so low key and controlled—that I was rather blown away. It was inevitable that I would be attracted to him, that I would look for the love and affection I so desperately needed after the crushing news of my father's death. But I was in for a rude, rude shock. He was cruel, verbally slashing me and endlessly putting me down, sneering and jibing at me. I found myself crying myself to sleep all over again.

My experience with the swamis up till then had been nothing but good. Swamis Pavitrananda and Sarvagatananda were always so sweet, so appreciative of anything I did, that this tongue-lashing for no obvious reason from this younger Indian man was impossible to take. I felt as if he were hitting me over the face with the cat o' nine tails, the fabled nine-tongued, knotted whip with which the Brits traditionally quelled any sort of insubordination. And it didn't matter what I said, trying to mollify him—he would lash out at me anyway. He seemed determined to "get" me, no matter what. This was the last thing I needed in my state of grief, and of course, it roused a lot of the old feeling I had had with my father's abusive behavior. And, underneath it, it also raised a great deal of anger and feelings of revolt. Why did I have to put up with this? Was this really a swami? Why did the devotees fawn over him as they did? What sort of organization would tolerate this kind of thing?

Swami Sarvagatananda was so busy with this guest swami and supervising some construction work going on at the retreat that he was not really available to talk with me. But one day he and I were alone for a few minutes. He asked me very kindly how I was. I said, quietly and deliberately, without any emotion: "My father died six weeks ago." He was thoroughly familiar with my difficulties with my father and was, therefore, in a position to understand what this news meant. He looked at me in silence, his eyes brimming with tears. I went on, "Why is this younger swami treating me the way he is? It is so like my father—it is very difficult to put up with, particularly now, when I have so much to cope with emotionally." He looked at me compassionately. "You must reach the place where you cannot be touched by such things," he said quietly. These few words, directing me back to my spiritual practice (the only real source of inner quiet), were very soothing, as was the deep empathy they conveyed. The next day, when the younger swami was really raking me over the coals in front of the large group of men who were doing the work at the retreat and had come for lunch, Swami Sarvagatananda suddenly said, with unexpected emphasis, "Be silent! Leave her alone!" I had never seen such a strong statement from a swami before and was deeply impressed by the energy behind what the older man had said. Swami A's eyes widened, and an expression of fear entered them. I realized that something highly complex and maybe unmentionable was going on, and was also deeply grateful for the support from the older, senior swami. With Indians the seniority thing is omnipotent, and Swami A. certainly toned down his attacks for the rest of my stay.

Back in New York and into the fall season, I began to argue with Swami again, perhaps as a reaction to my bad experience with Swami A. in Marshfield. Somehow I seemed to regard Swami as an all-purpose punch-bag, punishing him for the misdeeds of all others. Now I believe that this was part of the transference that was going on—my shifting my psychic load onto his shoulders and then working it out on him. I could not have chosen a better person to do this with, for Swami was extremely detached and remained completely unfazed by any of my manipulations. On the contrary, he would bring things right out into the open and tell me that I must stop putting the misdeeds of others on to him. "You must see me in your own way, and not let what others say or do affect our relationship." This was so very rational and much more promising than the nonsense I was trying to perpetrate, that I found it quite bracing and applied myself to thinking more constructively and seeing him through my own eyes, independent of Maman, Jeanne, Courtenaye, or Swami A. Or my father, the ghost always hovering over Swami's head.

I was terribly unsettled; and the news, breaking in October, that Swami A. would be staying at the Center for a month or so was most unwelcome, as was the notion that he might become Swami's assistant. Apparently the "deal" had not worked out in Boston. I felt sorry for the young swami—why was he being bounced from center to center like this? I had managed to find out that he had been kicked out of the center in Southern California, but not why. It was all very mysterious, and the mystery did not help me at all; if I had understood what was going on, I would have had a better chance of coping. As it was, his arrival, combined with the fact that Swami took sick and was not coming down to meals, was a dark day for me. Worse, Courtenaye was going through a terrible period (I had managed to find out that her ex-husband had just died in tragic circumstances), and was not going to cook for the young swami. The task was to fall to my lot. Under any other circumstances, or possibly with some other swami, this might have been a welcome assignment; but under the circumstances it was the curse of doom. I was being put in his power at a time when I had no resources to cope with it.

I decided to be quiet and submissive, as that is what he seemed to want and need. And it wasn't difficult, because the swami-swooners were there in force, talking, talking, talking. As usual, I found it sickening, but at least it protected me somewhat, for I did not have to speak. But he seemed determined to get at me, and would break off the swooners to torture me with his negative comments about my cooking or generally ripping me to shreds. I realized he was desperately unhappy and was most probably taking whatever his problem was out on me. This was not a role I needed just then, and I became very, very depressed.

Week after week dragged on. I thought of refusing to cook—but who else would do it? Courtenaye, who would never fail Swami, was failing me badly by refusing to cook. She had her sorrow—but so did I. Somehow I managed to soldier on, hating every moment of it. I began to feel the same helplessness as I had lived in for so long as a child, and coupled to it waves of self-reproach for the way I had behaved with my father. "If only I had not done that! Why did I do this?" would be my torture. I began to be wracked with guilt for not going to see him before he died. It was a really, really dark time—November in New York, and a re-descent into hell without Swami and all that he gave me. Occasionally, however, I would stop in the middle of my litany of guilt and one side of me would say, "Your father tried to get rid of you before he even knew you. Again, you were a kid of eight, of seventeen. How could you be expected to solve your father's problems? It didn't matter what you did—he always went at you." Or: "By the time he was finished, none of the family would allow him in their homes, he was so destructive and badly behaved. Why are you taking the full brunt of responsibility? They are good, responsible people—adults—and even they could not cope with him. Why put it all on yourself?" These were breaths of air, but only temporary in their effect.

One night I had an informative and important dream: I was the heroine in the myth of Bluebeard, the ogre who was noted for marrying women one after the other. He would take each new wife round his castle, showing her the keys to all the doors. There was one door at the bottom of a long flight of steps, deep in the basement of the castle, to which he would point and say: "This is the key to that door. But never, never, never go into it." Then he went off on business, and of course the young wife could not contain her curiosity. She would open the door and subsequently disappear. One particular wife, on opening the door, saw the bodies of all of his previous wives hanging from the ceiling with hooks through their necks, and was horrified to find that some blood had gotten on her clothes. She could not wash it out and realized that he would entrap her when he got back. More resourceful than her predecessors, she immediately summoned her brothers to protect her and managed to escape her doom.

That night, I was the young wife. I was standing on the stairs going down to the door, holding the key in my hand. I thought, "I know what is in there. I do not need to see it, nor am I going to put myself into the power of the ogre." I took the key and threw it out of a castle window as far as I could. I woke up feeling much better, even then understanding that this was my stand against male bullying and domineering. I was not going to play that game again; I was not going to let men drag me into darkness and despair. I was totally, totally through with all of that nonsense. Afterwards there were a few more weeks of disagreeable encounters with Swami A., but they bothered me a lot less. I was so glad to see him go, a few days before Thanksgiving. I felt sorry for the poor man, and at the same time glad I had learned such an important lesson from relating to him.

After he left, there were a few very dark days, still without seeing Swami. His absence from the scene had had a great deal to do with why things had been so difficult, and I really needed to see him, even for just one minute—or so it felt. One evening, as I worked away in the dark scullery, feeling exhausted and despairing, Jeanne came in and announced, "Swami is coming downstairs! He is feeling much better and wants to meet with everyone!" Somehow the whole group appeared, as if from nowhere—clearly, they, too, had been missing Swami very badly. I could hear them laughing and talking in the dining room. Then I could hear Swami's cane tapping on the stairs and the delighted cries of the group as he appeared at the doorway of the dining room.

I had so terribly wanted to see Swami over those desperate couple of months, but what was amazing was that, now he was actually there, I could hardly make myself go to the dining room. I delayed and delayed, struggling with my emotions. I remained, rooted to the spot. After a few minutes, Jeanne came in and told me that Swami was asking for me. Slowly I put down my work, dried my hands, took off my apron, and made my way to the dining room. I could hardly put one foot in front of the other, but I did make it to the dining room door and Swami's face lit up with a beatific smile. There is a line in English poetry, I think from Tennyson, about some heroic woman who finally breaks down under the pressure of long-suppressed emotion: "Like summer tempests came her tears." Well, that is what happened to me. I could not stop the tears from gushing down my face and, being aware that all of the others were staring at me, almost in disbelief, I turned and ran away without saying a word. What a débacle! Other people are happy and jolly, and I am crying!

What was important was that, before I turned and ran away, I saw Swami's face. He had immediately seen my anguish and become deeply concerned. His face was a study in compassion, concern and love. I saw him glancing quickly at the fruit plate on the table by the door and understood he wanted to give me something to make me feel better—but my tears had forced me away. That fruit plate was highly symbolic. It was huge, and Rabbi saw to it that it was always full with the best fruit money could buy—as often as not, Harry and David's, for which he always gave Swami a subscription. It was Swami's delight to give fruit to everyone who came through, and many times he had played a game with me over my selection. But this time I had run away, not waiting, even for one of Swami's wonderful fruits.

I went back to the sink in utter misery and despair. All the emotion suppressed since my father's death came welling up and overwhelming me. I felt like such a big drip, so unable to be happy with the group, so unable to get my act beyond this terrible struggle. Why couldn't I be like the others, simple-hearted, uncomplicated and straightforward? In this moment of black despair I suddenly saw Jeanne coming in and thought, "O, golly! Do I have to deal with her in this terrible situation?" Then I noticed that she was carrying in her hands, cradling it like a sacred object, a large, gorgeous, ripe persimmon. "Swami sent you this", she said, her eyes sparkling. This was the language she understood. "He picked this one out specially."

Persimmons are one of my top favorite things. How did he know? Perhaps from the previous two Novembers, of course. I accepted it gratefully, feeling immensely better. After Jeanne had left I felt as if something had given way inside me, like a huge dam bursting. Swami was still chatting and laughing with the group, while I was here, with all of the dammed-up distress gushing out, or as if an ugly, large abscess from deep within was bursting on the surface and draining all of the dead and dying trash from my past. I started to cry again, but this time from relief and gratitude. Swami had somehow known just how to do the one thing that would help me, in a domain completely removed from words. How very, very fortunate I was to be in the hands of such a guru!

This episode brought to an end the chapter of struggle with the archetype of my father and opened out a new chapter in my relationship with Swami. On the whole, it was much happier—or, if we had disagreements, they were friendly ones. I felt a lot more energy and clarity than I had had for quite some time, but nevertheless braced at Christmas time for a possible recurrence of my Christianity conflict. With my usual bluntness, I boycotted the Christmas program, fearing that Swami would again say something that would get me going again. But, as I sat in my room during the service, another wonderful thing happened. I actually saw Jesus and Ramakrishna looking at me and merging into each other, leaving the smiling and blissful form of Ramakrishna, whom I now understood in a mystical sense to be Jesus himself. This vision definitely calmed me down and made it possible to rise above not only my emotional tangles with Swami but also my lingering guilt over "abandoning" Jesus. I now felt perfectly comfortable with Ramakrishna whom, I understood, in no way excluded Jesus or indeed any other great spiritual figure. I was free to relate to and enjoy all of them. Perhaps my feelings were expressed in a sketch I made of Mary receiving the joyous baby Jesus from the hands of the Divine Mother herself, a happy synthesis of the best I had seen in Christianity and Vedanta.

But as the dark began to clear—even as early as November itself—I became aware of another, newer difficulty I was facing: What was I going to do with my life? In many ways, this had been the issue through this whole period, in the same way that making a decision about my career had dominated my life twenty years before. I was experiencing what spiritual life could mean and, despite the heavy "shadow work" I was going through, felt that it was what was most important to me. I wanted to clean up my act and live a life of self-reliance, poise and gracious response to the needs of others like Swami or Swami Sarvagatananda. Rightly or wrongly, I had assumed that in order to become spiritually developed, it would help me to live a monastic life like them. Swami would say that monasticism was the "full-time, Ph.D. of spiritual life"—and I was willing to believe him.

The two years I had now put in, living a life without romantic involvements with men and focusing fulltime on my meditation, study and work for the Center, had made me realize how meaningful and fulfilling such a lifestyle could be. What had impressed me particularly was how well I could focus on quite difficult ideas and lines of thought, such as I encountered in Indian philosophy and Vedanta—something that had not been possible previously. It took minimal effort to understand that this was because my energy was not being spent on emotional relationships with men, which of course, had never really been satisfactory, largely because I had not met anyone who really cared about Vedanta as I did. From the other side, what was interesting was that my intense relationship with Swami, though taking up almost my whole attention, did not seem to dissipate energy as romantic relationships did. Quite the contrary—it energized me and made me more focused on the principles I was working on understanding and trying to live.

One of the goals of Vedanta is to reach a state where one is so completely embedded in spiritual consciousness that "ordinary lifestyle" cannot touch you in the least. On the contrary, spirituality should be able to "digest" the "ordinary" and transmute it into the gold of the spirit. I could now see that this was a goal I cared about and wanted to aim for, and believed that the way to do so was to dedicate myself permanently to a celibate, monastic life. I had two wonderful exemplars before me, quite patently transforming all around them by their blazing—but

soothing—spirituality. And they were behind me, helping me to move forward in ways I could never have imagined. Even five years previously I could not have believed that my mind could be as clear of the toxins generated in my soul by my father—and here I was, exorcised and ready for a totally new life! It was all quite heady.

Such thoughts had been percolating underneath all of the excitement on the surface; but there was a problem. What was my responsibility to Mary? With what Uncle George had left her she had been able to get her own little home in Stamford, the quaint old town in Lincolnshire which was the nearest to the family home in Clipsham; and there she was, with her usual common sense and address, settling down to her new life. Her health was good and she was getting about quite nicely, but what would the future bring? For example, I knew that inflation was eating away at her resources, and I had always had the idea that I would take responsibility for her "golden years", but the question now was: How? Where did I fit in with her life in England, where she had been living now for about twenty years? Where would I get the money to support us? Was I going to have to go back to medicine, which I now felt was totally behind me? For Mary's sake, I was ready to go back to work at the little Stamford Hospital where I had done some work in my student days. I had found it boring and stuffy, but for her I would do anything. But now, aware of a totally different kind of life, of which she knew nothing and would almost certainly not understand, there was quite a bit of tension in my mind. Where did my duty lie?

With the huge storm over my father more or less over, the struggle over my responsibility to Mary now took center stage, and I realized that it had been drumming away in the background all along. I was going to have to face it, particularly as my savings were not going to last forever. Deciding to become a monastic was not going to be a simple matter, just as making the decision to be a doctor had not been easy. I could in no way get away from the idea that my primary responsibility was to her. She had been my mother, sacrificing for me her independence, comfort and career, and putting up with the most disagreeable situation at Grant Street for nearly a decade for my sake. No matter how idiotic I could be, she was always there for me, always welcoming, no questions asked. She had no inkling of what made me tick; in fact, I think she was a little afraid of the wild daemons that controlled my life. And she never asked. Possibly she did not want to hear. Maternal love is a strange and wondrous thing—it loves its object without any questions at all. Thank God for it.

Strangely, I had never told Mary how I felt about my commitment to her. I think it was just so obvious to me that I had not felt it necessary to express it. But, from her side, I had left home in a very decided frame of mind that I was going to be independent (though that was primarily aimed at my father), and had now been in the States for nearly eight years, though I had paid a visit back home in nineteen seventy-three. Almost certainly she had felt that I would get a career in the States and never return—and of course I had said nothing that would contradict such an impression. How could she possibly know how I was feeling—or that I was ready to give up everything I had done with my life to be with her?

However that might have been, one evening in November I received a long letter from her. I had just got in from the Center, a bit tired and vexed, perhaps. I decided to put on a kettle for tea, get settled in and really focus on what she had to tell me. I was utterly amazed to learn that Uncle George's family had created a trust fund to support Mary financially for the rest of her life. She would continue in her little house in Stamford, a central spot where the family could visit and keep in touch; and they would take care of all of her medical problems as they arose. I started to cry, I was so happy. Mary more than deserved every bit of it, she was so unselfish, so giving of herself. The family had recognized all this and, like the good souls they were, they were standing by her in her old age. I also felt that in many ways she would be more comfortable with them than with me. They were down-to-earth farmers and businessmen, straightforward, well-to-do Anglo-Saxons with none of the Celtic mists, selkies and banshees that haunted my life. Mary accepted me, loved me—but I was not really her type, and it was all to the good that she had found this wonderful family and been so completely accepted by them. Occasionally, the just really do get their reward.

After the first flush of emotion, I suddenly grasped the implications: I was off the hook! Mary did not need me economically at all. Indeed, compared to what the family could give her, anything I could do would have been a pittance. Very quietly a voice spoke to me: "If you want to join a convent, you are free to do so. Is that what you want? The way is open now."

FOURTH QUARTER

GROUND IT IS, AGAIN

CHAPTER 20

IN RECOVERY: 1976

By now I had learned that the fourth and last quarter of each turn of my life's spiral is one of settling down, getting myself behind whatever I had just discovered, and moving forward with it. Twenty years prior, it had been medicine. It was a struggle, but I got behind it—and, of course, ran into tremendous opposition and problems. This time the agenda was monastic life, which had emerged after the huge explosion of exorcising my father's influence on me. How it would work out I had, of course, no idea, though it was likely that it would be no bed of roses, as had been true of medicine. But, as a complete beginner, I did take it up with great thoroughness, studying the scriptures of not only Vedanta but also of other religions to understand its ground rules.

The main source of my information was, of course, the conduct of the two wonderful swamis who were molding my life at that time. For me, they were like my grandmother—loving, understanding, and intensely inspiring, encouraging me to think of myself in much greater and more spiritual terms that I possibly could on my own. And then, of course, there was the Ramakrishna literature, in which most of the main players were celibate monastics. Ramakrishna was celibate, initiated into one of the venerable monastic lineages of India; but was nevertheless married to a woman like himself, a powerful spiritual dynamo, for whom the life of the spirit was all that existed. They lived in the same temple grounds in Kolkata, seeing each other every day, for she cooked for him; but following, in actuality, the millennial lifestyle of brahmacharya, which means, literally, *moving in Brahman*. Brahman in Vedanta is the Absolute, impersonal Reality that lies behind everything and we interpret according to the way our minds are working. At best, most of us see Brahman as God, who is almost by definition somehow other than us and all we see; but some see Brahman as a living reality in and through all other experiences, without any specific form or name, but perfectly distinct and real.

Ramakrishna was such a person—and so was Sarada Devi, his much-younger wife and disciple. The two of them lived, moved and had their being in Brahman, which they experienced, not as some dry, burdensome dogma, but as a vibrant, living reality that filled them with unending and unquenchable serenity, compassion and bliss. When you read their lives, you can scarcely believe their sweetness, forbearance, humor and kindness—not just to this person or that, but to *all*, including those whom society rejected completely—Muslim bandits, prostitutes, and so on. These qualities, of course, are found in all of the really great spiritual leaders of the religions of the world. What was so riveting was that this all took place less than two hundred years ago, and was recorded by people who had been educated in Western science and reason, leaders of society and molders of thought, who had the ability to see and comment on things most of us want to know about.

Naturally, they had no biological children. But they did have spiritual sons and daughters, among whom was Swami Vivekananda, who had already captured my imagination. He was one of about twelve monastic disciples of Ramakrishna, most British-educated, who after the death of Ramakrishna had formed an organization to spread his teachings and serve Brahman, the living God, in all. Vivekananda, like other Vedantists, believed that a monastic order was necessary to preserve the tradition and transmit it to the world; and of course he called the order he founded *The Ramakrishna Order*. Ramakrishna himself was not an organizer—he was what inspires others to such activity. But he had given his "boys" the ochre-colored monastic cloth before he died, indicating that he would like them to become monks and form an order. Vivekananda succeeded in doing so in eighteen ninety-eight, creating a branch that was mainly for training monastics and another to work for the well-being of humankind. The training of monastics was to establish them, like Ramakrishna and Sarada Devi, in the same *moving in Brahman*, the direct vision of divinity, within themselves and in all other beings; and the work for others in which they participated and indeed took a leadership role, was the way that vision was meant to express itself.

One strand of Indian tradition has believed that in order to attain to such spiritual heights it is necessary to live a celibate life, and certainly that is the belief of the Ramakrishna Order. The earlier Vedantic literature, however, is full of highly developed spiritual people who were married and had children—the original rishis, or seers of the Vedic age (perhaps some three to four thousand years ago); Krishna, the great avatar of maybe one thousand BCE; Rama, the mythical king worshiped from one end of India to the other, and so on. Historically, Buddha was the first great spiritual leader of India who gave up family life to seek enlightenment, an example followed by Chaitanya, the great medieval saint. In the Abrahamic tradition, Jesus was a lifetime celibate, as far as is known, setting the tone in Christianity for a powerful monastic tradition. But as the spiritual leaders of the Jews and also Muhammad of Arabia were married men, their traditions do not support much in the way of monasticism, but have nevertheless produced some very great saints. I could not help thinking about my grandmother, Mary Anne, mother of six, who had laid the whole foundation of my own spiritual life.

I surveyed all of this and was unable to reach any decisions one way or the other. All I knew was that many of the really great spiritual leaders of the world had been celibates, particularly in the previous thousand years, and that this was what was before me at that moment in time. Of course, I had already found out how a life free from the distractions of dating was so much more calm, rational and purposeful, and how my mind could grapple with and digest ideas that otherwise would have been beyond my ken. With the kind of mind I have, that was important and played a big part in my moving toward the lifestyle permanently.

I therefore worked toward setting up my life in a more consciously monastic way, with regular periods of meditation and study, more controlled diet and sleep and—always difficult!—more control over speaking. As my mind settled down I began to make some important observations about my migraines, which were still very much with me. I still kept a record of them, as it had already proven so useful in bringing the attacks somewhat under control. I had given up coffee, tea, alcohol, late nights, various forms of gadding about, and things like that; but what I began to see in this new phase of my life was that, underneath all of the physical factors on the surface, the state of my mind was highly significant in triggering attacks. I particularly noticed that resentment was a very potent factor—and heaven knows, I had plenty of that! The behavior of the ladies at the Center was not easy to digest.

There was no doubt that my big explosion over my father had flushed a huge amount of negative feeling and resentment out of my soul. No matter what my father had done to me, I always tried not to hate him, for, although I could not really understand what was wrong with him, I always intuited that he was suffering terribly and in many ways could not help his behavior. And again, I knew full well that hatred is corroding and did not want to disfigure myself by giving in to it. But all that apart, I was beginning to understand that, when someone is preventing you from doing what is absolutely necessary for your growth and development, or forcing you to do something that is against it, frustration develops—and, if you can't work out a way to get what you want, anger and resentment starts to build up. As an adult, and through the grace of God and my family, I had been able to go my way independently of him, but there had been a reservoir of old, unresolved frustration and anger that had built up when I was a child and I could neither understand what was happening nor solve the problem. That was what had caused the huge abscess that had just burst; but now the question was: how to prevent such destructive emotions from ever building up again?

In my new, much calmer state of mind I could clearly see that permitting resentment to enter my mind was a potent trigger for my migraines. The notebook showed it and, because of my more controlled lifestyle, I was able to see it much more clearly. But then again, there was a lot of frustration with the little ladies, good as they were, and living in a tiny bubble, as far as I was concerned. How was I going to prevent myself from falling into bad habits of ill-feeling and long-term, corroding resentment? I tried telling Swami about my frustrations with Maman in particular, but he gave me a "glare" and said, with verve, "What will you be like when you are her age!" I realized at once that he was telling me: If you don't work on yourself now you will be like her when you are old, making life difficult for everyone. That was his way—putting the whole responsibility on me. And I liked and much preferred it to "empathy", which would actually have weakened me.

I understood that I was seriously starved for companionship, for it was not really possible with the ladies, and now I saw Daya and a few others only occasionally, as my duties at the Center were taking up more and more of my time. It was more or less inevitable that I would hang out with the Vedanta men, particularly Stanley, who now lived in the apartment below me. We were, quite simply, best friends.

He was, however, somewhat of a happy camper. He had found my terrible dark night over Swami A., my fight with Swami, and the hurricane over my father, incomprehensible and rather annoying. I could understand why he felt that way, but also grieved that he was unable to help me as much as I would have liked. I realized that I had too many expectations of him and therefore was setting myself up for disappointment, frustration and resentment over the long haul—though now I find it impossible to imagine being resentful of such a sunny, openhearted person. As I began to become more indrawn and calm, more conscious of living a monastic type of life, I realized I was depending on him too much and also that he was getting too attached to me. He would get angry with me for no apparent reason, which made me understand that he was attached to me and had unrealistic expectations of me. I began to understand what is meant by renunciation in monastic life. If you are going to retain your balance of mind, you cannot allow yourself to get involved in situations where there are unrealistic expectations on either side. Somehow you have to work to defuse such expectations, or adjust them to something more realistic. Mostly you can expect results only from yourself—you have to be the one that does the adjusting.

It was dawning on me that, if I wasn't careful, Stanley and I would be in a big emotional mess. I could see that I was going to have to draw back from him, because it was not going to be possible to explain anything and not hurt him. This was, in fact, my first conscious effort at "renunciation", giving up something that meant a lot to me in order to prevent anything toxic from developing. I discussed it with Swami at the beginning of February and he agreed that I would be best to cool it with Stanley. He asked me why I couldn't find companionship with the ladies, and did not seem at all surprised when I told him quite frankly that I lived in a totally different world from theirs. I went ahead and told Stanley that our Saturday jaunts would have to come to an end. He took it very well, most likely because he had also been realizing what was happening, but was perhaps less articulate about it than I. Though unsophisticated and simple-hearted he was, like all of the others at the Center, sensitive to issues pertaining to spiritual life, and, in fact, a man of considerable renunciation.

The immediate result was quite gratifying. My sleep, migraines, etc, definitely improved and, in addition, I took up a systematic, chronological study of Swami Vivekananda's letters, which were all higgledy-piggledy in his *Complete Works*, a project which involved quite a bit of original research and therefore gave quite a bit of depth and interest to my day. The project also took me more and more deeply into Swami Vivekananda's inner motivations and feelings, an enjoyable experience. I was discovering the humanity behind his magisterial greatness on the one hand, and the deep spirituality which I had experienced in his poetry. The tremendous drive I felt behind this work made me dimly aware that my energies had been released from the emotional level and were now moving more to the intellectual, a change that well suited me. My mind always needed "food", and research seemed to be its favorite, particularly on a subject that meant so much to me. This is the sublimation that is so central to any self-control. When you lose one thing you have to take the need to deeper level, where you find the gratification, but in another, more subtle way.

However, at the same time I did miss Stanley terribly and felt quite at a loss on Saturdays. I really needed companionship and, although I was finding deeper forms of gratification, there was nothing to immediately fill in the huge gap he left. It was really quite amazing how strongly this affected me: I felt a sort of vacuum round me, an eerie silence, a lack of warmth that was really quite numbing. As it got worse and worse, I finally told Swami about it. He looked at me intently for a few minutes and then said, "You can come to my lunches any time you like. We will talk there." This was an unexpected boon—to have access to Swami every day, without the gaggle of swooning women! But there was one problem. Lunchtime was Courtenaye's special opportunity to be alone with Swami, which as often as not was taken up with society business. I felt a little inhibited to crash this particular "party". But Swami said, "No, there is not so much business. If there is anything especially important, I will discuss it with her after my lunch."

I really could not believe this stroke of luck—or maybe, it was some sort of response to my effort to "renounce". At the same time, I felt reticent to encroach on Courtenaye's "turf": Swami was the world to her. Would she tolerate the kind of banter and argument that he and I engaged in? I decided to hedge my bets and come just occasionally, at least to begin with. Getting ready to go to the Center the first day of this new regimen, I could barely move my limbs, they felt so heavy and reluctant. I kept reminding myself that she would accept the arrangement because Swami had made it. That would be the saving grace. Of course, I had told her about it and she had taken it well; but words are one thing and actual fact is another.

Swami, of course, was delighted to see me and made me most welcome. I sat down, looking at Courtenaye from the corner of my eyes to see how she was reacting. All seemed well, at least for now. Then, before anything else could happen, Swami started to behave in the most unexpected way. He got a little excited and said, "As my medical advisor, I want you to look at my feet!" I was taken aback. We had gone through this a few times already during our private interviews: he would ask me to look at his feet and occasionally his chest, where he maintained there was some problem. However, I could never find anything significant, and any time I suggested treatment, he would simply smile, shake his head, and say nothing. After the second time I realized that this was some ploy of his, perhaps to bridge the huge gulf I was feeling between us at the time.

However, in front of Courtenaye was quite another matter. What would she think? I had suffered from the jealousy of so many women in my life that I dreaded any sort of display of my knowledge or skills in public. However, like it or not, Swami was busy taking off his shoe and sock and was determined that I make an "examination". Again, I could hardly make myself move, glancing nervously at Courtenaye. But Swami was taking no nay. "Here! Here!" he said, pointing to the usual spot. I looked at his foot closely, but without touching it. "Look at it properly!" he said peremptorily. I was forced to take his foot in my hands and go through the ritual of examining it. "Swami", I said, "as usual, I really can't find anything wrong." "Then look at the other foot!" he exclaimed. To my horror, he started taking off the other shoe and sock and actually put his foot on the table. I was utterly dumbstruck. Swami was the essence of control and manners, and to have him put his foot on the table! What would Jeanne think if she came in and saw his foot on her precious damask table cloth? That would be me out the door—and permanently!

I took a nervous side-glance at Courtenaye, but she was utterly impassive. I thought, "The sooner we get this over with, the better", and surrendered to the situation. I did a thorough examination and told Swami what I always told him, "I can't find anything significantly wrong." He seemed quite satisfied and without another word put his socks and shoes on again, with some help from me. Then he resumed his lunch and the conversation as if absolutely nothing had happened. I said not a word more.

Coming downtown to be present at Swami's lunch meant that I would be eating with the ladies and that was something I was not looking forward to particularly. However, to my surprise, it went off quite pleasantly. Perhaps my "promotion" from Swami had given me a better portfolio. But what was really significant was what Courtenaye said when the Genets had moved on to their post-lunch tête à tête, and she and I were savoring our after-lunch tea. "Once I touched Swami's hand by mistake, when we were going over some papers." Her voice was loaded with emotion; it was clear that Swami's pantomime had had a huge impact on her. I looked at her in total silence: With all of her dedicated work and unwavering feeling, she had never actually touched him—and here was I, a little pip-squeak, brash as all get out, and under a big cloud with the women on account of my "non-spiritualness", actually holding Swami's bare feet in my hands. In the Indian tradition, of course, there is a big thing about the guru's feet, which are considered sacred and the idea is to touch them reverently. Such a thing had never crossed my mind, I must say. For me it was a job and that was it. I was a medical doctor, beginning to realize that I was going through some kind of initiation, odd and at the same time encouraging. I thought I would say something to make Courtenaye feel better: "I am a medical doctor. That is why Swami asks me to look at his feet." She looked at me in silence, her large dark eyes filled with tears, but speaking volumes. I suddenly decided to shut up.

After this episode I was suddenly accepted in the ladies' circle once again. Whatever the alchemy, it worked. To this day I have no way of understanding it, but there are of course illustrations in the *Gospel*, where Ramakrishna would sometimes sit in the lap of one of his young disciples or put his foot on his lap as he sat cross-legged on the floor. As often as not, it was Swami Vivekananda on whom he bestowed this peculiar mark of recognition, for which no explanation was ever given. After what I experienced I am inclined to think that this was one way of demonstrating the particular "place" the recipient had in relationship to the guru; certainly Ramakrishna went to great lengths in many different ways to make it clear that Vivekananda was to be his successor and leader of the group. In my case, of course, there is no such implication, but nevertheless there is no doubt that it made a big difference to the ladies; and Courtenaye in particular took it very seriously and well. Her devotion to Swami was such that she took this strange episode as a mark of my closeness to him and thereafter she and I became like mother and daughter.

From the other side, these pantomimes put on by Swami were in some sense tailored precisely to my own personality. I never saw him or heard of him going through anything like it with anyone else, and I have come to the conclusion that somehow it was necessary for me to understand what my relationship with him was. The primary hypothesis is that he was simply bypassing my rational mind and connecting with me physically because of my formidable intellectuality. Perhaps, too, Ramakrishna had been constrained to do similar things with Vivekananda—certainly he touched him on the chest and sent him off into an unexpected and even unwanted trance at an early meeting, when Vivekananda was unwilling to believe what the Master was telling him. Who knows what the arsenals of these spiritual masters really are?

Yet another standpoint on this issue is the fact that Swami was a monk, strictly forbidden to have any physical contact with a woman. If he had been an "ordinary" man, he could have embraced me, and that would certainly have helped. But that was not possible. But the fact that I was a medical doctor in a sense put me in a different category, and hence this "medical advisor" business, through which I got a number of rather unusual opportunities. For myself, I always found these episodes a bit bemusing, but realized I had to go along with them for some inscrutable reason; and on the one or two instances when Swami "went public" with them I was terribly uncomfortable. I knew all too well the human capacity for jealousy and misunderstanding! But, of course, the close sisters and brothers were not of that stamp, and jealousy was one of the things that were mercifully absent in New York. And, if the truth be known, Swami did somehow convey to me an incredible sense of my own intrinsic worth, which had definitely been overshadowed by my early experiences and would be desperately needed—to a degree even I could not imagine—in the next (third) turn of the spiral I was shortly going to go through. It is true that he also was supportive and appreciative of me verbally, now that we were essentially over our Christianity struggle, but I rather think now that the "laying on of hands"—even if it was my hands that did the laying on—had something primal to do with the incredible strength and self-reliance I was to be able to summon in the descent into hell I was about to undergo a few years later.

For the meantime there was a little lull in the excitement. I had written to my father's sister Malina, asking her about our family's time in India, which she, as the oldest, would remember best. She sent me a photo of my grandparents in India in nineteen six, with Grannie's brother Willie, and Malina and Mary as little girls. My grandparents were in East Bengal for two years, probably between nineteen five and nineteen seven. I do not, however, know exactly when they went there. I recalled what Malina had told me about her Uncle Willie, Grannie's brother, who was apparently as spiritual as she. A sailor in the Merchant Marine, he traveled all over the world, but had a preference for India, where he would take off for the Himalayas, dress in a loincloth and turban and meditate with the yogis! When he came down to the plains he would of course visit Grannie and would take her to see any and all holy men who were in the vicinity.

I was fascinated; our family's connection with India was much deeper than I had realized. No matter that Lord MacAulay had been responsible for the Indian Education Bill, no matter than Grandpa was with the British Army (though as a non-combatant quartermaster)—there was a family connection with India going back several generations. And that Uncle Willie had taken Grannie to see Indian holy men! I remembered the book I had seen in Grannie's room after she died, with a swami looking out to the rising sun: *Swami—, Awakener of Modern India*. I was now sure that it had been Vivekananda, for he was indeed the awakener of modern India, and there was in fact a booklet of that name about him. So, she had known about him! And, with her brother taking her to see Indian holy men, it was entirely possible that she had met some of Ramakrishna's disciples! A woman of her spiritual stature would have been able to appreciate them, I felt sure; and maybe some of the stardust had rubbed off on me when I was living with her. I felt very excited and simply believed that it had happened.

I settled into my new routines quite quickly. The visits with Swami once or twice a week, along with eating at the Center helped me a lot, though I still felt periods of great loneliness. When I would mention this to Swami he would always emphasize how much good studying Vivekananda's works would do me, and I would redouble my efforts in that line. I found in Vivekananda so many answers to questions that no other reading had addressed, solutions to riddles that reading Plato, Descartes, Spinoza, Kant, and other Western stalwarts had merely intensified. Vivekananda was in fact coming from a standpoint that finally made sense of them. And he was not simplistic. A person who had been offered the chair of Oriental Philosophy at Harvard University was not one who simplified or boiled things down, although his English was remarkably direct and easy. Studying his works held my attention and gave me more and more understanding of what Vedanta could be and how it held so much together. Swami was quite right that this was the answer to my restlessness and spiritual discontent. My meditation, thus far a rather sorry excuse for the word, began to deepen and I could sit for much longer than the puny five minutes Swami had suggested at the beginning. I could now see that the issue was to tame and subdue my intellect, which was like a powerful racehorse, chomping on the bit and stamping on the ground, burning to prove its mettle. If there was anyone who could do that, it was Vivekananda—and I made the most of it.

In May of nineteen seventy-six, I finally got to cook for Swami and sit alone with him at lunchtime. Susan, a professional cellist, usually

Durga Mahishasura Mardini: A copy in gouache on paper
from an original, commissioned by one of Ramakrishna's
followers in the late nineteenth century.

cooked Swami's Monday lunches, but was away on tour so much that it was decided that I would do the cooking whenever she was away. Almost at once Swami and I settled in to a series of discussions that were to prove momentous later in my life. For one thing, he told me a great deal about his own life and experiences in the Ramakrishna Order, thus providing me with material for a biography which I undertook nearly twenty-five years later. And I shared with him some of my artwork, including a copy of an original painting of the Goddess Durga, whose energy protects the righteous from the demons of anger, lust, and the whole host of uncontrolled passions represented by the Great Demon of Pride (Mahishasura), who in the myth took the form of a giant buffalo.

Another subject he opened up at that time, much to my bemusement, was that of the convents which were being run by the order. I had studiously refrained from saying anything about my own aspirations in that line, partially because of my own doubts about it and partially because Pat, my spiritual sister, told me many times that Swami seemed unenthusiastic about any of us becoming nuns or monks. She, particularly, had had a hard time with him; he would not give his unqualified permission for her to become a nun and she was living in a sort of ongoing limbo, yearning to become a nun, and he simply not letting her.

This problem arose for one basic reason: the order had, after a long struggle with the two powerful swamis involved, permitted two convents to be started in California, but with the stipulation that no more would be started under any conditions. For the swamis at headquarters in Kolkata, the Ramakrishna Order was a man's order, not a woman's. For Indian women, Swami Vivekananda's dream of a separate, independent women's order had finally come to fruition in the nineteen forties and fifties; but in the order's mind, it was too early, either for the Western women to manage their own affairs or the Indian nuns to come to the West, and, under any conditions, not at all a good idea for swamis to be supervising convents.

But in many ways it had been Western women, their work, money and devotion, which had made it possible for the order to make as much headway as it had, and the two swamis in California were determined to create a sort of monastic "normal school" for Western women, to get something at least off the ground before too much more time went by. These were men with (by the order's standards) big followings, quite a bit of money and huge influence; and after a long struggle, the order relented and the swamis in Northern and Southern California were permitted to admit women as monastic aspirants.

Soon about twenty to thirty women were in the two convents and things looked hopeful, as the two swamis trained their disciples up in traditional Indian ways, while guiding their spiritual lives one-on-one. It was a good arrangement for women who were disciples of these swamis, or for women who blew in from the outside and were able to adjust to the swamis. But it was more difficult for women, like Pat and myself, who had worked with and been trained by another swami and wanted to become nuns. We would have to go to either Northern or Southern California and adjust to quite different conditions there.

There was also the problem of the rule about the upper age limit for joining. The swamis infinitely preferred younger women, whom they thought were "purer"—"untouched by the world"—and no doubt, more malleable psychologically. At that time the upper limit was thirty-five years, which Pat had already passed, and worried that she would never be accepted. At a mere thirty-four I had a little more time to think about the situation, but certainly time was moving forward. As was my way, I held my tongue about my thoughts and listened silently as the other women chittered about Pat and her "ego", which they interpreted her pleadings with Swami to indicate.

The other big factor in this situation was that Swami adamantly refused to start even a monastery for men at the Center, though he was within his rights to do so. The order was willing to accept Western men, and indeed there were already a number of quite distinguished American swamis: Swami Chidrupananda (Alfred Clifton) in San Francisco, Swamis Krishnananda (George Fitts) and Vidyatmananda (John Yale) from Southern California, as well as Swami Atmaghanananda (John Moffit), in New York, who had collaborated with Swami Nikhilananda on the *Gospel of Ramakrishna*. Many of our men had pleaded with Swami Pavitrananda to start a monastery in New York, but he simply refused, without giving any explanation, though I found out much later from Swami Sarvagatananda that Swami had felt that most Westerners were just not ready for monastic life. Swami was extremely rigorous about everything and was a hard nut to crack on this issue. Almost all the men who asked him to permit them to become monks got the reply, "If you think you are fit to be a monk, then go ahead!" One or two got more encouragement and went to India to face the situation there—and ended in failure. It was too hard for them.

The net result of all this was that the group in New York was not supportive of monasticism, particularly the women, who were reacting, as women almost always do, not so much to the principle as to the specific case before them. I had therefore been keeping my mouth shut and the last thing I expected was to hear about monasticism from Swami. However, raise the subject he did, and he came back to it again and again. He told me that when the subject of opening convents in the West came up at Indian headquarters in the nineteen forties, he was the Assistant General Secretary and therefore in a position of considerable power and influence. An avid follower of Vivekananda, he felt that the great leader's words: "Our right of interference [with women] is limited entirely to giving education. Women must be put in a position to solve their own problems in their own way. No one can or ought to do this for them,"[15] should be the guiding rule, and that having men running convents was not at all desirable. He would say, quite vehemently, "Western women can do this themselves! They *must* do it themselves!" After the surprise of the first few sessions like this, I pointed out to Swami that it would be incredibly difficult for Western women to get behind Vedanta, far less monasticism, which for most of us was extremely exotic. He seemed to nod his head slightly, but then again he reiterated, "It is much better that they do it themselves! They must create it themselves!"

Around this time I had made a new friend, Betty, a long-time member of the Ramakrishna-Vivekananda Center on East Ninety-Fourth Street. She had written a Masters' thesis on Sarada Math, the women's order started in India only about twenty years before. She had visited there, knew the nuns, and was very enthusiastic about this important new development in the work for women. Therefore, when Swami got vehement about the American convents, I finally asked him, rather tentatively, "What about the Indian nuns from Sarada Math? They are completely independent of the men and are saturated in Indian culture. Wouldn't the best thing be for Western women to join with them in their work, just as the Western men who become swamis are part and parcel of the Ramakrishna Order? They could come here and train us in scriptural study and all the other traditional aspects of Vedantic monasticism." Swami looked at me silently for a few minutes, then wrinkled his nose. "No", he said, "They will not

[15]   *Complete Works of Swami Vivekananda*, Vol.5: On Indian Women, p.229.

be able to do that. They do not lecture or take the sort of responsibilities that the swamis take in India. It will be too difficult for them to run the work here."

I thought silently that it would be only a matter of time before the Indian nuns were as effective and powerful as the swamis, but refrained from asking any more questions. I had absorbed from what Swami had said that there were deep issues in the idea of Indian and Western nuns working together; that for the moment it was beyond my understanding, and that was all. Moreover, if I did become a nun, it would be in America and in California, as going to India was out of the question. The heat, the diet, the threat to health, and no doubt adjusting to the culture would just be too much. From my now nine years in America I already knew how difficult it is to adjust to a foreign culture—and I was in my twenties when I did so, adjusting to an English-speaking culture. How much more difficult would it be in India, where English is spoken by only a few! I decided that I had spent enough energy on adjustment to culture; now I wanted to develop my inner life.

Swami's vehemence about the undesirability of monks running convents for women finally prompted me to ask him where did the problem lie—after all, hadn't the Buddhists and Christians done it for centuries? He replied, "It is such a responsibility." I wondered how much more responsibility it was than running monasteries for men, but he simply reiterated, with the maximum of solemnity, "It is a very serious responsibility." The whole subject was so new to me, as I had had absolutely no practical experience of it, and I said no more. I went home, wrote it all down and decided to say not a word about what was in my mind. As and when I knew more clearly what I felt, I would say something; but meantime, why bring down a hornets' nest of ladies or the bit N word from Swami?

Further consideration of this subject was soon put aside by Swami's decision not to go to California that summer. The swami in Hollywood, an old friend and brother-disciple of Swami, was desperately ill and Swami felt it would be an intrusion for him to go that year, too much of a strain on the staff in Hollywood, who were completely taken up with tending their sick guru. Swami had been going to Hollywood almost every summer since the mid fifties—over twenty years—partially to get a break in the company of his spiritual brother, and partially to give the devoted ladies in New York a rest. Unlike Swami, the Hollywood swami had built up a large, bustling center with a quite large monastery and convent, several wealthy devotees, and a following among the intellectuals and glitterati of Hollywood, including Christopher Isherwood, Aldous Huxley, Gerald Heard, Greta Garbo, Marlon Brando and other actors, artists and producers who had been known to mingle with the faithful, but not necessarily been "regulars". This was a center with facilities and staff to offer hospitality to guests; and Swami, of course, was more than welcome there. Our little group in New York was so much smaller, quieter and unglamorous by comparison (though it, too, had many distinguished, creative members), but there was a reason behind it, as I later came to understand.

Swami had decided to spend July at Erik's country home in upstate New York and August at Marshfield with Swami Sarvagatananda. Erik and his partner Jack would care for and cook for Swami at their place, but who would do the cooking at Marshfield? As Courtenaye would grimly tell me, "He never asks for anything. If he doesn't get what he can eat, he just doesn't eat and loses weight. He always loses six pounds every summer in California. They don't bother to follow his diet instructions." As Swami was nearly six feet tall and weighed about ninety pounds, losing six pounds was indeed a serious matter, and everyone agreed that Courtenaye, his regular cook, should go to Marshfield to cook for him. John, who was his personal attendant, would also go. But fate indeed has its twists and turns. In late spring Maman took seriously ill and was rushed to the hospital, raising the question: Who would be at the Center that summer to cope, should she get sick again? Swami would be away, as would Courtenaye and John, the two mainstays at the Center; and Jeanne, of course, could not really manage on her own. And then, Maman could not tolerate anyone but Jeanne and Courtenaye, ruling out myself and Pat, or anyone else who could conceivably be of help at the Center.

Finally Swami decided that Courtenaye should stay back in New York and I would go to Marshfield to cook for him. I was happy, and at the same time intimidated—how could I possibly learn the art of "doing it right" in a mere couple of months? Courtenaye, with her usual focus, showed no disappointment or other emotion and settled in to teaching me the how of this arcane art. The meals were not complicated, because Swami was on basically a sick diet, but the attention to detail was devastating—only ten grains of salt, to be measured out, and so on! I silently figured that all of this stemmed from the ladies' deep yearning to worship ritualistically. Swami was completely without any such tendencies and had not introduced to New York the heavy, complicated ritualism of Hinduism; but Jeanne was an ex-Catholic and doubtless was used to and preferred it. I had seen her waving a lighted incense stick—a ritual she performed when Swami was coming down through the chapel for lunch—and dragging it on and on, obviously grooving on it. For many, and especially for the Hindus, ritualism is an essential part of life, and if not built into the system (as was the case in New York), they will create it in all that they do—including counting grains of salt! Swami's meal preparations, I realized, were actually carefully crafted rituals, which I, as a Protestant of the most radical type was completely ignorant of and could see no point to at all. However, I wanted to feed Swami right, and so I went along with it, following my already established policy of *in Rome do as the Romans do*, until I knew enough to ask questions and bring about any changes that seemed necessary.

The importance of these precautions became apparent in early July, after Swami had gone up to Erik's and was there when the news arrived that the Hollywood swami had died on July fourth. Swami at once fell silent and deeply absorbed, showing no interest in food of any sort. Jack and Erik were extremely worried about him, especially as he seemed to be slipping away, among other things steadily losing weight. There had been a rule that there would be no visitors at Erik's while Swami was there, but as the news got worse and worse Courtenaye could stand it no longer and one day she drove me up to visit Swami anyhow. I wasn't sure how we would be received, but of course Erik was gracious and kind as always and Swami—whom we had expected to find completely indrawn—was radiantly happy to see us! We had a delightful lunch with Swami, Erik and Jack in the lovely dining room in Erik's house, decorated as only he and Jack—professional interior decorators—could do it. Although Swami was still rather indrawn over the Hollywood swami's death he was remarkably perky and, I distinctly remember, commented on President Ford dancing with Queen Elizabeth on her recent visit to the States. "I did not know that elderly people did such things!" was his ingenuous remark, much to our amusement.

After lunch Courtenaye and I went for a walk in the surrounding country while Swami took a nap. Around four we went to his room where he was sipping ginger ale, seated by the open window, outside of which a geranium in full bloom nodded in riotous color. Next to those blooms, Swami's tall, thin, ascetic frame, his silver hair, seemed quite ethereal and almost translucent. A gauze curtain lifted in the breeze and rays of light played across the room, seeming to express the happiness and blessedness of incredibly sweet presence. An indelible memory.

There was to be more of the same at Marshfield a month later, when I went to cook for him. Despite all of Erik's efforts, at his home Swami had indeed lost quite a bit of weight, and I felt as though I was really on the spot to get his weight back to normal. But his mind was deeply indrawn, focusing on the passing of his spiritual brother and on many events from the past, a feature that worried Swami Sarvagatananda. "Please try to distract Swami and get his mind back to the present," he requested of me and John. I, however, could do no such thing. Rather, I flowed along in the current of Swami's reminiscences, opening out like a fragrant garden otherwise hidden behind the high wall of his usual reserve. His mind was so utterly clear and pure, like a crystalline stream gushing from the rock, as I had seen at Mount Vitosha in Sofia—a distant echo of the Himalayas, which was Swami's natural element in many ways. He had spent twenty-four years living at a Himalayan ashrama, very remote and without any of the ritualistic distractions that keep Hindus busy in most of their institutions. Swami Vivekananda had started the ashrama, called Advaita Ashrama or Non-dual Retreat, where everything revolved around the formless, non-dual, undivided and indivisible God, the divine living in all hearts. Few of the swamis sent there from the plains could stand the silence, isolation and austerity of such a place, and ultimately a rule was made that they would stay up there for no more than ten years; but Swami had been able to live there for twenty-four years without any problems, no doubt on account of his intensely interior and detached approach to life. He would walk in the Himalayan jungles, seeing the divine in and through the natural beauty and would say, "Why do we need to perform rituals when nature itself is putting on such a glorious worship of the divine?"

This idyllic experience came particularly to a head one day after one of Swami's meals. His seat was facing a window, through which the sun was streaming, lighting up his face. He was in a quiet, sweet mood, hardly speaking, but communicating volumes. Finally he said, "Let us go now", and got up slowly, his face irradiated by the sun outside and from within by the exalted mood that had possessed him. I was sitting on his left, and as he rose I suddenly noticed a photograph of Sarada Devi on the wall to his right. In it, she too was in profile looking into a shaft of light. The similarity of the two profiles struck me profoundly, not just physically, but by the same serene inwardness and quiet joy that suffused them.

It came to me that the infinite motherliness of Sarada Devi had somehow taken the form of Swami and that, in effect, she was expressing herself to me through him, an impression that has always remained with me. As the Dark Mother in the form of Kali had brought me through the turbulent battles for survival of my childhood, Sarada Devi was now chastening and refining my emotions through the medium of my guru. Later I found out that Swami had met her, but only once. She had been veiled, as she was in her formal appearances before men, but he had nevertheless felt, in her presence, a vastly powerful, but at the same time serene and loving presence which had radically transformed him from an angry young man into a focused and deeply serious spiritual seeker. I was convinced that he was actually transmitting to me in his inimitable way the same spiritual inspiration that he had received from her. And as time passes, I can see that it was this immensely healing and soothing energy which had been reaching out to me, even through the terrible rupture with my father and the tsunami that swamped me afterwards. It was drawing me on, calling me to New York, and asking me to come and be healed and re-created in the relationship with Swami. His unconditional acceptance of me, his unwavering respect for and even admiration of me, even when I was far from my best, had built up a better, purer, more real me than what had been there before. That was what I had not wanted to sacrifice to the raging flames of my father during the last months of his life. Swami was drawing me out of that furnace and changing me into something vastly better, perhaps a somewhat blurry image in the holographic field of Sarada Devi, in which he himself was a much clearer, more recognizable reproduction of her.

Alongside this idyll another drama was playing out. The death of the swami in Hollywood had left a large, active Vedanta Center without a designated leader, and it was urgent to find a successor. Swami, once an Assistant General Secretary of the order and still a trustee, was the seniormost swami in America, and was therefore inevitably involved in any decision-making process. We therefore had, in quick succession, visits from the two swamis on the short list for the leadership of the Hollywood center. First came Swami B., a tall, imposing man who had been a shaker and mover in India. He was an outgoing man with strong political inclinations and wide influence, though professing to humility and doubts about any promotion to the much larger and more active Hollywood center.

I found Swami's response interesting: "You have been at your present posting for nearly seven years. The people there are devoted to you and with them you are building up the work. You should remain there and dedicate yourself to making it into a strong, spiritual center." This, of course, was his own agenda, a dedication to the transformation of the lives of American devotees. For Swami, political power in the order was the last consideration; but, glancing at Swami B., I knew he was of a different stamp and despite his show of humility was basically a power-broker, whom the order would probably choose in the end.

Against this scene of Swami exercising his authority over another swami I contrast another vignette that took place a few days later. Swami did not come on time for lunch—something most unusual, for, unlike most Indians, he was very exact about time. I went into his room to see if he was all right and found him sitting in his chair in an abstracted mood. Swami did go into ecstatic states, and I felt that his unusual lateness for lunch might be caused by some sort of abstracted or ecstatic state brought on, on this occasion, by unknown causes—perhaps meditation. He had a little difficulty recognizing me and focusing on getting up for dinner, never an event of much importance to him. "Oh," he said, "I haven't tied my shoelaces." It seemed as if he had been trying to get ready and had not been able to. He lay back in his chair, his eyes indrawn. "Can you tie my shoelaces?" he asked in a faraway voice. "OK, Swami," I said, getting down on my knees to move him toward his food before it got any colder. When I had finished, he said, more alert, "Now you go and wash your hands."

This was Hindu stuff. They have a horror of dirt, anything from the floor, touching the body—whatever—no doubt due to the ubiquitous disease germs that seem to lurk everywhere in India, combined with their poor preventative and therapeutic medical services, and their extreme obsession with "purity". Wanting to humor him and get him to the table, I got up to wash my hands. As I did so, he said very humbly, putting his hand to his heart, "Please excuse these Hindu superstitions." He was fully alert now and completely engaged with me. I couldn't believe this was the same person I had seen exerting his authority a day or two before; nor, when I thought of it, his reaction when something like this had come up before. Then he had been talking about how one of his senior friends in India put implicit faith in astrology, which Swami pronounced "pure superstition".[16] I listened for a while and then could not help saying, "Swami, you once went on a fast because you ate beef by mistake. Isn't that superstition, too?" For me, the total, compulsive Hindu taboo on eating beef was nothing but superstition, though from one point of view it made sense economically and ecologically. To make anything totally forbidden was, I felt, really a superstition; and, frankly, I was shocked that Swami, otherwise so rational, subscribed to it. He had looked at me earnestly for a moment and had rejoined, "You are right. It is a superstition, nothing but a superstition. It is not good to be ruled by these things." Even then I was struck by his humility and reasonableness, but now, having glimpsed his level of authority in the order, I was bowled over. This man was opening out to my needs to a degree I could never dream of, putting aside his culture, his position, and his authority. Quite amazing!

After Swami B. left, Swami C., the assistant swami from Southern California, visited Marshfield for a week. Coming to Southern California from India some ten years previously, he had survived his senior, Swami A. (my nemesis of the previous year) and was therefore theoretically in line to take over the Hollywood center. He was a much younger man than Swami B., a quite different type. Slim and boyish, he was primarily a writer with an interest in audio-visual projects. Political power and control were low on his agenda, and Swami had a hard time persuading him to even think of taking over the bustling, wealthy complex of centers in Southern California. "You have been there for nearly ten years," he said to the swami. "The members there know and love you; it will be best if you stay on and carry forward the work that has been begun." Swami's

---

[16]   On account of the Indian proclivity to passive dependence on it.

idea was that, as a trainee of the Hollywood swami, the founder and leader for over forty years of the Southern Californian Center, Swami C. would offer continuity for the members in Southern California, as Swami B., by staying at his post, would keep up the momentum he had already built up there.

It was clear where Swami stood. For him, the Western membership needed, above all, continuity and stability of leadership, spiritual guides who understood them and would stand by them as long as possible. That was his own commitment—and how fully he was doing it, in the political realm several notches "below" his previous prominent position in the hierarchy! Had he not confided in me how he regarded the work he was doing in America as the most important of his entire life? He had said, "The Center is small, but I have chosen the people very carefully." Then, with great intensity, "And I have *given* to them!" It was clear that the healing and transfiguration of souls came first for him. But, as Swami B. was primarily political, Swami C. was essentially interested in creating a literary world. To Swami's earnest exhortations he would burst out, in his boyish way, "But, Swami! I am a writer! I need a center that will help me publish and bring out the literature!"

As a person with literary leanings myself, I felt a lot more empathy for this younger swami and his goals than I had for Swami B.; but in both cases I was struck by how little concern they had for the Western devotees. No doubt good political organization and a copious, accurate literature were important; but I also knew from my own experience how vitally important was the kind of love and support Swami gave all of us and wanted to see in place for others. He had already transformed my life in a way that no amount of organization or literature ever could. I empathized totally with his earnest pleadings with the two swamis to put the devotees and their concerns first, to focus on the need for continuity and commitment to their flocks rather than political expediency or literary adventure. After all, I thought, if Swami B. wants to expand his present work, let him; and Swami C. can work with the already existing literary setup in Southern California. I hoped that Swami's seniority and accurate assessment would prevail, and that the swamis would somehow summon up the will to put the American devotees first, but did not have high hopes that it would be so. And that is how it was: at the end of the year Swami B. took over Southern California, leaving the devotees where he had been working to their fate, while Swami C. moved on as assistant in the small center in St. Louis, where the senior swami was a well-known scholar and writer and had established a strong literary and publishing tradition.

All of this was to have a huge impact on me later. For the moment, I was "safe in the arms of Jesus", as a Christian hymn puts it, under the protection of a deeply spiritual and loving soul, who put my spiritual and psychological well-being ahead of all other concerns. My bruising encounter with Swami A. the previous year, and now my overview of how other swamis were motivated, were warning signs of what might lie ahead, but at that moment they were mere blips on a large screen.

CHAPTER 21

THE CLOCK IS TICKING, TICKING . . .
1976-1977

The idyll at Marshfield was the last really happy time for me. Although I had more or less decided to become a nun, thus getting over a lot of struggle over my commitment to my medical career, there were serious problems before me. First was my diminishing supply of money, and then there was Swami's state of health. The deeply indrawn and distracted mood that had started after the death of the Hollywood swami showed little sign of abating and indeed seemed to be getting worse. His memory was failing, he was getting more and more unsteady on his feet and his ability to swallow was seriously impaired. It was truly agony to see him try to eat. Never much of an eater, he was so slow chewing and so excruciated in trying to swallow that it was truly torture to cook for him and be with him at the table. One evening at the library class I noticed him moving his lips in a certain way that I knew was diagnostic of serious damage to the frontal lobes of the brain—the seat of intelligence and insight—and realized he was suffering from dementia. The thought of this precious soul going down into a vegetative state such as I had seen in the Alzheimer's wards in the mental hospital in Sussex was too much for me, and I burst into tears, much to the surprise of everyone present.

Although I said nothing about such observations, it was clear that others were grasping what was going on, for bit by bit the other cooks and helpers started to drop out and more and more jobs and responsibilities began to fall on my shoulders. The work became more and more demanding and relentless, but I was determined to stick to my post. I knew where my best interests lay and made up my mind to stay with Swami as long as I possibly could. Only my money running out completely would stop me from staying with and serving him, so help me God.

Swami had been trying for some time to get an assistant swami from India and we finally learned that one would arrive in February. However, the new swami proved to be blustery, demanding and extremely defiant of Swami, who was trying to protect him from the worst impact of American society. He insisted on eating a full Indian diet, thus adding considerably to our work, on walking in the streets alone with women (a total no-no in monastic protocol), and on doing whatever he saw fit—understandable in a fifty-five year old man—but also fraught with problems, as when he went alone to Central Park and saw lovers making out to the max in the quieter, shady areas. He came back to the Center utterly distraught, for in India even holding hands and kissing in public is utterly taboo. "You might have been better off with one of our men to guide you!" I thought, realizing why Swami was being so protective of him. But the newcomer was utterly impervious to any sort of suggestion or guidance. And he kept laying into us, finding fault, heckling and harassing us, presumably well-meant, but so utterly insensitive and unlike Swami's subtle behavior with us, that all of us were mightily put out. Almost immediately the helpers at the Center completely dropped out, and Jeanne, Courtenaye and myself were left to carry on the work.

I could empathize with the difficulties the swami was facing: America and Americans are big, strong, and self-assertive, quite other than the quiet and self-effacing people and values of India or even Scotland, at least as relative to America. But along with such American self-assertion went a good-natured, enthusiastic willingness to move forward, to tackle new things and ideas, and to face difficulties squarely and very scientifically, which I deeply appreciated. No sweepings under the rug, no cover-ups; face the issue and get on with it—all virtues in tune with my own outlook. Over the years I had learned to adjust and expected the new swami to do so also. But whenever he would rant on about his problems and I would try to share some insight about dealing with Americans, he would shout, "You are a child! You know nothing!"

Instead of the divine patience, compassion and love of Swamis Pavitrananda and Sarvagatananda which extended a place of value and even importance to all, this man was offering only his preconceived ideas, which he seemed to feel were superior to ours and therefore absolved him from the need to work to understand us. I began to feel that perhaps some of this had been behind the rather cruel behavior of Swami A., which had caused me so much grief a year and a half previously.

Perhaps all of this could be put down simply to younger swamis going through the problems of adjusting to American life, and particularly to the self-assertiveness of American women, for which they were totally unprepared by their monastic training in India, at most seeing women occasionally, and adoring, simple-hearted Indian women at that. They were unused to women like myself who asked basic questions and expected cogent and adequate answers. Fluffing off with Hindu myth or Ramakrishna Order protocol just wouldn't do. We knew it, they knew it—but what other resources did they have? It was a difficult matter, and I felt for them. But I also had to live my life, and becoming a mindless swami-swooner or uncomplaining slavey just wasn't part of my equipment. Swami had commanded my allegiance through his amazing acceptance of and respect for me, and I would gladly do anything for him and deem it a privilege. But to slave over a stove preparing exotic Indian dishes for a person who so palpably had no respect for me was quite another matter.

As Swami began to move toward death and the drama with the new swami intensified, I realized that not only could I not live at the Center, but also that I could not remain in New York. I would have to move on if I was going to get the spiritual help I felt I needed. For me, the Spirit can only be manifested in an atmosphere of respect, and that was totally lacking now. The swami would protest that he loved me, but what does love mean without understanding and respect? Perhaps over time such respect might grow; but at that time I still felt too incomplete spiritually and too apprehensive of his agenda to want to remain. For her part, Jeanne had decided that he was "masterful", and made a point of specially attending on him. I was glad he had someone to turn to, but his reciprocation of her devotion by saying she was a goddess, a divine being, pointedly ignoring us or even putting us down, did nothing to help the situation. Jeanne had the qualities of a follower, an unquestioning devotee, which seemed to suit him, and I was happy that the pot had found its lid; but his impassioned denunciations of the rest of us as "cold, heartless, dry", both to our faces and during a visit he made that summer to Southern California simply widened the gulf between us.

The assistant had become increasingly defiant, even rude to Swami, and he was discussing him openly with whatever devotee would listen to him. And the content of such discussions soon came out. One evening as we were getting ready to leave the Center, Courtenaye came downstairs from the swamis' area, her face pale and her whole body shaking. She had had to deliver something to the swami, but on approaching his room had heard him talking loudly with John. "He said that Swami is senile," she whispered. "He said that we have to work around him, move him aside." Courtenaye had never heard such talk about Swami—she would not allow it. I, of course, knew that Swami was seriously incapacitated, but was appalled at how the assistant swami was handling the situation. There appeared to be no respect, no empathy, no consideration for the anguish we all were feeling, or even the basic respect for Swami that other swamis we knew extended to him and we were working so hard ourselves to develop. Indians usually show extreme respect for seniors—perhaps too much at times—but this man seemed to lack even a shred of it. What was wrong with him? Why was he so fixated on his own difficulties and not in the least interested in ours?

I got to the bottom of this problem one evening as I came downstairs to wash the supper dishes. For some reason Swami was not at supper, and Jeanne was talking alone with the assistant swami as he finished his meal; as usual, he was telling her "all", in his unusually loud voice. I couldn't help hearing what he was saying, and it rooted me to the spot. "I have difficulties with Pavitrananda Swami," he was saying, "because of difficulties I had with my father. He was very traditional, very domineering—and would thrash me to force me to obey." This was the first time I had heard a swami talk in such a psychological way or divulge anything so ugly. It surprised me, for I was used to the swamis being able to talk *above* problems like this, being able to draw us out of them to a deeper level where they ceased to have such a hold on us. I recognized that this man was terribly stressed by the cultural changes he was facing (in many ways because of his own intransigence) and far from being at his best, and I empathized with his struggles with his father—hadn't my own father set me up for so many of my own difficulties? I also realized that physical violence adds a whole new dimension to parental dominance and silently thanked the Lord that my father had never struck me.

I felt for the man, but at the same time asked myself, "Why does he impute domineering motives to Swami? Can't he understand the love and understanding behind his efforts to prepare him for work in the West?" I myself had had huge struggles with Swami's authority—including going off to Boston to escape from him—but had finally understood that the authority he wielded was spiritual, not even psychological, far less physical. He spoke from a place where there was no compulsion, just an appeal to one's deeper nature. He never demanded anything of me or even suggested anything without my asking. He had given me a mantra and a few instructions for meditation, a hint that singing every day as well as taking a couple of walks would help get rid of migraines—perceptions which I at first resisted, and then found to work very well. He had not stopped me from going to Boston, even though he knew how much I would suffer; he understood that I needed to learn for myself and gave me the space to do so. As I saw him, he met people where they were and helped them as they were. In my case, when he knew I was about to hang myself, he proffered me a rope, knowing I could learn from experience, keep my balance, and move on.

I was convinced that Swami's apparent assertion of authority with the assistant was geared to the man's competence and the fact that time was short. Swami was trying to get him trained up as quickly as possible, but the man was resisting to the utmost of his capacity. It seemed that the assistant did not want to open out to Swami—and now I knew the reason, at least as he saw it. From my own experience I knew how much damage an abusive parent can do to a child—but I also knew, from Swami's training, that spirituality includes a determined effort to resolve such issues and get beyond them, not to use them as an excuse for substandard behavior. That the assistant would in all seriousness dredge up such stuff was troubling to me, even though it was in the utter privacy of his mealtime with Jeanne. Was he trying to excuse himself? Had he any intention of resolving this issue and thereby making it possible to open himself out to the problems and struggles of others? These were the questions that were troubling me.

I had no delusions about my own areas of instability, and understood that to get beyond them I had to have a guide more advanced than myself, someone like Swami or Swami Sarvagatananda, both of whom always took me to a deeper level and showed me how to clean up and sublimate the conflicts. From overhearing this unfortunate confession, I understood that this man could never help me; he had the same problems as I, perhaps even worse, and any long-term association with him would simply be a case of the blind leading the blind, and both falling in the ditch. The writing was on the wall: After Swami left his body, I would head back to Boston and the sheltering grace of Swami Sarvagatananda, who never called me a "child", who saw my potential, as Swami did, and always extended to me so much appreciation and encouragement as I stumbled along my spiritual path. The dice were clearly cast. Like twenty years before, when I left the West of Scotland irrevocably and went to Edinburgh, I was going to be moving on to a new world. Then I was propelled by my longing to serve as a doctor, and now as a nun. I mulled this over internally, but never mentioned it to Swami. The clock was ticking, ticking, ticking . . . .

As this new conflict developed, the pieces were falling into place with Swami. After the persimmon episode I felt that huge barriers had been removed from between us and we began to communicate more and more closely. For whatever reason, Swami made a point of not getting "intellectual" with me, but we nevertheless found endless subjects to discuss: our lives (Swami had wanted to be a medical doctor, but had ended up as a writer—the opposite of my own life), the work, East-West communication, and the meaning of the teachings of Swami Vivekananda, who had by now become the central figure in my world.

Conversations like this were precisely what I needed to feed my soul, with its imperious intellect and adamant insistence on the freedom to work things out for myself and to put the solutions to tests of my own devising. During one such conversation I felt myself to be a huge condor flying over the Andes, with the wind rippling the tip feathers of my massive wings. With each beat of the conversation my wings would move majestically through the air and push me higher and higher into the empyrean. This, as far as I was concerned, was Vedanta, gushing forth like the crystalline springs I had encountered on Mount Vitosha near Sophia—fresh, clear, and deeply nourishing to the soul. This was the antidote to self-doubt, unhappiness and the addictive hero-worship which led to "swami-swooning" and cultishness, all of which Swami would roundly castigate, including the way his beloved brother monk in Hollywood had set up the centers in Southern California. Swami rejected any form of guruism as poisonous and would shudder at the expression of any sort of mindless cultism, such as he found rampant in Southern California. Apparently he loved the man, but not what he had set up around himself.

Despite Swami's physical decline, he and I were drawing closer and closer. I no longer felt any real conflict with him; now it was a case of learning all I could from him while he was still with us. An example: Any lingering doubts or conflicts on the Christianity issue were resolved one evening in the library class. The reading was from reminiscences about Swami Vivekananda, whom one close disciple saw at her first meeting with him as "a blaze of reddish gold, which seemed to have caught and concentrated the sun's rays . . . Young with an ageless youth and yet withal old with the wisdom of ancient times. For the first time we heard the age-old message of India, teaching of the Atman, the true Self."[17] Her words implied to me that this spiritual dynamo had poured himself out as an offering to the divine. It was an inspiring piece, which opened a door into my soul. When my turn came to speak I began, "This reading has helped me understand the meaning of the crucifixion." I could hear a gasp from the others: Not the Christian stuff again! But I had my epiphany to express, and I went ahead: "I see Christ as a radiant light, just like Vivekananda; and the crucifixion is like Swami Vivekananda's self-immolation for the good of people in the West and in India. He worked so hard for the sake of others that he died of diabetes at the early age of thirty-nine, at a time when there was no treatment for the disease. In the same way Christ poured himself out and was ready to face early death, if necessary, for what he considered most important and what he had to offer the world." Swami looked at me seriously for a long time and then said, "If that is what you really believe, I have nothing more to say." It was, and he didn't. That was the end of our struggle over Christianity.

The whole Christianity thing came to a gentle landing at Easter, when his Sunday talk contained no animus; and indeed, he put in several good remarks about Saint Paul, which was an added bonus. I had braced myself for the worst, but came out understanding that Swami was not antagonistic in himself, though he reflected the feelings of many Indians. He was merely responding to me and my issues, and indeed, maybe to many others'. Thus ended the lesson, and we had a very cordial lunch at the Center, with happy talk and, in my mind, a sense of complete closure. I felt that I had, indeed, put the Abrahamic focus on sin and atonement behind me and was moving into the Vedantic world of joy from which I was born, in which I lived, and to which I would return. This was not skirting the issue of good and evil; it was approaching it from another angle, for true bliss and spirituality can come only through ethical living and self-giving. As and when you have had a taste of that joy—which my relationship with Swami had definitely bestowed on me—wrong, self-centered behavior becomes less and less acceptable; it becomes so distasteful that leaving it behind becomes almost inevitable. That, at least, was how I understood the situation, and I experienced it as a happiness of the sort I had not previously encountered.

---

[17]   *Reminiscences of Swami Vivekananda,* Kolkata: Advaita Ashrama, 1964, p.161.

An incident in the library class around this time demonstrated to me just how cheeky I could still be and also how very tolerant and understanding Swami was. I don't remember what got me started, but I happened to mention, more or less casually, that Lord MacAulay, the

Thomas B. MacAulay, First Baron MacAulay (1800-1859).
A distant relative on my paternal grandmother's side of the family.

man who had been responsible for the British policy of denationalizing Indians through the Indian educational system (designed to all but delete the pre-existing culture) was a member of my family tree. Swami, whose generation was all too aware of the cultural atrocity the British had perpetrated on India in the name of commerce and modernization, sat bolt upright and glared at me with a glare to end all glares. I realized just what a tender nerve I had unwittingly struck, but instead of feeling contrite, I somehow felt inclined to strike another blow. "And, my grandparents were in India with the British army." Another shudder from Swami, and aghast looks or titters from the rest. Somehow I had gotten into a flow that only my shadow understood. I could not stop, even there. "And, of course, my main reason for going to medical school was to become a Christian missionary!" Swami was practically taking off like a helicopter, having become one huge, huge glare.

One side of me was thinking, "What do you mean you wanted to become a medical missionary! That was all over long before you went to medical school!" But something devilish in me wanted to make a statement. Perhaps this was a revolt against the Indian culture that pervaded the Vedanta Society, not so much from Swami as from the devotees, some of whom had a bit of a yen for things exotic and tended to push them down my throat. I was discovering, bit by bit, that I was a Westerner of Westerners, with no real interest in changing my cultural identity. I had had to struggle so hard to adjust to America—now at least ten years of it—that I had no inclination to adjust myself to becoming a Hindu. I had nothing against Indian culture in and of itself—indeed, I found it rather attractive, and of course I was totally committed to Vedanta—but I needed to follow my own culture and work things out that way, not flap about in a sari (not that Swami allowed us to do anything such thing—but the ladies would have done it, if they could), have a Sanskrit name, and endlessly bow and scrape in submission to authority, which seemed to be part and parcel of the Oriental way. Swami, of course, made a point of preventing us from "going Hindu", recognizing and honoring the fact that we were Western; but there is such a deeply ingrained attraction for the exotic and unusual, perhaps particularly in Americans, so many of whom seem to hunger for ethnic identity other than their Americanism—a phenomenon I could never understand. To me, being an American was something admirable and grand, but almost every American I met would introduce him or herself as an Italian, a Swede, a whatnot, much to my puzzlement. I would think, "My dear friend, you are utterly American! The Italians or Swedes wouldn't know what to make of you!" But that seemed to be the way it was.

For whatever reason, here I was asserting, not only my national identity, but also my links to all that was antagonistic to the Hindus. It was totally incongruous with the environment that Swami had worked to create, but was, alas, a very clear indication of all of the troubles I was about to face in the next turn of my life's spiral. There were few swamis who had transcended their own cultural identity to the degree that Swami had! Indeed, if I had met any other swami than he, I would never have been able to get on board with the Ramakrishna Order. But for the moment, he was registering amazement and perhaps annoyance at my impertinent challenge to Hindu culture which, after all, was so precious to him, though he did not push it on us. He held his cosmic glare for a few moments and then relaxed and began to smile. The tension in the room finally broke and we moved on to other things. This was a person of almost superhuman ability to understand and appreciate others, even across cultural barriers. Swami had risen above me, by several million miles, thus reinforcing my profound respect for him. At the same time, he was an ardent lover of his native land and would quite often talk about its struggles and aspirations, thus confirming my respect more and more. Here was someone who could respond to all sides of any issue—not only that, with the maximum of enthusiasm. An extremely rare bird, as I was soon to discover.

In April of nineteen seventy-seven Maman died. She was about ninety-six years old, working to the last. With regard to our relationship, things had not been good: Swami's usual "breakfasteers" had dropped out and Jeanne promoted to the task of making as well as serving Swami's breakfast. She would take his breakfast up to his room, her face a picture of bliss, with perhaps a hint of smugness—but let that pass. This meant that Maman was alone in the basement, something that could not be tolerated. There had to be someone there, and of course I, as the person with the least outside commitment, was asked to cover the situation. But there was one snag: Maman refused to have me in her space and would not let me in for anything but using the bathroom. I was, therefore, to sit in the dining room a few steps away from her room, to keep an eye and an ear out for her and any needs she might have. This meant that my now intense and sustained morning study of Vivekananda, which involved a lot of typing, had to be transferred down to the Center. Swami decreed that I would be set up in the dining room with a typewriter so that my studies could continue, a remarkable validation of my efforts, which was to carry a lot of weight for me in the struggles of the next turn of my life's spiral. Who knows what the Genets thought of my tip-tapping away next to their sanctum sanctorum! I detected a bit more frost, a bit more glitter in the eye—but Swami had given his imprimateur, and there was nothing they could say.

This enforced isolation in which I was sacrificing so much for the Genets was a bit hard to take, and I felt fresh waves of resentment coming on; but mercifully, a few days before Maman's death I made a huge effort to empathetically put myself in her position, a strategy Swami had suggested all along as the best way to cope with her. I saw how difficult it had been for this woman, brought up in luxury and used to her every command being obeyed, to humble herself and follow rather than lead her daughters into a religious group of which her understanding was limited, to say the least. There had been intermittent rebellion against the swamis, against the cramped quarters and imposed duties, but over time she had become more and more resigned. Her younger daughter

Rolande had managed everything by herself and more or less kept others out of her private space; but when others took over Rolande's work after her death in nineteen sixty-one, Maman had to endure the presence of Americans, many younger, sometimes noisy. It must have been difficult for her and it was perhaps natural that she had worked hard to hold on to her privacy and personal space, even to the length of treating some of the women in a callous and cruel way.

No doubt the Genets were modeling themselves on Sarada Devi, who had also had to live in a tiny, cramped room at the temple where Ramakrishna lived, with no chance of much of a social life, recreation or even seeing much of Ramakrishna. She had borne it all without a murmur, giving of herself totally to the Master and his followers, feeding them, mothering them, loving them, and asking nothing for herself. But, of course, Sarada Devi had had no resentment, never treated people badly or made anyone feel other than herself. That is why we revere her so much—such behavior is divine, not human. And of course it was most admirable that the Genets were following in her footsteps. Ours is to emulate to the best of our ability; but we cannot expect others to be saints—we have to work on our own case and try to forbear with the failings of others. One important thing I had understood along the way, when I could not get my mind off my resentment of Maman: If you constantly brood over what someone has done, you yourself start to behave like her. That had been a powerful incentive to me to struggle with my feelings and try to rise above them. As Swami said, who knew what I would be like at Maman's age! Would I be like her? Certainly, fixating on her would make it more likely.

I realized how difficult it is to be good, far less spiritual—a thought that was to become one of my mantras. Just to hang on in difficult circumstances was in and of itself an achievement, and this Maman had succeeded in doing for some forty years. My heart had expanded, and that last week, as I tiptoed around her, I had felt a lot less resentment than before. And, on the eve of her death, her trusting submission to Swami had been quite remarkable. She had requested him to sit with her, which he did, holding her hand for several hours till she died. Despite everything, she had come to understand his significance and had, despite her lifetime of defiance, actually died in his presence, a privilege none of the rest of us could claim.

This was the sort of thing that made me cleave to Vedanta. Despite many failings, some of them of quite serious proportions, adherents of

Vedanta were actively working on themselves, transforming themselves from imperious, self-centered matriarchs to uncomplaining and trusting devotees. And, of course, it was all fueled and supported by Swami, whose powerful spiritual personality, so uncompromising on the basic issues of commitment, self-discipline and making space for others, worked wonders on even the most hardened egotist. I had picked up all of this right from the beginning, when the contrast between these people and those I was struggling with at work was so evident. For me, "worldliness" meant, above all an unwillingness to look at one's faults and to try to rise above them.

As I knew to my cost, a false step with a worldly person could end in a lifetime feud of the greatest bitterness and several horrible "duels at dawn", fought to the death. But Vedantists, with all of their faults, made an effort to forgive and forget, and for me that was the pearl beyond price. In the case of Maman, it was *my* effort to do so that was involved; but of course that benefited me immeasurably more than if it had come from her. I realized I owed her a debt of gratitude for giving me the opportunity to work out the whole thing with her, and of course understood that none of it could have happened without Swami's benign, if very low-key, intervention. "It is not easy to be good, far less spiritual"—but it was possible to be "better", at least in small increments. I was intensely grateful that I had gotten over the worst of my resentment when she died, having suffered so much over my father's death, when huge waves of resentment and anger had assailed me, on occasion nearly drowning me. As it was, her passing was for me quiet, without either resentment or gloating, for it could have been easy to rejoice at her removal from the scene. No, she had "fought the good fight" and left me behind to carry it on with whomever stepped into her role in my life. How many were waiting in the wings! Another story—but the same, slow, difficult process we dub with the name *spirituality*.

While Erik was at the Center in connection with the brief memorial tribute Swami gave Maman in public, I took the opportunity to talk with him about Swami's medical condition, which was rapidly deteriorating. I especially shared with him my anxieties about Swami's diminishing memory and other neurological problems. It seemed to me that serious brain damage, for whatever reason, was going on—and of course Swami's adamant refusal to see a doctor about it was intensely frustrating and worrying. I knew that probably not much could be done, but as a medical doctor still wanted a diagnosis and to do whatever could be done to improve the situation. As I spoke with Erik—and I could not have talked about it with any of the others, as it would be too disturbing—I began to cry and confessed to my dear brother the anguish I felt at seeing Swami's mental condition deteriorate so rapidly.

Erik was sunny and good-natured (which made him the perfect foil for me), but there also was a deeper and more important dimension to

him. "Yes, Swami is losing his memory. But has he changed what he really is? Does physical ill health affect spirituality?" was his intelligent and deeply insightful reply. I stopped crying and looked at him for a few minutes as I processed his response. Of course! This was practical Vedanta! Vedanta insists that while we may have bodies, be emotional, intellectual and even intuitive, there is a yet deeper dimension which we call Spirit or Self. Spirit lies behind all the other faculties of our makeup and is not affected by them. When we train our faculties to let Spirit shine through and guide them, we are spiritual, and not before. This was what Erik was referring to; and as a long-term caregiver for Swami when he was sick, he had observed him closely over the years.

This precious insight helped me immensely. Instead of focusing on Swami's memory loss, his difficulty swallowing, and other distressing symptoms, I saw more clearly than ever how his interest in and love for each one of us was undiminished and perhaps more intense than ever. If I asked him a question, despite his disabilities he was as eager as ever to share information and to help me in any way he could. That was what really mattered to me. One day as I sat with him at lunchtime—blessedly free of the company of his ever-blustering assistant—he fell silent and became quite indrawn. The light from the window fell on him, a frail figure through whom the light seemed to pass and repass. Swami had always seemed transparent, but now I felt that he was transparency itself, posing no barrier whatever to the self-expression of the Spirit. The silence in the room was eternal, deeply serene and profoundly supportive, bestowing on me a peace that I had not experienced for a long, long time. As I gazed at him I suddenly felt that I was actually seeing the Atman, or spiritual Self, permeating him and the surroundings. A calm, steady current of joy was flooding through me, bringing me to the spiritual core he had worked so hard to open my eyes to. I was indeed experiencing the joy we are born in, are supported by and return to at death. Christianity and all the pain of separation between humanity and God it tends to stand for were now behind me and I would now move forward in the deeply supportive awareness of the Self, of which the best Christian expression is the "everlasting arms, ever underneath" of the Old Testament and the Comforter, the Holy Spirit of the New Testament. But, unlike the Abrahamic religions, divinity or the Self is not *other than* us. It is within us, our true nature to be discovered, embraced and expressed as fully in our own lives as possible.

It is not necessary for a Vedantist to have a church, a priesthood, rituals, though some seem to like and need them. Because we *are* the Self (or it is what we really are) it is theoretically possible to work out one's own salvation (as Buddha expected of his followers) without any external aids or intervention. Swami had shown me how to face, rise above and conquer some of the deep emotional problems lingering in my psyche from my childhood, largely encouraging me to face the issues and go into them directly, holding on to my conviction about who I really am and making up my mind to endure to the end. Of course, his presence and support had been vital to the task, but now that he was palpably preparing to leave this world, I realized I was going to have to face issues on my own without the possibility of talking directly to him. In a sense, this wonderful moment of communion with his inner source was a lighting of my own inner flame from his. Henceforth, nothing could dampen it, far less put it out; I would overcome everything in the strength and energy of the Self, my direct link to him. But, of course, I would have to tend it carefully and protect it from the harsh winds ever blowing in the world. As the Gita says, the Self can burn like a flame protected from the wind, unmoving, steady, and without smoke. (6.19) This would be my goal: to keep the flame burning steadily, to remove the obstacles to its burning brighter and brighter, and to feed it and fuel it in the form of cultivation of unselfish work, love for all without conditions, deeper and deeper self-knowledge and a universal all-encompassing view of the world.

CHAPTER 22

TWILIGHT AT MIDDAY: 1977

After Maman's death my freedom to come and go at the Center improved a little, and I could comfortably eat my meals there. However, the situation with the assistant swami steadily went downhill and I began to see why Swami was emphasizing the psychological independence of the women from male leadership. In addition, by the summer I was quite exhausted from carrying the now-crushing load of work at the Center, since almost all of our regular workers had dropped out. Swami was staying with Erik, while I was slated to go to Marshfield, partially for a rest and partially to set up for Swami's care when he went on there from Erik's within a week or so.

The night before leaving for Marshfield I was sleeping on a cot bed in the dining room of the Center, with all of my pots and pans and other paraphernalia stacked up around me, ready for departure the next day. It was a hot, sticky night, and I was having trouble sleeping. Suddenly everything went black and silent. The streetlights went out, the traffic came to a standstill, and Manhattan paused for a moment to take stock. It was the massive breakdown of the power grid that hit New York in the summer of nineteen seventy-seven, momentous in many different ways. It lasted two days and New York, sweltering without AC, melted down almost as much as the ice cream in the store freezers, which found its way to the storefronts for sale on tables before it became a soup. On the dark side, there was some serious looting all over the city, no means of communication and just a general sense of loss of control.

If I remember correctly, along with the blackout came the information from Erik that Swami had been admitted to hospital suddenly. He had to undergo some tests, the nature of which I do not now remember, though I was glad that at least one doctor was finally going to look into his problems. His doctor in New York, as far as I was concerned, was totally do-nothing, battling with whom was one of my heaviest crosses. Along with this news came Swami's instruction for me to proceed on to Marshfield nevertheless, as he would be going there after getting out of hospital. I had a hard time with this, sensing that Swami would not be in condition to go to Marshfield after all, and that indeed he might leave his body while I was up there. I was very reluctant to leave New York until I knew for sure that his condition was stabilized, and for the first time in my life I disobeyed him. I knew that he was keen for me to get some rest, and that was almost certainly why he had asked me to go on.

Marshfield, 1976, the year before Swami's death: Swami,
Rabbi Asher Block, and Swami Sarvagatananda.

But, at the same time, there were other considerations. For one thing, if Swami returned to the Center while I was in Marshfield, how would Jeanne cope? No, my "rest" would have to wait. Courtenaye and I visited Swami the next day and he was delighted to see us, making us feel, as ever, like goddesses. That was it! I would stay, along with Courtenaye and Jeanne, to take care of Swami in Manhattan, if necessary.

It was indeed a long, hot summer. Swami came back to the Center and we tended him as he struggled to keep up his energy and keep going. Mercifully, the assistant swami was away most of the time, bombing around the Western seaboard and letting off steam, denigrating Swami, the Center and its members to anyone who would listen to him. A day or two before the assistant's return from the West coast, Swami looked at me sadly and said, with a touch of conspiracy, "He thinks he is returning to a rat hole!" Certainly, everything was at low ebb, with Swami's health and energy so diminished and with no determined cause; the assistant so refractory and troublesome; and no one but Courtenaye, Jeanne and myself available to help. I realized that the devotion I had so longed for a few years before, envying the swami-swooners, could take different forms. Although I was no good at gushing, I was absolutely determined to stick with Swami till every cent of my savings ran out, to put up with the assistant in order to do so, and to somehow ignore Jeanne's inanity. That, too, was a form of devotion—my form.

Swami, too, was becoming increasingly difficult. His poor health prevented him from giving lectures and meeting with people—the essence of his work—and he was quite distraught over it. This was his reason for being, and now that it was taken away, he felt that his life had no further meaning. His apparent inability to surrender to divine will bothered me; but of course, that is another stage in the process. First comes the relinquishment of all that one has committed oneself to—in Swami's case very much against his meditative grain. Over and over he would say, "What a tragedy! I can't do the work any more!" I understood only later that such reactions were less about personal ego and more about a commitment to others than I could understand at the time. Certainly, seeing the performance of his assistant, Swami had little reason to feel hopeful about the future. As the assistant swami took over lectures and interviews, fewer and fewer Westerners were showing up, while a coterie of Indians was beginning to form, whose commitment was more to Indian culture than to inner spirituality as Swami had understood and taught it.

Swami had always been adamant that Vedanta work in the West was primarily for Westerners, with major emphasis on meditation, study and other inner practices, combined with work for the good of others rather than one's own aggrandizement. He, like Swami Vivekananda before him, understood that the West had had enough of organization, hierarchy, and outer action and achievement; what was needed now was to balance the West's massive control over the physical world with strong commitments to and practice of the science of inner experience. To that end, he heavily emphasized meditation and study of the Vedanta from a purely Western point of view. He wanted us to understand Vedanta *as Westerners*—that is, with our own reason and understanding—and not as Indians, whose minds, for the most part (though this is changing nowadays), are more taken up with myth and ritual and unthinking acceptance of the ancient, hierarchical status quo. To that end he strongly discouraged us from dabbling around in culty Indian myths, rituals, or assuming Indian names or social customs. He wanted us to remain Westerners and would say, "You are Westerners! Be Westerners! Assimilate Vedanta in your own way!" He well knew the lure of exotic culture and the degree to which identifying with it could totally distract students from the real work of self-transformation, transcendence and transfiguration—the hard, difficult and utterly essential stuff.

His clear position had resulted in a large following while he was stronger physically, and an utterly dedicated group of people like myself as he entered the twilight. But, before his very eyes, the assistant was pandering largely to Indians, dismantling all that he had worked for—and visibly driving Westerners away. Swami never spoke of all this; but it seems obvious that this undermining of his work was causing him great distress and fueling his pathetic lamentations.

This was the troubling background, but there was more. As Swami's health rapidly deteriorated and he felt more and more that he could no longer be effective, he put more and more pressure on me as his "medical advisor", letting off a lot of steam, which I interpreted as his expecting me to perform some miracle. On a number of occasions I had noticed his tendency to think of doctors as omniscient and omnipotent, (the old-fashioned view, which, of course, doctors themselves had done a lot to foster) and had told him every time that the patient is as responsible as the doctor for the ultimate result. But now he was reverting to type and expecting me to pull some rabbit out of a hat, all the more exasperating as he steadfastly refused to provide the lab specimens required to make a diagnosis from his devastating symptoms. The devotees were fraught with anxiety and Jeanne, in particular, was unusually aggressive and confrontational, accusing me of "doing nothing", of "dominating" the situation, "excluding others", and so on. I would have been only too glad to have had extra medical help, but knew full well that all of this was merely the symptoms of general systems failure in Swami's body. Inwardly, my mind was slowing beginning to visualize his deathbed and how his last moments might take place.

One day Swami spoke to me about his health situation, making me, an inexperienced medical doctor, feel tremendous pressure to do something, but completely stymied by his refusal to produce a specimen so we could make a diagnosis. Finally, frustrated by his irrationality (and also depressed by it, for it had been his rationality that had always attracted me) I simply told him, "Swami, if you can't cooperate with me, we cannot get a diagnosis or plan treatment. Without your cooperation there is nothing further that I can do. Please relieve me of the burden of 'medical advisor'." Needless to say, I felt like a rat. I did not have supernatural powers and if Swami could not be rational and cooperative, that was the end.

What I could not understand was that Swami, like anyone else, was under overwhelming pressure as he saw his life's work crumbling away, and had been letting off steam to me as the person who might be able to bear it. The swami-swooners would have shriveled up and died to hear Swami's lamentations and complaints—it was just too human; they had made an idol out of him. How difficult it must have been for him to live in that atmosphere! In many ways, he loved me because I was not the swooning type, but much more human and down to earth, dealing with his issues quite pragmatically. Later, as I became more familiar with the literature on Swami Vivekananda, I saw a similar relationship between him and his Irish disciple, Sister Nivedita. Vivekananda was totally lionized and idolized in India, but he knew he was dying of diabetes and had only a few years to live in which he could get his life's work underway. He was terribly agonized, but could not let off steam with his Indian followers, who totally relied on him for courage and inspiration, and looked up to him as a sort of father-figure. It was to Sister Nivedita, that sturdy Irishwoman with whom he had a much more human, spontaneous relationship than with most of his other followers, that he lamented and exposed his sufferings in letters that were sometimes utterly heart-breaking. Perhaps as a Westerner more attuned to the human condition, she had been able to absorb it all and still adore her leader with undiminished intensity, dedicating the remainder of her stormy life to bringing his work to fruition.

   In the depths of all this, one day Swami called me to his room, where I went with the utmost reluctance, not willing to go through any more charades. As I opened the door Swami came rapidly toward me, holding out the filled specimen container. "I got this, only because of your earnestness," he said with great animation, thrusting it into my hands. One side of me was vastly relieved, another impressed by his determination to respond despite his disabilities, and another wanted to laugh out loud. What a drama! For all I know his Hindu taboos, rising up from the collective subconscious, had taken him over and made him refuse to cooperate with Western medical science. In such a context I had succeeded in taking him beyond, to the level of rationality—no mean feat, as I was to discover with the swamis I would deal with later.

   However, the tests turned up nothing diagnostic and Swami was visibly sinking, while the hysteria at the Center was mounting up to the skies: Swami was the idol of so many—especially women—and they could not at all face what was going on. Finally, Erik, Courtenaye and I spoke with Swami together, urging him to go to hospital for further tests, with me explaining why. After a long struggle, he finally agreed, adding,

"They are going to kill me this time"—not exactly a soothing balm to my soul. And, as I had feared, no helpful results came out of Swami's brief hospitalization. I was totally in the doghouse with him, Jeanne, and the whole membership. The assistant was jabbering to whomever would listen about Swami's "senility", thus stirring everything up to the max, and weakening our resolve to serve to the end. I found him utterly intolerable and at the same time was disgusted with my own intellectuality, which seemed to be at the root of all my troubles. One morning I packed up all of my books on science and psychology and trundled them over to a senior citizen center, determined to put them to good use, now that I was finished with my intellect. I have no idea what the old folks made of books by the likes of Karl Popper and Michael Polyani, theoreticians in the world of science!

The final act in my drama with Swami took place near the beginning of November, nineteen seventy-seven. I was utterly baffled by his ongoing symptoms and their non-response to medical intervention and began to wonder if perhaps this was a case of vicarious atonement. Although Ramakrishna Vedantists reject the glorification of the notion of a life being taken for other lives, they do acknowledge that the holy, by removing the conflicts and bad habits of their disciples, can get physically sick from doing so, a fact that is supported, at least by circumstantial evidence, from medical science. This observation has been made in the lives of Ramakrishna, Sarada Devi, and Swami Vivekananda, though little was made of it in order to emphasize the importance of one's own efforts and will to grow spiritually. The great ones can and do shoulder the burdens of others—but lightly, not encouraging others to give up on their own responsibility for growth. Swami, particularly, was emphatic about this, screwing up his nose at the very term vicarious atonement, and therefore I hesitated to ask him about his own situation. But I knew he was the only person who would know, and finally made up my mind to tackle him on it.

He had not been seeing people for some time on account of his illness, but he agreed to see me. As I entered, he greeted me with great affection and my heart quailed, sensing that my mood was not altogether in tune with his. He was not in a mood for discussion, but this was my only opportunity and I had to take it. I sat down and looked at the ground, summoning all my self-confidence; and finally said, "Swami, I want to ask you about your illness." He looked at me kindly. I had already decided that he would not listen to a long introduction, so I went straight to the point. "Swami, your sickness is very mysterious and cannot be explained by medical science. Could it be psychological or spiritual in origin?" I was scrupulously avoiding the vicarious atonement trap, as I knew he would not like it, but in doing so I was also opening other doors with words of much less accuracy.

He stared at me for what seemed an eternity, and then came the deluge. "Psychological! How dare you use that word! Psychological!!! And spiritual!! What does sickness have to do with spirituality?" Taking up the book of his guru, Swami Brahmananda, in his hand, he said, "*This* is spiritual! It has nothing to do with physical illness." He was extremely agitated. After a pause he said, more calmly, "To ask me a question like this, you must be very unspiritual. Yes, you are very unspiritual."

I was totally unprepared for this and certainly unable to bear radical put-down from the one person who had helped me develop spiritually. It was especially difficult then, when I was so under attack from other quarters. Where on earth was he coming from? Didn't he know about psychosomatic disease, where spiritual or psychological states have definite effects on the body? Was there a complete divide in his mind between body, mind, and spirit—harking back to the old Medieval view, which, to me, Ramakrishna and Vivekananda had done so much to remove? What good would such Medievalism do me? After all was said and done, was he a traditional Hindu, emphasizing only the inner world and unable to relate it to other worlds of human existence? All of this hit me hard, but the worst pain was his high-handed dismissal of my aspirations to spirituality.

Ramakrishna once said that there are two kinds of bullock—those who sit down if you touch their tails, and those who frisk about. The latter are the better bullocks—and indeed, tail-touching is a test of the mettle of bullocks. I think I was the frisky kind, for I found myself saying, "Well, Swami! If I am not spiritual, I am wasting my time here. There is no point in sitting here any longer. Goodbye!" And I darted to the door, fully determined never to come back.

Swami was nothing if not a chameleon, able to change his tactics rapidly to deal with people. As my hand closed on the doorknob, he said quietly, "Come here and sit down." I stood there, holding the knob, extremely unwilling to go back. The simple equation was: If he rejected me, I rejected him. He repeated himself several times before I let go and most reluctantly went back and sat beside him. He said quietly, "At the moment you are unspiritual. But you will become spiritual." I said not a word, for this, to say the least, was cold comfort. I simply wanted to get out and get on with my life. But something made me sit there in the twilight until, finally, he said, "Alright. You may go now."

My self-esteem was mortally wounded and I was tempted to fall back into one of my black moods. But the work was so overwhelming that I had to keep going and somehow I did keep on with my routines, albeit with a deep pain in my soul. That he had dismissed me as unspiritual after all my struggles was terribly disheartening and I began to doubt that I would ever make spiritual progress at all. One evening after his supper he said to me mildly, "When I say things to people, I do it for their good." I felt sure that that was true, but did not connect it up with the scene of about two weeks before. It took ten years before I could do that.

In thinking all of this through at that time I saw three possibilities: One, he saw that I was getting swell-headed and wanted to deflate me before leaving his body. Two, he indeed did not understand psychosoma and his scolding was merely that of a traditional Hindu (emphasizing the world of spirit at the expense of that of the body) lashing out at a Western mind (which sees body and mind on a continuum), a scenario I was later to go through again and again with other swamis who refused to concede anything to Westerners in the way of spiritual knowledge or psychology. Three, he wanted to cut off any personal attachments I had for him personally, to prepare me for his impending death. All or none of these may be true; but certainly this episode gave me a good shaking and raised doubts in my mind about the swamis' ultimate understanding of the Western psyche. Swami had been outstanding in his ability to make space for me; to help me grow intellectually as well as spiritually, but his behavior since getting sick had made me wonder if indeed the Hindu mind can compass that of the West. It was as if his more flexible persona were slipping and the underlying Hindu root stock were expressing itself in his inability to deal with bodily ailments and the issue of psychosoma.

But there was another dimension, which I was able to understand in hindsight, thirty years later: He was getting me ready—perhaps unconsciously—for the truly dark night I was to go through on the next loop of the spiral, where all possible human support and love were to be taken away from me and I was to walk the spiritual path utterly alone, facing myself directly, with nothing between the unpleasant facts on the surface and the inner light shining so constantly and so brightly. I would have to face utter rejection, utter loneliness, utter self-doubt, with essentially no one who could understand and help me. I now realized that Swami's apparent cruelty was indeed a wake-up call for the next phase of my work. For five years he had given me an emotional bed of roses to lie on, speaking spiritually, but I am sure he knew that was to last not much longer and I would be called upon to go out into the dark and scout for the enemy without any contact with "base" or support system to give me confidence.

And finally, a thought that established itself in my mind even later: Even if I had been right, he would never have given a stamp of approval to the idea. To be able to offer vicarious atonement is the mark of an extremely developed spiritual personality, which he would never, never agree he was. Swami was always vehement in his rejection of the label *guru*, or even *teacher*; and would he agree to being called a saint, especially one with highly developed spiritual powers? His humility was radical, totally unwilling to accept any sort of label, particularly those which elevated him in any way whatsoever—a trait which I later discovered was more than unusual among the swamis. He was indeed immersed in the bliss of purity (Pavitrananda); refusing, even with a deeply damaged brain, to compromise on his understanding of himself as nothing but spirit, unconstricted by any name or human quality. This idea has taken hold in my mind because just before I left his room he gave me another chance to explain what I had meant by my impertinent question. I told him earnestly about my fears that the behavior of myself and others had somehow made him so desperately ill. Put that way and with so much sincerity, he received my words in silence, looking at me with what I can only describe as ineffable love, tinged with the admiration he so often expressed to me, even in words. He made the slightest shake of his head, a movement difficult to interpret; but it seemed to me that it was not so much denial of what I was saying as surprise that I would even think of, far less see, what he was up to.

But all of this is armchair philosophizing at a later date. The immediate concern was dramatic and urgent, leaving no time for analysis and digestion. Two weeks after the climactic "big scene" I had a dream around five am about Swami Vivekananda that was so clear and intense that I was quite dazzled by it; but its meaning and potential were to be revealed to me only twenty-four years later. Then I rose and sat to meditate.

About an hour later the phone rang and Jeanne asked me to come to the Center as Swami was "not well". No further specifications, but I realized something was not good, and immediately went over. Jeanne opened the door, her face unusually white and puffy. "He's upstairs," she said, uncharacteristically laconic. I ran up to his room and opened the door. I saw him lying on the bathroom floor with John kneeling beside him. Even from the distance of the door I could see he was dead, but went forward quickly, just in case. John looked up at me, watery-eyed and agitated. "I tried to do mouth to mouth resuscitation," he said pathetically. Good soul! Always willing to come forward and take responsibility.

John had found Swami's body after five-thirty, the time he usually went to help him with his morning's activities. The alarm was still ringing, set for five-thirty, so Swami had left the body before that. I examined the body and ascertained that it had been dead for a little over an hour. He had probably died at five am. No sooner had I ascertained that than I realized that that was when Vivekananda had appeared so vividly in my dream. That had been Swami's way of taking leave of me! I was flabbergasted; but of course there was a deep psychic bond between us, beyond the realm of words. It was in many ways quite natural that he should take his final leave of me on the psychic plane.

It was, however, a tremendous shock to have him leave so suddenly and without any formal farewells. We all knew he was close to death, but I for one had never imagined it would be like this. I had envisioned a process of slow detachment and formal separations—but Swami, always deeply adverse to rituals and formalities, had taken the quickest exit. In one dimension it fitted right on in with all he had been; but in another it was a terrible shock, from which it was to take me ten years to recover.

But again, there was no time to wallow in emotion. Swami's doctor was on vacation in Florida (as he always seemed to be!) and I had to call his son, also a doctor, to report Swami's death. He at once said, "Swami has not been seen medically for over three weeks; this will have to be a medical examiner's case." I expostulated with the doctor, reminding him that he knew full well what Swami's story was and that there was no need for the medical examiner, but he was adamant. Maybe he thought we were a cult, and that Swami's death was probably due to malfeasance. Within half an hour the police arrived in screaming cars and thundered up the stairs to Swami's room to make their investigations for the medical examiner. I was busy getting breakfast for Jeanne and Courtenaye, who were like limp rag dolls; but I got upstairs as quickly as I could. When I entered Swami's room I was horrified to see that the police had tied labels on to everything, including Swami's toe—exhibits, no doubt, for a potential court case.

"Get that thing off the swami's toe!" I barked. "How dare you come in here and treat us with so little respect!!!" The officers looked scared. "Where is the supervising officer?" I demanded. "Ma'am, he is on his way." "Well, don't you do one more thing till he gets here!" I shouted as I pounded downstairs to answer the doorbell. It was the police sergeant, whom I immediately took to task for the insensitivity of his officers. "Ma'am, just let me go upstairs and take a look at this. I will be right back." He was true to his word, and came back downstairs a few minutes later. "I have to apologize" he said. "Every day we get calls like this to what turn out to be cults and almost every time we find there are drugs, stolen goods and whatnot. But I can see at once that this place is not like that. This is a genuine religious organization. My men will remove the labels and leave."

Not long afterward the doctor from the medical examiner's office arrived and asked to speak with me. By this time the assistant swami had joined the fray, and I was rather surprised and put out that he tagged along with us. He had so habitually put me down and jeered at me that I felt extremely uncomfortable speaking with the doctor in his presence. However, there was no choice—he was, after all, now the swami in charge of the Center—and so I had to make the best of it. As I engaged in discussion with the doctor, of course, we got into increasingly technical language and I noted out of the corner of my eye that the assistant was looking back and forth between us as we hashed out the situation, not fully comprehending, but realizing that I knew what I was talking about. I was able to inform the doctor of Swami's increasingly serious neurological condition, my working diagnosis of dementia with arteriosclerosis and most likely a final stroke. He had little trouble accepting what I said, perhaps influenced by the fact that I had worked in neuropathology at Harvard Medical School, and quickly brought the matter to a close. "Dr. MacPhail," he said, "I am sorry you have been put to all this inconvenience. This case seems to be quite clear, and I will simply sign the death certificate and release the body to you." I longed to ask for an autopsy, feeling a real need to know exactly what had been going on in Swami's brain, but I also knew that it would raise a firestorm in the Center. Did we need that? I was pretty sure of the diagnosis, the medical examiner's officer had agreed with me, and I would have to settle for that. I had decided to save my energy for other struggles which I knew were ahead.

One problem solved. On to the next one, much more difficult: Dealing with the assistant. After the officer left, the swami turned to me, intensely emotional and out of control. "I had no idea that Pavitrananda Swami would die so soon! I am not ready to take over this Center! Why did you not warn me? You are a medical doctor! Don't you want to help me?" I stared at him in total disbelief. He was blaming me for not warning him that Swami could die any moment! Was he not capable of seeing that for himself? "Swami," I began, "I told you over and over and over how fragile he was." "I thought you were exaggerating, that you were just fussing over him!" "Well, Swami, if you chose to ignore what I said, there is nothing I can do about that. Now we just have to get on with what needs to be done."

He suddenly became very serious and said contritely, "I owe you an apology. I thought you were a foolish child, but now I realize that you are a medical doctor, that you are used to having authority. You dealt with the medical officer most efficiently." Again, I was flabbergasted. What was wrong with this man? Why couldn't he take people seriously and treat them with respect? What did it take to be given any sort of status at all in his world? Then I realized that, from his point of view, it was not a small thing to apologize to someone whom he had been treating with so much disrespect. I tried to warm up to him as I looked at him standing before me, all rumpled, out of joint and inadequate. I should have graciously said nothing and moved on; but as it was, there was so much that needed to be done at the Center, which he had been blocking with his blustering, that I foolishly said, "Swami, can you take seriously the various requests we have been making in order to run the Center more efficiently?" At once he snapped into his bossy stance and shouted, "Be quiet! You really are just a child!"

That was the end. There was so much to do for Swami's funeral and memorial service that there was no time to spend on emotional nonsense and I just plunged in and forgot completely about the swami. The next few weeks were such a vortex of activity that it passed like a blur. Swami Sarvagatananda arrived the day after Swami's death. He had been visiting in Sacramento, but came at once to be with us and help us through the unexpectedly abrupt transition. I made his breakfast and sat with him for most of the morning, telling him about my anxieties and particularly hopes for moving on and creating a new life for myself. We discussed convent life and the possibility of my moving on to it. Of what he said in the course of the conversation the one thing that remains with me is his comment, "The women still can't stand on their own feet. They need *real* leadership." If only I had fully understood the implications of that remark! Just what happens when there is inadequate leadership (and people who have no concept of what leadership means) was yet to be unveiled before me. If I had had any idea of what was in store I would have gladly returned to my profession and worked to make a go of it. But I had the dreamy idea that monasticism would be the best way to develop spiritually and was quite set in my resolve to move in that direction.

Swami had been an important figure in the order, both politically and spiritually. Every swami that could make the effort showed up at his memorial service some two weeks later. For me this meant getting through Thanksgiving (dinner for twenty or so) and then going full tilt into preparations to feed something like eight swamis for a week. I had a crew of ladies chopping onions and other basics for the Indian cooking that I was going to be immersed in almost day and night. It was so cold outside that we stored all of these items in the downstairs entranceway, where it froze over—saved refrigerator space! Courtenaye was so overwhelmed by Swami's death and the financial and administrative side of it (for which she, as the treasurer, was responsible) that she was, for all practical purposes, out of the domestic picture; and Jeanne, of course, was never really in it. Thankfully, several of the younger women came forward to help, so we managed without too much trouble. Annie, one of the nuns from Santa Barbara, showed up a few days before the swamis arrived, all ready to help out in any way she could. Her parents, particularly her father, were devoted to Vedanta and to Swami in particular, and she, like them, was his disciple. A trained nun, she was used to working in a group situation and immediately proved to be of the utmost help. Steady, available, and good-humored, she was a godsend in this quite desperate moment of my life.

And it was indeed desperate. The assistant swami was proving to be a total nightmare. Totally discombobulated emotionally, he kept yelling orders and commands at random, getting in the way and generally holding us up. I particularly resented the fact that regular batches of Indians kept showing up, the women howling and weeping in formal mourning (for someone they did not really know or, in some cases, had not even met), and him yelling at us to feed them and take care of them! I felt that Jeanne, as his "pet", should be taking care of such things, but she was completely unable to do anything; Swami's death had completely overwhelmed her. As I served up rice pudding and other such items to people I had never met—and who did not seem inclined to do any work whatsoever, including washing the dishes—I am sorry to say I was muttering imprecations under my breath. I remembered Sarada Devi's immortal words, "No one is a stranger. Learn to make the whole world your own", and wished that I could have felt that way about these people.

It was my first exposure to Indian culturalism, rather than to the lovely people Swami had drawn to himself, sincere, hardworking and identified with what was going on at the Center. Swami was almost notorious for the way he kept most Indians at arm's length—he maintained that most of them were merely cultural Hindus, with no real interest in serious spiritual life. To him, they were freeloaders, showing up mostly for the food at our various functions. That is why he had our functions in the morning, when breakfast was served rather than in the evening, with dinner; he knew it was more difficult for Indians—mostly family people who had to work—to show up in the morning than at night. He had been determined to weed out the Indian tares from the wheat and had been quite bloody-minded about it. From one side, it was terrible; but from another he had created an incredibly intense and focused group of both Westerners and Indians, all of them deeply serious about their spiritual practice and all closely-knit in shared aspiration and work. I was profoundly grateful to have had the experience of that wonderful companionship and regarded all who were in the circle as my own brothers and sisters, Indians as well as Westerners. That was the main reason I was so put out by this "social" attitude of the assistant—just because people were Indians, were we supposed to drop our work and jump to their tune?

It was really exhausting. And the assistant piled on insult to injury by constantly hollering that he had never seen such cold, unfeeling people as the devotees at our Center! "Why," he shouted at me, "you have not shed even one tear for your guru!" I glared at him, but said nothing. There was no point in speaking. But inwardly I thought, "Swami, there is no time for tears! I am too busy taking care of your Indian camp-followers!" Had I only realized that this is the way things were going to be from here on in, no matter where I went! Swami and his generation had been most unusual in their utter dedication to their Western flock; they saw their mission in the West as being primarily for the Americans, not for Indians, in line with the vision of Vivekananda. These swamis seldom, if ever, went back to visit India, for they identified so much with the West that they immersed themselves in American culture and history and indeed learned to "make Westerners their own".

But, of course, there were not too many Indians around before the sixties, when the immigration laws were changed and floods of Hindus began to arrive in the United States. Most of them were orthodox and built temples for themselves; but there was an increasing trickle to the Ramakrishna Mission centers, even though they were, to orthodox Hindus, rather heterodox and westernized. No doubt the swamis realized that they would have to accommodate these people, though with someone like Swami, it would not be at the cost of the Westerners or the quality of the work. In our assistant I was seeing for the first time the trend that was already taking over, of permitting Hindu culture to predominate, emphasizing more social and ritual aspects, while bypassing the intensive, inner work that I at least had come to expect from the swamis. Their minds were thoroughly Indian, as evidenced by their almost annual visits to India, the overwhelming emphasis on Indian custom and observance and the increasingly obvious élitism, paternalism, closed-mindedness and authoritarianism that became evident in short order.

Of course, at that time I did not realize that our assistant was simply part of a trend. I just found him exasperating. Had I realized that this was what I could now expect to find wherever I went, I would have made a completely different decision about my life—but as it was, my image of swamis was still that of Pavitrananda and Sarvagatananda, two men who had so radically improved my life that I was eternally grateful to them. And there were others, two of whom I met at Swami's memorial service. One was Swami Aseshananda, the eccentric, elf-like, and utterly adorable swami from Portland, Oregon, whose major claim to fame was that he was the disciple of Sarada Devi. One evening he gave a talk on his

association with her, of which I remember one particular highlight. The swami was rational and quite "Western", in some ways. He described how reluctant he had been, as a young man, to stop a tennis match he was playing to go and see Sarada Devi. But his friends had prevailed, and he had been ushered into the room where she was formally receiving men, her face veiled. Perhaps this had been a bit of a disappointment to him, for he had not been particularly impressed. And, as it happened, once he had gone outside he realized that he had left something important in her reception room, and had had to go back for it. He was a very young man, transparent and pure-hearted; when Mother's "bouncer" saw him, he permitted him to go upstairs to retrieve what he was looking for, without insisting on the usual protocols for men. All the other men had left and Mother was now relaxing with her women friends.

She had removed her veil and was sitting "at ease" when the young man entered. He said, "I went into her room, preoccupied about getting what I had lost—and then I saw her face!" At this he looked out at us, his own face beaming with indescribable joy. The whole room seemed to reverberate with spiritual rapture; it was obvious just how wonderful she had been and how radically this vision had affected the young man. Naturally, this moment was a highlight for me. Without words it conveyed something of the spiritual grandeur of Mother, whom I felt was holding me in her arms, always protecting me and guiding me at that time.

The other swami who made a big impression on me was Swami Shraddhananda from Sacramento, a tiny little man, always smiling and ever ready for some sort of innocent, spiritual mischief. He too

was a disciple of one of Ramakrishna's disciples, though junior to Swami Aseshananda. I don't remember anything particularly that he said; I just enjoyed the happy, impish atmosphere he carried with him, so open and welcoming. It was utterly different from the heavy, condemning, crushing atmosphere I had been feeling around the junior swamis with whom I had had difficulty in the previous year or two.

One day the younger swamis all went off on some excursion, led by Erik, if I remember rightly. The two older swamis stayed at the Center and had lunch together. As meal-coordinator, cook, and bottle-washer, I was present, along with Courtenaye and one or two other close women. Swami Shraddhananda asked me something about Swami's medical problem, which got me going on how much Swami had been incapacitated and how he had so amazingly remained totally above the whole physical drama. For, despite some of our passages-at-arms, he had been basically serene, loving, and always concerned for us—so utterly different from other patients with similar physical problems I had dealt with in my professional career. I may have mentioned the day when I felt I saw the Atman radiating from him—one of the high-water marks of my association with him, and something I felt these exalted spiritual swamis would appreciate. I suddenly realized that I was really shooting off my mouth and paused; how would these men take it—and what sort of effect was it having on the other women? People so often don't like to hear revelations of that sort.

But this time, with the two elderly, compassionate swamis, I felt something quite different. They were looking at me, their eyes beaming, and the women were also smiling gently. I felt that somehow I had said something that had helped to lift them above the smothering cloud of grief they were struggling with. It was a moment of blessedness, and one that created a strong bond between me and the two swamis, both of whom were to play a significant role in my ongoing development. They both made kindly and appreciative comments and invited me to come and visit them on the West Coast, an invitation I felt great enthusiasm to accept, though of course I had no money left to speak of.

That was the glory of Swami's memorial for me. But there was the other side, too. We had a gathering of all of the active swamis in America, and it was inevitable that they would get into discussions of protocol and policy, led almost always by Swami B., now leader of the large and wealthy Southern Californian Center, and an inveterate politician. Most of the swamis were Bengalis, but not all; so they spoke in English, and I was, therefore, able to understand what they were discussing. What particularly struck me was the introduction by Swami B. of the question as to what should be done with the monastic women. He made no bones about the fact that the swamis had to find a way of divesting themselves of the responsibility for these women, for whose right to monasticism, of course, the previous generation of swamis in Northern California and Southern California had fought so long and so fiercely. Swami B. seemed to feel that the time had come to set the women up on their own, handing over responsibility to them to run their own affairs, as had happened in India. I turned this over in my mind: Our founder, Swami Vivekananda, had always wanted the women to be completely independent, but it had taken fifty years before it had happened in India, while in the West, without a Vedantic tradition or, in many cases, even a monastic tradition behind them, the women were very new to the whole concept of a women's order. And hadn't Swami Sarvagatananda just told me that the women as yet had no real leadership? Without leadership, there can be no real organization or order worthy of the name.

This was, of course, of extreme interest to me, poised as I was to consider joining the order. Yes, Swami Vivekananda had definitely said that the women should manage their own affairs. Why, indeed, were they still dependent on the swamis? Why did there have to be this rather disagreeable discussion going on before me? What was wrong? It was clear that Swami B. was speaking for one side of the issue, coming from a place where he had had quite a battle with the nuns he supervised; but the other swamis, particularly the more senior ones, were not agreeing with him. They may, perhaps, have agreed that ultimately the women would have to take over their own responsibility, but they seemed to feel that, for the moment, they needed further training, further preparation, and development of leadership. All of this was of absorbing interest to me, along with the fact that these men were talking as if I was not there. It didn't seem to bother them a bit that a woman, a potential monastic candidate, was taking in all that they were saying—and registering it deeply, I may add. I thought that perhaps I just was able to merge with the woodwork more than some; but another explanation might have been that the swamis just didn't care, thinking I was yet another silly, airhead woman.

One of the swamis at the table was the head of the Vedanta Society of Northern California, who was running a convent there and was, therefore, the other person qualified to speak about the monastic women. He, however, said little, permitting Swami B., who was his senior (and, as I later learned, his adversary) to dominate the discussion. I had seen him speak at Swami Nikhilananda's memorial service and found his more up-to-date presentation, using current imagery, interesting. He was quiet, ultra serious, fair-skinned for an Indian, with large, yellowish eyes. On leaving New York, he came to take his leave of the ladies downstairs and said to me, "Please come and visit us in Northern California. We have a retreat in the country, a guest house in the city, and, for a select few, our convent." He said this very portentously, I felt; and I wondered if it was an invitation to join the convent. Things seemed to be moving in the direction I had been contemplating!

I became friends with Annie, the nun from Santa Barbara, and had many talks with her about monasticism and convents. "You should come and join our convent," she said hospitably. For some strange reason, when the actual C word was spoken, I started to imagine all the reasons why it would not be a good idea to go to one. Mostly I felt I was too freethinking, too independent, too secular. Recently I had seen the sleeve of an old LP record, with a Roman Catholic nun looking piously up into the light streaming from an altar, and had simply shuddered. I could never be pious, that I knew at once. I could never submit to anything I did not fully understand and believe in, nor could I mindlessly go along with the rather silly sentimentality most religious women are prone to. I said nothing about this to Annie, of course; but I did note that she, at least, seemed pretty normal and down to earth. Maybe the other nuns were like that, too; and if, so, maybe there would be a place for me.

The ensuing period was excruciating, learning to live without Swami, facing the fact that I had practically no money at all, and struggling inwardly with my conscience. I had invested so much of my time in medicine, for which the British Government and also my family had paid—was I going to throw that away? Was I going to turn my back on my idea of serving humanity? Then again, I had never gotten around to asking Swami about the decision to join a convent—would he have approved? I set myself to going through all I had written down of our conversations over the past five years to see if I could find guidelines, underlining anything that seemed to support the decision.

One side of me kept saying, "If monasticism helps you grow spiritually, you will be serving humanity, in some ways more than as a medical doctor. As a doctor you cured bodies; as a spiritually developed person, you may be able to cure souls." That made sense, particularly when I thought of how much Swami had done for me. How many doctors could have done anything like it? I could never expect to be as great spiritually as he, but to get anywhere near it would certainly be worthwhile. Then again, my intense study of our discussions led me to believe that Swami would have approved of my going on to formal monasticism. The previous five years had been for sure monastic, though of an informal type. I knew I had made huge strides forward, particularly with the deep conflicts that my parents had occasioned. The wheels were turning, turning, turning, and every week my money was less and less . . . In some ways the conclusion was foregone, but there was still a strong pull from the medical side. It seemed that it would not be difficult to call up Dr. Bill and get a job at Harvard, get back in the saddle and go on to research in neuropathology. That way, I would be fulfilling my original dream.

My approach to solving problems is to study the data intensely, ride the emotion and finally have some sort of psychic experience which points me in the right direction. This time was no different. I had a dream in which Dr. Bill, the symbol of my old life, and the swami from Northern California, the symbol of the possible new, met each other. All I remember is them staring at each other, each with large, limpid greenish-golden eyes. Their stares were fixed and purposeful, making me understand what was going on. Would Bill draw me back to neuropathology, or would the Northern California swami draw me over to the convent? Finally Bill lowered his eyes and I knew that it was to be the convent. Not a very "rational" method of making a decision, I suppose, but powerful. Of course, I believe it was really my own inner voice taking those forms to speak to me—it was not that I was invested in the actual men I was dreaming about. I had put in so many years of effort, so much thought, so much prayer, so much meditation; this was the resultant of all of it, my inner desire expressing itself. As always, I could not understand at all why my inner voice couldn't speak to me rationally, but somehow that is the way it is. My job was to learn how to listen, to watch, to become sensitive to the most subtle expression in this non-rational mode. Certainly this dream, coming at a time when a decision absolutely had to be made, was decisive.

CHAPTER 23

CALIFORNIA: THE SECOND SPIRAL WINDS ONWARD TO THE THIRD 1978

I was now thirty-seven years old, with fifteen hundred dollars to my name; cut loose from Swami, the person who had been most important to me during the strenuous cycle I had just come through; and contemplating a complete break with my past. I fled up to Boston for a few days to talk with Swami Sarvagatananda, and received his blessings on my plan to join one of the Californian convents. This positive input heartened me and gave me the courage to write to the heads of the Southern and Northern Californian convents respectively; to make plans to visit my family; and to get all of my things ready for the next departure in my life.

It was just a year shy of twenty years since I had gone to Edinburgh, making a definite break with all of the struggle and confusion of my childhood, moving on to the vocation of my choice in defiance of my father. During the twenty years of this second cycle I had become aware of the pattern in which my life seemed to be unfolding and, poised to move in a totally new direction, couldn't help noticing that in the same way that my father had cut me loose with his cruel reviling of my aspiration to be a doctor, Swami's death had similarly left me alone, having to make a difficult decision without his support and blessing. With no money and no enthusiasm to return to medicine, I was on a sticky wicket, from which I could see no way to fulfilling my dream. Would things work out now as they had then, or would I indeed have to return to my work? It was not that I did not like my work; by now I was convinced that I would do far more good with my life by deepening my conscious level, for I could see, as clear as day, that without spiritual depth nothing is really of avail. Despite the fact that I had worked hard, done well and indeed had accomplished a lot, it was my grandmother, Swami and Swami Sarvagatananda who had really mattered, and whose influence on me had accomplished something of enduring value. They had challenged me to become a deeper, better person, and had also helped me to do so.

However, the assistant swami's behavior was not helping me at all in this struggle. He would not stop badgering me about "throwing away" my medical work, which he felt was far more important than trying to live a deep spiritual life. "Why can't you live a spiritual life and be a doctor?" he kept shouting. I realized that he probably felt that Westerners, particularly women, were basically incapable of being inward and meditative, an attitude I was subsequently to run across in many Indians. Then again, he had not the slightest idea what it was like to work in reductionistic, materialistic America. I said as little as possible, but he did cause me a lot of anguish. I held on to what Swami had told me, to the recent dream, and to Swami Sarvagatananda's blessings. It was so excruciating that I finally realized that the swami, without realizing it, was doing this to help me leave the Center. I had become so utterly identified with the West Seventy-First Street Vedanta Society that I had feared I might not be able to leave it; but his endless stream of put-downs and haranguing were, minute by minute, severing all my connection with it. After all, what had made it so precious was Swami's presence. Now that he was gone, what was there, really? A narrow brownstone, dark inside, overheated on account of Jeanne's obsession with the swami's supposed comfort, on a nondescript street in central Manhattan, and now purveying a brand of Vedanta with which I could in no way identify.

That spring it snowed to the max. The roof of a large, brand new building in Connecticut collapsed under the weight of the snowfall, and the streets of Manhattan were either grist for cross-country skiers or mere footpaths between huge banks of shoveled snow, yellow with dog urine and hazardous with their poop. I felt rather woebegone as I sat in the JFK airport waiting to leave New York, but when I alighted in Los Angeles to bright sunshine, flowering trees and endless piles of garden flowers lying on the altar, I felt as if I had been transported to heaven while still in my body. I was to spend a week in the convent in Hollywood, and another in Santa Barbara. The nuns in Hollywood live near the 101 freeway with the endless noise of six-lane traffic, and at that time were almost all sick with flu, with one of the seniors heroically bringing them trays and waiting on them with the utmost devotion. That impressed me, but otherwise I felt there was a lot of stress and conflict, with some of the older nuns more or less chronic invalids, and the juniors conflicted and disaffected. Going for a walk with Swami B. who was also in charge of the convent—his way of conducting business—I learned that I would be useful to look after the sick, older women and to give lectures in the temple. I was not at all sure about that—I had spent so much time taking care of demented old people with conflicted minds that signing up for it permanently was not exactly a drawing card for me. In addition, I was still in an anti-intellectual mood and giving lectures was not what I had in mind at the time. I was interested in opportunities to meditate and think deeply, and the agenda the swami was offering seemed the complete opposite of what I craved.

I said nothing and proceeded on to my week at Santa Barbara. At the foot of the Santa Ynez hills overlooking the Pacific, with beautifully tended gardens loaded with flowers, it truly seemed heaven on earth. My friend Annie lived there; and indeed my interest was largely in that convent, because Swami always had such a happy time in Santa Barbara, and spoke of it with great enthusiasm and affection. Furthermore, I already knew from Courtenaye that this was the convent which was being run by the nuns themselves with a view to becoming independent one day. My natural inclination was to independence for women; and in, addition, my recent experience with the swamis was increasingly making me feel that perhaps the sooner it came the better. I was, therefore, extremely interested in Dorcas, the woman who was running the convent, having been trained by the previous Hollywood swami precisely for the job. Dorcas was from the South, with a strong accent, old-fashioned, gracious ways and manners and, as far as I could see, very warm-hearted and kind, as well as capable of holding the group together. She and I took to each other almost immediately, but did not speak one-on-one until I had spent several days exploring the routines of the convent.

I found that maintaining the house and garden was a large part of every day, that there was a deep-seated aversion to intellectualism, exhibited particularly during one of the superior's classes, where the sense of revolt was heavy in the air. This may have been due, of course, to resentment toward the new swami and his different agenda, a sentiment I could identify with after what we had been going through in New York. It was indeed difficult to change gears from the old, charismatic swamis to these more or less bureaucratic, unsympathetic hustlers. But the strong, strong anti-intellectualism I picked up did not bode so well for me and my inveterate pursuit of intellectual truth. I also found that there was a rather élitist sense there, that two candidates for the convent with whom I was working away in the garden, would be discussed at the meal table with a degree of contumely that I found disconcerting. Was this seeing God in all? Was this what Vedanta was about? How could these monastic women be so sure of their superiority to those whom I saw as patently sincere and earnest? Certainly it was clear that in Santa Barbara they stood very much on protocol, enforcing the age limits to joining with an iron hand. I was already two years over age, and despite the fact that I had spent the last five years under Swami's close supervision, living for all practical purposes like a nun, it seemed likely that they would reject me with the same degree of offhandedness as my two fellow "candidates".

I was, therefore, rather surprised at what Dorcas had to say to me when we finally met. She expressed great appreciation and affection for me, a soothing balm after all of the turmoil in New York and the rather strained atmosphere in Hollywood. Then she went on to say that she had a great deal of concern about the future of the Santa Barbara convent. She said, "There is really no one here who I think can manage this place after I and my generation go. The next generation does not have the understanding of what is needed, and the juniors are precisely that. Now you, dear—you have received so much training from Swami Pavitrananda and, in addition, are a medical doctor. You are used to taking responsibility and I can see you are good at it. I think you would be ideal as the manager here. I would see to it that you got intensive preparation and training for the position."

This was a total surprise. I said, "What about Annie and Jill? They are more or less seniors and have been training here for a long time." Annie was, of course, my dear friend, so kind, so helpful and so innocuous, while Jill was the highly energetic, dominant personality with the blonde hair and ice-blue eyes which stared at me with so much challenge. It was she, particularly, who seemed to lead the group in all of its condemnations, particularly of Swami B., who was in charge of their convent; but also in just about everything that came up. She certainly had energy; perhaps that could be trained and channeled into leadership.

"No, dear," Dorcas said. "These girls are not leadership material. You, on the other hand, quite clearly are." I was not at all sure that this was what I wanted. I was interested in meditation and study and these people in Southern California seemed determined to put me into situations through which I had already passed and, I hoped, graduated from. I couldn't see how these fractious women would be willing to have someone come out of the blue to take over the running of their everyday lives, and felt sure they would seize on the fact that I was over-age to block me from joining. Dorcas was quite aware of it, too. "If you are willing, I will bring up this issue at our next board meeting in ten days. I will try to get you admitted despite your age. Your years of training with Swami Pavitrananda will speak for you—we all know, love and revere him so much. That should speak for you very strongly." She added that, if she did succeed, she would like me to come down immediately to Santa Barbara to reinforce her case and get started immediately. What could I say? I rather reluctantly agreed, mainly because I really had fallen in love with Santa Barbara and wanted to be there. I knew that Hollywood did not appeal, and Northern California was, of course, a complete unknown. Better a bird in the hand than two in the bush.

I left shortly thereafter for the Northern California convent, about which I knew practically nothing, although the one fragment I had picked up from Pat in New York certainly did not whet my appetite. At the end of one of her many visits there she had hugged one of the nuns impulsively. "O dear!" the nun had said. "You have contaminated me. I was ready to do the worship, dressed in my pure clothes. Now I will have to take another bath and change again." I shuddered to think what *pure* meant. Wasn't Pat as pure as anyone else? What sort of madness was this? Now, here I was in the Northern Californian airport, trying to figure out which of the crowd around me might be the nuns that had treated Pat with so much disrespect.

Finally Lisbeth, the seniormost nun of the convent—a really good woman, but a total dilly—and Mandy, the nemesis-to-be of my entire life, connected up with me. I was struck by the contrast with the Southern Californian nuns, who were, on the whole, pretty jolly and self-assured. The Northern Californian women were rather self-deprecating and apologetic, vacillating and unsure of themselves, and I realized at once that my job was to somehow get through the visit without saying anything untoward. It also did not take me long to understand that, although this was a branch of the Ramakrishna Order, it was being run on totally different lines from the centers in New York, Boston, or Southern California, as far as I knew it. Here rules *ruled*. There was little scope for any sort of creativity or spontaneity—*regimented* was the word that came to my mind. Unlike Southern California, the food was skimpy and barely adequate, we were required to wear corsets (!!!!!), and everything we did was governed by some set of rules, either institutionalized or made up on the spur of the moment by whomever you were dealing with.

The one place where there seemed to be any sort of enthusiasm and jollity was at the Society Retreat in the Northern Californian countryside, where the sisters went twice a week to do maintenance work on the property. Bundling on to a World War II weapons-carrier driven by Tillie, our in-house Mighty Mouse, we bumped up the hills to our worksite and then threw ourselves and our mattocks at the job we were doing, hollering with great gusto. I realized that this was the built-in safety-valve in what was otherwise a hothouse of an institution.

And why it was like this was pretty quickly revealed to me. I was slated to have three private appointments with the head of the center and superior of the convent, whose yellow eyes had stared down Dr. Bill in my dream, intense and compelling. I had no particular attraction to him—he was simply a symbol for monastic life for me. He struck me as super-serious, rather portentous, perhaps, and without much of a sense of humor, at least of my variety. But, of course, my aspiration could be in his hands, so I went to see him with the best possible attitude and intentions. At the first interview he put me through what I can only describe as the third degree, grilling me about myself on subjects that I could not for the life of me see as relevant to monastic life. However, I strung along with him as best as I could. Toward the end of the first interview I could feel myself getting the nausea of early migraine and had an important vision. I saw myself as a little white dove imprisoned in a slatted wooden box, my head forced on to my chest and my folded wings rammed on to my back. I could barely breathe at all, I couldn't lift my head, and couldn't help remembering how with Swami I had felt like a condor in the Andes, breathing in the whole universe and soaring into the empyrean.

This vision was a warning, if there ever was one; a deep message from within, which, like so many of my intuitions, I simply ignored. Apart from anything else, I went on to a full-blown migraine, was sick for the rest of the day and was in no condition to think about anything. I put this reaction down to nervousness, but couldn't help remarking that I came down with migraines after the next two, heavy interviews with him as well. We seemed to be going nowhere; he was grilling me, not only ruthlessly, but also unnecessarily, almost undermining me; and in the meantime Dorcas had called me from Santa Barbara, telling me that she was readying herself to get me down with her as soon as possible. On the day I was slated to go to the sister-convent in the country I had a few minutes with the swami in charge, and took the opportunity to say to him, "Swami, we don't seem to be making any progress at all. There is a chance I may have to go down suddenly to Santa Barbara to be trained to take over the convent. Can you kindly let me know whether I have any chance here at all, or not? If not, I will simply go back to Southern California and waste no more of your time." His eyebrows shot to the back of his deeply receding hair line—something I was to notice on many occasions, with much amusement—and his eyes dilated to the max. Totally unused to being spoken to so directly, he was at a loss for words. The sisters were waiting to take me to the country, so I took a quick leave of him and left the city with no idea where I stood with him.

The city convent was an apartment building in the north part of the city, with a breathtaking view from the dining room; but it was on a hill, right next to heavy traffic grinding gears as it maneuvered up and down. The country convent, on the other hand, was at the outer perimeter of the town on a hill, but way off the main drag. It was surrounded by an acre of trees and grass and was blissfully quiet. From the corner of the attic to which I was assigned as a guest, I could see the sun rise in the morning and the moon when it was new. I felt, for the first time in a long, long, while, a degree of peace and inner calm which really soothed my soul. However, my body took the opportunity to get sick with a heavy chest cold, which kept me in bed for nearly the whole week I was slated to spend there. I remembered how extreme stress had had a tendency to affect my lungs, after the horrible scene with my father in the north of England, and also when I was in the Jewish in Brooklyn. Socially, it was an embarrassment, but spiritually it was ideal, for it let me off the feverish activity at the country convent, the sisters rushing every day to commute either to the city or the retreat. I realized within a couple of days that the country convent was merely a bedroom for workers in the city, a pity when the situation in the country was so ideal for being quiet, meditative and studious, as I was hoping to be.

Another feature of getting sick was that I got to know Gloria, one of the sisters who lived in the country. She was a few years older than I and her parents had been working-class immigrants from England. She, like over half of the convent, was a student of Swami Ashokananda, the swami who had preceded the present swami and had been an avid disciple of Swami Vivekananda. Swami Ashokananda had been a dominating intellect and had generated original research into Vivekananda's thought, which had not set well with the order, but had fired up generations of Americans. This was up my alley, and I gladly spent my time chatting with Gloria, who seemed terribly enthusiastic about me, partially because I was British.

Gloria's personality was very sweet, shy and kindly. She went all out to make lovely meals for me and generally fuss over me, a welcome change from the brutal way I had been living in New York since the assistant had come on the scene. I asked her why she was not feverishly commuting like the other sisters and she explained that someone always had to be in the house to take care of the shrine. "What do you need to do to 'take care' of it?" I asked. "Well, we have to keep the sun off the pictures, make sure it is not getting too hot or too cold, and that Sri Ramakrishna has someone to look after him." This was something completely new to me. That Ramakrishna was a person with "needs" was simply not a part of my thinking. For me he was a principle that expressed itself in and through everything that happened. I realized that here was a quite different way of doing things and wondered just how I would adjust to it.

"OK, I get the gist. But why is it always you who does this?" I asked. "Why don't the others take turns?" "Oh, they want to be with our superior," she replied. "They go wherever he is, to do his work." I looked at Gloria closely. Perhaps she, too, preferred to be quiet and unto herself rather than hanging out with an Indian "boss". I did not feel it appropriate to ask any questions directly, but silently decided that Gloria probably felt as I did, and was quite happy minding her own business off the main drag. There was such an intense yearning in me to be utterly quiet, inward and contemplative that even the idea of getting in a car to go anywhere was extremely painful. My aspiration now was to live a life of search for the inward Self, to which Swami had pointed so clearly and had indeed manifested to me in so many ways.

A few days after I had gone to the country, the swami in charge called me up at breakfast time to tell me that he had discussed my case with the trustees of the convent, Swamis Aseshananda and Shraddhananda, as well as Swami Sarvagatananda, all of whom had approved of my application. If I so wished, I was free to join, even though I was two years over age. He did not at all convey to me that he had approved; his whole statement rested on what the senior swamis had said. This may perhaps have been coming from a position of humility, of submission to seniority, which is always a big thing in monastic institutions; but at the back of my mind I had the thought that perhaps he didn't like it himself, an impression created by his remorseless grilling of me at those three horrible interviews—and, maybe, the testimony of my inner, intuitive self. However, it certainly was positive on the face of it, providing me with an alternative should Santa Barbara not work out.

Despite my deeply felt reservations about Northern California, there had been no agenda, as in Southern California, to make me work in all sorts of capacities such as a medical doctor, a situation about which I was quite ambivalent. I hoped to put my past behind me in the convent and move into a deeper world within myself, from which I could heal others much more profoundly than I ever could have as a medical doctor. Nor was I keen to become a "mother superior" at that stage of my life. However, although the Northern Californian setup was not trying to push me into organizational roles, there was something sinister—but what was it?

As I lay in bed in the attic of the country convent, sleeping a lot and otherwise gazing out the window at the sky, I was really rather enjoying myself. Wonderful meals, the TLC of Gloria, who seemed to have a bottomless capacity for it, and no responsibilities, far away from the haranguing of any swami whatsoever, it seemed like a good deal. The other sisters—swami-swooners all—were off the premises, burnishing their swooning over the superior, wherever he was, and I was enjoying the blessed quiet of the country, with nothing to distract or soothe me (as I took the fancy) but the trilling of birds or the whooshing of the wind through the California oaks that surrounded the house.

The only intrusion of "reality" was a call from Dorcas in Santa Barbara, who had had a rough time with the sisters at the board meeting. They had put up ferocious resistance to her proposal to draft me for the Santa Barbara Convent, ostensibly on account of my being overage, but doubtless because they had sniffed out her agenda of bringing in new blood to train for leadership. Dorcas seemed rather put out and distressed, and asked me if I couldn't come down immediately; she would try to make a last effort, perhaps backed by the head swami of the Center and the general board of directors, and having me there would make all the difference in the world. "Why, Dorcas," I said, "Thank you so much for all your efforts. I am sorry the sisters are being so intransigent. I will try to come down as soon as I can, but right now I have bronchitis and am in bed. Maybe next week." There was a moment's silence. "Jean, dear, I am so sorry you are not well. You are probably exhausted after all you went through with Swami Pavitrananda's death. But I have to have you now—it is absolutely crucial." "Dorcas, if I come now I may go on to pneumonia. I am very sick. Can't it wait for a week?" There was another pause. "I am up against tremendous opposition and pressure to bring this to an end. I feel sure that without you being actually there, I don't stand a chance." "Dorcas, I just don't know what to do. The superior here and the trustees of the Northern Californian Convent have said I can join here if I want to." Then she changed her tune. "Jean, dear, I think your sickness is sending us a message. When it is so difficult for you to come here—no matter how much I would like it—and the door is opening for you up there, perhaps that is what is meant to be." Her voice sounded much stronger and I detected a note of relief, too. "Perhaps we shall just have to let it be that way."

So, it was not to be Santa Barbara after all. One side of me was disappointed, but I was too exhausted to put up much of a fight. Like Dorcas, I would have to resign myself to divine will and make the best of the situation. I was lucky to have been accepted at all, even if it was in a convent which had the least appeal of the three I had visited. In some ways I couldn't really believe it was happening: I was so utterly not the pious, "nunny" type, but I was very, very serious about intensifying my spiritual life, and now, as with medical school, the door had finally opened to a world I aspired to deeply, and had really wondered if I would ever attain to.

But I was basically without roots in the Northern Californian Convent. I had met the sisters there sight unseen and with no common talking-points, which I had had in the south. On the whole they seemed to be good souls, well-meaning and apparently cheerful, though I couldn't help picking up a sense of desperate regimentation. It reminded me somewhat of Dollar, where the living was military, basically. I was not averse to that in and of itself; in fact, in many ways my own home, my grandfather's home, had been that of a military man, and I was more or less used to pretty strict discipline and austerity. There were, however, some ominous straws blowing in the wind, in the form of Hilary and Mandy, both of whom seemed to have something against me. Mandy held back from me the whole time I was there, and I kept wondering why. She was my age, artistic and intelligent, apparently similar to me in many ways; but there it was—a dead silence, a foreboding silence, a silence with roots down into depths that even now I cannot fathom. On the other hand, Hilary—some fifteen years older than I—was loquacious and basically gregarious, but somehow seemed to have difficulties with me. I picked this up intuitively, for nothing actually negative was said, other than a strange outburst from Hilary: "You said I am a madcap!" I stared at her in disbelief. I did not even know accurately what a madcap was, far less use the term, nor would I say anything negative on a first visit! What on earth was she talking about? I looked the word up in the dictionary later and simply marveled at her mentality. What sort of intelligence did she think I had to decide she was a mental case in the space of two weeks?

After I returned to New York with my report of the Californian visit Courtenaye, always one to get to basics, asked me point-blank: "Is there anyone there who is going to give you hell?" I started to laugh at her directness. But there was no delay in my reply: "Yes, Courtenaye, there are two women who are going to make my life hell. I have not the slightest idea why, but they have already assigned me to the torture chamber, and I am going to have to pay a heavy price." I said it laughing; but had I known the degree to which these women would torture me, how long it would go on, how ruthless it would be, and how it would have ended, I would never have put foot over the door of that convent. But that is getting ahead of myself. For the moment, I was going to be a nun, and that was enough. My immediate hurdle was to go to my family and explain what I was doing, and if possible, why.

On my five-week visit to Britain I made a point of visiting everyone: Mary, Uncle Willie, Aunt Jane, Aunt Malina, the Dunlops, Daisy, now married with two children, and Uncle Ian. The Northern California swami had made it clear that after I joined the convent I would no longer be allowed to be in touch with my family; traditionally monastics in India severed all family ties and that is what we would be observing. As I had now been away from home and essentially on my own for nearly twenty-five years, this did not seem to be anything too difficult. Somehow the quadruple whammy of Grannie's death, boarding school, Mary's marriage, and my father's marriage all coming together back in the fifties, had created in me a feeling of being basically independent of my family. Dollar had been the place where I had forged my own identity and of course America had just been a continuation of the same process. Living completely independently didn't seem too much to ask, particularly if it helped me to grow spiritually. At the same time, I was very fond of my family and held them in high esteem, and did want to take my leave of them with as much graciousness as possible.

I had braced myself for a lot of criticism and reproach, but was pleasantly surprised to find nothing of the sort. I got the impression that all of them wanted me to be happy. They already knew me, my headstrongness, my determination, my deviation from what they considered "normal". They could not understand me, but they were willing to let me "follow my bliss", a great phrase coined by Joseph Campbell I was to learn later. Mary was her usual self, well-ensconced in her new home and deep into the family issues of her English relatives. It was not possible for me to visit Uncle Willie at his home with his second wife, so I stayed with my cousin Murdo and his wife Brenda, at whose home I was to meet my uncle. I had met Uncle Willie's new wife and understood that she was very strange, and was therefore not surprised at this arrangement. What I was not prepared for was the condition I found my uncle in. He was unusually quiet, almost fearful and rather remote emotionally. I had hoped to communicate with him as before, but it was evident that something had changed radically. He would sit looking at me intently, but saying absolutely nothing. It was rather eerie, and also troubling. Something was going on, which I could not fathom—and my uncle was somehow disconnected from me. I felt sorry at not being able to "take my leave" of someone who had meant so much to me, but those were the breaks. I thought that perhaps he, as a committed Christian, didn't approve of my becoming a Hindu, but the fact was that he just didn't engage me in anything substantial at all. He was just too, too remote. This left a big question mark in my mind, a puzzlement to which I was to find a truly shocking answer some twenty-six years later.

By contrast, my visit with my Aunt Malina turned out to be very revealing. We met in a tearoom on Sauchiehall Street, transformed from its grimy, congested old self into a lovely mall, with baskets of geraniums and lobelia hanging from the lampposts. I could barely believe my eyes—Glasgow had emerged from its dark, dirty past and was becoming a contemporary city. As always, Malina was gracious; but in addition, she was far more forthcoming than I had ever known her. She told me that the whole family had been deeply concerned about me all through my childhood. "Your mother's suicide was a terrible thing for a child of your age to have had to cope with. And then, on top of that, your father's behavior was enough to destroy

Grannie and my Aunt Malina, around the 1930s.

any child. Mary did yeoman work to help you, but we all were afraid you would be permanently damaged psychologically." I was rather taken aback by this—no one in the family had ever spoken to me about any of it, and for all I knew, had even been aware of what was going on. Malina was beaming at me. "But, Jean, I see you seem to have survived and are none the worse. You seem to be a strong person, who doesn't let things hold you back." She told me that the whole family had felt, when I left for America, that I was in revolt and that I would never be heard from again. She was right about the revolt, as I fully understood by then, but of course I had been keeping in touch with Mary every week since I left. I just owed too much to her and could not turn my back on her. Malina went on, "We were all so surprised and happy that you have kept in touch. We were not expecting it at all. And, Jean, we would not have blamed you if you hadn't. The way you were treated as a child was quite dreadful. We did what we could for you, but we would have understood if you had just disappeared for ever. It has meant the world to Mary that you write to her so regularly." I took the opportunity to express to Malina what Grannie had done for me, and also the swamis in America, who for all practical purposes had saved me from nervous breakdown, thus opening up the possibility of discussion of my new venture. She took it all in her stride, showing her spiritual maturity in her easy acceptance of what I was saying.

This conversation gave me closure with my family and also a sense of their commitment to me, which they had never expressed to me directly in words. The Scots do not effuse or express themselves verbally; but they do take action—and, truth to tell, my family members had really stood behind me, supported me and done all they could for me, even if nary a word of encouragement was spoken. When you get down to it, it is that kind of commitment that really matters. Words are easy, as I had learned from being around the swami-swooners; but who stands with you and supports you, when the chips are down?

In many ways this was the highlight of the visit. My visit with Mary was not so smooth and easy. I could not bring myself to tell Mary directly what I was planning to do, but I did talk about Vedanta, the swamis, and the convents, and what they meant to me. A few days before I was to leave for America, Mary suddenly said, "Are you planning to join a convent?" It seems likely that Malina had told her something, but it was also true that Mary loved me intensely and had on many occasions been able to read my mind. I had been giving her hints and clues, of course, but now it was out in the open. I just told her yes, without any further prevarication. Her main concern was whether I would be allowed to keep in touch with her, a question to which I could not give a categorical yes; but I promised her to try to get permission to write as often as possible. That was all Mary wanted. She asked me no more questions, nor would she have been interested in anything I had to say. Mary was not at all religious, but she loved me intensely and would sacrifice her life for me—as for others—as she had demonstrated so totally in the thirty years I had known her. I owed practically everything to this wonderful, unselfish woman, and the last thing I wanted to do was to put her out of my life or hurt her in any way.

Back in New York, I had only a few more weeks left before departure, and was frenetically busy rearranging myself for a totally new way of life. I couldn't help remembering that twenty years before I had gone through something similar as I prepared to go to university, like this quite a triumph of will over matter. Preceding events had seemed so unpropitious to my aspiration, there had been moments of despair that I would succeed, but somehow things had worked out and I had been able to fulfill what I saw as my destiny. Becoming a nun seemed so different from becoming a doctor, but in my own mind there was a connecting link: serving humanity. My role model, of course, had been Swami, who had so radically helped me in my struggles to overcome my inner pain and darkness. If I could become even a shadow of what he was, I felt, I would have done something worthwhile and might indeed be able to serve others in a meaningful way. What I had forgotten, however, was the disappointment when I arrived at medical school; that had been something that had had to be worked out over the ensuing years. Perhaps I was going to have to face something similar with regard to the reality of the convent. It remained to be seen.

On my way to Northern California I spent a week with Swami Sarvagatananda in Boston and Providence. In Boston I stayed with Helga and Diane, two of the swami's students who were living a nun-like life and aspired to joining convents at a later date. I had met Helga at Marshfield in nineteen seventy-six. Originally from Germany, she had her blond braids wound round her head, just like a fraulein, but her manner was as open and friendly as any American, which of course she was. Dedicated to caring for people, particularly the old and the young, she was, like me, a free-spirited Aquarian, who was to become one of my ongoing correspondents and friends for the remainder of my monastic life. Diane, much more introverted and intensely intellectual, was destined to live in India and follow a checkered career.

In Providence I stayed with Pamela and Nora, also aspirants to monastic life, whom I had first met at Marshfield in the summer of nineteen seventy-three. They had already gotten themselves into a monastic routine, although still working at regular jobs. They were earnest young women, more devotional than Helga, perhaps, and certainly less independent in their thinking. They were waiting for Swami Sarvagatananda and me as we arrived from Boston by car, eager to see the "new nun"—who distinguished herself by throwing up copiously the moment she got out of the car. I was feeling as bad as I ever had with a migraine and simply collapsed into the gutter. The girls were all a-flutter, but Swami somehow got me taken up to the guest bedroom in the Center, rather than transporting me any further to the girls' apartment. By the evening I was able to move about somewhat and arrive at their place, which they had gotten up to welcome me with the utmost devotion. I felt like a big, fat toad, oozing slime and noxious chemicals. I so wanted to be able to chat and share with them, but the truth was that I was in the grips of a really dire revisit of some of my inner darkness—and who knows, perhaps was going through a quick flash forward to all that lay in store for me.

From there I went on to Portland, where I was to spend two weeks in the company of Swami Aseshananda, who had so entranced me at Swami's memorial week. He greeted me with the utmost affection and assigned me to live in the women's residence he had established. A one-of-a-kind swami, Swami Aseshananda had a masters degree in philosophy and at the same time was an inspired madman. He was short in stature, with a mop of hair sticking up like Albert Einstein's, and dark pigmentation around his eyes, which made him look something like a raccoon. He had a wild sense of humor and would tell the most off-the-wall jokes, such as a description of the famous "sleepers" in Vedanta—those devotees who make an art form of sleeping through the swamis' lectures. We heard about some of the early days, when one of the wealthy, important ladies involved in establishing the movement would make a grand entrance to the lecture hall, sweep down in her Victorian finery, ensconce herself in the front row and settle in to sleep for the entire lecture! There had been other distinguished nappers, one of whom I knew personally, an extremely nice university professor whom I had watched many times as his head fell backwards and his mouth open as the lecture wore on. Most people sag forward, but Michael sagged backward—apparently a refreshing change for the swamis, for Swami Aseshananda dwelt on his case at length and with great glee, imitating him over and over. The stories were utterly hilarious and an interesting swamis'-eye view of life.

Swami Aseshananda's wackiness was exactly what I needed at that moment in time. My bad migraine in Providence and its aftermath had made it crystal clear to me how unhappy I was about leaving New York behind and, perhaps, an omen of what the next part of my life would be like. The swami seemed to sense something of my mood, for he went all out to pay special attention to me, to make me laugh and generally be happy. As a special dispensation he permitted me to live alone at the country retreat of the Portland Center for a week, one of the most blissful times of my life. The retreat was out in the glorious Oregon woods, where a number of shrines to the different religions had been constructed by one of his monks, an erstwhile architect. All of the shrines were works of art and very uplifting, but the one that really spoke to me was the Native American shrine, a huge, stylized eagle with its wings outspread and its face looking out over the woods to the river in the distance. Swami had had it dedicated by a Native American medicine man, who returned every year to repeat the ceremony. Sitting inside the shrine, I felt a huge, spiritual presence and a sort of identification with the eagle itself, the symbol of freedom, of strength, of fearlessness. I would go there every day and meditate, completely detached from my forebodings and anxieties.

Swami Aseshananda was a great ritualist, quite unlike Swami, of whom he had, however, been extremely fond. As I set off for the retreat, he told me, "Be sure to do worship in the shrine every day." I agreed, not divulging at all that I had never done any such thing in my entire life nor had the slightest clue what was involved. The lady who took me to the retreat showed me where the shrine and the implements were, and gave me a rough idea of what to do. As I was doing this all alone, with no one to criticize or interfere, I was rather intrigued by the whole project. I followed instructions, picking large numbers of the glorious rhododendron heads that were all around me in a wide range of colors, and took them to the shrine room, where I sat down, meditated and improvised my own form of worship. All around me was silence, broken only by the chirping of birds and the rustle and squeak of mice under the floorboards. What I felt can only be described as ecstasy. Sitting at the heart of nature, with no responsibilities but to merge in What Is, and no one to nag me like the assistant in New York, I felt wonderfully uplifted and happy, poised in a universe of happiness and light.

Returning to Portland was difficult. I wanted to remain in the bliss of the retreat for the rest of my life. But of course, the wheels of life roll on and my day for departure for Northern California was at hand. The swami was all attention to me, and one day said, "In Northern California the swami in charge will look after you. But if you need anything more, please do get in touch with me." Though said in an affectionate and low key way, there was something to his manner struck me rather forcibly. Did it mean that I would have difficulties with the Northern California swami and would need help from another swami? The thought flitted through my mind and out the back door. This was not a time for negativity. I had to go into my new life with as much openness, trust and readiness as I could muster.

CHAPTER 24

TWO YEARS OF "HONEYMOON"
1978-1980

The Northern Californian Convent was located in a four-story apartment house on a steep hill. For the first four months I lived in the guest room on the second, dining room floor, which means it was rather noisy, as the sisters were coming and going all the time, cooking, getting snacks, talking, looking at the pin board to check where the cars and personnel were—for we had four cars and a group of women who seemed to be eternally in motion. The rules were that we did not travel on public transportation and that we always had to have a companion wherever we went, so there was endless dickering to snag someone to drag downtown, to the country, to the retreat and sometimes further afield to Novato. We had a system of coordinators, seniors appointed by the swami supervising the convent to organize the convent activities, and these ladies were ever hovering around on the second floor, talking, talking, talking and occasionally arguing or haranguing people. Another convent rule was that during the day we could not close the doors of our room. The principle was that nothing belonged to us, not even our personal space, and that a closed door signified a mentality that shut out others. Like the companionship rule, meant to protect us when venturing out, I could see the point of the open door policy, but in practice it meant that there was nothing to protect me from the eternal bustle and noise immediately outside my room, while the companionship rule meant that for the first ten days I spent most of my time schlepping around the city in the car, with my companion talking a mile a minute about things and problems I knew absolutely nothing about.

Although there were problems, in some ways I was more or less "anesthetized", being weary, weary, weary, to the depths of my being from the long, desperate struggle in New York (and perhaps resisting, in some way, what was going on around me). I distinguished myself, the very first week I was in the convent, by sleeping through a seven-alarm fire, which woke up everyone else in the convent. The sisters had all congregated on the second floor to look out of the large windows at the fire—but I had not heard a thing. Nor did I register, although I was in my room reading a book, an epochal fight in the kitchen between Peggy and Sue, who had wrastled each other on to the floor, ending in Peggy biting Sue in the armpit! If anything, all I heard was a strange thud, which, not being repeated, I had decided to ignore.

But the "wake up call" from all of this was an episode which happened one afternoon. For some reason I had a moment to myself and I decided to go to the fourth floor to read in the relative quiet up there. Our library and classroom were located there, with a few bedrooms at the back. The sisters on that floor were mostly close followers of our superior, meaning that they were up at the temple running around him and used the convent only for sleeping. I therefore looked forward to a nice, peaceful read and communing with my ideal in the lovely, large library commanding a wonderful view through its huge windows. After about a quarter of an hour a group of sisters started up a discussion in the middle bedroom, a short way down the hall. Their voices were for the most part low, but I couldn't help hearing what they were saying. They were discussing various other sisters in a none too pleasant way, dwelling on their faults and dissecting them almost clinically.

There were about four women in the group, three of them disciples of our superior, and Mandy, who had come in from the country for the day. She was a disciple of Swami Ashokananda, but somehow had made herself close to the students of the present swami, sisters who were closer to her in age. It didn't take me long to understand that it was Mandy who was at the center of this discussion, and it struck me forcibly that her victims were women who were her own sister-disciples. I wondered: Why is she shafting her own sister-disciples, "betraying" them to the younger women, who tended to gang up against them? I was utterly devoted to my own spiritual brothers and sisters, no matter what their faults, and could not imagine gossiping about them like this. I loved them too much. I wondered what on earth she was up to and was by then all ears to what was being said. She had selected for discussion one of the sisters who was always the butt of derision and contempt, but nevertheless a senior and, as far as I could tell, a sincere and goodhearted woman.

I could feel the ghoulish delight of the sisters as they launched into a feeding frenzy over the hapless sister they had selected for discussion. I closed my book and waited, almost trembling. But I was in no way prepared for what actually happened. As it unfolded, I realized that this was not just your average gossip-fest; it was a clinical, ruthless dissection, a character-assassination, a gloating carnage, which reminded me of the "experiments" that had gone on in the German concentration camps, with Mandy the chief inquisitor and dissector, magisterially leading her audience along, although I knew them to be decent women one-on-one. I began to feel faint, almost nauseous, for in my entire life I had never heard anything so destructive. Even normal gossip is considered injurious to spiritual life—but this was the *Grand Guignol* of all gossip, a hideous massacre being carried out in cold blood, dwelling lovingly on every last, hideous detail.

It did not take me long to decide that I could not take any more of this. I quietly got up and tiptoed off the floor, actually shaking with horror. Although it was a lovely quiet spot, a refuge from the racket downstairs, I never returned to it for over five years, I was so horrified by what I had heard. I had had a glimpse into the soul of Mandy, a person I intuitively knew to be my nemesis, for within her there was a deep, deep reservoir of negativity that was beyond my comprehension. And, of course, I had plenty of my own negativity, with which I was always struggling; but hers was cosmic, infinite, quite overwhelming—and, as I was to find as I went along, it could resist any attempt to neutralize or divert it. This was to be a long, drawn-out drama, as was my relationship with my superior. In both cases, I was given a glimpse right at the beginning of what was in store for me—and, in both, I just kept trucking, not understanding till much, much later, what I had been up against. Between them these two generated a field which I can only compare to that of the dementors in the Harry Potter series, beings who come in dark, ominous clouds and, hovering over their victims, draw out their souls.

But all of that was in the background for the moment. What affected me most at the time was that though there were large, generous cabinets to store my things, they were full of convent storage, this being the seldom-used guest room. Nor was there ever any sign of the stuff being moved on so I could unpack my bags, out of which I lived for four months. I did not have drawer-space either for several weeks, as the sisters had the notion that I might like to strip the chest of drawers and repaint it. As I had never done anything of the sort in my entire life, this presented quite a problem for me. I spent whatever time I was not barreling around the city struggling in one of the garages with vile-smelling chemicals on a project about which I had no idea whatsoever. I was altogether too exhausted to comment on all this, even to myself, but I did feel the inconvenience and also what seemed rather a cold-comfort welcome to my new life. Perhaps the acme of my discomfort and feeling of being unwelcome was Hilary's reaction to the picture of Mother Kali I had hung up on my wall to try to introduce a familiar, reassuring note to the rather desolate situation I was living in. Hilary happened to be coordinator then (for the job rotated every month) and, coming unannounced into my room one day, saw the picture freshly put up on the wall. She froze in horror and said animatedly, "You can't have that on the wall! Kali must have formal worship every day, or there will be very bad luck!"

"But I have had it on my wall in New York for years and there has been no problem! I am not a ritualist, and she doesn't expect that sort of thing from me. I have my own attitude toward her!" But Hilary was adamant, even ferocious. There would be no Kali images in that convent, she would see to it! She insisted that Swami Ashokananda, the swami who had founded the convent, had been totally against images of Kali, particularly if they were not formally worshiped—and that was that.

I could have told her about my relationship with Kali, my Dark Mother, how she had protected me, nurtured me, brought me through many terrible dark nights, and was the light and heat that stoked the furnace of my life. But I realized it would do no good. This woman was adamant, and ready for battle. Nor did it seem to matter to her that Kali was the deity whom Ramakrishna had worshipped above all, the outer form of Brahman, the Absolute Reality, the feminine dynamic force creating and also destroying the universe. Hilary's insistence on ritualistic criteria came as a shock, for we had had no such thing in New York.

In another dimension, this was my first experience of Hilary as a self-styled "supporter of convent tradition", a role she sometimes played so extremely that it actually became amusing. But it seemed to me that there was more to Hilary's attack than mere "coordinatorship". Had I not picked up her personal animus three months previously, when I came to visit? Something seemed to be burning in her soul, something I could not at all fathom, but definitely strong and acrimonious. And her violent opposition to my Kali picture cut my spiritual umbilical cord, leaving me to face the world alone. With a succession of episodes like this following one after the other, and particularly the relative calm that descended the following month when someone else took over the coordinatorship, I began to suspect that the lack of basic amenities and decent arrangement for my comfort was not so much due to a general lack on the part of the sisters as to Hilary's personal feeling toward me.

Law ruled the roost at the Northern Californian Convent. If some emergency arose, we had to wait till the appropriate coordinator was contacted, and, as far as I was concerned, her decision often had little to do with the actual need we were facing. She would hand down a fiat based on some rule or precedent, not on what I saw as actually happening. Almost immediately I realized that what was going on was a ruthless suppression of creativity and independent thinking, perhaps a necessary part of group living, but for me very oppressive. There was a lot of jealousy, and somehow there seemed to be no control over the negative emotions of those in authority. I would marvel at the way Hilary would get away with her various witch-hunts and other victimizations, with nary a word said. Within a couple of months I had receded into myself, feeling that nothing I had to offer was of any use. It was no use volunteering for anything—it would not be accepted; it was no use saying what you felt—people did not want to know; it was no use trying to solve problems from a deeper level—the interest lay in how many women-hours you were clocking in and how much you conformed to the routines.

Despite all this—and hadn't I been through so much difficult stuff already in my life?—I tried my utmost to live every moment in full awareness of the divine, doing everything with total concentration and care, impressing on my mind the new ways of doing things and trying to master them as quickly as possible. I had been so lucky to be admitted to the convent at my age, and I would make the very best of the situation. In many ways, how could I expect a group to love and understand as Swami had—and, despite some of the difficulties with the old ladies, even the devotees in New York? Of course, now I could not be in touch with them any more, for friends of any sort were as off limits as family, including even members of the Vedanta Society of Northern California.

Taking stock of my options, I understood that I would have to rely almost totally on myself to work everything through, and that, in turn, would depend on my meditation and self-awareness, as well as on controlling my intellect, which was quite obviously going to be a liability in this ferociously anti-intellectual environment. It was going to be a lot of work, and looked, at the moment, very bleak. But, I thought, isn't that the meat of spiritual life? Isn't struggling with issues like this the real "work" through which you clean the dust off the mirror of the heart, as the Indian saint Chaitanya—a contemporary of Teresa of Avila—had said so beautifully? The outlook was dark, but perhaps that was exactly what was wanted now. I also remembered that, according to my "scheme" about my life, "arrival at the goal" was not necessarily pleasant (as had been the case in Edinburgh). Moreover, I was on the cusp of the third turn of the spiral, a time of tremendous struggle, when there is open warfare between what you are at the moment and what you are to become, resolved only by a plunge deep into the vastness of the Self, which underlies everything. It certainly looked as if it was indeed going to be life and death struggle, between, perhaps, my longing for love and affection—which I had had so abundantly from Swami, and was so patently lacking in this new environment—and some other aspect of myself, which as yet I could not see. It was an agenda of rather titanic proportions, not the soothing "rosy glow" I was supposed to be having during my two years of "honeymoon" in a new spiritual environment.

If I had had any notion of getting help from my superior in this huge project, it was quickly squelched. To some extent, the problem came from me: I had felt so much pain from dealing with the younger swamis—and, of course, from Swami's death—that I was extremely leery of becoming attached to any more swamis. I felt that the time had come to stand on my own Self, my inner guide, not human beings who might not understand me—or, if they did, die on me, leaving me still deep in ignorance. I quite consciously did all I could to expect nothing and to ask for nothing, which meant, in practice, that I was inappropriately unforthcoming at the weekly meeting our superior accorded to each of the nuns on an individual basis. This was time-wise far more than Swami had ever offered, but it posed the problem of finding something to say. My native taciturnity returned, fostered perhaps by my intuitions about my superior and a mortal fear of suffering as much as I already had at the hands of the swamis. Both I and the swami were doing our best, but it just was not working.

Then again, I was beginning to understand more of the psychology of these younger men, who had been trained in a totally different environment than Swami and his contemporaries. Swami had been the disciple of Swami Brahmananda, one of Ramakrishna's own disciples, and was therefore close to the source of inspiration of our movement, rooted in the old, mystical India. The generation I was dealing with now had grown up during the height of the Indian fight for freedom from British domination and rule, and had reached maturity in free India, after it got its independence in the nineteen forties. Their outlook was radically different from that of Swami and his generation: they seemed to be more interested in promotion in the organization, *doing* things, building things, drawing crowds, and suchlike. Western things, I would say. The intense emphasis on the inner life and studying Vedanta just was not there, at least in ways that could help me, or that I could readily recognize. And, along with these external differences went a totally different way of behavior. On the one side was Swami and those of his spiritual brothers whom I had met, all of whom were almost unbelievably detached. They seemed to have no personal axe to grind, holding themselves ready to help us transform ourselves from consciousness of the physical world to that of the inner worlds we have within us and would never know about without the help of such altruistic and unselfish guides.

I gained some insight into all of this from a visit from a senior nun from Hollywood who had just returned from over a year's stay in India. She was extremely restless and talkative, but friendly and forthcoming. From her I learned the story of Swami A. and why three years ago he had been traveling round the States from center to center, trying to be accepted as an assistant. It seemed that he had been accused of molesting women in Hollywood, but that had been contested. The old swami who had founded the Hollywood Center had supported the accusations, apparently whipped up by a coterie of jealous women, with endless tales about Swami A. "O golly, I can recognize this hysteria!" I thought. "What lengths people go to!" The nun seemed to favor Swami A. in this unsavory tale, and insisted that he had been innocent, that he had been framed by angry, jealous women and also by the old swami. Despite the fact that the old swami had been her guru, she told me frankly that he had admitted to having a jealous personality; in her opinion, the younger and quite charismatic Swami A. had aroused the old man's jealousy and that was why he had ended up booting his assistant out. I was simply paralyzed on hearing this tale, so murky, so unfair and so utterly smelling of lack of self-control and spirituality. I remembered how Swami had told us that he was quite sure Swami A. had done nothing untoward, but that he had been incautious in his behavior with women—always a fault in a monk.

I kept thinking, "It is difficult to be good, far less spiritual." And, at the back of my mind, I was also wondering about the Northern California swami. Though he kept up a calm, serene, soft-spoken and gentle manner and seemed to be friendly, why was I reacting so violently to him? Why had I seen that vision of the dove forced into a box, why did I get migraine headaches after his Thursday morning class for the nuns? Why was I so reluctant to speak with him one-on-one? These were riddles I was not in a position to answer at the time, though the revelations about Southern California were now proof that all was indeed not as well as it might be with this generation of swamis (and indeed, even with Swami's, though hopefully that applied only to the one, "jealous" swami.)

Gradually I found myself taking a new position. I told myself, "You are Spirit! You can't let yourself be destabilized by your emotions any more—you have had just enough of that." This was one of the methods approved by Vedanta for solving problems, and in this case it actually worked. At the same time I had a vision of the Dark Mother Kali disappearing into the serene form of Sarada Devi, the ever-increasing light of the dawn on the dark horizon. From this I understood how Sarada, with her more gentle and soothing ways, had been taking over the guidance of my life and was standing with me even as I faced what looked like a rather ominous situation. As Swami had been the prime mover of the of this whole last cycle, Mother Sarada had been the presiding genius, quietly and surely drawing me forward—kicking and fighting, of course—and was now completely revealed to me. I felt comforted and reassured and quite consciously felt that, now that Swami had left his body, she would protect and guide me through my two year "honeymoon", which was promising to be a rather ghoulish one.

One of the good things about the Northern Californian Convent was the classes held three times a week in the convent itself. Swami Ashokananda

had wanted his nuns to get beyond the anti-intellectualism so prevalent in the United States and to have a magisterial grasp of the philosophical side of Vedanta. To that end he had set up classes run by the women themselves, guided at first by a number of the brilliant, professional women scholars he tended to attract. The result had been that quite a few of his students were indeed thoroughly familiar with the depth thinking of Vedanta, and the classes were really quite stimulating. After one such class in early September—a time when the advancing equinox always made my mind super-active—I saw more clearly than ever the four-fold "life-pattern" I had sensed in New York, not applying just to me, but to all that was going on around me. I got the distinct feeling that this was a system in which all of us are embedded, and that fully understanding how it works would be a worthwhile study.

In addition to the convent classes, our superior held a monastic class once a week, at which we were studying the *Vivekachudamani* (the Crest Jewel of Discrimination) by Shankaracharya, an eighth-century intellectual luminary of Vedanta. Such study was totally new to me, for Swami had taught us, not didactically, but holistically, drawing out from us ourselves the inner meaning of anything. He had also dwelt, while I knew him, primarily on our contemporary Vedantic leaders, who were so accessible and so loveable, unlike this Medieval teacher, speaking to a totally different period of history, embedded in theology and metaphysics. One interesting illustration of what I mean by *Medieval* can be found in the first or second verse of this text, which maintains that only humans can hope to attain spiritual liberation; and of humans, only men; of men, only brahmins, the highest caste; and of brahmins, only monks. Needless to say, there were several questions about this, which the swami explained away somehow; but I was left with a lingering shadow in my mind: Could these ideas still be at the back of the minds of some of these Indian men? I knew Swami had subscribed to nothing of the sort, but what about this generation, which I was beginning to realize belonged to a totally different reality than Swami's?

The remainder of the text in and of itself was an interesting new discovery, but the swami's remarks made me feel, once again, as if my head were in an enclosed box, and I found myself dozing off to sleep on a regular basis. This was embarrassing, and I moved to the back row where I might not be so conspicuous. I undertook a series of systematic observations on myself in the hopes of getting to the bottom of the problem, but with no conclusive results. This was to be the first of an endless series of observations and experiments, something I had done before when facing dire problems, but not as constantly as I did in the convent. I seemed to be moving to the position of an observer of my life, not an emotional participant. More and more I regarded my life as an experiment I was conducting, looking at myself as an object and gathering facts like any scientist, so that I could get to the bottom of what was going on.

All of this was, no doubt, precipitated by the situation I found myself in, but could also be thought of as the beginnings of a whole new way of seeing myself and the world, the outcome of my progression from a primarily emotional creature to one who relied on the intellect to guide me. Over time it made me more and more remote emotionally, to the extent that some of my sisters felt that I had no feelings at all. But such statements had little effect on me—I was learning who I am in a very direct way, and of course was no longer endlessly perturbed by my uncontrolled emotions, a luxury I simply could not afford in the land-mine strewn environment I found myself in. In order to survive I had to be constantly aware, in control of myself and what I was doing, and as informed about what was going on as possible. I became almost like a question-machine, endlessly quizzing people to find out the lie of the land and what storms were brewing on the horizon. Spiritual hurricane-watch, you could call it. Many of the others found this disturbing, but I could not help it. I had to survive, and, as I increasingly understood, knowledge really is power.

In October I learned that I was to move to the country, the sister-house of the city convent, but I was rather put out by the fact that Hilary would be also moving with me. It seemed that I was not going to be able to avoid this Scylla (in myth a dangerous rock off the coast of Italy); while, of course, Mandy was already there, the Charybis (or whirlpool off Sicily that traditionally trapped those trying to avoid Scylla) to complement her. Put in more American idiom, I was between a rock and a hard place: I already knew that these two women hated and resented me, though I had not the slightest notion why; it seemed that they had conceived their passion even before I joined. Later I learned that everyone knew that Hilary ate new girls for breakfast—why on earth had our superior knowingly sent me out with this Gorgon? He had told me privately that new women normally were not sent out to the country, as there were several problems associated with living there; but everyone agreed that I was unusually self-disciplined and would be able to deal with the issues. This, on the face of it, was flattering, but it could also have been a cover-up for getting me out of the main drag in the city, where I could have hoped to get down roots and be able to hold my own.

It would take me nearly twenty years to be able to see into the depths of why things were done as they were at the Northern Californian Convent. For one thing, it was less than a year since we had found Swami's body on the bathroom floor—I needed time to recover, even to grieve, for I still had not shed a tear over what was one of the major tragedies of my life. Perhaps because I was not showing any of this outwardly; perhaps because of the swami's implacable attitude toward the guru-disciple relationship (which he seemed to feel was something undesirable and trampled on whenever he got an opportunity); perhaps because of a basic lack of feelings all around, the fact that I might be in deep mourning was not considered at all in this almost sadistic assignment to the country.

As soon as I got there—to that beautiful, quiet country residence—I understood what was going on. There were only six of us there, of whom four were disciples of Swami Ashokananda; one was the current swami's closest disciple; and myself. The disciples of Swami Ashokananda were Hilary, Gloria (my friend from my previous visit), Mandy, and Gretchen, a woman in her eighties who was not a nun but had been admitted as a lay sister some twenty years prior. Although a respectable front was kept up it did not take me long to understand that Hilary, Gloria and Mandy were disaffected and disgruntled by the new régime. Eight years had passed since Ashokananda had died, and there had been time for the open negativity to be buried—but not to die down, as I was to learn to my cost as time went by. What was happening was a slow smolder, spreading and gaining in intensity, though seldom showing itself openly—a situation much, much worse than open warfare. What it could do to the human personality could only be understood by the events that were to unfold over the next twenty-four years. I think it was Byron who said, "Hell has no fury like a woman spurned"—which he, as a notorious womanizer, would of course know about. I was to live to see the hell created by spurned human souls, ardent and inflamed by the ideal of one swami, only to be crushed, suffocated and smothered by his successor. I had felt it myself in my vision of the dove in the box, though I had no idea it had such vast ramifications.

The situation was terribly exacerbated by the presence of Tillie, one of the current superior's most ardent disciples. She lived only to be around him and to implement his vision, in so many ways at total odds with all that the previous swami had built up. Tillie was tiny and terrifyingly energetic. A few years previously, the sisters had given her a denim jacket with a Mighty Mouse logo on it, ostensibly as a joke, but of course also expressing their utter exasperation at her relentless pushing and shoving to enforce the will of the current swami. It was impossible to escape Tillie, whose entire *raison d'être* was to make us conform to the new paradigm—unending activity, in which self-awareness, meditation, study, seemed to play no part. The pace was grueling, involving jumping in the car at the first possible moment and tootling off to some activity or other in the city or at the retreat.

There was another issue permanently on the simmer between Swami Ashokananda's students (who cared for the principles of Vedanta as a way of life adjusted to America rather than as an ethnic religion) and those of the current swami, who were basically being trained as cult Hindus. Their emphasis was on India, not the West, on learning Sanskrit, Vedic chanting, ritualistic worship, formal Indian methods of behavior and communication, and so on. Then there was a philosophical conflict between Ashokananda's non-dual viewpoint, which embraced the whole world as divine and the individual as a center from which the divine communicated with the divine—as far as I then knew, the sum and substance of Vedanta—and the much more limited, traditional, viewpoint of devotional Hinduism, in which the deity is the locus of the divine, not the individual human being. Ashokananda had been a fiery proponent of the Vedanta of Vivekananda, based squarely on what I like to call spiritual humanism, while the current swami was peddling the notion that somehow God is basically other than human (a position known technically as dualism); that some things are "spiritual", while others are not; and that we have to worship an abstract God rather than the living God in our fellow human beings and the world around us. In many ways, his view was much closer to the devotionalism of Christianity, in which God and human are permanently separate from each other—the very viewpoint I had rejected nearly twenty years previously. And certainly it is the majority view of Hindus, who on the whole are not too keen on spiritual humanism, for them a rather new-fangled way of thinking, something of a blend of East and West, which Swami Vivekananda, my hero, had come up with on the basis of Ramakrishna's amazingly integrative worldview.

What goes along with the dualistic type of thinking is heavy ritualism, involving the notion of "purity", attained by the way you eat, dress, speak, etc.—the hard core of cult Hinduism, built up over millennia—but utterly foreign to someone like myself, brought up in egalitarian Protestantism. Such ritual purity creates an atmosphere of "us versus them", "holier-than-thou", of superiority to others, and a whole host of attitudes which, up till then, I had regarded as anything but spiritual. It did not take me long (aided by my reading of Vivekananda) to understand that this attitude had a whole lot to do with the institution of caste in India, which Vivekananda pronounced to have "a mania for purity". On the basis of supposed ritual impurity, whole hosts of people had been treated as subhuman, as cesspools, and relegated to an inhuman, degrading way of life. I began to wonder if the swamis were in effect (though perhaps not consciously) training up Westerners to create a Western caste system, along with the "cruelty, heartlessness, callousness" that Vivekananda himself laid at the door of the brahmins, the upper caste who traditionally enforced the whole system. My soul cried out against such a travesty of spirituality—wasn't the crown-jewel of the West its humanism, its recognition of the innate dignity and value of each and every human being?

But, at that time, there wasn't time or energy to work on these problems in depth. I had to deal with "real time" in which there were desperate conflicts roiling round me. Not the least of these was the conflict between Tillie and Betsy, who were locked in mortal combat over the leadership at the retreat. Betsy was an older lay sister living in the city, who had been a stalwart of the Society for decades, and who had many of the macho tendencies that Tillie had. Both of them drove the trucks and weapons carrier at the retreat, oversaw the fieldwork—and when I went there, were having a huge showdown over who was going to be the ultimate "boss". Tillie was undisputed crew-leader on Tuesday (the day that our superior was at the retreat and therefore as many women as possible wanted to be there); while Betsy was leader on Saturday, when our superior was in the city and the crew was small. That way, her ego was somewhat mollified; but the problem was out in the open on Tuesday, when Betsy had to play second fiddle to Tillie. Although the chat was kept relatively light—as was the way with everything—the explosive emotions right below the surface impacted me seriously. By the end of Tuesday workdays, I was all wrung out and unable to meditate to any extent at all.

It was apparent that Tillie—also of large greenish-yellow eyes, like her guru—was staring down and overpowering Betsy, a woman already in her sixties and, as far as I could tell, suffering from some sort of organic brain damage. I always noticed when I spoke with her that her pupils were pinpoint and never seemed to dilate, a sign of serious damage to the brain. But, as she was the secretary of the Society and our superior's right-hand person, I kept wondering if my impression was right about her. She did sometimes talk incoherently, mixing up words, losing her meaning, and so on; but I kept thinking: How can she be secretary with as much brain damage as I think she has? It was a total mystery to me. It was clear that she was extremely agitated over her relationship with Tillie, though, like everyone else, she kept up appearances of friendliness. Again and again Tillie would best her, make her look silly and dysfunctional—much to my disgust—and poor Betsy would be left, her face bright red, her pupils still totally undilated, and completely at a loss for words of any kind, muddled or not.

The convent in the country had over an acre of landscape to be maintained, a job which had fallen on me, more or less. As everyone else was always running off to be with our superior's program in the city, I got to work in the fields and vegetable garden alone, a situation which suited me much better than the noisy, adversarial situation at the retreat, and it did not take me long to work out a deal in which I was permitted to focus more on the work in the country, rather than dragging my carcass off to the retreat to get involved in the open warfare going on there.

The other player in the country was Gretchen, an octogenarian lay-sister whom Swami Ashokananda had drafted for the convent, like Betsy, when they, as utterly devoted supporters and workers for decades, had fallen on hard times and could not manage financially any longer. Gretchen had grown up on a German-American farm with little formal education, had lived a hard life working herself to the bone to support her daughter—whose father had disappeared early on—and was nothing short of a complete trooper. She had had desperate, radical surgery for cancer something like twenty years before I met her, and was completely disabled by the malignant osteoporosis that was a result of the surgery. Despite all of her disabilities and impediments, Gretchen was as bright as a button, a bottomless pit of good suggestions, particularly to drivers (as she had worked most of her life at the triple A), an indefatigable worker at whatever she could still do, and afflicted from time to time with paranoid delusions, some of which were actually rather funny. She would call up the coastguard from time to time to report that Communist Chinese were in a boat in the wharf, plotting to take over the town. And it would not just be one phone call—she would do it over and over and over, no matter how we insisted she stop! Giving the coastguard guys a chance to practice forbearance, no doubt.

Gretchen's contribution to the seething cauldron in the country was as a noisy admirer and supporter of Tillie and all of her doings. Although a disciple of Ashokananda, she, like Betsy (who told me this herself), related much better to the current swami, who did not pack the intellectual and charismatic punch of his predecessor and was much more willing than he to surround himself with lesser lights. Gretchen would have followed Tillie to the ends of the earth, and often did so, as Tillie needed a companion to go on her endless errands all over the face of Northern California. It was quite comical to see them ensconced in the car, their heads barely visible over the dashboard, two little mighty mice off on a toot! And Gretchen ready to keep Tillie straight all of the way on the fine points of her driving!

This was the ménage I was destined to live with for nine years, although every alternate year one sister would be moved to the city as part of our rotation plan. In order to prevent any sort of entrenchment or ossification, there would be a big shakeup every two years: a rotation between the city and country; and, and in the city itself, room changes. One of the prime austerities was having a roommate. I had spent much of my life in Britain sharing a room with someone, but it was clear that for these American women, the very idea of sharing anything was a major proposition. Although the sisters in the country all had their own rooms (which were tiny), I was put up in the attic with Gretchen, which I did not mind at all, but which was, in fact, a poor assignment in the eyes of the others. For one thing, it had the same disadvantage as the guest room in the city, in that it was directly over the kitchen. Without doors of any sort, we had to live, not only with cooking noise, but also endless, noisy telephone calls, discussions, and often quarrels. I also had the distinct impression that Hilary made a point of making as much noise as possible in order to torture me. She would set up camp in the kitchen and carry on

long, angry discussions on the phone that just never seemed to come to
an end. Why she did not take herself to the utility room in the basement,
where there was a large table, a phone—and a door that would have kept
the noise in—baffled me.

Yes, there were many layers of conflict in the convent, which had
been going on, it seemed, ever since the arrival of the new superior in
nineteen-seventy. He had come as a new broom all ready to sweep the
nest of non-dual Vedantists into the comfy, dualistic embrace of cult
Hinduism, and in doing so had had many head-on collisions with the
aggressive, opinionated students of Swami Ashokananda, who had
been himself an assertive firebrand, flaming out the message of Swami
Vivekananda.

Swami Ashokananda had compromised the non-dual ideal to some
extent in that he had instituted ritualistic worship, probably to provide
ongoing activity for the monastics, who were notoriously difficult to
keep adequately employed. Some of the nuns had jumped at it (as
Jeanne in New York also clung to any little ritual she could perform),
and had soon turned it into a prestige thing, emphasizing its "holiness",
its "specialness" and demanding privilege above everyone else—all of the
things Vivekananda had disliked about the practice of ritual in India.
The rigid strictures followed by those who performed ritual soon became
enforced on all of us: there were rules about cooking, eating, the kind of
clothes you wore, even about when we had our periods. At that time we
were "impure" and ritually unclean. I was extremely taken aback, during
my first months in the convent to be constantly asked, "Are you pure?"
I would always say, quoting St. Paul: "To the pure, all things are pure."
I had a deep, natural revulsion to this sort of thing, which was basically
equating purity with the body rather than the mind, which, for me,
was the place where the work to become "pure" should really be taking
place. To make the natural functions of the body "impure" was for me
a regression to Medieval myth, which had already proven its capacity to
dehumanize the human race. Wasn't the five-hundred-year Inquisition
of the Middle Ages, fueled by a fanatical form of celibacy, enough of all
of this sort of stuff?

In addition to these built-in issues at the convent, I had my personal
battles. Although I had been living in the United States for eleven years
at that point, in many ways I had not really encountered American-
Americans at close quarters. Most of my close friends had been Europeans,

Asians or first generation Americans, who, I find, are quite a bit different from "full-blooded" Americans. I had worked closely with Americans at the New York Center, of course; but it is not quite the same as sharing a bathroom and otherwise being cheek-by-jowl with others. I found out very quickly how fussy Americans are, being used to a much higher standard of living than I; how intolerant of differences, how unwilling to see any cultural viewpoint but their own, how sure of their own "rightness", and how unrelenting in enforcing it. They all knew so much more than I about mechanical equipment, automobiles, chain saws, telephones—you name it—and openly despised me for being so wimpy in that domain. They would get furious with me when I defended such things as aristocracy—not as it had worked itself out historically, but as a principle by which some people require special circumstances in order to make their contribution to society. For the first time I experienced what C. S. Lewis had spoken of in the *Screwtape Letters*: Enforced mediocrity, the rule of the lowest common denominator, and savage anti-intellectualism. C. S. Lewis had seen all of this as the work of the devil; now I was having the opportunity to test his hypothesis!

And then there was the issue of the baby-boomers. This was the first time I had even heard the word, far less been aware of who or what the baby-boomers were. A member of the "Lost Generation" born during World War II, I had left the workplace just before the baby-boomers hit it, had been isolated from them in New York by virtue of being on the "geriatric shift" at the Center, and had not been reading popular literature for some time. About half the convent was baby-boomer, I realized after about six months. Their basic presuppositions quite simply had no place for mine: the notion that people mattered in and of themselves, that empathy and love are essential in human relationships, that kindness is a virtue, that bearing and forbearing are necessary if we are to get along at all. Sometimes I wondered if I was living with people at all—everything seemed utterly mechanical, without heart, understanding or love. Tillie, the "Mighty Mouse" was the arch incarnation of all of this, embodying in herself all the razzle-dazzle of Americanism, the mechanization, love for fast-foods, intolerance of opinions other than her own, ruthlessness in suppressing any view that competed with hers. Early on, she looked at me and said, with the maximum of rudeness, "What planet did you come from?", quite sure that her planet was the default. I stared at her, completely amazed. Even in America I had not been asked anything so rude, arrogant and unfeeling. I don't believe I replied, but inwardly I wondered just what planet she was living on herself.

There was so much to cope with in this new life! In many ways, however, the most immediate problem was living in an exclusively feminine environment, a first for me. Although my mother had been the only influence on me as a toddler, although I had attended an all girls school in Glasgow and had been at boarding school in my teens, the masculine had always been there to balance all the girls and women. First was the Scottish temperament, which is stoic and self-contained, not given to emotional outbursts or vaporizing. Then the fact that my mother and her sisters were all quite powerful intellectuals, which in those days also meant agnostic, atheistic, left-wing, more interested in issues than in personal emotions (though, again, it might have been better if my mother had had a better handle on hers!) After my mother died, my father had become my closest friend (and tormentor), and had exercised a great influence on me, taking me for long walks during which we had sustained intellectual discussion, combined with rowing on Loch Lomond, working on the Hoggs' farm, and nary a moment of sentimentality or emotion—other than his annoyance if I managed to beat him in an argument (which happened much more often than anyone would have imagined). At boarding school girls were outnumbered by two to one, and, being in the science and math stream, I was surrounded by boys, who made up most of my day. This was also true at medical school and even more so at my work, where women were outnumbered by at least five to one.

And then, the women who were closest to me—Grannie, Mary, Aunt Jane, Jean Irwin, and Mrs. Browne—were women of great character, purpose and restrained emotion. There was deep love and affection, but no sentimentality or gushing emotion. Getting on with it was the order of every day I ever lived. Sturdy self-reliance was everyone's motto, and infatuation, hero-worship, or any form of giving up your own self-respect or autonomy was unthinkable. We used to marvel at the women shrieking over Frank Sinatra, particularly when you looked at the scrawny, self-indulgent item himself. "The Americans are fery funny people!" Grannie would remark mildly after some unbelievable news item on the radio. "I haff no itea what it is all apouht!" Nor did we.

It was, therefore, totally beyond my comprehension how the women in the convent could have sold their souls so utterly to cult worship of our superior. I had, of course, seen swami-swooning in New York—and intensely disliked it and the silliness it gave rise to. But, compared with what I encountered in Northern California, the swooning of the New York ladies was a bagatelle. In Northern California it had progressed beyond mere swooning to serious cult-worship, in which everyone was expected to take part, with the thinly-veiled threat that, if you didn't, you would pay for it heavily. Tillie was the main enforcer of this situation, abetted by Lorie, her friend from Tennessee who had joined the convent at the same time. I could somewhat understand their attitude as they were our superior's key players and therefore enjoyed considerable prestige and privilege; but what stumped me completely was that the old-timers kept up a front of "swooning" and, more seriously, seemed to have totally abrogated any capacity to think in order to follow instructions coming down from His Holiness, as I came to dub our superior to myself. During my first year I would approach one or other of the seniors to learn something about how the convent was run, only to be met with a simper and, "You will have to ask Swami!" Once again, I could have understood this response if I had asked something of serious import, something "advanced", but I met it even with the most superficial inquiry.

I really wondered what was going on. Didn't these women have any minds at all? Were they totally powerless, as it certainly seemed on the surface? Why, O why were well-educated women, far more intelligent and experienced than Tillie, knuckling down to her imperious demands and compromising—as I saw it—their own beliefs and experience, even the grand tradition they had been trained in by Swami Ashokananda?

It was clear I had entered a dark, labyrinthine cave in which all manner of strange monsters were living, just waiting to entangle me in their slimy, and possibly electrocuting embrace. Apart from anything else, there was a huge vat of darkness and pain inside myself, with which I was going to have to cope as I tried to fend off all that was coming at me from outside. What would become of it all? Thus far my intuition— which, as ever, I resolutely ignored, much more focused on dealing with immediate issues. The first of these was to get some peace and quiet in which I could hear myself think. Study was a crucial part of my life and now of my spiritual practice, and I simply had to get time to work on it. Having memorized Swami Vivekananda's poems and systematized his letters, in which he reveals so much of himself, I was now moving on to a study of his comments on the *Bhagavad Gita*, the text that had brought me to Vedanta in the first place. By that time I had read over thirty

English translations of the Gita in an attempt to get to its core meaning, but remained dissatisfied overall. I was aware that Vivekananda often quoted the Gita—so helpful for everyday life, particularly that which involved work and emotion, but of course also meditation and higher knowledge—and realized I would be doing myself and others a favor by culling from his rather disorganized *Complete Works* all of his comments on the immortal Sanskrit text. Putting them together would be a vade mecum for me personally and perhaps for others as well.

As a background study for this work I had also embarked on a systematic study of the other Vedantic texts that lay behind the four yogas, beginning with karma, or the yoga of work. Vedanta has traditionally concerned itself much more with philosophy and what is called higher knowledge than with this-worldly matters, such as spiritualizing work, but there are a few classic texts, to which I applied myself diligently. One of these is the *Mahabharata*, an ancient classic on the subject of dharma, or obedience to cosmic law, usually translated into English as righteousness, and certainly tied in with questions of acceptable behavior. I found a twelve-volume translation in the Vedanta Society's library, and set about reading every word of it. And what a text it is! Telling a long-drawn-out tale of the epic struggle of two dynasties for the throne of India, it goes into every nook and cranny of the subject of dharma, leaving, as far as I could see, no stone unturned.

The Indian tradition is steeped in the awareness that there are several levels of reality, each with its own logic and conventions, making ethical choices much more complex and variable than for most of us in the traditional West. In facing any situation, it is imperative to determine which level is most in play, or in answering which the problem will best be resolved. The Mahabharata is, from one point of view, a work-book of how all of these priorities work themselves out in various situations, depending on the ability of the main players to tap fully into the situation and respond appropriately to the dominant level in play. Internalized rules and regulations as we understand them in the West are not anywhere near as important, for the main controlling feature of Indian life was the social system, which was divided into castes, nowhere near as rigidly as in modern times, but nevertheless a very compelling force. As illustrated by a story in the book, brahmins—members of the highest caste, most of whom were strict vegetarians—could in a pinch eat flesh, even human flesh, in a desperate famine; whereas the scavengers, outside the whole caste system, had license to do so, more or less by default. But, of course, the lower the caste to which one belonged, the less respect and prestige one had; indeed, the lowest were treated worse than animals, many of whom (especially the cow) were accorded almost divine status as symbols of the deities.

This was an exotic new world, which had thus far eluded me. Swami had been so contemporary and rational that we had not really had even a whiff of this Byzantine, incredibly complex world I was now encountering. The deeper I went into it, the more I marveled at how he had succeeded in going beyond it—and also how much it still lingered in the minds of most of the swamis I was to meet from thenceforward, though in forms that followed the letter rather than the spirit of this highly interior "law". On the other side of the equation, my sisters were so strikingly Western, with their emphasis on the rightness of only one aspect of anything that came up: words could have only one meaning, and there was only one way to do things (incongruously, often the Indian way, the relevance of which to what we were and were doing was sometimes extremely hard to see).

This little incident illustrated very clearly the difference between me and my sisters. I was interested in principles, they were focused, Western-style, on rules and regulations—and, by golly, they would see that they were enforced! I continued on with my studies, however, finding in them the sort of reality that was so lacking in my everyday surroundings.

I kept undertaking systematic studies of myself—my sleep, emotions, migraines, and so on—to see if I could get to the bottom of what was bothering me, but with no clear results. There were two episodes which did throw light on my situation, however. One was the visit of Annie, my sister from Santa Barbara. Some of us went with her to our retreat in the hills near San Jose, which had been pioneered in the first years of the twentieth century by no less than Swami Turiyananda, one of Ramakrishna's disciples and Swami's main mentors, a man of deep spirituality and meditativeness. It was wonderful being out in the silence, the endless chaparral, the wildflowers, with just Annie and a couple of empathetic sisters. Annie and I sat in the meditation cabin where Turiyananda had so often gone deep into himself, and both enjoyed a long, deeply satisfying meditation. It was the only really good meditation I had had since I went to Northern California, and the last one for a long, long time. However, it had the effect of reminding me why I was living this new life and giving me hope that I was still in touch with what mattered most to me.

Myself in Edinburgh just before joining the convent.
Obviously in a blissful mood!

The other episode that helped me a great deal was a visit from Pat, who had returned from her year-long visit to India, where she had been accepted as a nun in the women's order. She had to return to America for six months in order to await a visa, if I remember rightly, and spent much of that time with us at the country convent. She was naturally in an upbeat mood, having finally achieved her heart's desire, and provided for me the utterly vital link with Swami and all that he stood for. We talked a lot, laughed a lot, and had an all-round jolly good time, the first such unmeditated, "careless rapture" since I had gone to Northern California. This release from the grinding mechanism of the convent (the matrix, if you will, that we were embedded in) was an utter godsend, and served to reground me in ways that nothing else could. Certainly I could see that any exposure to Swami's way of doing things was highly remedial, an antidote to the regimentation and coercion of the convent.

I often wondered if group life necessarily had to be so mechanical and lacking in spontaneity and life, not to mention love, but of course could get nowhere at that time. The data just wasn't in, though the portents were certainly not promising. If this was my "honeymoon period", what would the actual "marriage" be like? I was much too busy just surviving to ask myself such questions, but it might have been better had I really examined the question then and there, even with the limited information I had at hand. But, for the moment I had now completed the second turn of my life's spiral and was poised to enter the third, at the doors of which dementors and other denizens of the disordered human mind were ominously gathering. Just how bad might it get? And how was I going to cope with it? Perhaps in a way similar to how I had negotiated through the rather disappointing experiences at medical school. Or, again, in view of my more mature outlook on life, perhaps not.